Positive Psychology and Disabl

MW00862149

Series Editors

Michael L. Wehmeyer, Beach Center on Disability, University of Kansas,
Lawrence, KS, USA
Karrie A. Shogren, Kansas University Center on Developmental Disabilities,
University of Kansas, Lawrence, KS, USA

The **Positive Psychology and Disability** book series provides comprehensive coverage of research and practice issues pertaining to the application of constructs and principles from the discipline of positive psychology across the disability context. In addition, books in the series address the application of strengths-based approaches to understanding disability and designing and implementing supports to enable people with disabilities to live, learn, work, and play as meaningful participants in their communities. Drawing from traditional areas of focus in positive psychology, series books:

- Provide cutting-edge research and practice that can improve the quality of life and well-being of people with disabilities.
- Address theory and research across such areas as hope, optimism, self-determination, and character strengths.
- Examine research- and evidence-based practices to promote involvement in goal setting, problem solving, and decision making.
- Synthesize research and practice from multiple disciplines and apply strengths-based approaches to disability.

Volumes published in this series are must-have resources for researchers, professors, clinicians and related professionals, and graduate students in developmental and positive psychology, special education, social work, child and school psychology, and other allied disciplines.

More information about this series at http://www.springer.com/series/15589

Roger J. Stancliffe
Michael L. Wehmeyer
Karrie A. Shogren
Brian H. Abery

Editors

Choice, Preference, and Disability

Promoting Self-Determination
Across the Lifespan

 Springer

Editors
Roger J. Stancliffe
Centre for Disability Research and Policy
The University of Sydney
Sydney, NSW, Australia

Michael L. Wehmeyer
Beach Center on Disability
University of Kansas
Lawrence, KS, USA

Karrie A. Shogren
Kansas University Center on Developmental
Disabilities
University of Kansas
Lawrence, KS, USA

Brian H. Abery
Institute on Community Integration
University of Minnesota
Minneapolis, MN, USA

Positive Psychology and Disability
ISBN 978-3-030-35685-9   ISBN 978-3-030-35683-5   (eBook)
https://doi.org/10.1007/978-3-030-35683-5

This Springer imprint is published by the registered company Springer Nature Switzerland AG
The registered company address is: Gewerbestrasse 11, 6330 Cham, Switzerland

This book is dedicated to self-advocates with disability and their efforts to exercise their basic human right to self-determination. Through advocating both within and outside of existing systems to demand their personal self-determination and enhance the choices available to others, they are making their voices heard around the world. They inspire us to do more, aim higher, and work to eliminate structural discrimination and systemic oppression.

Foreword

A decent society is one whose institutions do not humiliate people. A civilized society is one whose members do not humiliate one another. – Avishai Margalit

And yet, there is a solitude, which each and every one of us has always carried with him more inaccessible than the ice-cold mountains, more profound than the midnight sea; the solitude of self… Such is individual life. Who, I ask you, can take, dare take, on himself the rights, the duties, the responsibilities of another human soul? – Elizabeth Cady Stanton

It is commonplace in this century for family members of people with complex disabilities to say that living with disability opened their minds in ways they had never anticipated. That has been my experience over the last 36 years as a parent, advocate, advocacy organization leader, government official, and now president of Inclusion International. The doorway to the deepest thinking about human rights – and about all that makes us human – is opened wide by the old mistakes and new problems, the persistent paradoxes and changing issues that surround us. People with disabilities themselves often lead the way. The authors whose contributions appear in this volume have thought deeply about the questions that often confound us, whether we are politicians, mothers, or disabled advocates. A central question, in my experience, is how to support the individual freedom of persons with intellectual, cognitive, or complex cognitive disabilities.

We live in times when more people with more complex disabilities can be supported longer and better in families and communities than was ever possible in the past centuries. Then, resources, tools, and even ideas were scarce. Now, we have better systems, better technologies, and better expectations. We continue to develop better ideas, often in response to cultural shifts.

Thinking about self-determination is ever more challenging as proponents of neoliberal thought attempt to extend its reach in the world. Clearly, it is worth pursuing the idea that disabled persons can be in charge of their own destiny, but the overemphasis on individual control and personal responsibility can be isolating, illogical, and damaging. The idea that the person alone is responsible for their choices and their outcomes is laughable for families who see clearly that despite abstract theoretic doctrines, the practicable options available are often severely limited by systems, cultures, communities, and policies based on long-held ideas of scarce resources and even by family circumstances. Systems can be disabling, sometimes more than impairments are disabling. Economies and cultures can destroy capabilities or provide no opportunities for exercising atypical capacities. Alas, families and loved ones sometimes can be disabling, too.

I have been responsible for systems and have had shared responsibility for a family. We do the best we can. Sometimes we fail. Often, our reach exceeds our grasp. We are always grateful when our best researchers and thinkers take on the bigger questions, as the authors of these chapters have done.

One error most of us make, especially when we are failing or when systems fail us, is to believe that our own city, state, or nation is unlike any other and that all of our problems can be solved by political action and policy initiatives within our own systems. These authors have addressed the problems and opportunities of freedom, choice, and self-determination around the world, giving us a rare opportunity to think globally and from a human and plural perspective.

The Universal Declaration of Human Rights (UDHR) as reflected in its Conventions has become a touchstone that many working on problems associated with human disability use to test proposals and guide joint inquiry and activism. The process by which scholars from around the world drafted the Declaration deserves to be better known than it is. It did not involve first agreeing on a common scientific or philosophic or cultural doctrine as the basis of human rights; rather, the participants sought and found common grounds of human rights, enumeration of particular rights, and agreement on the actions required to achieve and protect them. The plurality of research approaches and views in this volume reflect that approach.

Another error that is often repeated, but not here, is to hold that the ultimate goal of self-determination is to control financial resources. The focus on control of resources can nudge us toward greed. As the famous self-advocacy battle cry "Nothing about us without us" morphs into "Nothing about me without me," it leaves social responsibility in the dust. In my own country, problems caused by the inequitable distribution of wealth seem to be mirrored in the inequitable distribution of human services. The neolibertarians who would reorder our world into a gilded age on steroids seldom acknowledge that not everything is about money and regulation. Disabled people and their families – even young children – are now serving as one of the last and most powerful political and cultural reminders that we owe something to one another.

That is one of the most important lessons one learns when living with disability: dignity is about much more than money and regulation. Freedom from external control or limitations is only part of liberty; the other and probably more important part is to be free of internal errors such as greed, avarice, or ignorance that can cause one to make choices that will ultimately bring harm to oneself or others. Thus, greedy people are never free, even if they are wealthy beyond measure. Access to education is one of the positive contributions society can make to the individual capabilities that support liberty, and inclusive education provides the benefit of helping students with and without disabilities in their attainment of genuine positive liberty.

I have often noticed that ideas and technologies first developed to aid people with intellectual disabilities end up being useful to all of humanity. As we react to cultural shifts, sometimes we cause them, too. It does not escape my notice that we need much better understanding of choice, preference, and self-determination and how to support them in many aspects of human life and endeavor as we continue to balance on the razor's edge of both climate and economic disaster. Perhaps humanity is showing signs of some new form of collective intellectual disability when it comes to addressing climate and economic collapse. Perhaps ideas here will help.

If "recognition of the inherent dignity and of the equal and inalienable rights of all members of the human family is the foundation of freedom, justice and peace in the world" [UDHR, preamble], then we have work to do together. The Convention on the Rights of Persons with Disabilities is helping us understand the Sustainable Development Goals, and vice versa. Families and policymakers in cultures around the world are wrestling now with the connections among freedom, choice, and disability. All cultural views are welcome to the discussion, if we hold to no insistence that only one view can be correct. Experts in all scientific, practical, and artistic disciplines can contribute, as the authors here are doing.

Sue Swenson, MBA, is the current President of Inclusion International, a global network of persons with IDD and their families who work to advance the rights and inclusion of persons with intellectual disabilities in all parts of the world. Prior to her association with Inclusion International, she served as the Deputy Assistant Secretary for the Office of Special Education and Rehabilitative Services (OSERS) at the US Department of Education during the recent Obama Administration. In this capacity, she advised the US Secretary of Education on matters related to the education of children and youth with disabilities, as well as employment and community living for youth and adults with disabilities. Prior to assuming her responsibilities at the OSERS, she served in the Clinton Administration as the Commissioner for Developmental Disabilities in the US Department of Health and Human Services as well as Executive Director of the Joseph P. Kennedy Jr. Foundation and CEO of The Arc of the United States. She became involved with disability advocacy because her middle son, Charlie, had profound disabilities. She was active in the Minneapolis, Minnesota, public schools as well as in state and federal policy while working as a Professional Services Marketing Director before being named a Kennedy Fellow in the US Senate in 1996. Sue earned her AM at the University of Chicago as well as an MBA at the University of Minnesota.

Bethesda, MD, USA   Sue Swenson

Contents

Part III Choice and Preference Across the Lifespan

Part IV Implications for Policy and Practice

About the Editors

Roger J. Stancliffe, PhD, FAAIDD, FIASSIDD is Professor of Intellectual Disability at the University of Sydney's Centre for Disability Research and Policy. He has an ongoing 25-year affiliation with the Research and Training Center on Community Living at the University of Minnesota. His applied research focuses on making a difference in the everyday lives of people with intellectual and developmental disability, ranging from research on transition to work to studies on ageing. His interests include participation, choice, self-determination, support, and the operation of service systems. He has published extensively and has presented papers at research conferences in five continents. He edited the *Journal of Intellectual & Developmental Disability* from 2003 to 2008. He is the recipient of the 2011 AAIDD Research Award. His most recent book is *Transition to Retirement: A Guide to Inclusive Practice.*

Michael L. Wehmeyer, PhD is the Ross and Marianna Beach Distinguished Professor in Special Education and Chair, Department of Special Education, University of Kansas. He is also Director and Senior Scientist at the Beach Center on Disability, also at KU. His research focuses on issues pertaining to self-determination, the application of positive psychology to the disability context, applied cognitive technologies, and the education of learners with intellectual disability and extensive support needs. He is a Fellow of the American Psychological Association (Division on Intellectual and Developmental Disabilities), the International Association for the Scientific Study of Intellectual and Developmental Disabilities, and the American Association on Intellectual and Developmental Disabilities, the latter of which he is also a Past President. He is currently the President of the Council for Exceptional Children's Division on Autism and Developmental Disabilities.

Karrie A. Shogren, PhD is a Professor in the Department of Special Education, Senior Scientist in the Life Span Institute, and Director of the Kansas University Center on Developmental Disabilities. Her research focuses on self-determination and systems of support for people with disabilities, and she has a specific interest in the multiple, nested contextual factors that impact outcomes. She has published over 130 articles in peer-reviewed journals, is the Author or Coauthor of 10 books, and is one of the coauthors of *Intellectual Disability: Definition, Classification, and Systems of Support* (11th edition) of the American Association on Intellectual and Developmental Disabilities' seminal definition of intellectual disability as well as the Supports Intensity Scale – Children's and Adult Version. Dr. Shogren is also the lead author of the *Self-Determination Inventory System*, a newly development measurement system for self-determination. Dr. Shogren has received grant funding from several sources, including the Institute of Education Sciences (IES) and National Institute on Disability, Independent Living, and Rehabilitation Research (NIDILRR). Dr. Shogren is co-Editor of *Remedial and Special Education*.

Brian H. Abery, PhD is a Senior Research Associate at the University of Minnesota's Institute on Community Integration as well as an Adjunct Faculty Member within the Special Education Program. He serves as the Co-director of the Institute's Research and Training Center on HCBS Outcome Measurement and Global Disability Rights and Inclusion Program. He holds a doctorate in Educational Psychology and has been a Principal Investigator and Director of numerous government- and foundation-funded projects designed to promote the self-determination, healthcare coordination, social inclusion, and quality of life of persons with disabilities. He has published journal articles, technical reports, and products on self-determination, inclusive education, and residential services, as well as presented at numerous national and international conferences. He is Coauthor of the tripartite ecological model of self-determination as well as several instruments designed to assess the self-determination of children, youth, and adults with disabilities.

About the Contributors

Lynda Lahti Anderson, PhD, MPH is a Research Associate at the University of Minnesota's Institute on Community Integration. She holds a PhD in Rehabilitation Science with a focus on self-management of disability and chronic conditions as well as master's degrees in public health and health administration. She has extensive experience managing residential programs, working with families in home and school settings, and as a Case Manager for recipients of home- and community-based services. Her research interests include qualitative and mixed methods research as well as analysis of disability-focused secondary datasets. Her work at the University of Minnesota includes refinement of national survey (FINDS) on the experiences of family caregivers, secondary data analyses and data briefs related to family caregiver outcomes, and serving as Project Director for a Family Information Systems Project.

Marjorie Aunos, PhD is an internationally renowned Researcher, Adjunct Professor at two Canadian universities, and Clinical Psychologist. She was a Director of Professional Services within a health and social service agency in Montreal, Canada, and founded an evidence-based program for parents with an intellectual disability that is nationally recognized and deemed as best and promising practice by Accreditation Canada. She is also the Chair of the International Association for the Scientific Study of Intellectual and Developmental Disabilities (IASSIDD) Special Interest Research Group on Parents and Parenting with Intellectual Disabilities (SIRG/PID) and has led a number of book chapters and presented at national and international conferences. She was a Coeditor of a double special issue of the *Journal of Applied Research in Intellectual Disabilities* and has published many and various peer-reviewed manuscripts.

Christine Bigby, PhD, FIASSIDD is Professor and Director of the Living with Disability Research Centre at La Trobe University, Melbourne, Australia. She has a long track record of working in partnership with disability support organizations investigating the effectiveness of social programs and policies that aim to support the social inclusion of adults and older people with intellectual disability. She has won the Research Prize of the Australasian Society for Intellectual Disability three times since 1993. She is a Member of the College of Experts of the Australian Research Council and has published 6 books, 35 book chapters, over 135 journal articles, and numerous research reports. She is Founding Editor of the journal *Research and Practice in Intellectual and Developmental Disabilities* (RAPIDD) and was Editor of *Australian Social Work* from 2008 to 2013.

Helen I. Cannella-Malone, PhD is Professor of Special Education at The Ohio State University. She has taught students of all ages who have significant disabilities and has been involved in special education teacher education both at the pre- and in-service levels. She has been at Ohio State since 2005. Her research focuses on teaching people with severe to profound disabilities new skills and the assessment of preferences and provision of choice for students with significant physical and intellectual disabilities. She has worked in public schools, private educational behavioral programs, and homes developing behavioral programs. She also serves as the Vice Provost for Academic Policy and Faculty Resources.

Nicholas P. Cocchiarella, BA is a strong advocate for equality among all humans, no matter the shape of our bodies and minds. He graduated from the University of St. Thomas in 2014 with a degree in communications and journalism and is planning on furthering his education in the area of vocational rehabilitation. His interests include long walks through nature, nerding out over Harry Potter, and enjoying craft beer.

Bernadette Curryer, MHlthSc (Dev Disability) is currently a PhD Candidate at The University of Sydney, researching self-determination of adults with intellectual disability within the context of family relationships. Beginning her career as a Registered Nurse, she later moved into the disability sector and worked primarily in the fields of advocacy and adult education. As a Board Director of the Australasian Society for Intellectual Disability, she is actively involved in the promotion of quality practice through research dissemination. These professional roles, together with her experience of parenting an adult daughter with an intellectual disability, have resulted in a strong belief in the right of people with disability to live a life of choice, purpose, and inclusion.

Angela Dew, PhD is Associate Professor of Disability and Inclusion at Deakin University Melbourne, Australia. She has worked for over 35 years as a Practitioner, Manager, and Academic in the Australian disability sector. Her research focuses on understanding the lived experience of people with disability and their families with a particular interest in those with complex support needs. She uses participatory, action research and arts-based approaches to ensure her research is inclusive of end users. She is the recipient of the 2016 Centre for Disability Studies Trevor Parmenter Research Excellence Award for her work in translating research into practice. She has published extensively and regularly presents at national and international conferences.

Karen R. Fisher, PhD is a Professor at the Social Policy Research Centre, UNSW, Sydney, where she leads the Disability Research Program. Her research interests are the organization of social services in Australia and China, including disability and mental health community services, inclusive research and evaluation methodology, and social policy process.

Jacinta Douglas is Professor and Deputy Director of the Living with Disability Research Centre at La Trobe University in Melbourne, Australia. Her qualifications span the disciplines of speech pathology, clinical psychology and neuropsychology. She has extensive research and clinical experience in the rehabilitation of adults with traumatic brain injury and has authored over 130 journal articles and 10 book chapters. Her research contribution has advanced knowledge particularly in the domains of interpersonal communication and psychosocial functioning. She is a fellow and past president of the Australasian Society for the Study of Brain Impairment and a fellow of Speech Pathology Australia.

Marja W. Hodes, PhD is Clinical Psychologist and Head of the Psychologists of the Dutch service organization ASVZ, Department of Family Services. She has worked for the past 35 years with families headed by parents with intellectual disabilities. Together with her colleagues, she developed the toolkit "Talking About Children." This toolkit supports future parents with intellectual disabilities to think carefully about the consequences of having and raising a child. In 2010, she won a national award for this toolkit. With the money from this award, she built a website with free downloadable tools to support future parents. In addition to her clinical work, in 2008, she started scientific research concerning parenting by parents with intellectual disabilities at the VU Amsterdam. She developed the Video-Feedback Intervention to Promote Positive Parenting for Parents with Learning Difficulties (VIPP-LD) with a focus on harmonious parent-child interactions and sensitive discipline.

Berit Höglund is a Registered Nurse and Midwife in Sweden. For nearly 30 years, she worked as a Midwife at the delivery ward, in antenatal care, and with family planning. In the 1990s, she became interested in midwifery care for women with intellectual disability. In the early 2000s, she received a masters' degree in medical science, which led to her further studies. She completed her doctoral studies in 2012 at the Department of Women's and Children's Health at Uppsala University, Sweden. The overall aim of her thesis was to investigate pregnancy and childbirth in women with intellectual disability and the health of their newborns in Sweden. Her postdoctoral studies have focused among other things on the health of pre-school children born to women with intellectual disability and on contraception in women with intellectual disability.

Roni Holler, PhD is a Lecturer at the Paul Baerwald School of Social Work and Social Welfare at the Hebrew University of Jerusalem and a Member of the Center for Disability Studies. His research is situated at the intersection of social policy, disability studies, and social work. Within this broad field, one of his primary research interests is the living conditions of people with disabilities and the ways in which the welfare state and its key agents – social workers – take part in constructing these conditions. His current research projects focus on guardianship for people with disabilities and take-up of social security benefits.

Gunnel Janeslätt, PhD, MSc, OT(reg) is an employed Researcher at SUF Resource Center in Uppsala and is associated with the Department of Public Health and Caring Sciences, Disability and Habilitation and Center for Clinical Research Dalarna, both at Uppsala University, Sweden. Her research focuses on assessment and intervention to make daily life manageable for children, youth, adults, and elderly with difficulties related to cognitive limitations including time processing ability. She was engaged in developing the ISO Guidelines for Daily Time Management and General Guideline for Cognitive Accessibility and in developing national guidelines on support for parents with children in care. She is presently involved in culturally adapting and evaluating clinically useful methods for support in daily time management and in parental competencies. She leads the Nordic Research and Practitioner Network for research about children and parents when parents have cognitive limitations.

Laurie Kincade, MA is a Doctoral Candidate in the School Psychology PhD Program at the University of Minnesota. She has worked for nearly 4 years as a Graduate Assistant at the Institute on Community Integration with research focusing on the importance of self-determination for individuals with disabilities. She has also assisted on projects focusing on smart home technology, reading assessments, and implementation science. She has coauthored publications in these areas and is currently working on two other manuscripts. Her own research interests include the importance of student-teacher relationships and social-emotional learning programs and practices at a universal and school- and class-wide level. She has deep passion for diversity and equity within all of her work.

Dušan Klapko, PhD has been a Faculty Member at the Department of Social Pedagogy at Masaryk University in Brno, Czech Republic, since 2005. In his teaching, he focuses on social theories, social inclusion, history of social pedagogy, as well as methodological approaches and courses in experiential pedagogy. In his research, he analyzes textbooks, power discourses in the area of socialization of Roma children, and the impact of theater on education and experiential learning. His most notable accomplishments include the completion of two large-scale projects focused on the education and opportunities for social inclusion of Roma students and a project of the National Heritage Institute of the Czech Republic for which he received the Europa Nostra Award.

Carmel Laragy, PhD is an Accredited AASW Member and a Senior Research Fellow at the School of Social and Political Sciences, The University of Melbourne, Australia. After working as a Social Work Practitioner in several fields, she has contributed to the introduction of individual funding into disability services since the early 2000s. She has a deep commitment to promoting services and supports that empower people and give them maximum choice and control over their lives. She has studied individual funding programs internationally, evaluated national programs, and published widely. She is on the committee of management of a self-advocacy service for people with intellectual disability and convenes a peer support group for social workers navigating the National Disability Insurance Scheme (NDIS).

Gwynnyth Llewellyn, PhD, FIASSIDD is Professor of Family and Disability Studies at the University of Sydney. She is Co-director of the Centre of Research Excellence in Disability and Health, Leader in the WHO Collaborating Centre on Strengthening Rehabilitation Capacity in Health Systems, and a Stream Leader in the Centre for Disability Research and Policy. Her research aims to bring about inclusive societies for children with disabilities and families headed by parents with disabilities. Her work focuses on inequities with a particular focus on discrimination, abuse and neglect, and the lifelong impact on health and well-being. She has published extensively with colleagues and graduate students on this topic. Her latest contribution to this field is the chapter on parents with disabilities in the *Handbook of Parenting* (third edition) published by Routledge in early 2019.

Charlotta Löfgren-Mårtenson, PhD is Professor of Health and Society in the field of Sexology and Sexuality Studies at Malmö University in Sweden. Her main research area is on sexuality and young people with intellectual disabilities, focusing on societal and cultural norms as well as digital social arenas. "Hip to be Crip? About Crip Theory, Sexuality and People with Intellectual Disabilities" (Löfgren-Mårtenson, 2013) and "We Need Culture Bridges: Challenges in Sex Education for Youths with Intellectual Disabilities in a Multicultural Society" (Löfgren-Mårtenson & Ouis, 2018) are some of her publications. She has received the RFSU Prize Award and Intra-award for her groundbreaking work in the field.

Philip McCallion, PhD is Professor and Director of the School of Social Work within the College of Public Health at Temple University. His research advances evidence-based interventions in health promotion, falls reduction, caregiver support, dementia management, and service system redesign. He is Co-founder/Co-principal investigator/Co-applicant of the Intellectual Disability Supplement to the Irish Longitudinal Study on Aging and Co-investigator on longitudinal studies of dementia in persons with Down syndrome. He is Visiting/Adjunct Professor at Trinity College Dublin, a John A. Hartford Foundation Social Work Faculty Scholar and Mentor, and a Fellow of the International Association for the Scientific Study of Intellectual and Developmental Disabilities and of the Gerontological Society of America. Serving on international consensus panels and the Steering Committee of the National Task Group on Intellectual Disabilities and Dementia, he is the National Consultant on Intellectual Disabilities and Dementia for the US National Alzheimer's and Dementia Resource Center.

Mary McCarron, PhD, MA, RN ID, RGN, BNS, FTCD is Professor of Ageing and Intellectual Disability and Director of the Trinity Centre for Excellence in Ageing and Intellectual Disability. She is the Founder and Principal Investigator for the first ever Intellectual Disability Supplement to the Irish Longitudinal Study on Ageing (IDS-TILDA) in persons with intellectual disability conducted in Ireland or internationally. This study is a supplement to The Irish Longitudinal Study on Ageing (TILDA). She has led large longitudinal cohort studies in the area of dementia in people with Down syndrome spanning over 25 years focused on early detection and presentation of dementia and the development of humane approaches to care and support. Award-winning approaches on environmental design and technology innovations sustain and improve quality of life. She is currently setting up a national memory service for people with Down syndrome. In 2019, her work was awarded the inaugural HRB Impact Award.

Darren McCausland, PhD is Research Fellow at the Trinity Centre for Ageing and Intellectual Disability and the Intellectual Disability Supplement to the Irish Longitudinal Study on Ageing (IDS-TILDA) at Trinity College Dublin, where he leads on social and community research. His research interests broadly include social inclusion and community participation for adults with an intellectual disability. He has published and presented research papers on a range of topics including relationships and social connection, choice, human rights and citizenship, family caring, future care planning, person-centered support, transport, employment, and occupation.

Mary-Ann O'Donovan, PhD is Assistant Professor in Intellectual Disability and Inclusion and Coordinator of a 2-year accredited program for students with intellectual disability in Trinity College Dublin. She is Research Lead on the theme of transitions on the Intellectual Disability Supplement to the Irish Longitudinal Study on Ageing. Her main research interests include key life transitions, particularly housing and education transitions, inclusive practice in education and physical activity, related issues of choice and self-determination, policy analysis, health service utilization, and access to health services for people with an intellectual disability.

Terje Olsen, PhD (Sociology) is Research Director at Fafo Institute for Labour and Social Research in Oslo, Norway. His research interests are welfare state issues, disability studies, youth research, marginalization, participation in the labor market, legal rights, and access to justice for persons with disabilities. His PhD thesis is based on ethnographic fieldwork and participatory observation in work settings with persons with intellectual disabilities. He is Editor of the journal *Nordic Welfare Research*.

Wenwei Ouyang, BS is Principal of Shenzhen Yuanping Special Education School in Guangdong Province in China and Chairperson of the Special Education Steering Committee in Guangdong Vocational and Technical Education Association. He has been working in the field of vocational education and special education for 29 years.

Laura Pacheco, MSW, PhD is a Clinician Researcher in an evidence-based parenting service for persons with intellectual disability at the CUISSS-ODIM in Montreal, Quebec. Her research and practice are focused on improving the quality of life and fostering equality in the lives of parents with intellectual disability and their children. Her research interests include participation and self-advocacy, improving services, practices and systems capacity, narratives, integrating critical disability, and intersectionality theory in research and practice. She has published various peer-reviewed manuscripts and has presented in various international workshops and conferences.

Miriam Pomerantz is a Bachelor's degree student at the Paul Baerwald School of Social Work and the Faculty of Law at the Hebrew University of Jerusalem. She is a Leading Research Assistant at the Center for Disability Studies and has participated in the Legal Rights Clinic for People with Disabilities.

Linsey M. Sabielny, PhD, BCBA-D is an Assistant Professor of Special Education at DePaul University's College of Education. With diverse work experiences in home-, clinic-, and school-based programs across the United States and other countries, she has continuously aimed to improve the education of individuals with more significant developmental, intellectual, and physical disabilities. Her research focuses on identifying the most effective instructional, prompting, and assessment methods for this population. Specifically, her work centers on preference assessment methodology, prompting strategies, and daily living and vocational and leisure skill acquisition. Her work has been published in a variety of peer-reviewed outlets including the *Journal of Applied Behavior Analysis*, *Journal of Developmental and Physical Disabilities*, and *Exceptional Children*.

Aaron D. Schaper, BA is a Research Assistant at the Institute on Community Integration and a graduate student in the Counseling and Student Personnel Psychology Program at the University of Minnesota. He has worked with individuals with varying disabilities both as a direct support professional and as an advocate seeking to improve support services. He currently works on the Care Profiler project which analyzes the implementation of training techniques and their utility to in-home care supervisors. He also serves as a mental health practitioner at Christian Family Solutions in Lakeville, MN, facilitating group skills work for individuals and groups with mental health challenges.

Jan Šiška, PhD is an Associate Professor at the Faculty of Education, Charles University, and West Bohemia University in the Czech Republic. For the last decade, he has been serving as a country representative for the Academic Network of European Disability Experts and has conducted research both within the Czech Republic and internationally into deinstitutionalization and community living, active citizenship, access to education for learners with disabilities, policy development in the EU, and staff training, for example, in Cambodia, Bhutan, India, and Ethiopia. He recently served as a Lead Consultant on special and inclusive education for Federal Ministry of Education in Ethiopia.

John G. Smith, MSW is a Coordinator at the Institute on Community Integration at the University of Minnesota. He has assisted with applied research and led program evaluations in community programs serving persons with intellectual and developmental disabilities (IDDs) for the past 25 years. His primary goal is to improve the lives of people with IDDs, and his interests include promoting self-determination and self-advocacy, translating knowledge to make it useful to families and people with IDDs, and measuring quality in services and supports. He also has lived experience as a person with cerebral palsy and professional experience in supporting the self-advocacy movement and serving as an advocate for people with IDDs.

Margaret Spencer, PhD has over 30 years' experience working with parents with intellectual disability and their children. Her doctoral research resulted in the development of the UPS – a novel supported decision-making process to assist family workers and parents with intellectual disability work together to understand and plan support for parenting. She currently lectures in the Social Work Program in the Faculty of Arts and Social Science at the University of Sydney.

Lydia Springer is a Licensed Clinical Psychologist with an advanced specialist degree within the area of disability and works at the Habilitation and at SUF Resource Center, Region Uppsala, Sweden. For over 20 years, she has been contributing with her knowledge about disability and parenting to increase best practice for families at a local, regional, and national level. She has been involved in research, developing national guidelines and collaboration strategies, as well as culturally adapting and evaluating clinically useful methods for supporting children and parents when parents have cognitive limitations.

Juan Tang, MS is a Doctoral Student in the School of Psychology at the University of Newcastle in Australia. Her research focuses on intergroup contact, with a particular focus on the motivational predictors of intergroup contact and how it works to reduce prejudice. She is a Co-investigator of several national projects on employment services for persons with disabilities in China.

Beth Tarleton, MPhil, PGCE is a Senior Research Fellow at the Norah Fry Centre for Disability Studies, School for Policy Studies, University of Bristol. For the last 14 years, her research has mainly focused on positive support strategies for parents with intellectual disabilities. She coordinates the Working Together with Parents Network (wtpn.co.uk) which is a free network for professionals supporting parents with intellectual disabilities. Her teaching focuses mainly on inclusive research methods, research ethics, and support for parents with intellectual disabilities.

Olha Telna, PhD is an Associate Professor in the Department of Correctional Education and Special Psychology at the Kharkiv Academy for Humanitarian and Pedagogical Studies. Her applied research focuses on education and upbringing of children with visual and speech disabilities, both in special and inclusive schools.

Her interests include independent living, participation, self-determination, motivation, support, as well as legal, financial, and human resource provision. She is an Activist in the Ukrainian disability movement. She regularly participates in regional and national seminars and conferences and has numerous publications in Ukraine. She is a Coordinator of the project on international cooperation (with the University of Minnesota's Global Resource Centre) Without Borders: Developing and Sustaining Inclusive Educational Community and a Member of the National Special Educators' Union of Ukraine.

Renáta Tichá, PhD is a Research Director and a Co-director of the Global Resource Center on Inclusive Education at the University of Minnesota's Institute on Community Integration. She has extensive experience in the development, implementation, and evaluation of assessments and interventions for children and adults with different types of disabilities. She has been a Principal Investigator (PI) or a Co-PI on multiple national and international grants, including the National Core Indicators, a national dataset on outcomes of people with intellectual and developmental disabilities, Research and Training Center on Home- and Community-Based Services Outcomes Measurement, and a UNICEF project focused on enhancing the inclusion of children and youth with disabilities in Armenia. Her international work has focused on issues of inclusive education and the rights of people with disabilities in post-Soviet and Asian countries. She serves as the Editor of the *Journal of the International Association of Special Education.*

Yotam Tolub, MA is an international expert on legal capacity. He is an Israeli Disability Rights Lawyer and currently working on his PhD on disability rights and elderly rights. He is the Former Executive Director of Bizchut – the Israel Human Rights Center for People with Disabilities – and was one of the leaders of the Israeli legal capacity reform. He has represented hundreds of clients with disabilities throughout the last decade. He has been working on the international sphere supporting local and international efforts to promote law reforms on legal capacity and disability rights in over a dozen countries and has been active in developing practice models in this field and publishing research on these issues.

Jan Tøssebro, PhD (Sociology) is Professor of Social Work at the Norwegian University of Science and Technology (NTNU) in Trondheim, Norway. His research profile is the study of ideal-reality gaps in disability policies, thus contrasting policy ideals with the experiences of disabled people. His research addresses among others deinstitutionalization, service systems, growing up with disability, family issues, education, employment, and living conditions. He has been a Member of public committees on disability policy and was the President of the Norwegian State Council on Disability for 4 years. He was the First President of the Nordic Network on Disability Research and Editor of the *Scandinavian Journal of Disability Research* from 2002 to 2004. He has published extensively on disability issues in both English and Scandinavian languages.

Irene Tuffrey-Wijne, PhD, RN is Professor of Intellectual Disability and Palliative Care at the Joint Faculty of Kingston University and St George's, University of London. A nurse by background, she has extensive clinical experience in palliative care. She also spent many years as a support worker for people with intellectual disabilities. Since 2001, she has focused on doing research to improve the end-of-life care and bereavement care of people with intellectual disabilities, with a particular focus on breaking bad news, communication, and involvement of people with intellectual disabilities in their own care. She is Chair of the UK-based Palliative Care of People with Learning Disabilities (PCPLD) Network and of the Reference Group on Intellectual Disabilities of the European Association for Palliative Care (EAPC), which published a White Paper on Palliative Care for People with Intellectual Disabilities in 2015. She received the 2017 EAPC Postdoctoral Research Award.

Shirli Werner, PhD is an Associate Professor at the Paul Baerwald School of Social Work and Social Welfare and Head of the Center for Disability Studies at the Hebrew University of Jerusalem. Her applied research aims to improve the quality of life of individuals with disabilities and secure their rights. As such, her main research interests are on community inclusion and participation, school inclusion, choice, self-determination, and stigma focusing most specifically on individuals with intellectual disabilities. She has presented papers at numerous research conferences and has published extensively on these issues including coediting the book *Intellectual Disability and Stigma: Stepping Out from the Margins*.

Michele Y. Wiese, PhD, MA, PS, FASID is Lecturer in Applied Psychology at Western Sydney University, Australia. She has worked as a Clinician, Educator, and Researcher in the intellectual disability sector for over 30 years. For the last 10 years, her research focus has been end-of-life care. She is Honorary Senior Research Fellow at the University of Sydney's Centre for Disability Research and Policy, Faculty of Health Sciences, and Fellow of the Australasian Society for Intellectual Disability. She has published extensively and is Consulting Editor to two international peer-reviewed journals.

Tianxi Xu, PhD is an Associate Professor of Special Education and Disabilities Studies in the Department of Special Education in the School of Education at the Central China Normal University and an Honorary Senior Research Fellow at the University of Sydney's Centre for Disability Research and Policy. His research focuses on school-to-work transition for students with intellectual and developmental disabilities. He is Chair and Principal Investigator of the post-school transition and support projects for people with intellectual disability and autism.

Yuan Zhou, BEd is Director of the Vocational Education Department at Shenzhen Yuanping Special Education School in Guangdong Province in China. She has been working in the field of special education, vocational training, and supported employment services for 16 years.

Part I
Overview of Choice and Preference

Choice Availability and People with Intellectual Disability

Roger J. Stancliffe

This chapter begins with a reflection on the range of reasons why choice is important. Definitions of choice are considered next, including examination of common misunderstandings of choice. Next, I describe and analyse major assessments of choice availability, with attention to assessment involving self-reported choice versus choices reported by proxies. This section is followed by an examination of the major research findings concerning choice availability for adults with intellectual disability. This chapter also engages with the under-researched topic of choice within various types of relationships. Implementing choices with and without support is considered in the context of the implicit tension between autonomy-as-independence and autonomy-as-volition (see chapter "The Development of Choice-Making and Implications for Promoting Choice and Autonomy for Children and Youth with Intellectual and Developmental Disabilities"). This chapter concludes with a brief examination of 'what works': interventions that purport to enhance choice availability. A number of the issues canvassed are examined in more detail in other chapters of the book, so where appropriate, reference is made to the relevant chapters.

Why Is Choice Important?

There are multiple reasons why choice is particularly important for and to people with intellectual disability. First, people with disabilities themselves have stated repeatedly that they want to control their own lives (Miller, Cooper, Cook, & Petch, 2008). As New Zealand self-advocate Robert Martin put it, 'We want to live in a community that encourages us to learn about decision-making and to take

R. J. Stancliffe (✉)
Centre for Disability Research and Policy, The University of Sydney, Sydney, NSW, Australia
e-mail: roger.stancliffe@sydney.edu.au

© Springer Nature Switzerland AG 2020
R. J. Stancliffe et al. (eds.), *Choice, Preference, and Disability*, Positive Psychology and Disability Series, https://doi.org/10.1007/978-3-030-35683-5_1

responsibility for our own decisions. Until this happens, true empowerment and self-determination can only be a dream' (Martin, 2006, p. 127). This issue is taken up in depth in the chapter "Reflections on Choice: The Stories of Self-Advocates" of this volume which reports the views of prominent US self-advocates about choice.

Second, there is a problem of restricted availability of choice to people with intellectual disability compared to the general community. Research shows people with intellectual disability make far fewer choices (Sheppard-Jones, Prout, & Kleinert, 2005; Wehmeyer & Abery, 2013).

Third, because of these issues, choice and self-determination have become prominent features of national legislation and policy in many countries. For example, in the chapter "Choice, Control and Individual Funding: The Australian National Disability Insurance Scheme", Laragy and Fisher discuss Australia's *National Disability Insurance Scheme,* which is designed with choice and control by people with a disability as fundamental and explicit design principles. Xu and his co-authors in the chapter "Choices and Transition from School to Adult Life: Experiences in China" comment that self-determination and choice for people with disability are relatively new concepts in China, but also note that these ideas are beginning to appear in school curricula, suggesting a more positive climate may be developing. By contrast, recent changes in regulations that limit support available to Norwegians with intellectual disability for choosing integrated employment are examined by Tøssebro and Olsen in the chapter "Employment Opportunities for People with Intellectual Disabilities".

Fourth, choice is central to the Convention on the Rights of Persons with Disabilities (United Nations [UN], 2006), where choice is identified as a human right. For example, Article 19 states that 'Persons with disabilities have the opportunity to choose their place of residence and where and with whom they live on an equal basis with others'. However, Tichá and her co-authors in the chapter "Choices, Preferences and Disability: A View from Central and Eastern Europe" discuss the numerous attitudinal, service-provision and policy barriers that continue to substantially constrain choice by people with intellectual disability in Central and Eastern Europe, despite many countries there having signed and ratified the United Nations Convention on the Rights of Persons with Disabilities (UN, 2006).

Fifth, self-determination and choice comprise a fundamental domain of quality of life (QOL) (Schalock, Verdugo, Gomez, & Reinders, 2016). For example, Neely-Barnes, Marcenko and Weber (2008) showed empirically that exercising more choice was positively related to better QOL outcomes for other QOL factors such as rights, community inclusion and relationships.

Sixth, having choice has positive effects on other outcomes. For example, choice improves activity engagement and reduces challenging behaviours (Tullis et al., 2011; Zelinsky & Shadish, 2018; the chapter "Preference Assessments, Choice, and Quality of Life for People with Significant Disabilities" of this book by Cannella-Malone & Sabielny).

What Is Choice?

A number of similar definitions of choice have been proposed in the intellectual disability literature. Stancliffe (2001) reviewed earlier definitions of choice and identified elements such as (a) actively making a choice based on one's preference and not passively accepting decisions made by others, (b) selection from a minimum of two options and (c) free choice without coercion. Based on these three components, Stancliffe proposed the following definition: 'making an unforced selection of a preferred alternative from two or more options' (Stancliffe, 2001, p. 92). This definition appears compatible with more recent definitions such as 'choice-making requires that a person … can choose without coercion, and can express a preference to others' (Wehmeyer, 2007, p. 19).

Choices take place in a context, and appropriate environmental conditions are necessary to access, make and communicate choices. As described by Cannella-Malone and Sabielny in the chapter "Preference Assessments, Choice, and Quality of Life for People with Significant Disabilities", for people with significant disabilities and limited communication repertoires, opportunities for choice may require the support person to present alternatives carefully and to respond to selection methods, such as eye gaze, used by the person to communicate preferences. These authors also emphasise the importance of routinely incorporating many opportunities for choice throughout the day.

In addition to the immediate here-and-now context, developmental factors underpin choice. As Wehmeyer and Shogren point out in their chapter "The Development of Choice-Making and Implications for Promoting Choice and Autonomy for Children and Youth with Intellectual and Developmental Disabilities", making and communicating selections in childhood, and experiencing the consequences of these choices, provides the foundation for more complex choice and decision making in later life.

Stancliffe's (2001) definition describes minimum requirements for choice to exist, but there are other factors at play when considering more fully developed choice. Ideally, there would be many more than two options, and the individual would generate the options, rather than someone else controlling the available alternatives. Choice between two or more unattractive options is often viewed as a dilemma rather than a real choice. For example, one's day activity options being restricted to sheltered employment, unpaid day activities at a disability centre or having no structured daytime activity may all be unattractive to a person who is seeking a fully paid job in the mainstream workforce. However, as noted in the chapter "Employment Opportunities for People with Intellectual Disabilities" on employment, a key consideration is the individual's appraisal of the options. If one or more of these options are considered valued and attractive, then the person has a real choice.

In addition, there is an important distinction between making a choice and implementing it. Wehmeyer and Shogren in their chapter "The Development of Choice-Making and Implications for Promoting Choice and Autonomy for Children and

Youth with Intellectual and Developmental Disabilities" propose the concept of *autonomy-as-volition*. This approach focuses on the person *making* their own choice with *implementation* of the choice involving whatever support is needed.

Misunderstandings about choice A misguided interpretation of choice has some-times been used to try to justify poor support of people with intellectual disability. For example, some may see a person with intellectual disability spending large amounts of time doing nothing (euphemistically described as *relaxing*) as an active choice and an indication of a preference for inactivity. Logically, a preference for inactivity requires evidence that the person rejects activity alternatives and opts to do nothing, that the activity offered is known to be enjoyed by the person and that appropriate support for participation is provided. By contrast, an approach called *Active Support* 'assumes that people with severe ID are disengaged not through their own active choice, but because the assistance needed to participate is unavail-able' (Stancliffe, Jones, Mansell & Lowe, 2008, p. 209). Active Support is a well-developed approach that involves carefully structured support for participation in chosen activities and is particularly relevant to people with more severe disability who may not be able to initiate a desired activity without support.

Brown and Brown (2009) commented on another misunderstanding of choice which proposes that people with intellectual disability should choose anything they like, with any unpleasant consequences simply seen as an unavoidable result of the choice made. This approach overlooks the possibility that the person is making an uninformed choice, unaware of some negative outcomes. Brown and Brown pro-posed an educative approach, whereby the person is supported to think through the consequences and given the opportunity to change their mind or to experience and learn from the consequences if they proceed with their choice. van Hooren, Widdershoven, van den Borne and Curfs (2002) described a similar joint learning approach as a means of dealing with the ethical dilemma of managing risk and pre-serving choice.

Assessing Choice Availability

As noted elsewhere in this chapter, fundamental research findings include (a) that people with intellectual disability have access to fewer choices than their peers and (b) that other people either make the choice for the person or provide the person with restricted choice or limited control. Therefore, major objectives of policy and practice are to increase access to choice and to enhance the person's level of control over the outcomes of these choices. Having assessments that can provide informa-tion on these issues is necessary to document, understand and change these restricted opportunities. The assessments examined in this section have largely been devel-oped to assess these dimensions of choice making – availability of choice and control over choices.

Assessment methods for identifying specific individual preferences (e.g. preferring tea to coffee or hot chocolate) have also been the focus of considerable research attention, especially relating to individuals who are unable to state their preferences. These issues of preference assessment are examined in the chapter "Preference Assessments, Choice, and Quality of Life for People with Significant Disabilities" of this book and will not be considered in the present chapter. Other aspects of choice assessment, such as measuring the steps involved in making choices or identifying the sources of support for choice making, have received much less attention from researchers developing choice assessments. One likely reason for this approach is that these other factors tend to be moot if the choice is not available to the person.

Stancliffe (2001, Table 1) listed four scales designed to assess choices available to people with intellectual disability (Kearney, Durand, & Mindell, 1995; Kishi, Teelucksingh,, Zollers, & Meyer, 1988; Schalock & Keith, 1993; Stancliffe & Parmenter, 1999). More recently, O'Donovan et al. (2017, Table 1) described eight scales. Table 1 below is a revised and expanded version of Stancliffe's (2001) Table 1. It does not claim to be comprehensive listing of every available scale. To help readers who seek access to the item content of the scales listed in Table 1, the studies which include full information about scale item wording and scoring are identified with a superscript 'a' in the second column.

Item content   Very large numbers of choices are potentially available to people every day. A comprehensive listing would generate unwieldy and impractical assessment tools. Instead, the available assessment tools listed in Table 1 each include items on a limited selection of choices (ranging from 3 to 26 items) intended to serve as indicators of choice availability more generally. This approach to content selection requires items that are applicable to most people and representative of choices more generally. This selection issue has been dealt with by:

- Choosing item content related to choice within activities that most people engage with often (e.g. what to eat, when to go to bed, leisure activities) so as to minimise missing data due to non-applicable items and to capture the person's typical level of control because the item involves a choice that occurs very regularly
- Framing questions to relate to broader choice issues not specific options, such as 'Who decides your daily schedule [like when to get up, when to eat, when to go to sleep]?' (Lakin et al., 2008, p. 330)

It is notable that there is similarity in the item content of a number of the scales listed in Table 1. One reason is that new scales have often borrowed or adapted items from earlier assessments. For example, the choice items used by Kishi et al. (1988) provided most of the items in the scales examined by Heller et al. (2000) and by O'Donovan et al. (2017). O'Donovan et al. (p. 475, parenthetical material added) also noted that 'of the 9 items in the NCI scales (used by Lakin et al., 2008 and Tichá et al., 2012), 6 of these items are included in the adapted Heller et al. (2000) used in this study'. The scales set out in Table 1 mostly focus on residential, community and leisure issues, with limited attention to other settings. One exception is the scale used by Agran, Storey and Krupp (2010) which examines choices at work.

Table 1 Scales assessing choice

Scale	Authors	Item content	Respondent (self or proxy)	Response scale
Life Choices Survey	Kishi et al. (1988)[a]	11-item scale (including a 'lie' item)	Self-report or proxy	5-point Likert scale ranging from choice *not available/ appropriate to me* to *I can make this choice when I want to*
Resident Choice Assessment Scale	Kearney et al. (1995)	25-item scale about adults	Proxies (direct-care staff)	7-point Likert scale ranging from *Never* to *Always*
Quality of Life Questionnaire – Empowerment factor	Schalock and Keith (1993)[b]	10-item scale about choices and control over one's life	Self-report or completed by two proxies	3-point scale – item-specific options, each ranging from free choice to very little/no choice
Choice Questionnaire	Stancliffe and Parmenter (1999)[a]	26-item scale dealing with a variety of choices for adults	Self-report or proxy	3-point scale – item-specific options, each ranging from free choice to others decide/I am not allowed
Daily Choice Inventory Scale	Heller, Miller, Hsieh and Sterns (2000)[a]	12 items	Proxy	2-point scale – choice made by self; others
The Resident Choice Scale	Hatton, Emerson and Robertson (2004)[a]	26-item scale on opportunities for choice in residential settings	Proxy	4-point scale: No supports/ opportunities for choice; Little real choice; expresses preference but does not have final say; Person's expressed preference is the final say
Everyday Choice Scale Support-Related Choice Scale	Lakin et al. (2008)[a] Tichá et al. (2012)[a]	3 items (everyday choice) and 6 items (support-related choice) from the *National Core Indicators Adult Consumer Survey*	Self-report or proxy	3 response options: person chooses; person has help choosing/has some input/can request a change; someone else chooses
Unnamed scale	Agran, Storey and Krupp (2010)	6-item scale about the availability of choices and support for choice making at work	Self-report	2-point (yes/no)
		7-item scale about work-related choices (a) made today and (b) usually made	Self-report	2-point (yes/no)

(continued)

Table 1 (continued)

Scale	Authors	Item content	Respondent (self or proxy)	Response scale
The Adapted Daily Choice Inventory Scale	O'Donovan, Byrne, McCallion and McCarron (2017)[a]	14-item scale	Self-report or proxy	3-point scale (I chose, supported choice, someone else chose), or 4-point scale (as for 3-point scale plus a *no choice* category for choices that were not a part of the person's life)
Resident Choice Assessment Scale – 18	Ratti, Vickerstaff, Crabtree and Hassiotis (2017)[a]	18-item scale	Proxy	7-point Likert scale ranging from Never to Always

[a]Scale items and scoring provided in the journal article
[b]Commercially published scale

Some choice scales contain seemingly anomalous item content. The *Resident Choice Assessment Scale* (Kearney et al., 1995) and the closely related *Resident Choice Assessment Scale - 18* (Ratti et al., 2017) both include multiple items on participation in household activities, such as 'Does the client participate in the cleanup after meals?' (Ratti et al., 2017, p. 205). This wording appears to be about participation not choice. Having the opportunity to participate is different from having a choice about whether, when or how to participate. This assertion is strongly supported by Ratti et al.'s finding that there was a separate 5-item factor of the *Resident Choice Assessment Scale - 18* that measured participation in household activities as distinct from its 13-item factor measuring everyday choices.

Several important and challenging topics have received almost no attention in choice assessment scales. For example, choices related to sexuality, parenting and end of life do not appear in any of the scales listed in Table 1, except for a lone item on 'looking at sexy magazines, videos or movies' in the *Choice Questionnaire* (Stancliffe & Parmenter, 1999). Stancliffe (1995) undertook a detailed item content analysis of nine choice assessment instruments. Among the 84 different topics addressed, there was a single item in one scale on 'sexual behaviour' (unspecified) and no items dealing with the choice of becoming a parent or with choices related to end of life, such as whether to attend a funeral. Partly as a response to the absence of these seemingly taboo issues within the broader choice literature, the chapter "Choice, Relationships, and Sexuality: Sexual and Reproductive Health and Rights" of this book deals with sexuality and relationships, the chapter "The Choice of Becoming a Parent" with parenting, while the chapter "End-of-Life Choices" addresses end of life.

Factor analysis of different types of choices There are many ways that different choices could be classified according the content and circumstances of the choice. Choices about everyday matters (daily activities, what to wear, when to go to bed) have consistently been found to be more available to people with intellectual disability than choices about more major life issues (where to live, with whom to live, choice of disability staff) in research conducted in the USA (Lakin et al., 2008; Mehling, & Tassé, 2015; Tichá et al. 2012) and Ireland (O'Donovan et al., 2017 and the chapter "Choice as People Age with Intellectual Disability: An Irish Perspective"). Moreover, factor analysis has repeatedly shown these two types of choices to be empirically distinct, suggesting the importance of assessing both domains (Lakin et al., 2008; Mehling, & Tassé, 2015; O'Donovan et al., 2017; Tichá et al. 2012). That said, as noted in the section on item content above, Ratti et al. (2017) reported a somewhat different two-factor structure when they factor analysed the Resident Choice Assessment Scale (Kearney et al., 1995) – Ratti et al.'s second factor, *Participation in Household Activities* – differed from other factor-analytic studies. This divergent finding likely reflects the item content of the Resident Choice Assessment Scale that Ratti et al. examined. As noted, this scale includes multiple items related to domestic participation, such as 'Does the client participate in doing his/her laundry?' (Ratti et al., 2017, p. 205). This wording may be contrasted with items that focus on choice concerning domestic participation, such as 'Who decides which jobs you do around the house?' (Stancliffe & Parmenter, 1999, p. 126).

Response options and item scoring As the final column of Table 1 shows, scoring of individual items is mostly based on the degree of control exercised by the person with intellectual disability when making a choice. Typically, this ranges from the lowest score for no choice (e.g. others decide or the choice is not available), through some degree of choice (e.g. the person has some say but not full control), to full choice and control, which receives the highest score. Thus, total scores across items are affected both by the number of items where the person exercises some degree of choice and the degree of control exercised. That is, item scoring reflects both the availability of choice and the degree of control. There has been much less emphasis in these assessment scales on the frequency of choice, with most scales including items involving daily choices (e.g. what to wear) and items that arise rarely (e.g. where to live), without any attempt to quantify the number of such choices made.

Self-reporting and proxy reports Nine of the ten of the scales listed in Table 1 can be answered by proxies, whereas only six explicitly indicate that self-reports are appropriate. As noted by Stancliffe (2000), there has been a growing trend towards people with intellectual disability being active participants in research and express- ing their own views about their lives, instead of or in addition to the views of others (proxies). Therefore, it is surprising to see recent studies of choice availability (e.g. Ratti et al., 2017) that focus solely on proxy data.

There is ample evidence that reliable and valid self-report data can be obtained by using a number of the choice scales listed in Table 1. Clearly, many people with intellectual disability can report the choices they do and do not make, provided that appropriate instruments are used that are specifically designed to take into account their difficulties with understanding and communication. One challenge is that these instruments are usually answered orally and so tend to require verbal self-report participants with milder intellectual disability (e.g. O'Donovan et al., 2017). Findings obtained from these participants are presumed also to apply to people with more severe intellectual disability, but there is little or no direct self-report data from that population to evaluate the validity of such assumptions. Instead, most available data about the latter group comes from proxy reports. Non-verbal preference and choice assessment methods can be used with people with quite severe intellectual disability (see the chapter "Preference Assessments, Choice, and Quality of Life for People with Significant Disabilities" of this book), but these approaches are generally limited to here-and-now choices and cannot easily be applied to past or future choices such as selecting where to live or who to live with.

Data from some choice scales indicate reasonable agreement between self- and proxy reports of choice availability, such as the *Choice Questionnaire* (Perry & Felce, 2005; Stancliffe & Parmenter, 1999) and for the *Quality of Life Questionnaire - Empowerment factor* (Schalock & Keith, 1993; Stancliffe, 1999). However, there are also multiple papers showing that self- and proxy reports of choice availability can differ (see Stancliffe, 2000). Under these circumstances, it seems wise to be cautious about uncritically combining data about choice availability from self-reports and proxies. In cases where both sources of data are obtained, Stancliffe's (2000, p. 90) recommendations for data analysis likely still apply, to 'analyze self report and proxy data separately (or)... correct statistically for the influence of proxies'. An ongoing challenge is to develop reliable methods to enable more people with severe disabilities to self-report. These approaches may include (a) having symbols depicting the available response options to which respondents can point (Cuthill, Espie, & Cooper, 2003), (b) using pictures of choice options (Anderson, Sherman, Sheldon, & McAdam, 1997) and (c) emerging technologies. In their chapter "Preference Assessments, Choice, and Quality of Life for People with Significant Disabilities", Cannella-Malone and Sabielny describe non-verbal response methods for communicating preferences.

Major Research Findings About Choice Availability

This section deals with research on choice availability to people with intellectual disability and is mostly focussed on adults. The chapter "The Development of Choice-Making and Implications for Promoting Choice and Autonomy for Children and Youth with Intellectual and Developmental Disabilities" by Wehmeyer and Shogren examines key aspects of the development of preference and choice in children and youth. Adult research has generated a number of notable findings that are summarised in this section. Quite a few of the studies referred to have used one of the choice scales listed in Table 1 as the data source for their research. This section examines the fundamental issue of choice availability, a focus that was also evident in the section on assessing choice. Research on the availability of choice includes comparison with the general community, comparisons among different living arrangements and comparisons between people with different characteristics. Several environmental influences on choice availability are discussed. In addition, choice availability has been used as an outcome variable used to evaluate policies (e.g. individualised funding) and service-delivery practices.

As mentioned in the section on assessing choice availability, multiple factor-analytic studies have identified two separate types of choice: *everyday choices* that are available frequently and over which adults within intellectual disability have greater choice and control relative to the second type of choice, which involves more infrequent *major life choices* where much less choice and control are available (Lakin et al., 2008; Mehling, & Tassé, 2015; O'Donovan et al., 2017; Tichá et al. 2012). This difference appears to stem partly from other people (family, disability staff) seeking to protect the person and/or others from the enduring negative consequences of an unwise major choice, whereas everyday choices have short-lived and quite minor consequences that may only affect the individual (e.g. choices about food or clothing) (Saaltink, MacKinnon, Owen, & Tardif-Williams, 2012).

Comparison with the general community There is consistent evidence that adults with intellectual disability experience substantially less choice than their peers without disability (Kishi et al., 1988). Choices that are unavailable are all too often made by others, without even consulting the person with disability. For example, in the USA, Sheppard-Jones et al. (2005) reported that more members of the general community exercised choice on *every* issue that they assessed. The magnitude of many of the group differences was very large. For the major life choice of who to live with (roommates), on a 0 (no choice) to 2 (full choice) scale, participants with disability average score was 0.73 (37% of the scale maximum), whereas the general population averaged 1.70 (85% of the scale maximum), with a very large effect size (Cohen's $d > 1.2$, where $d = 0.8$ is usually described as a large effect).

Comparison by living arrangements Outcomes experienced by people with intellectual disability residing in different living arrangements, including choice availability, have been a major focus of research from the early years of the deinstitutionalisation era. For example, in one of the few controlled intervention studies reporting longitudinal data about choice, Stancliffe and Abery (1997) found that people who moved from an institution to community living experienced more choice than stayers who remained institutionalised. However, the authors noted that both groups had quite low levels of choice. A number of other cross-sectional studies have reported similar findings when comparing institutional and community living arrangements (Houseworth, Tichá, Smith, & Ajaj, 2018; O'Donovan et al., 2017; Tichá et al., 2012).

In addition, there are important variations in choice availability across different types and sizes of community living arrangements. Overall these findings show that people living in smaller more normalised living environments, and living more independently, experience more choice (Felce et al., 2008; Houseworth, Tichá et al.,

2018; Stancliffe & Keane, 2000; Tichá et al. 2012). People living independently in their own home experienced the most choice, whereas those in larger group homes had the least. Factors such as the constraints of group living on individual choice (e.g. Stancliffe, 1991) and the continuous presence of staff (Felce et al., 2008; Stancliffe & Keane, 2000) have been proposed as variables limiting choice in congregate community settings such as group homes.

In examining the findings of studies that compared choice availability by living arrangements, it is important to recognise that the people who live in the various settings often differ on important personal characteristics such as severity of disability. As is noted in more detail below, level of intellectual disability is strongly related to choice availability, so it is essential for meaningful comparisons that personal characteristics are controlled appropriately, for example, through matching (e.g. Stancliffe & Keane, 2000) or by statistical control (e.g. Tichá et al. 2012).

The studies considered in this section mostly reported data about disability service residential settings. With some exceptions, there has been much less focus on examining choices available to adults living in their family home. This issue is also reflected in the service-focussed item content of a number of major choice assessments. For example, the Resident Choice Scale 'was designed to assess service practices for promoting resident choice' (Hatton et al., 2004, p. 103).

Choice of where to live Later in this chapter, in the section on relationships, I discuss the availability and benefits of choosing who you live with. Everyday experience indicates that choosing where and with whom to live fundamentally influences the quality of one's domestic life, yet these choices are often not available to people with intellectual disability (Sheppard-Jones et al., 2005; Stancliffe et al., 2011). Research examining choice of where to live revealed that people with milder disability had more choice (Stancliffe et al., 2011). There were marked availability differences by type of living arrangement. As might be expected, most people (83%) living in institutions had no involvement at all in the choice to live there, whereas only 23% of those living in their own home had no choice of where to live (Stancliffe et al., 2011).

Of course, even for those who live in their own home, financial factors such as poverty and rental costs may severely limit the range of affordable choices about where to live (Stancliffe & Lakin, 2007). Increasing the income of people with ID may be one effective means of improving choice and personal control (Stancliffe, Abery, & Smith, 2000). One way to increase income is to support the person to work in mainstream community employment (Cimera, 2012).

Importantly, there is evidence, albeit cross-sectional, that choosing where to live is associated with other positive quality of life outcomes. Stancliffe, Lakin, Taub, Chiri and Byun (2009) found that individuals with greater choice of where to live also enjoyed significantly better outcomes regarding liking where they live and feeling happy and reported having staff at home who are nice and polite.

Disability service funding and regulations One important environmental factor related to choice availability is disability service funding and regulations. For example, in the USA, there is consistent evidence that residents in settings funded and regulated under the more institutional and prescriptive Intermediate Care Facility (ICF) funding experience less choice than their counterparts who use the much more flexible Home and Community-Based Services (HCBS) funding (e.g. Lakin et al., 2008). The chapter "Preference, Choice, and Self-Determination in the Health Care Context" by Abery and Anderson provides an example of such system-related impacts on choice by examining issues of choice in the American health service context. One of the stated purposes of individualised disability funding is to increase the choice and control exercised by people with disability. A randomised control trial in the UK provided strong evidence of more choice and control for recipients of such funding (Glendinning et al., 2008). In their chapter "Choice, Control and Individual Funding: The Australian National Disability Insurance Scheme" of this volume, Laragy and Fisher examine Australia's National Disability Insurance Scheme (NDIS) which has individualised funding as a fundamental design feature for all participants. These authors provide a detailed analysis of the effect of switching to individualised NDIS funding and the benefits for choice and control.

In the USA, there is consistent evidence that choice for adult service users with intellectual disability varies substantially from state to state (Houseworth, Stancliffe & Tichá, 2018; Lakin et al., 2008; Tichá et al. 2012). It seems reasonable to assume that these differences arise from between-state variability in disability funding, regulations and service provision, but evidence is limited as to which specific factors are the most important. Houseworth, Stancliffe et al.'s (2018) multivariate, multi-level analysis found that states with a larger percentage of people with disability in independent living had higher levels of support-related choice (choice of where and with whom to live, of disability staff and of type of work or day activity). The researchers argued that these types of choices are strongly affected by the state's disability service system and proposed that this factor may reflect 'a shift in state culture toward more independent living and choice' (p. 87). Importantly, this state level variable was independently related to choice in addition to an individual-level independent-living variable.

Comparison of people with intellectual disability with different personal characteristics A highly consistent research finding is that level of intellectual disability is strongly associated to choice availability. Controlling for other important factors using multivariate analysis, studies have found that those with milder intellectual disability exercise more choice (Hatton et al., 2004; Lakin et al., 2008; Ratti et al., 2017; Stancliffe et al., 2011; Tichá et al. 2012). Possible reasons for this result are discussed more fully later in this chapter in the section on implementing choices with and without support. One important research implication of this finding is that comparisons of choice availability involving other factors, such as living or working arrangements, need to control for differences in level of intellectual disability to ensure valid comparisons are made. Other issues that may help explain differences in choice availability by level of intellectual functioning have not yet received detailed research attention in this context. These include the availability of appropriate environmental supports and the expectations of support providers.

Communication skills are also closely related to choice (Brown, Gothelf, Guess, & Lehr, 1998). Both receptive (understanding a choice presented verbally) and expressive (communicating your choice) communication skills are obviously helpful in negotiating choice. For example, individuals with intellectual disability who demonstrate their communicative competence by *self-reporting* their own access to choices consistently score higher on scales of choice availability than participants who do not self-report and use a proxy (Lakin et al., 2008; Tichá et al., 2012). Several other personal characteristics such as gender and age (among adults) have been found to be unrelated to choice availability (Lakin et al., 2008). Further details on supports for those with complex communication needs are presented in the chapter "Preference Assessments, Choice, and Quality of Life for People with Significant Disabilities".

Relationships

The issue of relationships with other people and their impact on choice has received intermittent research attention. In the context of support for decision making, Bigby et al. (2017) emphasised the centrality of a positive, trusting relationship between the person with disability and the person providing the support. These issues are taken up in greater depth in the chapter "Supported Decision Making" of this volume in relation to the emergence of supported decision making as an alternative to guardianship. Likewise, in the chapter "Choice within the Israeli Welfare State: Lessons Learned From Legal Capacity and Housing Services", Holler and colleagues from Israel emphasise understanding choice in the context of relationships and interdependence. In this section, I consider the associations between choice and relationships with a range of partners: family members, friends, co-residents and disability staff.

Relationships within families Varied findings have been reported regarding family support for making choices. Studies describe different points on the continuum between protection and self-determination, but all indicate that involved family members often have a strong influence on choice making across the life span. Barriers to choice making are evident, such as overprotection by parents and encouragement or pressure to make choices consistent with family values (Saaltink et al., 2012; Shogren & Broussard, 2011). Indeed, some individuals with intellectual disability have chosen to move out of their parents' home into disability accommodation to escape parental restrictions and to obtain greater freedom to go out and participate in social activities (Cattermole, Jahoda & Markova, 1988) although other individuals may choose to remain within the family culture and engage in interdependent choice and decision making.

Curryer and her collaborators (Curryer, Stancliffe, Dew, & Wiese, 2018) have described some adults with intellectual disability actively seeking guidance from a trusted family member with a close relationship (often a mother) and apparent voluntary acceptance of limits on choice and control because of factors such as (a) the person's own recognition of their need for support to make well-informed choices, notably choices about money; (b) involvement by trusted family members in choices was accepted as being motivated by love and concern; and (c) while choices were mostly negotiated, some participants seemingly accepted the family member's right of veto. Importantly, the nature of the relationship was central. It was not any family member who was chosen for such roles, but only trusted family members with whom the person with intellectual disability had a strong positive relationship. As noted by Curryer et al. (2018, p. 197), 'Participants clearly differentiated who in their family they trusted and turned to for support'. These topics are explored more fully in the chapter "Adults with Intellectual Disability: Choice and Control in the Context of Family" as well as in the context of supported decision making in the chapter "Supported Decision Making".

Relationships with friends Friedman and Rizzolo (2018) reported that having friends (apart from staff and family) and being satisfied with the number of friends and the frequency of contact with them was positively associated with a large number of quality of life outcomes, including choice. Individuals with friends experienced significantly more choice about where and with whom to live, where to work, services and personal goals.

As is inevitable with cross-sectional research, Friedman and Rizzolo (2018) were not able to attribute causality. Reciprocal causality was likely operating, where having more choice overall opens up opportunities to choose friends and to choose to participate in activities (e.g. integrated employment) where making new friends may be possible. Likewise, having friends other than family and staff may enhance choice by making the person aware of more options to choose from (e.g. living arrangements, leisure activities) and/or exposing them to role models (e.g. friends) who exercise greater self-determination.

Two other studies reported cross-sectional analyses of National Core Indicators survey data concerning relationships (e.g. having friends and a best friend) and choice. Mehling and Tassé (2015) used structural equation modelling and reported that greater choice of disability staff (direct support staff and case manager) was associated with higher levels of a composite variable involving community participation and relationships. Neely-Barnes et al. (2008) reported similar findings for adults with mild/moderate intellectual disability. Those who made more choices also experienced better quality of life, with relationships representing one of three factors contributing to the latent quality of life variable. The two studies differed in the extent to which they controlled statistically for confounds due to factors known to be related to choice, such as level of intellectual disability, proxy responding and living arrangements. Their findings addressed friendship/relationship data in the context of an overall quality of life variable, not just friendship data alone. Nevertheless, both studies report some potentially important associations between choice, community participation and relationships, associations that likely involve reciprocal causality, as discussed previously.

Relationship with co-residents Compared to people who live alone, those who live with others exercise less choice and control (Kishi et al., 1988; Stancliffe et al., 2000). This finding should be understood in the context of *voluntarily* opting to take into account co-residents' wishes and preferences, for example, during joint decision making about a shared meal or leisure activity. When we choose to spend time with others and do things together, this often involves choosing an activity that all will enjoy, rather than one individual's preference prevailing without compromise. However, when the outcome is dictated by others and is no longer voluntary, choice is diminished. For example, in a group home, meal choices or community leisure options may be determined by co-residents' vote – the tyranny of the majority (Stancliffe, 1991). Moreover, staff often require that all co-residents participate, regardless of individual preferences (Stancliffe, 1991).

A particular case of relationships with co-residents arises with choosing one's living companions, a choice that is not available to many people with intellectual disability (Stancliffe et al., 2011). Stancliffe et al. (2011) found that choice of who to live with (or to live alone) was strongly associated with the type of living arrangements, in that people who lived in their own home exercised much more such choice than, for example, group home residents. Choice of living companions has been associated with several important QOL outcomes (Stancliffe et al., 2009). Individuals who chose who they lived with also experienced less loneliness and were more likely to report liking their home and being happy, all outcomes that would seem logically related to living with people you like, or living alone if there is no one you want to live with. Taken together, these findings appear to paint a common-sense picture of (a) choice of who to live with being more available in non-congregate settings such as one's own home, (b) people choosing living companions who they enjoy being with and (c) consequent QOL benefits. However, the studies cited are cross-sectional and, despite the use of statistical control of key personal characteristics, did not demonstrate cause and effect. Likewise, none of the studies reported data on the basis on which people choose their co-residents, so it is simply presumed that they choose wisely. Nevertheless, these studies provide important evidence that choosing who one lives with remains unavailable to many people with ID and provides another example that choice and relationships have important associations.

Relationships with disability support staff Continuity of contact between individuals is a fundamental feature of relationships. Many people with intellectual and developmental disabilities report that disability staff are their friends (Friedman & Rizzolo, 2018), but high levels of staff turnover frequently disrupt staff-client relationships. Friedman (2018) found that the majority (56%) of adult users of disability services had experienced changes in direct support staff in the past 2 years. Friedman (2018) reported a significant association between staff turnover and poorer outcomes in a wide range of quality of life domains compared to those with consistent staffing, including being significantly less likely to choose where and with whom to live or to choose their services. Once again, the cross-sectional design precludes determination of case and effect. There were also possible confounds with residence type. Not surprisingly, those living in congregate settings experienced both higher staff turnover and lower resident choice. Nevertheless, it seems reasonable to propose that disability staff who know the individual well through working with the person over an extended time are better placed to support choice making, to help identify the person's true preferences and to be more familiar with how the person communicates choice than new staff who have just started working with the individual.

A different aspect of this issue has been illuminated by studies in Australia (Stancliffe & Keane, 2000) and the UK (Felce et al., 2008) examining the choices available to people living semi-independently (i.e. with drop-in disability staff support, not continuous staff presence). The consistent finding was that *less* staff presence was associated with *more* choice making. Although not explored directly in any of these papers, the implicit conclusion was that merely by being present, staff inadvertently or by design reduced choice. Viewed another way, the *absence* of staff effectively requires the person to make the choice (e.g. when to go to bed, whether to go out) for themselves, as there is no 'authority figure' to consult or decide for you and who may have inaccurate expectations about the ability or right of people with intellectual disability to engage in choices about their lives. However, the authors of both studies emphasised the important point that staff support needs to be matched to the individual's support needs. Too little staff support will result in neglect, not more choice, although the support should be based on high expectations and aligned with the needs of the person being supported.

Conclusions about relationships There is growing evidence that relationships affect choice, a finding that appears true for a variety of relationships with family, friends, co-residents and disability staff. The role of other people can range from choice denying to choice enhancing. However, the field of choice and self-determination has only given limited research attention to this seemingly pervasive issue and the complex factors that shape opportunities for and expectations of choice making. Issues of research design, such as the predominance of cross-sectional studies, as well as the limited range of questions addressed both constrain the available conclusions about choice and relationships. That said, there appears to be scope for future intervention research. In addition to understanding how relationships and choice interact, relationships presumably provide a potential avenue for interventions to enhance choice. Working with family or friends to encourage them to be more supportive of self-determined choices and to be more skilled at supporting these choices is a potentially fruitful avenue for future research. Indeed, Brown and Brown (2009, p. 16) proposed that one important way to enhance choice is to 'Increase skill of support personnel and family members to encourage and support choice'. Emerging models of supported decision making that focus on building supports for choice and decision making and ensuring the right to legal agency remains with the person with disability (versus substituted decision making under guardianship arrangements) are more fully addressed in the chapter "Supported Decision Making".

The exact mechanisms of what is required within these relationships to more effectively support choice have not been fully explored. One interesting line of work has been led by Charles Antaki (e.g. Antaki, Finlay, Walton, & Pate, 2008) exploring the nature of choice interactions between disability staff and people with intellectual disability. This research has begun to identify staff communication behaviours that are supportive (or not) of choice. These same issues may well characterise choice-related interactions involving family or friends of the person with intellectual disability.

Implementing Choices with and Without Support

As noted elsewhere in this chapter, choice has been strongly and consistently associated with level of intellectual disability. Those with milder intellectual disability exercise more choice (Hatton et al., 2004; Lakin et al., 2008; Ratti et al., 2017; Tichá et al., 2012). There appear to be several reasons for this finding. First, individuals with more severe disability typically have more difficulty with communication, so will often find it harder to convey their preferences and choices, particularly as many individuals are not able to access meaningful communication systems aligned with their needs (Stancliffe et al., 2010). Second, more complex and abstract choices may be related to cognitive functioning. For example, financial choices and money management require relatively complex understanding and reasoning that even many adults with mild intellectual disability find challenging (Suto, Clare, Holland & Watson, 2005). Third, it is likely that caregivers (family, disability staff) will have lower expectations of the choice-making capacity of people with more severe disability and so provide fewer opportunities for choice. Fourth, caregivers may be unwilling or unskilled at providing the more detailed supports needed by individuals with severe disability to make and implement choices.

However, there is a fifth factor, the ability of the individual to *implement their choices without direct support*, which also favours people with milder disability who typically have better-developed functional skills. In their chapter "The Development of Choice-Making and Implications for Promoting Choice and Autonomy for Children and Youth with Intellectual and Developmental Disabilities", Wehmeyer and Shogren characterise this approach as *autonomy-as-independence,* but argue for an alternative conceptualisation they call *autonomy-as-volition.* One important dimension of this distinction is that autonomy-as-volition does not require the individual to *implement* their choice without support, so long as the person *makes* the choice freely and in accord with their own values and preferences. When needed, they receive support to enact their choices. In an ideal world, appropriate support would always be available. However, this ideal is often not attained, usually because the required support is provided by another person who is unavailable, unskilled or unwilling to give the support when needed (e.g. Friedman & Rizzolo, 2016; McVilly, Stancliffe, Parmenter, & Burton-Smith, 2006).

Transportation represents one form of support that can affect the practical implementation of choices about community participation and social interaction if, for example, a parent is unwilling to drive her adult son/daughter where they want to go. One of McVilly et al.'s (2006, p. 701) participants stated, 'it's hard when you got too far to travel …[Q]… like mum has to drive and she's got lots of shopping to do and then I can't see my friends'. In the USA, Friedman and Rizzolo (2016) found that Medicaid funding for disability transportation was often restricted to non-emergency medical transportation and travel to and from disability employment or day programs, with other aspects of community access not supported, likely closing off many choices regarding community participation to individuals unable to travel without support.

Controlling for characteristics such as mobility and level of intellectual disability, Stancliffe and Anderson (2017) found that adults with IDD who accessed the community alone and without support for exercise did so much more often. Presumably, these individuals went out more often because they chose to do so. Their ability to access the community without support meant that they could go out whenever *they* chose, without having to wait for a support person to be available to them. Emerging technologies (e.g. cognitive supports for navigating transportation systems, self-driving cars) have the potential to change the supports available; however, ensuring access for people with disabilities will be critical.

The capacity to implement a choice without *direct* support is not an all-or-nothing phenomenon. Instead, it depends on the interplay between the person's skills and environmental factors, such as task setup and indirect support. For example, a man with severe disability has been taught how to get himself a hot drink safely, so he does not need someone else to be available at the time to provide *direct* support by helping him make the beverage. The items needed (cups, coffee, teabags, teaspoon, long-life milk sachets, sweetener, hot water urn with safe dispensing mechanism) are always set up in a consistent manner at a specific location in the kitchen. He has learned that he can choose to make himself a hot drink whenever *he* wants and can select tea or coffee, with or without milk. He needs no *direct* support to do this, but does need the *indirect* help of an environment in which a consistent task setup is maintained by others (e.g. by restocking the supplies). Unfortunately, this type of skilled indirect support is all too often not available, thereby condemning the man to wait for others to be available and willing to implement his choice.

Despite the appeal of an *autonomy-as-volition* approach, the need for direct support can come at a cost – compromise of what to do or how and when to do it. Clearly, better availability of direct and indirect support to enact choice would result in more choices being implemented. However, these issues suggest other avenues to increase enactment of choice: enhancement of key functional skills and improving caregivers' support skills.

Individuals who can contact friends and family by phone or social media can choose to do so when *they* want, particularly when they do not have to rely on others to directly support their use of communication technology. Likewise, a person who can travel in the community without supports can more readily implement their choice of community activity. That is, enhancement of key functional skills and achieving independence provides another route to enabling people with ID to make *and implement* choices more often.

Similarly, enhancing the capacity of caregivers to provide skilled (indirect) support (e.g. through Active Support training, Beadle-Brown, Hutchinson, & Whelton, 2012; Stancliffe et al., 2008) can also allow people to implement their choices without direct support. For example, setting up the person's phone for easy one-touch dialling will enable the individual to make phone calls without direct support. Similarly, a person may be physically able to walk to a local gym for exercise, but could initially need support to plan and follow a safe walking route. Once the person has learned that route, no further direct support may be needed. Teaching caregivers how to provide that initial support may well enable the person to use their phone or implement their choice of when to go to the gym without ongoing direct support.

What Works

In this final section of the chapter, information is presented on a number of methods thought to enhance choice. The strongest evidence of effectiveness comes from a limited number of controlled intervention studies (e.g. Stancliffe & Abery, 1997; Heller et al., 2000). A larger number of cross-sectional multivariate analyses (e.g. Tichá et al., 2012) and qualitative studies (e.g. Antaki et al., 2008) suggest possible interventions (e.g. moving to live in one's own home) but do not report direct effectiveness data based on actually implementing the intervention. That is, the methods outlined in this section are based on the best available evidence, but the quality of that evidence varies.

Methods to enhance choice include:

- Changing living environment from larger, more restrictive living arrangements to smaller, more individualised and more independent living, such as living in one's own home (Felce et al., 2008; Houseworth, Tichá et al., 2018; Stancliffe & Abery, 1997; Stancliffe & Keane, 2000; Stancliffe et al., 2011; Tichá et al., 2012).
- Implementing a multi-session, multi-component training curriculum, with each participant with intellectual disability having an individual support person attend the training alongside them (Heller et al., 2000).
- Non-verbal support with communication regarding choices and choice making such as using pictorial activity schedules (Anderson et al., 1997), using objects (e.g. table game, book, video game) to offer a choice of leisure activities (Wilson, Reid, & Green, 2006), recognising individual behaviours that indicate choice (e.g. pointing, grasping, vocalising) (Wilson et al., 2006) and emerging technologies.
- When choices are presented verbally, Antaki et al. (2008) found it is best to keep choices simple and try to avoid asking for repeated clarifications and checks which can unintentionally confuse the person and cause them to abandon their

original choice. Antaki et al. recommended against offering multiple alternatives verbally because of the risk of confusion and increased susceptibility to recency response bias. Antaki et al. recommended offering tangible alternatives so the person can point to or name their choice. The chapter "Preference Assessments, Choice, and Quality of Life for People with Significant Disabilities" provides additional suggestions and best practices.

- Implement *active support* (Beadle-Brown et al., 2012; Koritsas, Iacono, Hamilton, & Leighton, 2008). Active support is an evidence-based approach to training disability staff to support people with intellectual disability to be active participants in everyday activities (Flynn et al., 2018). This approach includes offering the person a choice of activities and/or support for individually preferred activities, rather than the activity being selected by the support person. Beadle-Brown et al. (2012) reported that the types of choices that increased (e.g. choosing what activity to do, how to do it and choosing to change activities) were logically related to the activities supported.
- Similar to active support, Wilson et al. (2006) trained staff to embed choice of activities when supporting people with severe disability to participate in leisure activities at home. Training resulted in large increases in choices offered by staff and choices made by residents and in leisure activity participation.
- Use technology to support the expression of choice. Photovoice is a technique to teach people with intellectual disability to use cameras to take photos that express interests and preferences and can easily be used to support learning how to identify preferences (Jurkowski, 2008).

These examples reveal a variety of approaches to increasing choice ranging from environmental interventions such as changing one's living environment to a number of training interventions aimed at people with disability themselves or at support providers, such as disability staff, with a view to staff making choices more consistently available as a matter of routine daily support practice, thereby respecting the rights and enhancing the self-determination of people with intellectual and developmental disabilities. In terms of research priorities, one evident need is for more controlled intervention studies to test the feasibility and effectiveness of interventions suggested by non-intervention research.

References

Agran, M., Storey, K., & Krupp, M. (2010). Choosing and choice making are not the same: Asking "what do you want for lunch?" is not self-determination. *Journal of Vocational Rehabilitation, 33*, 77–88.

Anderson, M. D., Sherman, J. A., Sheldon, J. B., & McAdam, D. (1997). Picture activity schedules and engagement of adults with mental retardation in a group home. *Research in Developmental Disabilities, 18*, 231–250.

Antaki, C., Finlay, W., Walton, C., & Pate, L. (2008). Offering choices to people with intellectual disabilities: An interactional study. *Journal of Intellectual Disability Research, 52*(12), 1165–1175.

Beadle-Brown, J., Hutchinson, A., & Whelton, B. (2012). Person-centred active support – Increasing choice, promoting independence and reducing challenging behaviour. *Journal of Applied Research in Intellectual Disabilities, 25*(4), 291–307. https://doi.org/10.1111/j.1468-3148.2011.00666.x

Bigby, C., Douglas, J., Carney, T., Then, S-N., Wiesel, I., & Smith. E. (2017). Delivering decision making support to people with cognitive disability — What has been learned from pilot programs in Australia from 2010 to 2015. *Australian Journal of Social Issues, 52*(3), 222–240. https://doi.org/10.1002/ajs4.19

Brown, F., Gothelf, C. R., Guess, D., & Lehr, D. H. (1998). Self-determination for individuals with the most severe disabilities: Moving beyond chimera. *Journal of the Association for Persons with Severe Handicaps, 23*, 17–26.

Brown, I., & Brown, R. I. (2009). Choice as an aspect of quality of life for people with intellectual disabilities. *Journal of Policy and Practice in Intellectual Disabilities, 6*(1), 11–18.

Cattermole, M., Jahoda, A., & Markova, I. (1988). Leaving home: The experience of people with a mental handicap. *Journal of Mental Deficiency Research, 32*(1), 47–57.

Cimera, R. E. (2012). The economics of supported employment: What new data tell us. *Journal of Vocational Rehabilitation, 37*, 109–117. https://doi.org/10.3233/JVR-2012-0604

Curryer, B., Stancliffe, R. J., Dew, A., & Wiese, M. Y. (2018). Choice and control within family relationships: The lived experience of adults with intellectual disability. *Intellectual and Developmental Disabilities, 56*(3), 188–201. https://doi.org/10.1352/1934-9556-56.3.188

Cuthill, F. M., Espie, C. A., & Cooper, S. A. (2003). Development and psychometric properties of the Glasgow Depression Scale for people with a learning disability. *Individual and carer supplement version. British Journal of Psychiatry, 182*, 347–353.

Felce, D., Perry, J., Romeo, R., Robertson, J., Meek, A., Emerson, E., & Knapp, M. (2008). Outcomes and costs of community living: Semi-independent living and fully staffed group homes. *American Journal on Mental Retardation, 113*, 87–101. https://doi.org/10.1352/0895-8017(2008)113[87:OACOCL]2.0.CO;2

Flynn, S., Totsika, V., Hastings, R. P., Hood, K., Toogood, S., & Felce, D. (2018). Effectiveness of active support for adults with intellectual disability in residential settings: Systematic review and meta-analysis. *Journal of Applied Research in Intellectual Disabilities*, Advance online publication. https://doi.org/10.1111/jar.12491

Friedman, C. (2018). Direct support professionals and quality of life of people with intellectual and developmental disabilities. *Intellectual and Developmental Disabilities, 56*(4), 234–250.

Friedman, C., & Rizzolo, M. C. (2016). The state of transportation for people with intellectual and developmental disabilities in Medicaid Home and Community-Based Services 1915 (c) waivers. *Journal of Disability Policy Studies, 27*, 168–177.

Friedman, C., & Rizzolo, M. C. (2018). Friendship, quality of life, and people with intellectual and developmental disabilities. *Journal of Development and Physical Disabilities, 30*, 39–54. https://doi.org/10.1007/s10882-017-9576-7

Glendinning, C., Challis, D., Fernández, J.-L., Jacobs, S., Jones, K., Knapp, M., … Wilberforce, M. (2008). *Evaluation of the individual budgets pilot programme: Summary report.* Social Policy Research Unit, University of York. Retrieved from https://www.york.ac.uk/inst/spru/pubs/pdf/IBSENSummaryReport.pdf

Hatton, C., Emerson, E., & Robertson, J. (2004). The Resident Choice Scale: A measure to assess opportunities for self-determination in residential settings. *Journal of Intellectual Disability Research, 48*(2), 103–113.

Heller, T., Miller, A. B., Hsieh, K., & Sterns, H. (2000). Later-life planning: Promoting knowledge of options and choice-making. *Mental Retardation, 38*(5), 395–406.

Houseworth, J., Stancliffe, R. J., & Tichá, R. (2018). Association of state-level and individual-level factors with choice making of individuals with intellectual and developmental disabilities. *Research in Developmental Disabilities, 83*, 77–90. https://doi.org/10.1016/j.ridd.2018.08.008

Houseworth, J., Tichá, R., Smith, J., & Ajaj, R. (2018). Developments in living arrangements and choice for persons with intellectual and developmental disabilities. *Policy Research Brief,*

27(1), University of Minnesota, Institute on Community Integration. Downloaded from https://ici.umn.edu/products/view/972

Jurkowski, J. M. (2008). Photovoice as participatory action research tool for engaging people with intellectual disabilities in research and program development. *Intellectual and Developmental Disabilities, 46*, 1–11.

Kearney, C. A., Durand, V. M., & Mindell, J. A. (1995). Choice assessment in residential settings. *Journal of Developmental and Physical Disabilities, 7*, 203–213.

Kishi, G., Teelucksingh, B., Zollers, S. P., & Meyer, L. (1988). Daily decision making in community residences: A social comparison of adults with and without mental retardation. *American Journal on Mental Retardation, 92*, 430–435.

Koritsas, S., Iacono, T., Hamilton, D., & Leighton, D. (2008). The effect of active support training on engagement, opportunities for choice, challenging behaviour and support needs. *Journal of Intellectual and Developmental Disability, 33*(3), 247–256. https://doi.org/10.1080/13668250802282944

Lakin, K. C., Doljanac, R., Byun, S., Stancliffe, R. J., Taub, S., & Chiri, G. (2008). Choice making among Medicaid Home and Community-Based Services (HCBS) and ICF/MR recipients in six states. *American Journal on Mental Retardation, 113*(5), 325–342.

Martin, R. (2006). A real life – A real community: The empowerment and full participation of people with an intellectual disability in their community. *Journal of Intellectual & Developmental Disability, 31*(2), 125–127. https://doi.org/10.1080/13668250600681511

McVilly, K. R., Stancliffe, R. J., Parmenter, T. R., & Burton-Smith, R. M. (2006). Self-advocates have the last say on friendship. *Disability & Society, 21*(7), 693–708.

Mehling, M. H., & Tassé, M. J. (2015). Impact of choice on social outcomes of adults with ASD. *Journal of Autism and Developmental Disorders, 45*(6), 1588–1602.

Miller, E., Cooper, S., Cook, A., & Petch, A. (2008). Outcomes important to people with intellectual disabilities. *Journal of Policy and Practice in Intellectual Disabilities, 5*(3), 150–158.

Neely-Barnes, S., Marcenko, M., & Weber, L. (2008). Does choice influence quality of life for people with mild intellectual disabilities? *Intellectual and Developmental Disabilities, 46*(1), 12–26.

O'Donovan, M.-A., Byrne, E., McCallion, P., & McCarron, M. (2017). Measuring choice for adults with an intellectual disability – A factor analysis of the adapted daily choice inventory scale. *Journal of Intellectual Disability Research, 61*(5), 471–487. https://doi.org/10.1111/jir.12364

Perry, J., & Felce, D. (2005). Correlation between subjective and objective measures of outcome in staffed community housing. *Journal of Intellectual Disability Research, 49*(4), 278–287. https://doi.org/10.1111/j.1365-2788.2005.00652.x

Ratti, V., Vickerstaff, V., Crabtree, J., & Hassiotis, A. (2017). An exploratory factor analysis and construct validity of the resident choice assessment scale with paid carers of adults with intellectual disabilities and challenging behavior in community settings. *Journal of Mental Health Research in Intellectual Disabilities, 10*(3), 198–216. https://doi.org/10.1080/19315864.2016.1277287

Saaltink, R., MacKinnon, G., Owen, F., & Tardif-Williams, C. (2012). Protection, participation and protection through participation: Young people with intellectual disabilities and decision making in the family context. *Journal of Intellectual Disability Research, 56*, 1076–1086. https://doi.org/10.1111/j.1365-2788.2012.01649.x

Schalock, R. L., & Keith, K. D. (1993). *Quality of life questionnaire*. Worthington, OH: IDS Publishing.

Schalock, R. L., Verdugo, M. A., Gomez, L. E., & Reinders, H. S. (2016). Moving us toward a theory of individual quality of life. *American Journal on Intellectual and Developmental Disabilities, 121*(1), 1–12. https://doi.org/10.1352/1944-7558-121.1.1

Sheppard-Jones, K., Prout, H., & Kleinert, H. (2005). Quality of life dimensions for adults with developmental disabilities: A comparative study. *Mental Retardation, 43*, 281–291.

Shogren, K. A., & Broussard, R. (2011). Exploring the perceptions of self-determination of individuals with intellectual disability. *Intellectual and Developmental Disabilities, 49*, 86–102. https://doi.org/10.1352/1934-9556-49.2.86

Stancliffe, R. J. (1991). Choice making by adults in supported community accommodation: Hobson's choice? *Interactions, 5*(4), 23–33.

Stancliffe, R. J. (1995). *Choice and decision making and adults with intellectual disability.* Unpublished doctoral thesis, Macquarie University, Sydney.

Stancliffe, R. J. (1999). Proxy respondents and the Quality of Life Questionnaire empowerment factor. *Journal of Intellectual Disability Research, 43*, 185–193.

Stancliffe, R. J. (2000). Proxy respondents and quality of life. *Evaluation and Program Planning, 23*, 89–93.

Stancliffe, R. J. (2001). Living with support in the community: Predictors of choice and self-determination. *Mental Retardation and Developmental Disabilities Research Reviews, 7*, 91–98.

Stancliffe, R. J., & Abery, B. H. (1997). Longitudinal study of deinstitutionalization and the exercise of choice. *Mental Retardation, 35*, 159–169.

Stancliffe, R. J., Abery, B. H., & Smith, J. (2000). Personal control and the ecology of community living settings: Beyond living-unit size and type. *American Journal on Mental Retardation, 105*, 431–454.

Stancliffe, R. J., & Anderson, L. L. (2017). Factors associated with meeting physical activity guidelines by adults with intellectual and developmental disabilities. *Research in Developmental Disabilities, 62*, 1–14. https://doi.org/10.1016/j.ridd.2017.01.009

Stancliffe, R. J., Jones, E., Mansell, J., & Lowe, K. (2008). Active support: A critical review and commentary. *Journal of Intellectual & Developmental Disability, 33*(3), 196–214. https://doi.org/10.1080/13668250802315397

Stancliffe, R. J., & Keane, S. (2000). Outcomes and costs of community living: A matched comparison of group homes and semi-independent living. *Journal of Intellectual & Developmental Disability, 25*, 281–305. https://doi.org/10.1080/13668250020019584

Stancliffe, R. J., & Lakin, K. C. (2007). Independent living. In S. L. Odom, R. H. Horner, M. Snell, & J. Blacher (Eds.), *Handbook on developmental disabilities* (pp. 429–448). New York, NY: Guilford Publications, Inc..

Stancliffe, R. J., Lakin, K. C., Larson, S. A., Engler, J., Taub, S., & Fortune, J. (2011). Choice of living arrangements. *Journal of Intellectual Disability Research, 55*(8), 746–762. https://doi.org/10.1111/j.1365-2788.2010.01336.x

Stancliffe, R. J., Lakin, K. C., Taub, S., Chiri, G., & Byun, S. (2009). Satisfaction and sense of well-being among Medicaid ICF/MR and HCBS recipients in six states. *Intellectual and Developmental Disabilities, 47*(2), 63–83. https://doi.org/10.1352/1934-9556-47.2.63

Stancliffe, R. J., Larson, S. A., Auerbach, K., Engler, J., Taub, S., & Lakin, K. C. (2010). Individuals with intellectual disabilities and augmentative and alternative communication: Analysis of survey data on uptake of aided AAC, and loneliness experiences. *Augmentative and Alternative Communication, 26*(2), 87–96. https://doi.org/10.3109/07434618.2010.481564

Stancliffe, R. J., & Parmenter, T. R. (1999). The Choice Questionnaire: A scale to assess choices exercised by adults with intellectual disability. *Journal of Intellectual & Developmental Disability, 24*, 107–132.

Suto, W. M. I., Clare, I. C. H., Holland, A. J., & Watson, P. C. (2005). Capacity to make financial decisions among people with mild intellectual disabilities. *Journal of Intellectual Disability Research, 49*(3), 199–209.

Tichá, R., Lakin, K. C., Larson, S., Stancliffe, R. J., Taub, S., Engler, J., … Moseley, C. (2012). Correlates of everyday choice and support-related choice for 8,892 randomly sampled adults with intellectual and developmental disabilities in 19 states. *Intellectual and Developmental Disabilities, 50*(6), 486–504. https://doi.org/10.1352/1934-9556-50.06.486

Tullis, C. A., Cannella-Malone, H. I., Basbagill, A. R., Yeager, A., Fleming, C. V., Payne, D., & Wu, P. (2011). A review of the choice and preference assessment literature for individuals with severe to profound disabilities. *Education and Training in Autism and Developmental Disabilities, 46*, 576–595.

United Nations [UN]. (2006). *Convention on the rights of persons with disabilities and optional protocol.* New York, NY: United Nations.

van Hooren, R. H., Widdershoven, G. A. M., van den Borne, H. W., & Curfs, L. M. G. (2002). Autonomy and intellectual disability: The case of prevention of obesity in Prader-Willi syndrome. *Journal of Intellectual Disability Research, 46*, 560–568.

Wehmeyer, M. L. (2007). *Promoting self-determination in students with developmental disabilities.* New York, NY: Guilford Press.

Wehmeyer, M. L., & Abery, B. (2013). Self-determination and choice. *Intellectual and Developmental Disabilities, 51*, 399–411.

Wilson, P. G., Reid, D. H., & Green, C. W. (2006). Evaluating and increasing in-home leisure activity among adults with severe disabilities in supported independent living. *Research and Training in Developmental Disabilities, 27*(1), 93–107.

Zelinsky, N. A. M., & Shadish, W. (2018). A demonstration of how to do a meta-analysis that combines single-case designs with between-groups experiments: The effects of choice making on challenging behaviors performed by people with disabilities. *Developmental Neurorehabilitation, 21*(4), 266–278.

Self-Determination, Preference, and Choice

Karrie A. Shogren

The right of all people, including people with intellectual and developmental disabilities, to self-determine their own lives is acknowledged in research, policy, and practice (Shogren & Ward, 2018). Opportunities for choice and the expression of preference are associated with the development and expression of self-determination (Wehmeyer & Shogren, 2017) and are relevant to the application of positive psychology to the lives of people with intellectual and developmental disabilities (Shogren, Wehmeyer, & Singh, 2017). Policy initiatives, such as the United Nation's Convention on the Rights of Persons with Disabilities (United Nations, 2006) and the United States' Americans with Disabilities Act, (1990) identify choice as a fundamental right and promote the full participation of people with disabilities in all aspects of their lives and communities. The purpose of this chapter is to examine and more fully describe the relationship between self-determination, preference, and choice. I will define each of these constructs, describing the relationship of preference and choice to the development and expression of self-determination across the life span. Research on the impact of preference expression and choice making on self-determination and other valued outcomes will be described. We will conclude with a discussion of "what works" for enhancing choice opportunities and self-determination.

Defining Self-Determination

Self-determination has received significant attention in the disability field since the 1990s (Shogren & Ward, 2018). Several factors contributed to the emergence of the focus on self-determination. First, new frameworks for understanding disability

K. A. Shogren (✉)
Kansas University Center on Developmental Disabilities,
University of Kansas, Lawrence, KS, USA
e-mail: shogren@ku.edu

© Springer Nature Switzerland AG 2020
R. J. Stancliffe et al. (eds.), *Choice, Preference, and Disability*, Positive
Psychology and Disability Series, https://doi.org/10.1007/978-3-030-35683-5_2

were emerging and influencing research, policy, and practice. Social-ecological or person-environment fit models (Luckasson et al., 1992; Schalock et al., 2010; World Health Organization, 2001) began to conceptualize disability as a function of the interaction between personal competencies and environmental or contextual demands. Such models paved the way for a shift to focusing on the support needs that emerged from mismatches between a person's capabilities and the demands of their environment and using an understanding of support needs to build individualized supports to enhance personal outcomes (Thompson et al., 2009). This necessitated an increased focus on the fundamental right of people with disabilities to be involved in choices about their supports and services as well as where and how they lived and worked. It also raised awareness of the need to focus on supporting the goals, values, and interests of people with disabilities and creating opportunities for people with intellectual and developmental disabilities to have access to opportunities to develop preferences and make choices. Second, the emergence of positive psychology in the 2000s (Snyder & Lopez, 2002) further supported the growing emphasis on building on the strengths and capabilities of people with disabilities and leveraging these strengths and capabilities to enhance outcomes (Shogren, Wehmeyer, & Singh, 2017; Wehmeyer, 2013).

Third, data was emerging from large, national outcome studies in the United States as well as in other countries confirming the disparate outcomes experienced by people with disabilities. This included documentation of significantly lower employment rates, access to postsecondary education, and engagement in the community for adults with disabilities (compared to their peers without disabilities), particularly after the transition from school to adult services and supports (Blackorby & Wagner, 1996). The outcomes for young adults with intellectual and developmental disabilities were particularly troubling. This led to attention in the fields of special education, rehabilitation, and disability services and supports on the need to enable a more effective transition from school to the adult world for young people with disabilities, and self-determination was identified as a mechanism to more fully engage people with disabilities in this process. This coincided with the growing self-advocacy movement led by people with disabilities which asserted the right of people with disabilities to have choices and decisions in their lives respected (Wehmeyer, Bersani Jr., & Gagne, 2000).

As a result of these factors, between 1990 and 1994, the US Department of Education's Office of Special Education Programs funded 26 model demonstration projects to develop methods, materials, and strategies to promote the self-determination of youth and young adults with disabilities during the transition from school to post-school environments (Sands & Wehmeyer, 1996; Ward, 1996). These projects mirrored efforts around the world focused on enhancing choice and the right of people with disabilities to be agents over their lives, with needed individualized supports to do so.

Causal Agency Theory

Building on the intersecting factors that raised awareness of the critical need for supports for self-determination, choice, and preference in the disability field, researchers began to develop frameworks to define the self-determination construct and its development in people with disabilities (Abery, 1994; Field, 1996; Field & Hoffman, 1994; Mithaug, 1996; Powers et al., 1996; Wehmeyer, 1996; Wehmeyer, Abery, Mithaug, & Stancliffe, 2003; Wehmeyer, Kelchner, & Richards, 1996). These frameworks led to numerous assessments and interventions designed to shift the focus from other-direction to self-direction in the disability field, enabling people with disabilities to be at the center of decisions and choices made about their lives.

Causal Agency Theory (Shogren et al., 2015) builds on the theoretical work on self-determination that emerged in the 1990s and provides a contemporary framework for understanding the development of self-determination. Causal Agency Theory describes how all people, including people with intellectual and developmental disabilities, develop the actions and beliefs necessary to act to cause things to happen in their lives. Causal Agency Theory integrates ongoing developments in understanding self-determination and its development, developments emerging from positive psychology, including theoretical advances in related theories that describe human motivation (Ryan, 2012).

Definition of self-determination Causal Agency Theory defines self-determination as a

> … dispositional characteristic manifested as acting as the causal agent in one's life. Self-determined *people* (i.e., causal agents) act in service to freely chosen goals. Self-determined *actions* function to enable a person to be the causal agent in his or her life (Shogren, Wehmeyer, Palmer, Forber-Pratt, et al., 2015).

Embedded in this definition are several key terms. First, self-determination is conceptualized as a dispositional characteristic, meaning that self-determination can be measured, will differ across individuals based on previous experiences, and can be influenced by changes in the context. Second is the notion of self-determined people as causal agents over their lives. This notion is critical to understanding self-determination and differentiating self-determination from other terms or outcomes such as independence. A causal agent acts or causes things to happen in their lives; they may not necessarily make these things happen independently (e.g., delegating a decision or activities to someone else can still be self-determined, so long as the person is fully engaged in making that choice). Causal agency, therefore, reflects the fact that self-determined people engage in actions to *cause* an effect to *accomplish* a *specific end*. This is where acting in service to goals becomes critical; only when acting to accomplish an end (i.e., make progress toward a goal) can a person link their actions with the ends they wish to experience. As such, self-determined actions enable a person to act as a causal agent, promoting movement toward personally valued goals.

Essential characteristics of self-determined actions Causal Agency Theory further elaborates on the characteristics that define self-determination actions, as well as the skills and attitudes that contribute to the development of these constructs. Figure 1 provides an overview of the relationship between the three essential characteristics defined by Causal Agency Theory – volitional action, agentic action, and action-control beliefs – and associated skills and component constructs that are further defined in this section.

Volitional action Self-determined people act volitionally, which means that they can use choice-making, decision-making, goal-setting, problem-solving, and planning skills to identify what they want in their life (i.e., set goals based on personal interests, preferences, and values). As such, acting volitionally involves making conscious choices that reflect one's preferences and interests. Conscious choices are intentionally conceived, deliberate acts that occur without direct external influence, although one's choices and preferences are influenced by previous opportunities and experiences, and cultural values. Volitional actions are therefore defined in Causal Agency Theory as being self-initiated and contributing to greater autonomy (component constructs associated with volitional action, as shown in Fig. 1). Essentially, volitional actions involve the initiation and activation of a person's ability to identify personally meaningful goals based on their interests, preferences, and options – initiating the process of making things happen in one's life.

Agentic action Self-determined people also act agentically, meaning they have the skills and abilities to identify and use pathways to self-regulated actions toward

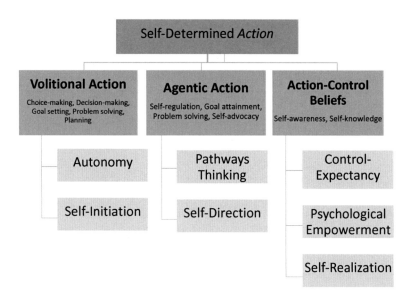

Fig. 1 Self-determination and its essential characteristics. (Reprinted with permission from Shogren (2018))

their goals. When acting agentically, people use self-regulation, goal-attainment, problem-solving, and self-advocacy skills. The use of these skills leads to the use of self-direction and pathways thinking. People who use pathways thinking can identify multiple ways to achieve their goals, and when they encounter barriers, they use problem-solving and decision-making skills to find other pathways to attain their goal. In doing so, people self-regulate their behavior, directing actions that guide them to a specific end. The identification of pathways, or pathways thinking, is a proactive, purposive process and leads to the capacity to sustain action toward a goal.

Action-control beliefs Self-determined people, in applying volitional and agentic actions over the life span, develop action-control beliefs. Action-control beliefs contribute to a person feeling that they have what it takes to attain their goals. People with adaptive action-control beliefs have self-awareness and self-knowledge that they use to inform their selection of goals and the actions that they take to achieve their goals. They perceive a link between their actions and the outcomes they experience and develop a sense of control expectancy (i.e., that their environment will be responsive to their actions) and psychological empowerment (i.e., feeling empowered to take steps toward their goals). People with adaptive action-control beliefs also experience self-realization; they recognize the value of understanding themselves and their support needs and aligning their actions toward that understanding.

Assessment of self-determination Shogren and colleagues (in press a, b) recently introduced the *Self-Determination Inventory System*, which includes the *Self-Determination Inventory: Student Report* (SDI:SR), the *Self-Determination Inventory: Parent/Teacher Report* (SDI:PTR), and the *Self-Determination Inventory: Adult Report* (SDI:AR). All assessments were designed to provide information on overall self-determination as well as the three essential characteristics and component constructs defined by Causal Agency Theory, with the SDI:SR and SDI:AR self-report measures for adolescents aged 13–22 and adults aged 18 and over, respectively. The SDI:PTR is parallel to the SDI:SR but allows for parallel reporting by an adult that knows the adolescent well. All assessments include 21 items that are delivered online (see www.self-determination.org), and a recent validation study of the SDI:SR that included over 4500 students confirmed the theoretical structure of the scale and Causal Agency Theory (Shogren, Little, et al., in press). Other research has suggested that the SDI:SR identifies differences in self-determination based on personal and environmental factors including disability status, gender, age, race/ethnicity, and socioeconomic status (Shogren, Shaw, Raley, & Wehmeyer, in press-a, in press-b). Notably, because self-determination has meaning for all adolescents, not just those with disabilities, the tool was validated with adolescents without disabilities as well as those with varying disability labels (learning disability, intellectual disability, autism spectrum disorders, and other health impairment) increasing its applicability in inclusive general education contexts. Ongoing research is underway with the Parent/Teacher Report version of the tool as well as the Adult Report version. The SDI has been translated and validated in Spanish (Mumbardó-Adam, Guàrdia-Olmos, Giné, Raley, & Shogren, 2017), and translation activities are underway in American Sign Language, Korean, French, and Chinese.

Environmental and Contextual Influences on Self-Determination

The development of self-determination, as defined by Causal Agency Theory, is shaped by environment opportunities to (a) develop self-determination skills, (b) apply these skills across contexts, and (c) receive individualized supports necessary to express and use self-determination skills. Having opportunities to respond to challenges in one's environment (e.g., the need to set a goal or develop and implement an action plan to achieve that goal) creates a natural opportunity for the use of volitional and agentic actions, supported by action-control beliefs, to enable people to initiate and direct their behavior to achieve a desired change or maintain a preferred circumstance or situation. Self-determined people will use volitional actions to initiate a *goal generation process* leading to the identification and prioritization of needed actions. The person frames the most urgent action need in terms of a goal state and engages in a *goal discrepancy analysis* to compare current status with goal status and identify agentic actions that lead to pathways that direct progress toward the goal. A person can then, over time, evaluate progress toward the goal and determine through self-evaluation, if changes are needed in the goal, the action plan, or if a new goal needs to be generated. Essentially, throughout life, people engage in goal setting, action planning, and evaluation cycle allowing goals to be identified and chosen based on values, preferences, and interests.

Thus, choice and preference are critical to self-determined action, particularly the act of selecting goals and appropriate action plans based on an understanding of one's strengths, needs, preferences, and interests. In the following section, we will further define choice and preference and their role in the development of volitional action and ultimately self-determination.

Preference, Choice, and Self-Determination

Having opportunities to express preferences and make choices is critical across the life span, although the nature of preferences and the complexity of choice making evolve throughout development. Having early opportunities to explore one's environment and test preferences and interests is important in early childhood to inform later choice making and self-awareness. Feeling empowered to explore and develop preferences across the life span is important, particularly as choices become more diverse and complex (e.g., what type of career does a young adult want to pursue).

Choice opportunities and the level of complexity and risk of choices increase as children age, but a strong foundation in exploring preferences and making choices is a critical foundation for the development of volitional action. Exploring one's preferences and having the skills and motivation to make choices contribute to self-initiation and autonomy in the goal generation process. Introducing early choice-making opportunities can also have positive collateral benefits. For example, Dominguez et al. (2013) studied the relationship between choice opportunities, preferences, and the vegetable consumption of 4- to 6-year-old children without disabilities. Children either had a chance to choose a vegetable to eat prior to their meal, to choose between multiple vegetables during their meal, or were provided no choice in vegetables. When choice was provided either before or during the meal, children ate significantly more vegetables than those in the no-choice condition, even when the no-choice condition included a vegetable that the child had identified as their preferred vegetable. This line of work suggests the power of choice for promoting engagement across multiple life domains, even beyond accessing preferred items. In synthesizing the international research on the impact of opportunities for basic choice making across the school years (e.g., the order of activities, timing of activities, etc.), researchers have found that providing choice opportunities can impact engagement in learning activities as well as reduce problem behavior (Shogren, Faggella-Luby, Bae, & Wehmeyer, 2004). Ongoing research continues to explore the relationship between choice and preference and how to leverage both preference and choice-making opportunities to lead to long term benefits.

Defining Preference and Choice Making

Although choice and preference will be discussed throughout this text, it is important to understand how choice and preference are defined and to differentiate them from other skills associated with self-determination. For example, choice making and decision making are often used synonymously, but under Causal Agency Theory choice making is a distinct skill that can be taught and supported, with unique opportunities provided for using and practicing these skills based on situational demands.

At its simplest, making a choice involves expressing a preference between two or more alternatives. Expressing a preference involves indicating that one likes or enjoys something (i.e., thing, person, activity) relatively more than something else. As such, exposure to various options is necessary to develop preferences and make meaningful choices. Additionally, and particularly for people with complex communication needs, having means to express preferences and have them respected by the environment is critical. Other chapters (see chapter "Preference Assessments, Choice, and Quality of Life for People with Significant Disabilities") will focus more on supports that enable preference assessment and expression for people with significant disabilities; however, in relation to self-determination, providing access to a wide array of opportunities across life domains (e.g., work, living, recreation leisure) is critical to the development of self-determination across the life span (Almeida, Allen, Maguire, & Maguire, 2018; Cobigo, Morin, & Lachapelle, 2009).

As such, expressing preferences and making choices are directly linked to the development of volitional action and therefore self-determination. As noted previously, volitional action is action based upon making a conscious choice; that is understanding and being able to express preferences and making choices about options. It is important to note that making conscious choices does not necessarily mean making choices without considering the opinions of others or the impact that choices may have on others. In some cultures and families, choices may be informed by an array of familial or cultural factors. However, the notion that the choice is conscious and made volitionally (not independently) is what is central to the development of self-determination.

The question that can be raised then is what is the difference between expressing a preference and making a choice? Theorists have addressed this issue, and it relates to the development of feelings of volition and action-control beliefs. Beyond expressing preferences, choice provides more agency for the person, allowing the person to see themselves as the origin of their actions (whatever the ultimate outcome or choice may be). Deci and Ryan (1985) – leading motivation and self-determination theorists – argue that choice occurs when a person has entertained the options (rather than just expressing which is preferred); essentially, they differentiate choice by focusing on ensuring the person has the opportunity to consider not engaging in the behavior or action (Deci & Ryan, 1985).

So, in defining a choice versus the expression of a preference, choice is choosing between multiple options that were fully entertained – suggesting the person must have enough experience with the options to fully entertain them – and consider not doing what is being selected from. To truly have choice opportunities, people must (a) have experience and exposure to the options so as to have developed preferences and (b) have the opportunity to consider engaging in the choice options. For example, if a choice is between two things, one of which is something the person has not experienced or has not been able to engage with in their environment, then it is not a real and meaningful choice.

Development of Preference and Choice Making

Children learn to identify and communicate preferences, and as these capacities develop, children grow in their capabilities to make choices (e.g., to entertain possibilities and choose between them). This process begins early in life, as young children begin to explore their environment, manipulating and interacting with objects they encounter and finding that some objects hold their interest more than others (Odom & Wolery, 2003). As children learn what holds their interest, they begin to develop a sense of identity and autonomy, recognizing that their interests may differ from others, such as caregivers. The level of support in environments for exploration and interactions with diverse materials and activities shapes the development and expression of preferences and later the ability to make choices (Brown & Cohen, 1996; Erikson, 1963; Wehmeyer & Palmer, 2000).

Choice-making skills emerge as children can have various alternatives and choose between them, which again requires supportive environments. Building choice-making skills is central to the development of other skills associated with self-determination, such as decision making. Decision making also involves identifying possible options and consequences of each option, making it more complex than choice making. But, decision making, in the final step, involves making a choice of the preferred option. Adolescents develop the ability to make choices and decisions through early experiences and continue to learn to respond to contextual and environmental challenges (opportunities, threats) that motivate them to continue to express preferences, make choices, and weigh decision options leading to volitional action and the development of self-determination. Repeated opportunities to act volitionally lead to enhanced self-determination.

Role of the Environment in Shaping Preference Expression and Choice Opportunities

Issues related to choice – and the restricted choice opportunities that all too often characterized the lives of people with intellectual and developmental disabilities – were central to the emergence of self-determination as a key outcome in the disability field. Self-advocates with disabilities brought attention to their fundamental right to make choices about where to live, where to work, with who to socialize, as well as the systematic barriers to doing so that were (and unfortunately continue to be) present throughout the world. The self-advocacy movement brought emerging recognition of the lack of choice-making opportunities available to people with intellectual and developmental disabilities, and researchers began to document the detrimental effects of the lack of such opportunities on multiple life domains (Brotherson, Cook, Erwin, & Weigel, 2008; Carr et al., 2002; Dunlap, Kern-Dunlap, Clarke, & Robbins, 1994; Neely-Barnes, Marcenko, & Weber, 2008; Stancliffe & Wehmeyer, 1995; Wehmeyer, 2002; Wehmeyer & Abery, 2013; Wehmeyer & Bolding, 1999, 2001). Without opportunities to experience diverse people and environments across the life span, the ability to learn to act autonomously and volitionally is limited. This is particularly important during adolescence and early adulthood as preferences and choices have to be made about social relationships (Fisher & Shogren, 2016), employment opportunities (Martin, Woods, Sylvester, & Gardner, 2005), living arrangements, and so forth.

Unfortunately, however, the literature clearly shows that people with disabilities, including people with intellectual and developmental disabilities, continue to have far fewer opportunities to make choices and express preferences in their lives (Stancliffe et al., 2011; Tichá et al., 2012; Wehmeyer & Abery, 2013). Early research established extreme disparities. For example, compared to peers without disabilities, people with disabilities experienced significantly fewer choice opportunities pertaining to where they lived and worked. In a sample of people without disabilities, 77% indicated that they chose their current job, while Wehmeyer and Metzler (1995) found that only 11% of people with intellectual disability made such choices. Similar discrepancies were found in relation to choices about where to live (46–6%) and with whom to live (59–9%). And, when people lived and worked in segregated settings (i.e., congregate living environments, sheltered workshops), fewer choice opportunities were provided (Stancliffe and Wehmeyer (1995). However, even in more integrated and inclusive settings, barriers to choice can still be identified. This suggests the need for education of supporters, as well as a systematic focus on creating opportunities for exposure to diverse opportunities to develop preferences and opportunities for choice and self-determination for people with intellectual and developmental disabilities.

Research on Preference and Choice and Personal Outcomes

As noted, research suggests that in children with disabilities, the provision of basic choice opportunities (e.g., order of tasks, materials to complete a task, etc.) has positive impacts on engagement (Shogren et al., 2004) although more research is needed to distinguish between the impacts of preference expression and choice making as well as to explore the linkages between access to choice and preference opportunities on the development of self-determination across the life span. There is literature, however, that suggests more wide ranging impacts of choice making and enhanced self-determination on personal outcomes for adults with intellectual and developmental disabilities (Hassan, 2017; McDermott & Edwards, 2012; Neely-Barnes et al., 2008; Nota, Ferrari, Soresi, & Wehmeyer, 2007; Nota, Soresi, Ferrari, & Wehmeyer, 2011; Shogren, Lopez, Wehmeyer, Little, & Pressgrove, 2006; Shogren, Wehmeyer, Palmer, Rifenbark, & Little, 2015; Timmons, Hall, Bose, Wolfe, & Winsor, 2011). For example, researchers have found that living arrangements associated with greater choice opportunities are also associated with higher quality of life in adults with intellectual disability and developmental disability (Neely-Barnes et al., 2008). Other researchers have established the importance of – in the work context – access to early work experiences to build preferences and enable choice and self-determination in employment (Timmons et al., 2011). Researchers have also discussed the importance of supporting choice in retirement for older adults with intellectual and developmental disabilities (McDermott & Edwards, 2012). Despite, however, the clear identification of the benefits of choice making, which is enabled by opportunities to learn and practice preference expression, research also suggests that there remain significant limitations in the opportunities for people with intellectual and developmental disabilities to make choices about their lives, particularly for adults with more complex communication needs (Agran, Storey, & Krupp, 2010).

What Works: Enhancing Preference Expression, Choice Opportunities, and Self-Determination

To enhance opportunities to develop and express preferences and make choices to lead to enhanced self-determination, there are multiple ways to create opportunities for preference development and choice making throughout the life span. This starts in childhood, by providing exposure to a variety of opportunities and activities so that children can develop an understanding of their interests and preferences. Researchers have identified an array of effective ways to embed choice opportunities into practice. For example, choice can be provided:

- Between activities (e.g., which toy to engage with, which activity to participate in)
- The order of activities (e.g., what task should be completed first)
- Not to participate in an activity (e.g., allow choice over what to participate in)
- Location of an activity (e.g., do the activity in the front of the room or back, at the desk or on the floor)
- Materials/reinforcers (e.g., decide to use a blue pen or red pen for writing)
- Within the context of transitions (do you want to go left or right)

While each of these may seem minor, together, they can establish a foundation for the establishment of choices-making skills and preferences that leads to the development of action-control beliefs and volition.

Over time, as children grow into adolescents, choices become more impactful and require exposure to various options as well as opportunities to explore and build interests and enable meaningful choice. Multiple researchers have suggested that, for example, employment for adults with intellectual disability and developmental disabilities is shaped by various contextual factors in childhood and adolescence (Carter, Austin, & Trainor, 2012; Timmons et al., 2011). For example, early work experiences are consistently identified as a strong predictor of post-school employment. In practice, then, considerations of actively engaging people with disabilities in a range of career development activities over the life span is critical to later preference development and expression of choice as well as employment outcomes. However, attitudes of family members and service providers are also highly impactful, particularly as this can shape the opportunities provided. Remember, if a person has never experienced something, it is difficult to know if one prefers it. Interventions, such as the Family Empowerment Awareness Training (Francis, Gross, Turnbull, & Turnbull, 2013) can be used to educate family members about what integrated employment and community participation can look like, raising expectations and creating supportive contexts. These ideas of providing exposure to options even extend to older adults with intellectual and developmental disabilities, as choices about retirement need to be made. For example, McDermott and Edwards (2012) explored the supports available for adults with intellectual disability in supported employment in Australia, finding that there were systematic barriers that limited choice making about retirement. While providers felt it was important to provide choice and promote self-determination during retirement, it was identified that – in practice – opportunities for people with intellectual disability to have exposure to experiences related to retirement were needed to develop preferences and make informed choices.

Ultimately, as the need for increasingly consequential choices emerges, supporting an understanding of the relationship between actions and outcomes or consequence will become more important, supporting the development of action-control beliefs, as well as the ability to act volitionally, using knowledge of preferences to inform the selection of goals and initiation of actions to reach desired outcomes across life domains (e.g., employment, community living, and social relationships). Shevin and Klein (1984), in an early article on choice making that still has relevance today, suggested the importance of using the following steps, in practice, to enhance choice opportunities over time:

1. Incorporate choice early.
2. Increase the number of choices available over time.
3. Increase the number of domains in which choices are made.
4. Raise the significance in terms of risk and long-term consequences of the choices made.
5. Clearly communicate areas of possible choice (after exposure to develop preferences has occurred) and begin to talk about the limits within which choice can be made.

This last point, providing education around the limits of choice making and external factors that can influence choice making, is particularly important in practice, yet remains an area in need of further research and development in the disability field.

Providing these opportunities is impactful not only for people with disabilities but also for those that support them. Providing choice opportunities and hearing choices made by people with disabilities have been found to shape the perceptions of supporters regarding the capacities of people with intellectual disability to be involved in their lives as well as the opportunities provided (Shogren, Plotner, Palmer, Wehmeyer, & Paek, 2014). Essentially, policy and practice changes that enable supporters to provide more choice opportunities can actually change supporters' perceptions of the capacity for choice of people with disabilities.

Systematic interventions that can be used to shape how teachers and other support providers create opportunities for choice within the context of goal setting, such as the Self-Determined Learning Model of Instruction (Shogren, Wehmeyer, Burke, & Palmer, 2017), have been developed and can be used to support both student and teacher change. Other interventions, such as the *Pathways of Decision Processing* model (Hickson & Khemka, 2013), have been developed to support decision making, which necessitates the use of choice-making skills.

As noted throughout this chapter, preference and choice are important across the life span, and there are unique considerations across life domains and cultural contexts in supporting meaningful choice that will be explored in greater depth in subsequent chapters. For example, implications of choice in multiple cultural contexts will be explored, including Israel (chapter "Choice within the Israeli Welfare State:

Lessons Learned From Legal Capacity and Housing Services"), Central and Eastern Europe (chapter "Choices, Preferences and Disability: A View from Central and Eastern Europe"), and China (chapter "Choices and Transition from School to Adult Life: Experiences in China"). Chapters will also highlight the role of choice across life domains. Chapters will discuss how to support meaningful choice in the context of individualized funding (chapter "Choice, Control and Individual Funding: The Australian National Disability Insurance Scheme"), healthcare (chapter "Preference, Choice, and Self-Determination in the Health Care Context"), relationships (chapter "Choice, Relationships, and Sexuality: Sexual and Reproductive Health and Rights"), and aging (chapter "Choice as People Age with Intellectual Disability: An Irish Perspective"), for example. And researchers and practitioners are increasingly exploring innovative ways to provide supports that enable meaningful choice, leading to enhanced self-determination, for example, initiatives to ensure access to alternatives to guardianship, such as supported decision making, as discussed in chapter "Supported Decision Making", as well as to support parenting (chapter "The Choice of Becoming a Parent") and end-of-life decision making (chapter "End-of-Life Choices").

Ultimately promoting self-determination, a valued goal of disability policy throughout the world (Shogren, Luckasson, & Schalock, 2015; United Nations, 2006), is shaped by access to meaningful choice opportunities across the life span that enable the development of volitional action and ultimately self-determination. There is a compelling need to continue to innovate to create opportunities for preference development and expression and *meaningful* choice.

References

Abery, B. H. (1994). A conceptual framework for enhancing self-determination. In M. F. Hayden & B. H. Abery (Eds.), *Challenges for a service system in transition: Ensuring quality community experiences for persons with developmental disabilities* (pp. 345–380). Baltimore, MD: Paul H. Brookes.

Agran, M., Storey, K., & Krupp, M. (2010). Choosing and choice making are not the same: Asking "what do you want for lunch?" is not self-determination. *Journal of Vocational Rehabilitation, 33*(2), 77–88.

Almeida, D. A., Allen, R., Maguire, R. W., & Maguire, K. (2018). Identifying community-based reinforcers of adults with autism and related disabilities. *Journal of Behavioral Education, 27*(3), 375–394. https://doi.org/10.1007/s10864-018-9295-x

Americans with Disabilities Act of 1990, 42 U.S.C. § 12101 et seq.

Blackorby, J., & Wagner, M. (1996). Longitudinal postschool outcomes of youth with disabilities: Findings from the National Longitudinal Transition Study. *Exceptional Children, 62*, 399–413.

Brotherson, M. J., Cook, C. C., Erwin, E. E., & Weigel, C. J. (2008). Understanding self-determination and families of young children with disabilities in home environments. *Journal of Early Intervention, 31*, 22–43.

Brown, F., & Cohen, S. (1996). Self-determination and young children. *Journal of the Association for Persons with Severe Handicaps, 21*, 22–30.

Carr, E. G., Dunlap, G., Horner, R. H., Koegel, R. L., Turnbull, A. P., Sailor, W., … Fox, L. (2002). Positive behavior support: Evolution of an applied science. *Journal of Positive Behavior Interventions, 4*(4–16), 20.

Carter, E. W., Austin, D., & Trainor, A. (2012). Predictors of postschool employment outcomes for young adults with severe disabilities. *Journal of Disability Policy Studies, 23,* 50–63. https://doi.org/10.1177/1044207311414680

Cobigo, V., Morin, D., & Lachapelle, Y. (2009). A method to assess work task preferences. *Education and Training in Developmental Disabilities, 44*(4), 561–572.

Deci, E. L., & Ryan, R. M. (1985). Intrinsic motivation and self-determination in human behavior. New York: Plenum.

Dominguez, P. R., Gamiz, F., Gil, M., Moreno, H., Zamora, R. M., Gallo, M., & Brugada, I. (2013). Providing choice increases children's vegetable intake. *Food Quality and Preference, 30,* 108–113.

Dunlap, G., Kern-Dunlap, L., Clarke, S., & Robbins, F. R. (1994). Some characteristics of nonaversive intervention for severe behavior problems. In E. Schopler & G. B. Mesibov (Eds.), *Behavioral issues in autism* (pp. 227–245). New York, NY: Plenum.

Erikson, E. H. (1963). *Childhood and society* (2nd ed.). New York, NY: Norton.

Field, S. (1996). Self-determination instructional strategies for youth with learning disabilities. *Journal of Learning Disabilities, 29,* 40–52.

Field, S., & Hoffman, A. (1994). Development of a model for self-determination. *Career Development for Exceptional Individuals, 17,* 159–169.

Fisher, K. W., & Shogren, K. A. (2016). Does academic tracking impact adolescents' access to social capital? *Remedial and Special Education, 37,* 89–100. https://doi.org/10.1177/0741932515616758

Francis, G. L., Gross, J. M. S., Turnbull, A. P., & Turnbull, H. R. (2013). The Family Empowerment Awareness Training (FEAT): A mixed-method follow-up. *Journal of Vocational Rehabilitation, 39,* 167–181.

Hassan, N. (2017). 'Putting music on': Everyday leisure activities, choice-making and person-centred planning in a supported living scheme. *British Journal of Learning Disabilities, 45*(1), 73–80. https://doi.org/10.1111/bld.12178

Hickson, L., & Khemka, I. (2013). Problem solving and decision making. In M. L. Wehmeyer (Ed.), *The Oxford Handbook of positive psychology and disability* (pp. 198–225). New York, NY: Oxford University Press.

Luckasson, R., Coulter, D. L., Polloway, E. A., Reiss, S., Schalock, R. L., Snell, M. E., … Stark, J. A. (1992). *Mental retardation: Definition, classification, and systems of supports* (9th ed.). Washington, DC: American Association on Mental Retardation.

Martin, J. E., Woods, L. L., Sylvester, L., & Gardner, J. E. (2005). A challenge to self-determination: Disagreement between the vocational choices made by individuals with severe disabilities and their caregivers. *Research and Practice for Persons with Severe Disabilities, 30,* 147–153.

McDermott, S., & Edwards, R. (2012). Enabling self-determination for older workers with intellectual disabilities in supported employment in Australia. *Journal of Applied Research in Intellectual Disabilities, 25*(5), 423–432. https://doi.org/10.1111/j.1468-3148.2012.00683.x

Mithaug, D. E. (1996). The optimal prospects principle: A theoretical basis for rethinking instructional practices for self-determination. In D. J. Sands & M. L. Wehmeyer (Eds.), *Self-determination across the lifespan: Independence and choice for people with disabilities* (pp. 147–165). Baltimore, MD: Paul H. Brookes.

Mumbardó-Adam, C., Guàrdia-Olmos, J., Giné, C., Raley, S. K., & Shogren, K. A. (2017). The Spanish version of the Self-Determination Inventory Student Report: Application of item response theory to self-determination measurement. *Journal of Intellectual Disability Research, 62,* 303–311. https://doi.org/10.1111/jir.12466

Neely-Barnes, S., Marcenko, M., & Weber, L. (2008). Does choice influence quality of life for people with mild intellectual disabilities? *Intellectual and Developmental Disabilities, 46,* 12–26. https://doi.org/10.1352/0047-6765(2008)46[12:DCIQOL]2.0.CO;2

Nota, L., Ferrari, L., Soresi, S., & Wehmeyer, M. (2007). Self-determination, social abilities and the quality of life of people with intellectual disability. *Journal of Intellectual Disability Research, 51,* 850–865. https://doi.org/10.1111/j.1365-2788.2006.00939.x

Nota, L., Soresi, S., Ferrari, L., & Wehmeyer, M. L. (2011). A multivariate analysis of the self-determination of adolescents. *Journal of Happiness Studies, 12*(2), 245–266. https://doi.org/10.1007/s10902-010-9191-0

Odom, S. L., & Wolery, M. (2003). A unified theory of practice in early intervention/early childhood special education: Evidence-based practices. *Journal of Special Education, 37*(3), 164–173.

Powers, L. E., Sowers, J., Turner, A., Nesbitt, M., Knowles, E., & Ellison, R. (1996). TAKE CHARGE! A model for promoting self-determination among adolescents with challenges. In L. E. Powers, G. H. S. Singer, & J. Sowers (Eds.), *On the road to autonomy: Promoting self-competence in children and youth with disabilities* (pp. 69–92). Baltimore, MD: Paul H. Brookes.

Ryan, R. M. (Ed.). (2012). *The Oxford handbook of human motivation.* Oxford, UK: Oxford University Press.

Sands, D. J., & Wehmeyer, M. L. (Eds.). (1996). *Self-determination across the life span: Independence and choice for people with disabilities.* Baltimore, MD: Paul H. Brookes.

Schalock, R. L., Borthwick-Duffy, S., Bradley, V., Buntix, W. H. E., Coulter, D. L., Craig, E. P. M., … Yeager, M. H. (2010). *Intellectual disability: Definition, classification, and systems of support* (11th ed.). Washington, DC: American Association on Intellectual and Developmental Disabilities.

Shevin, M., & Klein, N. K. (1984). The importance of choice-making skills for students with severe disabilities. *Journal of the Association for Persons with Severe Handicaps, 9*, 159–166.

Shogren, K. A. (2018). *Self-determination theoretical framework.* Lawrence, KS: Kansas University Center on Developmental Disabilities.

Shogren, K. A., Faggella-Luby, M., Bae, S. J., & Wehmeyer, M. L. (2004). The effect of choice-making as an intervention for problem behavior: A meta-analysis. *Journal of Positive Behavior Interventions, 6*(4), 228–237.

Shogren, K. A., Little, T. D., Grandfield, B., Raley, S. K., Wehmeyer, M. L., Lang, K., & Shaw, L. A. (in press). The self-determination inventory-student report: Identification of items for a new measure of self-determination. *Assessment for Effective Intervention.*

Shogren, K. A., Lopez, S. J., Wehmeyer, M. L., Little, T. D., & Pressgrove, C. L. (2006). The role of positive psychology constructs in predicting life satisfaction in adolescents with and without cognitive disabilities: An exploratory study. *The Journal of Positive Psychology, 1*, 37–52. https://doi.org/10.1080/17439760500373174

Shogren, K. A., Luckasson, R., & Schalock, R. L. (2015). Using context as an integrative framework to align policy goals, supports, and outcomes in intellectual disability. *Intellectual and Developmental Disabilities, 53*, 367–376. https://doi.org/10.1352/1934-9556-53.5.367

Shogren, K. A., Plotner, A. J., Palmer, S. B., Wehmeyer, M. L., & Paek, Y. (2014). Impact of the self-determined learning model of instruction on teacher perceptions of student capacity and opportunity for self-determination. *Education and Training in Autism and Developmental Disabilities, 49*, 440–448.

Shogren, K. A., Shaw, L. A., Raley, S. K., & Wehmeyer, M. L. (in press-a). Exploring the effect of disability, race/ethnicity, and socioeconomic status on scores on the Self-Determination Inventory: Student Report. *Exceptional Children.*

Shogren, K. A., Shaw, L. A., Raley, S. K., & Wehmeyer, M. L. (in press-b). The impact of personal characteristics on scores on the Self-Determination Inventory: Student Report in adolescents with and without disabilities. *Psychology in the Schools.*

Shogren, K. A., & Ward, M. J. (2018). Promoting and enhancing self-determination to improve the post-school outcomes of people with disabilities. *Journal of Vocational Rehabilitation, 48*, 187–196.

Shogren, K. A., Wehmeyer, M. L., Burke, K. M., & Palmer, S. B. (2017). *The self-determination learning model of instruction: Teacher's Guide.* Lawrence, KS: Kansas University Center on Developmental Disabilities.

Shogren, K. A., Wehmeyer, M. L., Palmer, S. B., Forber-Pratt, A. J., Little, T. J., & Lopez, S. J. (2015). Causal agency theory: Reconceptualizing a functional model of self-determination. *Education and Training in Autism and Developmental Disabilities, 50*, 251–263.

Shogren, K. A., Wehmeyer, M. L., Palmer, S. B., Rifenbark, G. G., & Little, T. D. (2015). Relationships between self-determination and postschool outcomes for youth with disabilities. *Journal of Special Education, 53*, 30–41. https://doi.org/10.1177/0022466913489733

Shogren, K. A., Wehmeyer, M. L., & Singh, N. N. (Eds.). (2017). *Handbook of positive psychology in intellectual and developmental disabilities: Translating research into practice*. New York, NY: Springer.

Snyder, C. R., & Lopez, S. J. (Eds.). (2002). *Handbook of positive psychology*. London, UK: Oxford University Press.

Stancliffe, R. J., Lakin, K. C., Larson, S., Engler, J., Taub, S., & Fortune, J. (2011). Choice of living arrangements. *Journal of Intellectual Disability Research, 55*(8), 746–762. https://doi.org/10.1111/j.1365-2788.2010.01336.x

Stancliffe, R. J., & Wehmeyer, M. L. (1995). Variability in the availability of choice to adults with mental retardation. *Journal of Vocational Rehabilitation, 5*, 319–328.

Thompson, J. R., Bradley, V., Buntinx, W. H. E., Schalock, R. L., Shogren, K. A., Snell, M. E., … Yeager, M. H. (2009). Conceptualizing supports and the support needs of people with intellectual disability. *Intellectual and Developmental Disabilities, 47*, 135–146.

Tichá, R., Lakin, K. C., Larson, S. A., Stancliffe, R. J., Taub, S., Engler, J., … Moseley, C. (2012). Correlates of everyday choice and support-related choice for 8,892 randomly sampled adults with intellectual and developmental disabilities in 19 states. *Intellectual and Developmental Disabilities, 50*, 486–504. https://doi.org/10.1352/1934-9556-50.06.486

Timmons, J. C., Hall, A. C., Bose, J., Wolfe, A., & Winsor, J. (2011). Choosing employment: Factors that impact employment decisions for individuals with intellectual disability. *Intellectual and Developmental Disabilities, 49*(4), 285–299. https://doi.org/10.1352/1934-9556-49.4.285

United Nations. (2006). Convention on the rights of persons with disability. Retrieved from http://www.un.org/disabilities/default.asp?navid=14&pid=150

Ward, M. J. (1996). Coming of age in the age of self-determination: A historical and personal perspective. In D. J. Sands & M. L. Wehmeyer (Eds.), *Self-determination across the life span: Independence and choice for people with disabilities*. Baltimore, MD: Paul H. Brookes.

Wehmeyer, M. L. (1996). Self-determination as an educational outcome: Why is it important to children, youth and adults with disabilities? In D. J. Sands & M. L. Wehmeyer (Eds.), *Self-determination across the life span: Independence and choice for people with disabilities* (pp. 15–34). Baltimore, MD: Paul H. Brookes.

Wehmeyer, M. L. (2002). The confluence of person-centered planning and self-determination. In S. Holburn & P. M. Vietze (Eds.), *Person centered planning: Research, practice, and future directions* (pp. 51–69). Baltimore, MD: Paul H. Brookes Publishing Co..

Wehmeyer, M. L. (Ed.). (2013). *The Oxford handbook of positive psychology and disability*. Oxford, UK: Oxford University Press.

Wehmeyer, M. L., Abery, B., Mithaug, D. E., & Stancliffe, R. (2003). *Theory in self-determination: Foundations for educational practice*. Springfield, IL: Charles C. Thomas Publishing Company.

Wehmeyer, M. L., & Abery, B. H. (2013). Self-determination and choice. *Intellectual and Developmental Disabilities, 51*, 399–411. https://doi.org/10.1352/1934-9556-51.5.399

Wehmeyer, M. L., Bersani, H., Jr., & Gagne, R. (2000). Riding the third wave: Self-determination and self-advocacy in the 21st century. *Focus on Autism and Other Developmental Disabilities, 15*, 106–115.

Wehmeyer, M. L., & Bolding, N. (1999). Self-determination across living and working environments: A matched-samples study of adults with mental retardation. *Mental Retardation, 37*, 353–363.

Wehmeyer, M. L., & Bolding, N. (2001). Enhanced self-determination of adults with intellectual disability as an outcome of moving to community-based work or living environments. *Journal of Intellectual Disability Research, 45*, 371–383.

Wehmeyer, M. L., Kelchner, K., & Richards, S. (1996). Essential characteristics of self-determined behavior of individuals with mental retardation. *American Journal on Mental Retardation, 100*, 632–642.

Wehmeyer, M. L., & Metzler, C. A. (1995). How self-determined are people with mental retardation? The National Consumer Survey. *Mental Retardation, 33*, 111–119.

Wehmeyer, M. L., & Palmer, S. B. (2000). Promoting the acquisition and development of self-determination in young children with disabilities. *Early Education and Development, 11*(4), 465–481.

Wehmeyer, M. L., & Shogren, K. A. (2017). The development of self-determination during adolescence. In M. L. Wehmeyer, K. A. Shogren, T. D. Little, & S. J. Lopez (Eds.), *Handbook on the development of self-determination*. New York, NY: Springer.

World Health Organization. (2001). *International classification of functioning, disability, and health*. Geneva, Switzerland: Author.

Supported Decision Making

Christine Bigby and Jacinta Douglas

> With its rejection of the idea of incapacity and its enunciation
> of an entitlement to receive assistance, supported decision-
> making essentially shifts the focus from the capacity of the
> person being assisted to the adequacy or otherwise of the
> capacity of those providing assistance.
>
> (Carney, 2017, p. 48)

Decision Making: Why Is It Important

Choice and decision making are seldom clearly defined, and the terms are often used interchangeably. We argue that choice making is just one part of decision making, which involves far more than the exercise of choice. For example, choice making does not necessarily lead to a decision, as choice may not be acted upon or only constitute a small part of a decision. Illustrating this distinction, decision making is defined in the International Classification of Functioning as "making a choice among options, implementing the choice, and evaluating the effects of the choice..." (World Health Organization, 2001, d177).

Making decisions about one's own life is important to personal well-being. It is one way of controlling your life and ensuring your own preferences and values take priority. The benefits of decision making for people with intellectual disability or acquired brain injury (whom we refer to as people with cognitive disabilities in this chapter) are no different from others. These include an increased sense of self-identity, psychological wellbeing and quality of life (Brown & Brown, 2009; Knox, Douglas, & Bigby, 2016a; Nota, Ferrari, Soresi, & Wehmeyer, 2007). Everyone needs support to make decisions, and most adults draw on their social as well as cognitive resources. A critical realist perspective (Shakespeare, 2006) suggests that adults with cognitive disabilities are likely to need significant support with decision making due both to their difficulties with executive function, self-direction and

C. Bigby (✉) · J. Douglas
La Trobe University, Living with Disability Research Centre, Bundoora, VIC, Australia
e-mail: c.bigby@latrobe.edu.au

© Springer Nature Switzerland AG 2020
R. J. Stancliffe et al. (eds.), *Choice, Preference, and Disability*, Positive
Psychology and Disability Series, https://doi.org/10.1007/978-3-030-35683-5_3

communication, and the discriminatory structures and limiting social attitudes that compound these difficulties often depriving them of rights, respect and dignity.

Informal support for decision making is an integral part of day-to-day support provided by families, friends and paid supporters to people with cognitive disabilities. It is also at the heart of the support, given by health and social care professionals, for person-centred planning, health care and support coordination. In most jurisdictions, particularly when support is provided by families or friends, there are no real mechanisms to guide, monitor or regulate it, other than professional codes of ethics or practice frameworks (Bigby & Frawley, 2010; Carney & Beaupert, 2013).

Some aspects of decision-making support are regulated by law for people with cognitive disabilities; their right to make some types of decisions can be removed, and who provides support can be prescribed, as well as the principles by which they do so (Then, Carney, Bigby & Douglas, 2018). Most commonly this involves the imposition of a substitute decision making through guardianship. The law dictates the principles and processes guardians use to make decisions, often requiring a lens of 'best interests' rather than prioritising an individual's preferences. There is, however, a dearth of empirical evidence about how these play out in practice. Nevertheless, too often guardianship conjures up images of past paternalism that denied self-determination and citizenship were feasible for people with cognitive disabiliies because they lacked rationality (Kittay & Carlson, 2010). Removal of the right to make decisions, and legal regulation of decision making through guardianship, is increasingly critiqued by disability rights advocates and law reform commissions (Then et al., 2018).

The Need for Change

The case for more empowering alternatives to restrictrive legal frameworks and reliance on unregulated informal support is embedded in the United Nation's Convention on the Rights of Persons with Disabilities (UNCRPD) and continues to be made by the disability rights movement (Bach, 2017). Article 12 of the UNCRPD affirms the equal recognition before the law of people with disabilities and has been interpreted as breaking the nexus between mental and legal capacity, asserting that everyone has the right to make decisions about their own life, irrespective of cognitive ability (Bach, 2017; Series, 2015). Article 12 places a clear obligation on member states to take measures to 'provide access by persons with disabilities to the support they may require in exercising their legal capacity'. The General Comment on Article 12 and academic debate has promoted supported decision making as the means of doing this (Arstein-Kerslake, 2017; Committee on the Rights of Persons with Disabilities, 2014), which Bach (2017, p.11) summarises as 'support needed to compliment unique decision making abilities sufficient to exercise power over our lives and legal relationships...an interdependent way to exercise legal capacity with the communicative and interpretative assistance of trusted others'.

Service system reforms based on personalisation and individualised funding have increased decision-making opportunities exponentially for people with cognitive disabilities and brought to the forefront the significance of decision-making support (Bigby, 2016; Carney, 2013). For example, approximately 480,000 people with severe disabilities, who are eligible for an individual plan and funding package, will have the opportunity to make decisions about their support services when the Australian National Disability Insurance Scheme (NDIS) is fully implemented in 2020 (NDIS, 2013). It is increasingly clear, however, that such systems do little to redress existing inequalities, and those with strong family support do better in accessing individualised resources (Carey, Malbon, Reeders, Kavanagh, & Llewllyn, 2017; Jilke, 2015; Neely-Barnes, Graff, Marcenko, & Weber, 2008). Many people with cognitive disabilities simply do not possess the type of social capital needed to take advantage of opportunities for decision making in individualised systems (Bigby, 2008; O'Connor, 2014).

In addition to inequities from the lottery of social capital, other issues suggest drawbacks of relying on unregulated informal support for decision making, adding to the case for change. A body of evidence suggests that informal decision support does not always reflect expectations about furthering the rights, empowerment and self-determination of people with cognitive disabilities embedded in reformed service systems (for review, see Bigby, Whiteside, & Douglas, 2015). Too often individuals' preferences are overridden, and their rights compromised by power and control exerted by informal decision supporters, be they families or paid workers. The bulk of this research concerns people with intellectual disability and is small scale and qualitative. Nevertheless, it portrays common patterns of limited involvement in major or minor decisions that affect their lives (Antaki, Finlay, & Walton, 2009; Bigby & Knox, 2009; Bowey & McGlaughlin, 2005; Kirkendall, Linton, & Farris, 2016) and the paternalistic, controlling or risk averse nature of decision support often experienced including:

- Support that reflects the values of others rather than their own or driven by perceptions of risk or resource constraints (Bigby, Bowers, & Webber, 2011; Bigby, Whiteside, & Douglas, 2017; Dunn, Clare, & Holland, 2010; Hodges & Luken, 2006; Kjellberg, 2002; Sowney & Barr, 2007)
- Support that is paternalistic (Bigby et al., 2011; Bowey & McGlaughlin, 2005; Kohn & Blumenthal, 2014; Nunnelley, 2015)
- Support that is unduly influenced by risk averse organisational management (Hawkins, Redley, & Holland, 2011)
- Support that is negatively affected by supporters' lack of communication skills, poor knowledge about cognitive disability and unawareness of the influence of their own preferences and values (Antaki et al., 2009; Dunn et al., 2010; Ferguson, Jarrett, & Terras, 2011; Sowney & Barr, 2007)
- Meetings conducted by professionals that are disempowering and obstruct rather than facilitate involvement in decision making (Abreu, Zhang, Seale, Primeau, & Jones, 2002; Pilnick, Clegg, Murphy, & Almack, 2010)

Qualitative studies are beginning to show that decision-making support can be an onerous and complex task which has been likened to 'twirling plates on a stick' as supporters simultaneously draw on ideas about rights, practicalities and risks (Bigby, Whiteside, & Douglas, 2017 p.11). Evaluations of small pilot decision support programs in Australia demonstrate the benefits of support to supporters through training or individual consultations, but that training packages are often based on expert opinion and practice wisdom rather than rigorously developed empirical evidence.

Resistance from others involved in a person's life and their refusal to act on decisions can undermine decision support, creating uncertain boundaries between decision support and advocacy (Bigby et al., 2017). Program evaluations as well as other studies identify uncertainty about roles of family, service providers and others in decision support; the difficulties in resolving competing perspectives when supporters have no formal standing; and the confusion this can cause for third parties (Bigby, Webber, & Bower, 2015; Kohn & Blumenthal, 2014). As this emerging body of evidence about decision support suggests, informal support for decision making often lacks systematic guidance to supporters, resources to build their capacity or mechanisms for accountability and runs the risk of being undermined by conflict or uncertainty, paternalism and becoming simply informal substitute decision making.

The Promise of Supported Decision Making

Supported decision making was developed in the 1990s by Canadian parent groups, as a less restrictive alternative to guardianship, as it became apparent that informal supporters would require some type of formal standing in the emerging models of individualised funding (Gordon, 2000). It gained prominence through debate about Article 12 of the UNCRPD and has become an omnibus rather than a precisely defined concept. Supported decision making is referred to both as the practice of rights-based support for decision making and as a legal scheme that formally recognises supporters who assist decision making or co-construct decisions with people with cognitive disabilities (Browning, Bigby, & Douglas, 2014).

The underlying premise of supported decision making is that everyone has the right to exercise legal capacity and participate in decision making and can express their preferences with support in the context of trusting relationships. The role of supporters is to explain issues, explore options and support the expression of preferences (Carney & Beaupert, 2013). They may engage others in decision-making processes, make agreements that give effect to decisions or implement decisions (Bach & Kerzner, 2010). Supporters' roles with people with more severe intellectual disability may extend to interpreting signs and preferences, ascribing agency to a person's actions or co-constructing preferences or decisions (Series, 2015).

Carney suggests that by recognising decision making as a shared process and acknowledging the role of supporters, supported decision making

...replicates how citizens already decide things: mirroring informal collaborative ways advice is sought or accepted within family and other networks of daily life, and avoiding any real loss of 'ownership' of the decision made. The person receiving support keeps rather than loses their formal individual autonomy; is treated as capable rather than incapable of making decisions; and retains a social and legal equality with other citizens that would be lost should a substitute decision-maker step into their shoes. (Carney, 2017, p.44)

Supported decision making as either practice or legal scheme holds the promise of enabling better decision support for people with cognitive disabilities than previous approaches through:

- Retaining their rights to make decisions while ensuring access to necesssary support and safeguarding mechanisms
- Recognising informal support arrangements
- Taking least restrictive options and enhancing autonomy by putting the person's will and preferences at the centre of decision making
- Shifting practices of support through better guidance, capacity building and accountability of supporters to principles of rights-based support
- Providing criteria for judging or challenging the quality of decision support
- Identifying where support is lacking in the informal sphere and a need for additional formal resources

Adoption of Supported Decision-Making Schemes

Despite the considerable value proposition of supported decision making, Then et al. (2018) suggest it exists more often on paper than in practice. Their examination of nine law reform commission reports from various states or provinces in Canada, Australia, the United States and the United Kingdom found that although all proposed legal recognition of some form of supported decision making as an adjunct to substitute decision making, none recommended complete replacement. Remarkably, very few of the recommendations from these reports have been implemented.

Some jurisdictions, such as the Canadian states of British Columbia and Alberta, the US states of Texas and Delaware, Sweden, Israel and Ireland, have reformed legal systems to incorporate supported decision making. Mostly such schemes have been designed as alternatives rather than replacements for guardianship (Kanter & Tolub, 2017). For example, Texas, the first US state to legislate supported decision making in 2015, retains provisions for guardianship where evidence suggests other alternatives are not feasible. Sweden, one of the few countries to have fully dismantled guardianship for non-financial matters, created the position of Godman, to which family or paid staff may be appointed to manage an individual's affairs according to their wishes. The Irish legislation requires that any decision support be guided by a person' will and preferences rather than a best-interests perspective. It includes three different forms of supported decision making according to the severity of a persons' intellectual impairment, decision-making assistance agreements, co-decision-making agreements and appointment of decision-making representatives with power to make a decision on a person's behalf (Kanter & Tolub, 2017).

Another approach to supported decision making has been reducing the need for guardianship through support agreements for specific types of decisions and easing capacity thresholds to ensure accessibility to people with cognitive disabilities. An Australian example is the Victorian Medical Treatment Planning and Decisions Act, 2016, which states that a person has decision-making capacity to make an advanced care directive if 'they are able to make a decision with practicable and appropriate support'.

Various safeguards have been built into supported decision-making schemes for supported adults and third parties involved in their decisions. These include oversight by appointed monitors, courts or tribunals with power to conduct reviews and provisions for agreements to be registered or revoked. The Australian medical treatment example above requires a general practitioner to witness an advance care directive and certify that the person has been provided with practicable and appropriate support in making it.

Evidence About Supported Decision Making

There is very little empirical evidence about the effectiveness of supported decision-making schemes or safeguarding mechanisms, and this together with the vulnerability of people with cognitive disabilities may account for hesitancy about its adoption (Boundy & Fleischner, 2013; Then, 2013). The early Canadian and Swedish adopters have not investigated how the ideals of supported decision making have been translated into practice, and it remains unclear whether schemes have delivered on promise. Kohn, Blumenthal and Campbell (2014) assert, for example, that it is

> …impossible to know whether supported decision making actually empowers persons with cognitive and intellectual disabilities. Furthermore, there is reason to be concerned that supported decision making might actually have the opposite effect, disempowering such individuals or making them more vulnerable to manipulation, coercion, or abuse. (p. 1114)

The only in-depth qualitative study of decision support in the context of Representation Agreements in British Columbia, Canada, provides some evidence to support these concerns (Browning, 2018). Although assessing practice against principles was not a primary aim, Browning's study suggests that legal recognition did help supporters to navigate the practicalities of providing support but their practice did not always reflect the ideals embedded in the scheme. She states:

> …decision making support in the context of Representation Agreements and Microboards sometimes involved undue influence, and informal coercion… the presence of legal mechanisms did not substantially shape how central participants were supported with their decision making. (Browning, 2018, p.191)

As the quote at the beginning of this chapter suggests, it is the adequacy of support practice that lies at the heart of supported decision making. Assembling evidence about the processes of decision support, what constitutes effective supported decision-making practice, and using this to develop tools to build the capacity of supporters may be necessary before supported decision making can be more entrenched in legal systems.

Support for Decision-Making Practice

As indicated earlier, a plethora of factors, such as supporters' skills, attitudes and legal context, influence decision support. These can facilitate participation in decision making by people with cognitive disabilities or deny or reduce opportunities and actively shape decisions to avoid risk or reflect primarily the preferences of supporters.

A substantial body of knowledge exists about some of the underpinning aspects of decision support, such as skill development, choice making, communication and the impact of cognitive impairment on capacity. Use of this knowledge is reflected in the practical strategies identified in research about effective decision support, for example, simple adapted communication strategies like color-coded buttons on a TV controller to enhance decision making for residents with intellectual disability in an accommodation service (Rossow-Kimball & Goodwin, 2009); 'cognitive scaffolding' to break down a big decision into smaller steps to involve people with acquired brain injury in decision making (Knox, Douglas, & Bigby, 2015); active support practice, based on concepts such as task analysis, to enable choice and control about everyday matters (Beadle-Brown, Hutchinson, & Whelton, 2012); and training programs to improve decision-making skills of people with cognitive disability about topics such as sexuality (Agran, Storey, & Krupp, 2010; Dukes & McGuire, 2009), later life options (Heller, Miller, Hsieh, & Sterns, 2000), avoiding abuse (Khemka, 2000; Khemka, Hickson, & Reynolds, 2005) and health-care systems (Webb & Stanton, 2009).

A smaller body of research, primarily small-scale and qualitative studies, has considered decision support. Many of these studies confound choice and decision making, and only a few have focused solely on decision making. There is no consistent typology that makes sense of the different types of decisions, though magnitude, subject matter or life domains are often used, and prominence given to 'big' decisions or those about sex and health (Ferguson et al., 2011). Despite the limitations, there are some consistent findings about the nature of decision support that facilitates participation by people with cognitive disabilities.

The pivotal role of relationships in enabling good support for decision making is consistently identified (Burgen, 2010; Kjellberg, 2002; Knox, Douglas, & Bigby, 2013; Knox et al., 2015, 2016a; Knox, Douglas, & Bigby, 2016b; Watson, 2016). Relationships based on trust where supporters perceive the person with cognitive disabilities as capable of participating in decision making, have a positive attitude towards risk, give importance to choice and control, and are committed to upholding their rights and create opportunities for decision making are all identified as characteristics of good decision support (Agran et al., 2010; Bigby, Webber, & Bower, 2015; Caldwell, 2010; Kjellberg, 2002; Knox et al., 2015; Mill, Mayes, & McConnell, 2010; Renblad, 2003; Timmons, Hall, Bose, Wolfe, & Winsor, 2011). Studies have included decision supporters with different types of ties to the person they support, including volunteers without any pre-existing connection, and suggest that the quality of a relationship is more important than its type or length (Bigby, Douglas, et al., 2017; Knox, 2016; Knox, Douglas, & Bigby, 2017). Watson, Wilson, and Hagiliassis (2017) point to the positive influence of a close relationship on responsiveness of supporters to the expression of a person's will, asserting they 'were most effective in providing decision support… and had knowledge of the person's life story, particularly in relation to events that demonstrated preferences' (p.1022). Crisp (2018) illustrates why trusting relationships are important to decision support, showing they are a medium through which supporters can influence and challenge a person's preferences, but which also give them confidence that supporters will respect their preferences if they choose to reject the new opportunities. Another characteristic of relationships that enable participation in decision making is self-awareness of supporters and their ability to suspend their own judgments and adopt a neutral and non-judgmental stance (Ellem, O'Connor, Wilson, & Williams, 2013; Knox et al., 2017).

Notably, empirical findings about the importance of relationships to decision support mesh with feminist conceptions of relational agency and autonomy that contend 'beliefs, values and decisions that inform autonomous acts are constituted within social relations of interdependence' (Mackenzie & Stoljar, 2000). They highlight the significance of enabling environments and personal relationships in promoting self-determination and decision making as central to the ethics of care (Kittay & Carlson, 2010; Morris, 2001; Silvers & Francis, 2009; Wong, 2010). Silvers and Francis, for example, use the term 'prosthetic rationality' to draw an analogy between the support of a prosthetic limb and supporting a person to make decisions or express preferences, suggesting that 'a trustee's reasoning and communicating can execute part or all of subject's own thinking processes without substituting the trustee's own ideas as if they were subject's own' (2009, p. 485).

The importance of supporters knowing the person and enabling support to be tailored to their preferences is implicit in Watson et al.'s description of closeness and consistently reported by other studies (Antaki, Finlay, Walton, & Pate, 2008; Conder, Mirfin-Veitch, Sanders, & Munford, 2011; Espiner & Hartnett, 2012; Knox et al., 2015, 2016a, 2016b; Rossow-Kimball & Goodwin, 2009; Schelly, 2008). Most commonly highlighted is knowing about a person's cognitive impairment in order to adjust communication and the presentation of abstract concepts and a capacity of 'deep listening' informed by knowledge about the person to look for the core message behind their actions (Ellem et al., 2013; Espiner & Hartnett, 2012). In the case of people with acquired brain injury, Knox et al. (2015) suggest that supporters' understanding of changes that have occurred since the injury and how different a person may be is important.

Knox's doctoral study is one of the most in-depth studies exploring the decision-making experiences of people with traumatic brain injury and identified four overarching constructs important to understanding decision support (Knox, 2016). First is the importance of supporters understanding the multifaceted context in which decisions are made, including the individual, such as their life course stage or support networks; the social milieu, such as cultural or social norms; and legal frameworks, such as guardianship provisions. Second is the influence of participation in decision making in shaping a person's self-concept after injury and, in turn, self-concept of participation in decision making. Third is the 'complex, messy and recursive' nature of decision support that often involves shaping and reshaping the decision before reaching a conclusion. Supporters can facilitate participation by taking account of the decision's impact on the person as well as others involved with them, recognising that sometimes decision making can be overwhelming, and magnitude does not necessarily reflect significance of a decision to the person. Lastly, similar to other studies, this study recognised the saliency of relationships in facilitating participation in decision making especially those characterised by trust, closeness, honest and effective communication and where supporters know the person well. Additionally, Knox identified the benefits of having more than one person acting as a decision supporter and supporters who actively build connections by recruiting others to the support network.

Two other empirical doctoral studies have explored the experiences of decision support, primarily from the perspective of supporters of people with intellectual disability, using in-depth qualitative methods of data collection (Browning, 2018; Watson, 2016). They have developed fairly similar models describing the processes by which decision support occurs and factors influencing it. The context of Browning's study was Canadian and involved people with intellectual disability for whom either a Representation Agreement or Microboard was in place and supporters were family members, paid support workers or friends. She describes the process of decision-making support as

> …a dynamic interaction between the person's will and preferences in relation to a decision opportunity and their supporter's responses. This interaction was shaped by five influencing factors: the experiences and attributes the person and their supporter brought to the process; the quality of their relationship; the environment in which decision making occurred and the nature and consequences of the decision. The elements and influencing factors involved in the process were always the same, however because the nature of each and the way they interacted differed for each decision, the type of support provided and the outcomes observed varied significantly. (Browning, 2018, p.iii)

Her study, with its detailed vignette examples, demonstrates clearly the highly individualised and contextually dependent nature of the process of decision-making support.

Watson's study, set in Australia where there are no legal supported decision-making schemes, focussed more specifically on decision support for people with severe or profound intellectual disability in the context of intentional circles of support. Her model proposes support for decision making as a bidirectional process where the role of the person with cognitive disabilities is to express their will and preference using a range of unintentional and informal behaviours and that of the supporters to respond to the expression of preferences by acknowledging, interpreting and acting on that preference (Watson et al., 2017). This interaction and supporters' responsiveness are influenced by five factors: the person's communication in terms of intentionality, supporter attitudes and perceptions, their relational closeness to the person, the functioning and makeup of the circle of support and characteristics of the service system (Watson et al., 2017).

These two studies make important contributions to the limited knowledge about decision support which provide glimpses of understanding what good practice looks like and the factors associated with it. Like other studies, they emphasise the relational aspects of decision support, dynamic interactions between a person's expression of preferences and supporter responsiveness and the impact of context on support. They are, however, generic models of the process of support and neither set out to explore the specific factors associated with effective support. Browning's study, for example, demonstrated that similar processes of decision support can lead to empowering as well as disempowering support practice, depending on the nature of the influencing factors.

> …there were instances when the interaction of elements and factors led the supporter to respond by accepting or trying to clarify the person's will and preferences which increased the person's agency during the process. When the person was supported in a way that increased their agency it resulted in the outcome (the decision) closely aligning with their will and preferences. In other situations, the interaction of elements and factors led the supporter to respond by trying to change or disregard the person's will and preferences which decreased the person's agency, and resulted in the outcome (the decision) deviating from their will and preferences. (2018, p. 179)

What Works: A Practice Framework for Decision-Making Support Practice

A set of propositions about features of support for decision making and effective support for decision-making practice with people with cognitive disabilities is summarised in Table 1.

The La Trobe Support for Decision Practice Framework was developed from the program of research we have led at La Trobe University (Douglas & Bigby, 2018). It is based on the four-phase approach to the development and evaluation of complex interventions suggested by Craig et al. (2008). The first phase was a systematic review of the peer-reviewed literature on decision-making support for people with cognitive disabilities and series of qualitative studies, including those with our doctoral students (Browning, 2018; Crisp, 2018; Knox, 2016) exploring experiences of decision support from the perspectives of supporters and people with cognitive disabilities. From this knowledge, much of which has been discussed throughout this chapter, we developed an initial practice framework and education program for supporters. In phase two, these were piloted with 45 support workers and health professionals working with people with cognitive disabilities in a large residential setting, and revisions made from feedback of participants and the reference group. The third

Table 1 Summary of features of decision support and effective practice

Features of decision-making support	Features of effective support for decision-making practice
A complex process with discernible, interacting and overlapping components	Occurs in context of trusting relationships with supporters who have positive expectations of involvement of the person with cognitive disabilities in decision making and create opportunities for this
An iterative rather than linear process that does not necessarily proceed in a fixed order and may be fulfilled in a recursive manner	Requires a commitment to upholding the person's rights, self awareness of values and regular self-reflection and review of support
Involves multiple players, the person with cognitive disability, supporters and others involved in influencing or impacted by the decision	Requires knowing or getting to know all facets of the person
Participation and support needs change with every decision	Requires an understanding of the decision, its features, potential consequences and potential constraining factor
Each component requires ongoing tailoring to the individual based on knowing their personal attributes and the characteristics of the physical, social and organisational environment	Requires knowledge of the person's will and preferences around the specific decision and exploration of all possible options
Shaped by the context in which it takes place	Requires that communication is tailored to strengths and weakness of the individual
Decision must be implementable, and this may not rest with decision-making supporters who may need to engage advocates to support implementation	Can be onerous and supporters require support for their role

phase, evaluation, is work in progress and has various arms. The largest are two parallel, randomised controlled trials of an educational program with follow-up mentoring for supporters that involves dyads of primary decision supporters and people with either intellectual disability or acquired brain injury across eastern Australia. The education program is delivered to supporters, but data about change to decision support, both quantitative and qualitative, is collected from both members of the dyad. In a subsample, data is only collected from supporters to ensure the inclusion of those who support people with more severe and profound cognitive disabilities, recognising the difficulties this group have in giving verbal feedback on their experiences of support. Additional arms of the study involve less rigorous pre- and post-evaluation of delivering the education program to social care professionals in various roles who provide short-term support for decision making for people with cognitive disabilities seeking services. Preliminary analysis of the qualitative data is promising about the efficacy of the education program for supporters.

The practice framework is intended as a guide for supporters of people with intellectual disability or acquired brain injury (see Bigby, Douglas & Vassallo, 2019). Its central purpose, with the associated training materials, is to assist supporters to focus on understanding and acting on the will and preferences of people with cognitive disabilities, be they families, support workers, guardians or health

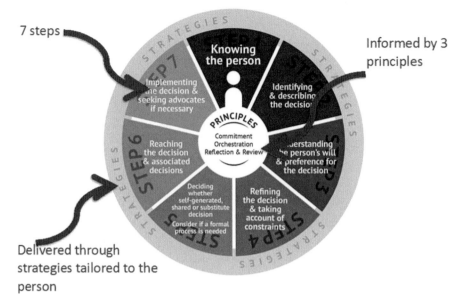

Fig. 1 Support for decision-making practice framework. (Bigby & Douglas, 2015)

and social care professionals. The framework is designed to be applicable to the varying and evolving contexts of decision support. It can, for example, be used by informal supporters in the current least restrictive alternative regime of Australian jurisdictions and the National Disability Insurance Schemes, by more formally appointed supporters in the context of the various types of supported decision-making schemes developing around the world, and potentially by formally appointed guardians charged with making substitute decisions that give priority to a person's will and preferences.

Figure 1 is a schematic representation of the framework which conceptualises support for decision making as having seven components or steps, delivered through individually tailored strategies and informed by three principles. This diagram illustrates the necessary components of decision support, but does not intend to suggest they occur in an orderly sequence. Rather support occurs iteratively, with supporters' attention moving backwards and forwards between the components or dealing with them simultaneously, during the process of supporting any single decision.

Principles of Support for Decision Making

The actions of supporters should be informed by three principles: commitment, orchestration and reflection and review.

Commitment Supporters must accept that the person they support has preferences, no matter their level of cognitive disability, and be committed to upholding their right to participate in decision making. The relationship does not have to be of a particular type or longevity but must be respectful and unconditionally regard the person as a human being of equal value and a holder of rights. When equality and rights are foundational beliefs, supporters are more likely to have positive expectations about the person's participation in decision making and to respect their preferences rather than subordinating them to those of others in the decision-making space who may exert power, such as family members, staff or professionals.

Orchestration Making decisions can involve a range of people who are differently engaged and know the person in different ways, such as a friend, a family member, a person for whom they are advocating, a long-term client who requires intensive and costly support with everyday activities or a short-term patient occupying an expensive hospital bed. Supporters may include immediate or extended family, direct support workers, managerial staff and subject matter experts. Someone must lead, whom we term a primary supporter, in orchestrating the process by drawing in other supporters from various parts of the person's life, as well as mediating any differences between supporters or others potentially affected by the decision. If such a lead person is not evident then, for some decisions, it will be necessary to find someone willing to take on that role.

Reflection and Review Supporters must hold a neutral, non-judgmental stance that puts aside their own preferences, to avoid exerting subtle influence. They need self-awareness and continuous reflection about their own values, their own stake in the decision and their potential to influence the person being supported to ensure the decision-making agenda remains firmly on the preferences and rights of the person they are supporting. Supporters need to employ a self-questioning strategy, applying self-checks and balances to each decision situation, and remain vigilant to points where they are particularly vulnerable to providing biased, value-laden or constrained support. Effective support for decision making should be transparent and accountable, meaning that supporters should be open to review by others, able to articulate their reasoning processes, describe the observations, experience and knowledge they have used to inform their support and track this through to the point of decision.

Strategies for Practice

Strategies are needed for turning principles into action and tailoring support to the individual throughout the various components of the process. Supporters require a repertoire of strategies that can be adapted to the person being supported and the particular task at hand. Many strategies are underpinned by knowledge about choice making, communication and the impact of cognitive disability as well as knowledge about the person being supported. They often revolve around locating and providing access to information and/or opportunities to widen experiences of what might be possible; enabling, ascertaining or interpreting a person's preferences; and helping to understand constraints and consequences. To be effective, strategies need to be person centred and attuned to the timing and situational factors, the significance, scope and nature of the decision, and who else might be involved in or affected by the decision. Figure 2 groups and illustrates some of the strategies.

Attention to communication

- Pitching information and communication methods at the right level
- Being aware of verbal and non-verbal behavioural clues
- Checking back for understanding
- Reviewing information presented

Education about consequences and practicalities

- Making the decision and consequences understandable to the individual
- Doing the research to gather information
- Presenting the options and related pros and cons
- Identifying associated smaller decisions and consequences
- Explaining the consequences and that priorities can be undermined by small decisions

Listening and engaging to ensure all options are considered

- Being attentive to will and preferences
- Taking sufficient time
- Using others as sounding boards

Creating opportunities

- Using active reframing that invites participation
- Providing a sounding board
- Acknowledging low expectations and building confidence
- Testing options
- Introducing and nurturing the seeds of ideas
- Bringing in others to trial a situation
- Creating distance to enable greater autonomy

Breaking things down
- Breaking decisions into smaller components
- Teaching and shaping skills to identify steps and smaller components

Fig. 2 Strategies for decision support. (Adapted from Bigby & Douglas, 2015)

Components of Decision Support

As represented in Fig. 1, there are seven components of decision support which must be worked through though in an iterative rather than sequential manner.

Knowing the Person The person being supported must be at the centre of all support, and supporters need to 'know' the person well or get to know them well. This means knowing all aspects of the person and having a sense of their self-identity or self-concept (who I am and how I feel about myself). This straddles many different aspects including knowing about their attributes and style, personal characteristics, likes, dislikes, preferences, skills, the effect on their understanding of their specific cognitive impairments, social connections, history and personal story. Part of knowing a person also means understanding the way they are seen by others in their network including the various 'experts' who have been involved in their life. Knowledge of what defines the person provides the conceptual context for understanding their preferences.

Identifying and Describing the Decision Decisions come in all shapes and sizes and are rather like Babushka (nesting) dolls embedded in each other. Bigger decisions open up opportunities for lots of other smaller decisions. They are also cumulative; decisions made in one part of a person's life will have implications in other parts and often set parameters for smaller decisions by either making or curtailing further opportunities for decision making.

Effective support requires the decision to be made or the opportunity for a decision to be identified and its features described in full, including its scope; how likely it is to impact on a person's life; the other decisions that might flow from it; who should be involved in helping the person to make the decision or the formal organisations that may be involved, such as the criminal justice system or health system; the time frame available in which to make the decision; and the potential consequences of choosing one decision option over others. Describing a decision helps to focus attention on the core issues, guide who to involve, identify tensions that might arise and constraining factors that might be amenable to change and clarify the potential flow-on effects of this decision to other parts of a person's life.

Understanding a Person's Will and Preferences About the Decision This is the 'blue sky' part of the process, when supporters need to think widely about the decision, and explore with the person all the possible options, the person's preferences about all the things that will be encompassed in the decision, and the consequences of different options. Everyone has preferences. They stem from experiences, knowledge and available information, personal values or cultural norms. They are communicated in many ways – through words, signs, gestures, expressions, behaviour, actions or lack thereof. For some people preferences have to be interpreted by supporters based on their knowledge of the person, or garnered from the perspectives of others who know the person well or in different contexts. In this component, preferences and options considered should not be constrained by parameters imposed by things such as resources or risks. In some decisions, this component is as similar to the dreaming or aspirational elements of some approaches to person centred planning but more focused on a specific decision.

Refining the Decision and Taking Account of Constraints A decision must be more than a dream or hopeful statement in a plan; it must be implementable. Once aspects of the decision have been explored and preferences are beginning to be understood, the support process involves prioritising and refining preferences with the person to take into account constraints such as time, money, impact on other people and safety. Ways will need to be considered to ensure the decision can be implemented, enabling any risks that might be involved and questioning or creatively managing resource constraints.

Risk can feature heavily in some decisions. The scale, frequency, likelihood and severity of potentially negative consequences of a decision may need to be scoped. There are no prescriptive procedures for weighing dignity and positives associated with risk against the negatives of risky decisions. A risk enablement approach suggests supporting risks to be understood, thinking about ways of respecting preferences that might also minimise the impact of the consequence or harm to the person or others if things go wrong and the risk eventuates (reducing the harm) (Bigby, Douglas, & Hamilton, 2018). Essential principles for thinking about enabling decisions involving risk are staying true to preferences, minimising harm, being proactive and putting positives first (see Bigby, Douglas, & Vassallo, 2018).

Consider if a formal process is needed This component distils the knowledge gained about the decision, preferences, priorities, constraints and consequences. The manner in which the decision is to be reached is based on the knowledge accumulated about the specific decision and the person's own skills. Indeed, it may well become clear that the person can self-generate the decision with little support or a shared decision can be made collaboratively by the person and their supporters. The principles of the framework and of contemporary disability policy, in many jurisdictions, suggest that a person's preferences should only be overridden where they cannot be realised without harm to themselves or others or breaching the law, and they do not fully understand the consequences of their preferences. Rather than informal substitute decisions occurring without scrutiny or due process in situations where there is serious anticipated harm to self or others or unresolved conflict about reaching a shared decision, recourse to the formal processes relevant to the jurisdiction, such as an application to a guardianship tribunal, may be necessary. In situations where a person already has a guardian in place, then supporters provide the guardian with all the relevant information to support a decision that reflects the person's will and preferences.

Reaching the decision and associated decisions A decision is made to reflect prioritised preferences as closely as possible. The many consequential decisions that will flow from a major decision will become clearer. In supporting each of these smaller decisions, the support for decision-making cycle loops back and components are repeated. Depending on the decision, it may be formally recorded and communicated to others involved in the person's life, formal or informal, who will support its implementation.

Implementing a decision and seeking out advocates if necessary Decision making often falters because the tasks, power or resources necessary to implement the decision may be beyond the scope of the supporters involved in earlier stages of the decision-making process. Responsibility to support implementation of a decision may not rest with decision-making supporters, and they may need to seek out advocates to make sure the decision is followed through by actions. The processes of support do not stop here, as the person being supported is likely to be involved in making consequential decisions and other unrelated decisions for which support might be needed. Having an advocate or a case manager to help implement a decision will not remove the need for continuing support with decision making.

Next Steps

Legal reforms that embrace schemes for supported decision making will only flourish if there is evidence about the type of decision support practice that translates rights-based ideals into everyday reality for people with cognitive disabilities. As research about practice gathers pace, it will also be important to consider the notion of dedifferentiation, if and when it might be necessary to develop specialist knowledge or training for supporters of specific subgroups of people with cognitive disabilities, or how to make adjustments to practice that take specific account of issues relevant to particular groups (Clegg & Bigby, 2017). It may also be the case that supporters may need specialist knowledge for specific types of decision, such as end of life directives. The focus of our research and practice framework has been adults with intellectual disabilities or acquired brain injury, whose levels of cognitive impairment remain relatively stable. Other research groups have focused on people with dementia whose cognitive impairment increases over time (Sinclair et al., 2018), or people with mental illness whose support needs may be episodic (Gooding, 2017). Much can be learned about support practice by comparing and contrasting practice with different groups as this research unfolds.

Importantly, the essential ingredients of supported decision making are supporters committed to upholding a person's rights and knowing them well. Attention must be given to building the social capital of people with cognitive disabilities if supported decision making is to be a viable alternative for everyone and redress the inequalities entrenched in individualised funding models. This means that supported decision-making schemes must incorporate not only capacity building strategies for supporters but mechanisms that proactively reach out to find, encourage and nurture supporters for the many people who do not have strong existing support networks. Formal rights can only create space for action, and as Reinders argues, people with cognitive disabilities need to be included in informal relationships as well institutions (Reinders, 2002).

References

Abreu, B. C., Zhang, L., Seale, G., Primeau, L., & Jones, J. S. (2002). Interdisciplinary meetings: Investigating the collaboration between persons with brain injury and treatment teams. *Brain Injury, 16*, 691–704. https://doi.org/10.1080/02699050210128942

Agran, M., Storey, K., & Krupp, M. (2010). Choosing and choice making are not the same: Asking "what do you want for lunch?" is not self-determination. *Journal of Vocational Rehabilitation, 33*, 77–88. https://doi.org/10.3233/JVR-2010-0517

Antaki, C., Finlay, W., & Walton, C. (2009). Choices for people with intellectual disabilities: Official discourse and everyday practice. *Journal of Policy and Practice in Intellectual Disabilities, 6*, 260–266. https://doi.org/10.1111/j.1741-1130.2009.00230.x

Antaki, C., Finlay, W., Walton, C., & Pate, L. (2008). Offering choices to people with intellectual disabilities: An interactional study. *Journal of Intellectual Disability Research, 52*, 1165–1175. https://doi.org/10.1111/j.1365-2788.2008.01101.x

Arstein-Kerslake, A. (2017). *Restoring voice to people with cognitive disabilities: Realizing the right to equal recognition before the law*. Cambridge, UK: Cambridge University Press.

Bach, M. (2017). Inclusive citizenship: Refusing the construction of "cognitive foreigners" in neoliberal times. *Research and Practice in Intellectual and Developmental Disabilities, 4*, 4–25. https://doi.org/10.1080/23297018.2017.1306794

Bach, M., & Kerzner, L. (2010). *A new paradigm for protecting autonomy and the right to legal capacity*. Ontario: Law Commission of Ontario. Retrieved from: https://www.lco-cdo.org/wp-content/uploads/2010/11/disabilities-commissioned-paper-bach-kerzner.pdf

Beadle-Brown, J., Hutchinson, A., & Whelton, B. (2012). Person-centred active support–increasing choice, promoting independence and reducing challenging behaviour. *Journal of Applied Research in Intellectual Disabilities, 25*, 291–307. https://doi.org/10.1111/j.1468-3148.2011.00666.x

Bigby, C. (2008). Known well by no one. Trends of the informal social networks of people with intellectual disability five years after moving to the community. *Journal of Intellectual and Developmental Disabilities, 33*, 148–157. https://doi.org/10.1080/13668250802094141

Bigby, C. (2016). Commentary by Christine Bigby on "Reducing the inequality of luck: Keynote address at the 2015 Australasian Society for Intellectual Disability National Conference" (Bonyhady, 2016). *Research and Practice in Intellectual and Developmental Disabilities, 3*, 134–139. https://doi.org/10.1080/23297018.2016.1230835

Bigby, C., Bowers, B., & Webber, R. (2011). Planning and decision making about the future care of older group home residents and transition to residential aged care. *Journal of Intellectual Disability Research, 55*, 777–789. https://doi.org/10.1111/j.1365-2788.2010.01297.x

Bigby, C., & Douglas, J. (2015). Support for decision making – A practice framework. Living with Disability Research Centre, La Trobe University. http://hdl.handle.net/1959.9/556875

Bigby, C., Douglas, J., Carney, T., Then, S., Wiesel, I., & Smith, E. (2017). Delivering decision making support to people with cognitive disability – What has been learned from pilot programs in Australia from 2010 to 2015. *Australian Journal of Social Issues, 52*, 222–240. https://doi.org/10.1002/ajs4.19

Bigby, C., Douglas, J., & Hamilton, L. (2018). *Overview of literature about enabling risk for people with cognitive disabilities in context of disability support services*. Melbourne, VIC: La Trobe University. Retrieved from: http://hdl.handle.net/1959.9/563495

Bigby, C., Douglas, J.M., & Vassallo, S. (2018). *Enabling risk: Putting positives first. An online learning resource for disability support workers*. Retrieved from: www.enablingriskresource.com.au

Bigby, C., Douglas, J., & Vassallo, S. (2019). The La Trobe Support for Decision Making Practice Framework. An online learning resource. Retrieved from: www.supportfordecision-makingresource.com.au

Bigby, C., & Frawley, P. (2010). *Social work and intellectual disability: Working for change*. London, UK: Palgrave Macmillan.

Bigby, C., & Knox, M. (2009). "I want to see the Queen": Experiences of service use by ageing people with an intellectual disability. *Australian Social Work, 62*, 216–231. https://doi.org/10.1080/03124070902748910

Bigby, C., Webber, R., & Bower, B. (2015). Sibling roles in the lives of older group home residents with intellectual disability: Working with staff to safeguard wellbeing. *Australian Social Work, 68*, 453–468. https://doi.org/10.1080/0312407X.2014.950678

Bigby, C., Whiteside, M., & Douglas, J. (2017). Providing support for decision making to adults with intellectual disability: perspectives of family members and workers in disability support services. *Journal of Intellectual and Developmental Disability*. Advance online publication. https://doi.org/10.3109/13668250.2017.1378873

Bigby, C., Whiteside, M., & Douglas, M. (2015). *Supporting people with cognitive disabilities in decision making – Processes and dilemmas*. Melbourne, VIC: Living with Disability Research Centre, http://hdl.handle.net/1959.9/319333

Boundy, M., & Fleischner, B. (2013). *Supported Decision Making Instead of Guardianship: An international overview Washington: TASC* [Training & Advocacy Support Center]. National Disability Rights Network.

Bowey, L., & McGlaughlin, A. (2005). Assessing the barriers to achieving genuine housing choice for adults with a learning disability: The views of family carers and professionals. *British Journal of Social Work, 35*, 139–148. https://doi.org/10.1093/bjsw/bch167

Brown, I., & Brown, R. I. (2009). Choice as an aspect of quality of life for people with intellectual disabilities. *Journal of Policy and Practice in Intellectual Disabilities, 6*, 11–18.

Browning, M., Bigby, C., & Douglas, J. (2014). Supported decision making: Understanding how its conceptual link to legal capacity is influencing the development of practice. *Research and Practice in Intellectual and Developmental Disabilities, 1*, 34–45. https://doi.org/10.1080/23297018.2014.902726

Browning, M. J. (2018). *Developing an understanding of supported decision making practice in Canada: The experiences of people with intellectual disabilities and their supporters.* (Doctoral thesis, La Trobe University, Melbourne, Australia).

Burgen, B. (2010). Women with cognitive impairment and unplanned or unwanted pregnancy: A 2-year audit of women contacting the pregnancy advisory service. *Australian Social Work, 63*, 18–34. https://doi.org/10.1080/03124070903471033

Caldwell, J. (2010). Leadership development of individuals with developmental disabilities in the self-advocacy movement. *Journal of Intellectual Disability Research, 54*, 1004–1014. https://doi.org/10.1111/j.1365-2788.2010.01326.x

Carey, G., Malbon, E., Reeders, D., Kavanagh, A., & Llewllyn, G. (2017). Redressing or entrenching social and health inequities through policy implementation? Examining personalised budgets through the Australian National Disability Insurance Scheme. *International Journal for Equity in Health, 16*(192). https://doi.org/10.1186/s12939-017-0682-z.

Carney, T. (2013). Participation and service access rights for people with intellectual disability: A role for law. *Journal of Intellectual and Developmental Disability, 38*, 59–69. https://doi.org/10.3109/13668250.2012.738810

Carney, T. (2017). Supported decision making in Australia: Meeting the challenge of moving from capacity to capacity-building? *Law in Context, 35*(2), 44–63.

Carney, T., & Beaupert, F. (2013). Public and private bricolage-challenges balancing law, services & civil society in advancing CRPD supported decision making. *The University of New South Wales Law Journal, 36*, 175–201.

Clegg, J., & Bigby, C. (2017). Debates about dedifferentiation. *Research and Practice in Intellectual and Developmental Disabilities, 4*, 80–97. https://doi.org/10.1080/23297018.2017.1309987

Committee on the Rights of Persons with Disabilities. (2014). *General comment No. 1, Article 12: Equal recognition before the law*. Geneva, Switzerland: Author.

Conder, J., Mirfin-Veitch, B., Sanders, J., & Munford, R. (2011). Planned pregnancy, planned parenting: Enabling choice for adults with a learning disability. *British Journal of Learning Disabilities, 39*, 105–112. https://doi.org/10.1111/j.1468-3156.2010.00625.x

Craig, P., Dieppe, P., Macintyre, S., Michie, S., Nazareth, I., & Petticrew, M. (2008). Developing and evaluating complex interventions: The new medical research council guidance. *British Medical Journal, 33*, 1655. https://doi.org/10.1136/bmj.a1655

Crisp, W. (2018). *"She proudly announced she has a boyfriend from her day placement and wants him to sleep over." The grounded theory of the process of guiding self-determination.* (Doctoral Thesis, La Trobe University, Melbourne, Australia).

Douglas, J., & Bigby, C. (2018). Development of an evidence-based practice framework to guide support for decision making. *Disability and Rehabilitation*, 391–392. https://doi.org/10.1080/09638288.2018.1498546

Dukes, E., & McGuire, B. E. (2009). Enhancing capacity to make sexuality-related decisions in people with an intellectual disability. *Journal of Intellectual Disability Research, 53*, 727–734. https://doi.org/10.1111/j.1365-2788.2009.01186.x

Dunn, M., Clare, I., & Holland, A. (2010). Living 'a life like ours': Support workers' accounts of substitute decision-making in residential care homes for adults with intellectual disabilities. *Journal of Intellectual Disability Research, 54*, 144–160. https://doi.org/10.1111/j.1365-2788.2009.01228.x

Ellem, K., O'Connor, M., Wilson, J., & Williams, S. (2013). Social work with marginalised people who have a mild or borderline intellectual disability: Practicing gentleness and encouraging hope. *Australian Social Work, 66*, 56–71. https://doi.org/10.1080/0312407X.2012.710244

Espiner, D., & Hartnett, F. M. (2012). 'I felt I was in control of the meeting': Facilitating planning with adults with an intellectual disability. *British Journal of Learning Disabilities, 40*, 62–70. https://doi.org/10.1111/j.1468-3156.2011.00684.x

Ferguson, M., Jarrett, D., & Terras, M. (2011). Inclusion and healthcare choices: The experiences of adults with learning disabilities. *British Journal of Learning Disabilities, 39*, 73–83. https://doi.org/10.1111/j.1468-3156.2010.00620.x

Gooding, P. (2017). *A new era for mental health law and policy: Supported decision-making and the UN convention on the rights of persons with disabilities.* Cambridge, UK: Cambridge University Press.

Gordon, R. (2000). The emergence of assisted (supported) decision-making in the Canadian law of adult guardianship and substitute decision-making. *International Journal of Law and Psychiatry, 23*, 61–77. https://doi.org/10.1016/S0160-2527(99)00034-5

Hawkins, R., Redley, M., & Holland, A. (2011). Duty of care and autonomy: How support workers managed the tension between protecting service users from risk and promoting their independence in a specialist group home. *Journal of Intellectual Disability Research, 55*, 873–884. https://doi.org/10.1111/j.1365-2788.2011.01445.x

Heller, T., Miller, A. B., Hsieh, K., & Sterns, H. (2000). Later-life planning: Promoting knowledge of options and choice-making. *Mental Retardation, 38*, 395–406. https://doi.org/10.1352/0047-6765(2000)038<0395:LPPKOO>2.0.CO;2

Hodges, J. S., & Luken, K. (2006). Stakeholders' perceptions of planning needs to support retirement choices by persons with developmental disabilities. *Therapeutic Recreation Journal, 40*, 94–106.

Jilke, S. (2015). Choice and equality: Are vulnerable citizens worse off after liberalization reforms? *Public Administration, 93*, 68–85. https://doi.org/10.1111/padm.12102

Kanter, A. S., & Tolub, Y. (2017). The fight for personhood, legal capacity, and equal recognition under law for people with disabilities in Israel and beyond. *Cardozo Law Review, 39*, 557–610.

Khemka, I. (2000). Increasing independent decision-making skills of women with mental retardation in simulated interpersonal situations of abuse. *American Journal on Mental Retardation, 105*, 387–401. https://doi.org/10.1352/0895-8017(2000)105<0387:IIDSOW>2.0.CO;2

Khemka, I., Hickson, L., & Reynolds, G. (2005). Evaluation of a decision-making curriculum designed to empower women with mental retardation to resist abuse. *Journal Information, 110*, 193–204. https://doi.org/10.1352/0895-8017(2005)110<193:EOADCD>2.0.CO;2

Kirkendall, A., Linton, K., & Farris, S. (2016). Intellectual disabilities and decision making at end of life: A literature review. *Journal of Applied Research in Intellectual Disabilities, 30*, 982–994. https://doi.org/10.1111/jar.12270

Kittay, F., & Carlson, M. (2010). *Cognitive disability and its challenge to moral philosophy.* Chichester, England: Wiley-Blackwell.

Kjellberg, A. (2002). More or less independent. *Disability & Rehabilitation, 24*, 828–840. https://doi.org/10.1080/09638280210131745

Knox, L. (2016). *The experience of being supported to participate in decision making after severe traumatic brain injury.* (Doctoral Thesis, La Trobe University, Melbourne, Australia). Retrieved from: http://hdl.handle.net/1959.9/559896

Knox, L., Douglas, J., & Bigby, C. (2013). Whose decision is it anyway? How clinicians support decision-making participation after acquired brain injury. *Disability & Rehabilitation, 35*, 1926–1932. https://doi.org/10.3109/09638288.2013.766270

Knox, L., Douglas, J., & Bigby, C. (2015). "The biggest thing is trying to live for two people": Spousal experiences of supporting decision-making participation for partners with TBI. *Brain Injury, 29*, 747–757. https://doi.org/10.3109/02699052.2015.1004753

Knox, L., Douglas, J., & Bigby, C. (2016a). Becoming a decision-making supporter for someone with acquired cognitive disability following TBI. *Research and Practice in Intellectual and Developmental Disabilities, 3*, 12–21. https://doi.org/10.1080/23297018.2015.1077341

Knox, L., Douglas, J., & Bigby, C. (2016b). "I won't be around forever": Understanding the decision-making experiences of adults with severe TBI and their parents. *Neuropsychological Rehabilitation, 26*, 236–260. https://doi.org/10.1080/09602011.2015.1019519

Knox, L., Douglas, J., & Bigby, C. (2017). "I've never been a yes person": Decision-making participation and self-conceptualisation after severe traumatic brain injury. *Disability Rehabilitation, 39*, 2250–2260. https://doi.org/10.1080/09638288.2016.1219925

Kohn, N. A., & Blumenthal, J. A. (2014). A critical assessment of supported decision-making for persons aging with intellectual disabilities. *Disability and Health Journal, 7*, 40–43. https://doi.org/10.1016/j.dhjo.2013.03.005

Kohn, N. A., Blumenthal, J. A., & Campbell, A. T. (2014). Supported decision-making: A viable alternative to guardianship? *Penn State Law Review, 177*, 1111–1157.

Mackenzie, C., & Stoljar, N. (2000). Autonomy refigured. In C. Mackenzie & N. Stoljar (Eds.), *Relational autonomy. Feminist perspectives on autonomy, agency, and the social self* (pp. 3–31). New York, NY: Oxford University Press.

Mill, A., Mayes, R., & McConnell, D. (2010). Negotiating autonomy within the family: The experiences of young adults with intellectual disabilities. *British Journal of Learning Disabilities, 38*, 194–200. https://doi.org/10.1111/j.1468-3156.2009.00575.x

Morris, J. (2001). Impairment and disability: Constructing an ethics of care that promotes human rights. *Hypatia, 16*(4), 1–16.

National Disability Insurance Scheme Act 2013 (Cth.) (Austl.). Retrieved from: https://www.legislation.gov.au/Details/C2013A00020

Neely-Barnes, S., Graff, J. C., Marcenko, M., & Weber, L. (2008). Family decision making: Benefits to persons with developmental disabilities and their family members. *Intellectual and Developmental Disabilities, 46*, 93–105. https://doi.org/10.1352/0047-6765(2008)46[93:FDMBTP]2.0.CO;2

Nota, L., Ferrari, L., Soresi, S., & Wehmeyer, M. (2007). Self-determination, social abilities and the quality of life of people with intellectual disability. *Journal of Intellectual Disability Research, 51*, 850–865.

Nunnelley, S. (2015). *Personal support networks in practice and theory: Assessing the implications for supported decision-making law.* Ontario: Law Commission of Ontario. Retrieved from: https://www.lco-cdo.org/wp-content/uploads/2015/04/capacity-guardianship-commissioned-paper-nunnelley.pdf

O'Connor, M. (2014). The National Disability Insurance Scheme and people with mild intellectual disability: Potential pitfalls for consideration. *Research and Practice in Intellectual and Developmental Disabilities, 1*, 17–23. https://doi.org/10.1080/23297018.2014.908815

Pilnick, A., Clegg, J., Murphy, E., & Almack, K. (2010). Questioning the answer: Questioning style, choice and self-determination in interactions with young people with intellectual disabilities. *Sociology of Health & Illness, 32*, 415–436. https://doi.org/10.1111/j.1467-9566.2009.01223.x

Reinders, J. (2002). The good life for citizens with intellectual disability. *Journal of Intellectual Disability Research, 46*, 1–5. https://doi.org/10.1046/j.1365-2788.2002.00386.x

Renblad, K. (2003). How do people with intellectual disabilities think about empowerment and information and communication technology (ICT)? *International Journal of Rehabilitation Research, 26*, 175–182.

Rossow-Kimball, B., & Goodwin, D. (2009). Self-determination and leisure experiences of women living in two group homes. *Adapted Physical Activity Quarterly, 26*, 1–20.

Schelly, D. (2008). Problems associated with choice and quality of life for an individual with intellectual disability: A personal assistant's reflexive ethnography. *Disability & Society, 23*, 719–732. https://doi.org/10.1080/09687590802469206

Series, L. (2015). The development of disability rights under international law: From charity to human rights. *Disability & Society, 30*, 1590–1593. https://doi.org/10.1080/09687599.2015.1066975

Shakespeare, T. (2006). *Disability rights and wrongs*. Abingdon, England: Routledge.

Silvers, A., & Francis, L. (2009). Thinking about the good: Reconfiguring liberal metaphysics (or not) for people with cognitive disabilities. *Metaphilosophy, 40*, 475–498.

Sinclair, C., Field, S., Williams, K., Blake, M., Bucks, R., Auret, K., … Kurrle, S. (2018). *Supporting decision-making: A guide for people living with dementia, family members and carers*. Sydney, NSW: Cognitive Decline Partnership Centre. Retrieved from: http://sydney.edu.au/medicine/cdpc/documents/resources/SDM_Handbook_Online_Consumers-ReducedSize.pdf

Sowney, M., & Barr, O. (2007). The challenges for nurses communicating with and gaining valid consent from adults with intellectual disabilities within the accident and emergency care service. *Journal of Clinical Nursing, 16*, 1678–1686. https://doi.org/10.1111/j.1365-2702.2006.01642.x

Then, S., Carney, T., Bigby, C., & Douglas, J. (2018). Supporting decision-making of adults with cognitive disabilities: the role of Law Reform Agencies – Recommendations, rationales and influence. *International Journal of Law and Psychiatry*. https://doi.org/10.1016/j.ijlp.2018.09.001.

Then, S.-N. (2013). Evolution and innovation in guardianship laws: Assisted decision-making. *Sydney Law Review, 35*, 133–166.

Timmons, J. C., Hall, A. C., Bose, J., Wolfe, A., & Winsor, J. (2011). Choosing employment: Factors that impact employment decisions for individuals with intellectual disability. *Intellectual and Developmental Disabilities, 49*, 285–299. https://doi.org/10.1352/1934-9556-49.4.285

Victorian Medical Treatment Planning and Decisions Act 2016 (Vic.) (Austl.)

Watson, J. (2016). *The right to supported decision-making for people rarely heard*. (Doctoral thesis, Deakin University, Melbourne, Australia). Retrieved from http://dro.deakin.edu.au/eserv/DU:30083812/watson-theright-2016A.pdf

Watson, J., Wilson, E., & Hagiliassis, N. (2017). Supporting end of life decision making: Case studies of relational closeness in supported decision making for people with severe or profound intellectual disability. *Journal of Applied Research in Intellectual Disabilities, 30*, 1022–1034. https://doi.org/10.1111/jar.12393

Webb, J., & Stanton, M. (2009). Better access to primary healthcare for adults with learning disabilities: Evaluation of a group programme to improve knowledge and skills. *British Journal of Learning Disabilities, 37*, 116–122. https://doi.org/10.1111/j.1468-3156.2008.00527.x

Wong, S. J. (2010). *Duties of justice to citizens with cognitive disabilities*. Chichester, England: John Wiley & Sons.

World Health Organisation. (2001). *International classification of functioning, disability and health: ICF*. Geneva, Switzerland: Author.

Reflections on Choice: The Stories of Self-Advocates

John G. Smith, Nicholas P. Cocchiarella, and Aaron D. Schaper

Introduction

There are two predominant conceptualizations of self-advocacy and people with intellectual and developmental disabilities. One meaning views self-advocacy as a skill that people with intellectual and developmental disabilities need to develop and/or acquire to make their needs known in requesting necessary supports and accommodations, while the other meaning frames self-advocacy as a civil rights movement that has empowered people with intellectual and developmental disabilities to shift power from professionals and parents to people with disabilities, and laid the groundwork for important innovations in service delivery, such as the use of person-centered planning and services and self-directed supports (Abery, Olson, Poetz, & Smith, 2019). Both of these conceptualizations frame self-advocacy as a means to empower people with intellectual and developmental disabilities to take greater control of their circumstances and lead more high-quality lives.

This chapter is based on interviews with eight people who experience intellectual and developmental disabilities and identify as self-advocates. All have achieved a high quality of life as active members of their communities. Many are also active in the self-advocacy movement in the United States. Though the chapter will include stories that explain more fully who they are, here are some brief introductions of these experts.

1. Katie McDermott is a young adult with intellectual and developmental disabilities who is a leader in the self-advocacy movement in Minnesota and who works professionally as coordinator for self-advocacy for The Arc Minnesota, an advocacy organization for people with intellectual and developmental disabilities and their families. Katie grew up with her family, which included her father, mother,

J. G. Smith (✉) · N. P. Cocchiarella · A. D. Schaper
Institute on Community Integration, University of Minnesota, Minneapolis, MN, USA
e-mail: smith144@umn.edu

© Springer Nature Switzerland AG 2020
R. J. Stancliffe et al. (eds.), *Choice, Preference, and Disability*, Positive Psychology and Disability Series, https://doi.org/10.1007/978-3-030-35683-5_4

and an older sister. Katie's experiences include moving out of her family home at an early age, then returning after falling in with the "wrong people." She later found her own apartment, where she has lived independently for the past 3 years.

2. Joe Meadours is a person with intellectual and developmental disabilities who is a national leader in the self-advocacy movement in the United States. Joe grew up in a large family with five brothers and one sister. He began his career in self-advocacy as a member and, eventually, the president of People First of Oklahoma. Joe has traveled extensively as an expert in presenting a self-advocate's perspective at national gatherings of policymakers, researchers, and others interested in quality supports for people with intellectual and developmental disabilities. Most recently, he has worked as the Executive Director of People First of California and continues as a mentor for its Board of Directors.

3. Heidi Myhre is a middle-aged woman with an intellectual and developmental disability who has been involved with the self-advocacy movement since she was in her early twenties. Heidi was adopted as a baby and grew up in her family's home. As a young adult, Heidi lived in an institution for a short time, then spent several years living in community-based group homes, before eventually moving into her own apartment, where she has lived for several years. Heidi takes pride in her independence and chooses to volunteer her time as an advocate for people with intellectual and developmental disabilities. This has led her to become a leader in local self-advocacy activities and a dynamic public speaker who shares her story to push for better services for all people with disabilities.

4. Tia Nelis is a national leader in the self-advocacy movement among people with intellectual and developmental disabilities in the United States and a founding board member of both People First of Illinois and Self-Advocates Becoming Empowered (SABE), a national organization of self-advocates. Tia grew up in Illinois where she was introduced to self-advocacy and worked for 25 years as a staff member of Institute on Disability and Health (UCEDD) at the University of Illinois. Tia currently works as the Policy and Advocacy Director for TASH and self-identifies as a person with learning disabilities.

5. Cliff Poetz is an elder with intellectual and developmental disabilities who was among the founders of the self-advocacy movement in Minnesota. Cliff grew up living with his family in a rural area and then chose to move to a community-based institution in a large metropolitan area and worked in segregated employment for people with disabilities. In time, Cliff left this sheltered employment situation to become a leader in the self-advocacy movement in his state and nationally and left the institution, first to live in an apartment training program, and for the past 40 years, he has lived independently in the community. Cliff is currently employed at the Institute on Community Integration at the University of Minnesota as a community liaison and takes pride in his decision to purchase a condominium 10 years ago.

6. Dan Roherty is a writer with autism spectrum disorder (ASD). Dan is most proud of his apartment where he lives independently with his cat named Tyson, has a job at a local library, and takes writing classes around the Twin Cities metropolitan area. He also has a partner, Sara, with whom he hopes to 1 day be wed. Dan

is keenly interested in the economic and systems-based barriers that sometimes limit his choices and the choices of other people with disabilities and is an emerging self-advocate.

7. Hunter Sargent is a Native American man who has fetal alcohol syndrome (FAS). He grew up in his grandmother's care, whom he credits for teaching him to advocate for himself. As a young adult, Hunter lived in an apartment training program before moving out on his own. Hunter has lived independently for most of his adult life and receives some support with budgeting his money and managing his home.

8. Holly Turley-Sargent grew up in a large family and had other siblings who had disabilities. She was born with a hearing impairment. Holly moved out of her family home to live with her sister after high school. After that did not work out, she returned home to live with her family as a young adult until she was married. Holly began working competitively in high school and has continued to do so her entire adult life.

Hunter and Holly have been married for 9 years and live together in a condominium they purchased. Holly has chosen to continue working as a Direct Support Professional (DSP) for Hunter, while Hunter has chosen a career as a public speaker and consultant on issues around living with FAS and being an active member of the many communities to which he belongs. Hunter and Holly report making many decisions together, including looking for a new home to buy since they are being harassed by a neighbor.

These eight people told stories and recalled key events to explain both successes and challenges in making meaningful choices. Additionally, they provided recommendations on how choice, freedom, and the opportunity to live life on ones' own terms might be expanded for all people with disabilities. Their stories suggest several themes and recommendations.

Themes and Recommendations for Expanding Choice and Opportunity

Making Meaningful Choices and Decisions Leads to Personal Pride

A common theme among the self-advocates we interviewed was the sense of empowerment they felt when they had control over choices and decisions in their lives. Being successful in making important decisions allows self-advocates to prove to themselves and those around them that they can and will make the right choices when given the opportunity. Everyone had stories of choices that they were particularly proud of and that influenced the direction of their lives, as well as recollections of the satisfaction they felt when having control over the many small, day-to-day decisions that most people take for granted. When asked about the choices and decisions that had made their lives better, most people talked about those choices and decisions that enhanced their involvement in the community and their sense of wellness, lead to new employment opportunities, and those choices and decisions they are making to prepare for their future. The examples that follow flesh this out.

> So, like last night at 11:30 at night, I decided I wanted to go out to eat, so I walked down the street to Denny's. That was my choice, you know, and I had a good time.

Heidi's quote above expresses the satisfaction she feels in being able to make spontaneous choices, which is central to being able to engage in many typical leisure activities. In order to be involved in the life of the community, Heidi chose to begin using public transit while in high school and still uses it regularly to do things like visit friends, go out to eat, and shop. Katie values accessing the community as well, recounting the pleasure in discovering a new record shop when looking for a Father's Day gift, and enjoys exploring new places with her boyfriend.

Katie also takes pride in her efforts to improve her health as she chose to quit smoking 7 years ago and is currently learning how to cook healthier meals. Likewise, Hunter and Holly described how they recently decided to improve their health by quitting smoking, drinking, and reducing the amount of soda they drink. They plan to have children and have decided to improve their health and their lives in preparation. It is important to them that they provide a good example of healthy living for their future family. Hunter also recalled a wellness choice he made as he tried many different religious traditions before discovering that Native American powwows fit best with his sense of spirituality, saying it provided a space "where I can interact, be connected, and be working with the man (sic) upstairs."

> It makes me feel good inside that I'm making a difference in my life and I'm making a difference in the community.

For four of these self-advocates, their choice to maintain involvement in the self-advocacy movement has led them into professional careers. Joe cherishes the opportunities he has had to travel and meet new people and to share his experiences as a consultant on self-advocacy. As reflected in the quote above, Joe feels a sense of accomplishment when he has opportunities to share his personal struggles and successes with others. Cliff also relishes his role in the self-advocacy movement, his biggest pride being that he was one of the founding members of the movement itself. He proudly notes, "People now have more rights than they used to have." His most memorable moment was when he became the first person with intellectual and developmental disabilities to testify before the US Congress in 1973. Likewise, Tia explained that her proudest accomplishment has been working at TASH and helping others become stronger self-advocates. Her most memorable moment was getting to meet US President Obama and being selected as a Google Hero.

> We would like to have a house or townhouse with a little backyard for our dog to run around. We would like more dogs. Hunter wants a German shepherd and I want a golden retriever.

Another theme common among the self-advocates' stories was the importance of having dreams and goals and making choices about their futures. Everyone could describe choices they made in the past that had opened new opportunities for them and goals they are currently working toward for their futures. Holly's quote above refers to her and Hunter's plans to sell their condominium and find a place to live that offers new opportunities. They are considering options, such as buying another place that has an association to share costs or applying with Habitat for Humanity for assistance in building a small house of their own. Dan is working to convince his parents, who also are his guardians, to allow him to get married, and Cliff recently made a move to assisted living to proactively prepare for his changing support needs that come with old age. These kinds of long-term goals and dreams lead to action steps and add to one's better quality of life. The self-advocacy experts also shared stories of pride about their long-term accomplishments, such as Heidi relating that she felt like a strong, independent woman when she moved into the apartment she selected after a long search. Hunter, Holly, and Joe expressed pride in improving their health by focusing on making better choices about their diet and how they care for themselves.

Developing Choice-Making Skills

The successes of these self-advocates did not happen by chance, but stemmed from a lifetime of learning the skills necessary to make good choices, practicing choice making, and working through the barriers often experienced by people with disabilities as they pursue their life dreams. The stories and ideas they shared illustrate the role of early learning and family support, learning to problem solve, and, most importantly, developing the self-advocacy skills necessary to obtain the kinds of supports and assistance they needed to be successful. The stories also demonstrate the value of being allowed to take "risky" choices and learn from the results, be they positive or negative. Some examples follow.

The Role of Families in Facilitating Choice

> My grandmother raised me. She was pretty much the steward who helped me learn about advocacy and speaking up for what I wanted.

In reflecting on the ways they learned to express preferences and make valued choices, most of the self-advocates interviewed recalled the important roles played by their family members. There were examples of ways that families supported them to learn to make important choices and examples of ways they felt overprotected and left out of choice-making opportunities.

There were many stories about how parents and family members taught these self-advocates to express their preferences and make choices at an early age. The quote above came from Hunter, who recalled how his grandmother encouraged him to begin making small choices at home. With his grandmother's support, Hunter began attending his Individualized Education Program meetings while he was still in elementary school. She then supported him to learn to voice his opinions about what he would do during the school day when he was in secondary school. Katie shared a very different experience, recalling how her mother's mental health challenges sometimes meant she had a great deal of control over choosing her friends and activities at an early age. Hunter and Katie both had stories of how these very different experiences of support, or the lack thereof, caused them each to get into a bit of trouble, but also provided them with many rich learning opportunities.

While other self-advocates could not recall particular choice-making opportunities at home when they were young, they relayed many stories of how parents equipped them with the information and judgement skills necessary to make good choices as they got older. Dan credited his father with encouraging his independence and teaching him the social and independent living skills that helped him with the choices that made his life in the community possible today. Joe remembered his mother teaching him how to make practical time management and hygiene choices as a teenager that led him to success in employment as an adult. Finally, Heidi remembered implementing the self-advocacy skills she learned from her father by choosing to stand up for herself and summon help from the principal when being bullied by peers in middle school.

> I was seeing all my brothers and sisters getting married, [I thought to myself] I hope I get married someday.

The stories also point to the helpful role that siblings played in encouraging these self-advocates to express their preferences and make choices. As reflected in the quote above, Holly remembered watching all her brothers and sisters getting married and moving out of the family home and hoping that she would do the same. She later explained how her siblings were supportive of her decision to get married and were eager to lend their help with the wedding plans. Katie had a similar experience in watching her sister move out of home to get an apartment, then asking for her advice and support when searching for an apartment of her own. Cliff fondly remembered how his brothers included him in all of their activities.

Family-Based Barriers to Choice/Overprotection

> I love my dad, and I love my mom, but when it came to something that they felt would put me in harm's way, I guess, they would say I shouldn't do it.

> I didn't have a lot of choices because I was a girl, I was disabled… my dad was protecting me. I wanted to do some of the cool stuff my brothers were doing.

There were also stories about families that self-advocates characterized as being "overprotective," causing them to miss out on opportunities as reflected in both Dan's and Heidi's comment above. Dan was recalling wanting badly to attend a rock concert as a young adult, but being prevented from doing so by his father, who warned him that "'all there was going to be there were teenaged girls and stuff,' and I was like 24 or 25." Heidi had similar memories of wanting to go to the drive-in theater, but not being allowed to do so, even though her younger brother was allowed to go. Interestingly, Cliff reminisced about times his parents had urges to overprotect him, but his older brothers supported him in taking the risks typical for a person his age.

The Role of Risk-Taking

> We need to be allowed to make mistakes and learn from those mistakes.

> How do you learn from your mistakes if you're not given the possibility of making a mistake?

All of these self-advocates felt strongly about the issue of being allowed to make some mistakes and learn from them, as reflected in Dan's and Tia's comment above. Their stories pointed to the value of risk-taking in helping them to become successful adults.

Cliff living in his own condominium and working professionally came after a lifetime of taking graduated risks. This began by leaving his family home in rural Minnesota to live in the large city of Minneapolis and later leaving the protection of a supervised living situation to live on his own in an apartment. During this time, Cliff also quit his job at a sheltered workshop due to low wages and became a community advocate with no formal pay. These moves each involved a certain amount of risk, but they allowed Cliff to become an active member of his community, an important and visible leader in the self-advocacy movement, both locally and nationally, and eventually a staff member at the University of Minnesota specializing in self-advocacy issues. He remembered his Dad's initial reservations about his leaving home to begin his journey and his mother's support to take the leap with her words: "He is moving to the city, end of discussion."

Similarly, Joe has led a very adventuresome life that has seen him "pack up and move" around the United States several times chasing interesting job opportunities in the self-advocacy movement. This eventually led to his current role as a professional staff member for People First of California. On a smaller scale, but still with some trepidation, Heidi recalled taking the risk of learning to use public transit as a young adult and quickly finding that it opened a wide range of opportunities to her. These are all examples of the kinds of "risky choices" that people with intellectual and developmental disabilities are often not allowed to make due to their perceived inability to understand what is at risk.

> You can learn from all the bad choices you make; life is like a journey; you never know what's going to come about; you never know what obstacle you have to jump through; you don't know your life is going to turn out.

Many of these self-advocates also recalled some risky choices they considered "bad" in hindsight and the adjustments they made when things did not work out as planned. Katie recalled moving out of her parent's house before she was ready, …"I moved in with people who were taking advantage of me, abusing me mentally and emotionally, thinking 'oh, they love me,' but they just wanted my money or they were stealing my paychecks while I was working." Similarly, Joe recalled his early choices of friends and how they were giving him a reputation he did not like. Katie and Joe both acknowledged the role of peer pressure leading to poor choices. Both also were able to conclude these stories with how they had learned from them and did things differently in the future.

There was nearly unanimous agreement on the importance of taking risks and learning from choices that did not work out as planned. Hunter observed that "for every negative, there is a positive," referring to some of his choices that turned out badly. Too often, people with intellectual and developmental disabilities are not allowed to make certain choices because of the risks involved. As Sanders (2006) observed, lowered expectations and sheltering people with disabilities from making important choices can deprive them from receiving constructive feedback and keep them in an inferior position compared to their peers without similar disabilities.

Community-Based Barriers to Choice Making

Being an active, healthy participant in the community is a desire that each self-advocate named in their own fashion, be it as working in a meaningful job, living in an accessible, affordable apartment, or, even, having the opportunity to attend a local rock concert. While there were many success stories, each person also shared stories of the barriers they encountered while following through with their choices and decisions.

> So that kind of sucked … they did not know where to put me, so they put me in fast food –
> McDonald's, you know, the stereotype.

While all of the self-advocates had experience working, a common theme was the difficulty finding a meaningful job that matched their skills and interests. When talking about her entry into community living as a young adult, Heidi remembered the importance that the people who were supporting her placed on employment, but her words above convey her frustration with the options she was offered. Heidi quickly chose to leave this job, and as she has gained greater independence, Heidi has chosen to work as a volunteer advocate and sometimes shares her work as a freelance artist. Tia's dream was to be a teacher's aide, but was turned down in a hiring process when the employer found out she had received special education supports while in high school. Cliff's vocational rehabilitation counselor placed him in a sheltered workshop, a job he ended up leaving due to poor pay and lack of challenge. Dan, despite having a job he enjoys, recognized that his low wage often limits his options when making choices. These stories convey the community attitudes and even attitudes among some professionals, which limit the employment options many self-advocates are offered. In turn, their interests and talents are often overlooked based on low expectations. This experience of having limited options showed up in other life domains.

Some of the most challenging and "high-stakes" choices these self-advocates discussed revolved around finding safe, accessible housing. The barriers they faced included inconsiderate people taking advantage of their vulnerabilities, the lack of affordable housing, and/or a service system that did not offer options that matched their preferences or honored their abilities.

> I wanted to prepare myself for when my parents passed on so I knew I could take care of myself.

Katie's words above reflect the goals of most young adults, including people with intellectual and developmental disabilities, to find a place to live that is their own. But the journey to her comfortable, suburban apartment was far from easy. She described her first attempt at living away from her parents as being with people who were taking her money (described in the previous section). After being forced to live on the street, then returning to her parents' home, Katie eventually got involved with the self-advocacy movement and met some peers who became positive role models and gave her new ideas. Moving into the role of a paid DSP, Katie's sister helped her resume her search for an apartment with assistance through a progressive service provider agency. Katie then faced another barrier: the cost of many apartments was beyond her budget. After a year of apartment searching, she finally found a place that fit her budget.

> I ended up not being able to move out into my own place because I didn't have enough money or skills yet ... And then one day I said it's time for me to go because it ended up like they were babysitting me.

Like Katie, Heidi initially struggled with her living situation, but the barriers she faced were caused by an unresponsive service system that was not honoring her preferences. She started her life away from home by being forced to live in an institution and then moving to two different group homes. She recalls life in the group homes as being "great but not great." Heidi appreciated learning skills but tired of having no control of the people she lived with or the rules she lived under. Eventually, she saw the group home to be less of a "benefit" to her and more of a "waste of money." Like Katie, Heidi didn't have enough of her own money to afford mainstream housing. Due to her persistent self-advocacy, Heidi's support staff finally "allowed" her to live more independently in an apartment, but only if she had a roommate to share expenses. While not her first choice, her new living situation opened up a vista of new opportunities, and she eventually did get her own apartment. She now enjoys the freedom of independent living. For example, she noted: "I can go to bed whenever I want to, I can eat whatever I want, and I can watch TV when I want." When talking about similar barriers he faced, Hunter wisely noted: "The system should not force you somewhere; you should fit where you want."

> ... they didn't know what to do with me!

A final barrier that limited the options available to these self-advocates was a some-times disjointed system of supports provided through government systems, which were based on a person's disability status. Hunter and Heidi both have uncommon disabilities that sometimes befuddled their case managers and service providers. This caused problems with not being eligible for helpful government-funded ser-vices (e.g., income supports like SSI/SSDI or food assistance) or being provided services that did not match either their needs or preferences. As a person with sig-nificant learning disabilities, Tia found that although she had support needs, she was not eligible for any government programs providing support to people based on disability status.

Communication Is Key

The act of making a choice, and having it honored, usually includes communicating with others. Effective communication can be difficult even in the best of circum-stances, but for a person with a disability, communicating one's preferences can seem downright impossible at times. The stories from these self-advocates show some ways they got around such barriers.

For example, from an early age, Hunter remembers needing to persevere to have his messages heard. The key, he says, was to find a way to communicate his needs in a way that others could understand. He says this reduced the number of "shame-ful reactions" to his requests, meaning people misunderstanding or ignoring him. When referring to how he works and communicates with his DSPs, Hunter observed: "They serve me; I don't serve them; they're not here to educate me; I'm here to educate them."

The stories of these self-advocates demonstrate how being able to communicate effectively makes them less vulnerable. Despite having different neurological con-ditions, Dan has faced challenges similar to those of Hunter. Dan described how many people on the autism spectrum "see things more to the point and more literal," which often means that more subtle methods of communication get lost in transla-tion. Dan said that: "It can be hard to grasp social cues and .... to know when I am being taken advantage of." As illustrated in her experiences with roommates, Katie also had trouble seeing that people were taking advantage of her until it was too late to stop it. Similarly, Joe learned to choose his friends after hanging out with people who were guiding him toward making "bad" choices.

> You have the right to live in the community, but you need to know how you will get the support you need.

Heidi learned how to ask people in the community for help, because her mental processing challenges led her into making choices that would get her into trouble. For example, Heidi became frustrated when an electronic device she purchased did not work out as planned. Self-advocacy has been important to her since childhood; learning how to do it in community contexts was the key. It was life experience that showed her how to do everything from asking a store clerk for clear information and advice when buying a new phone to doing the same with a case manager or service provider when changing support services.

Support That Is Helpful

It is natural for anyone to sometimes want assistance or advice when making an important decision. This may be because of limited expert knowledge (e.g., asking for a physician's advice on a medical decision), a need for emotional support (e.g., asking for advice and ideas from a family member when making end-of-life decisions), or a desire for support to implement decisions (e.g., asking a friend's advice before leaving a job if you want their help in finding a new one). But asking for support can sometimes involve ceding some control. Being able to recognize when help is needed and accurately describing what kind of help is desired can actually be empowering when making important decisions. Self-advocates do not want people to simply do things for them, but instead want the kind of support necessary to act in a self-determined manner. For example, Hunter, Holly, and Katie have all chosen to have someone help them manage their personal finances. They recognize their need for support in this area and have chosen to seek out a qualified person to help.

> So, with some of those [big] decisions, I have people who support me in either doing a PATH or looking at pluses and minuses stuff depending on what it is.

The self-advocates offered many examples of how others provided them with support in making choices and decisions. Tia's quote above refers to the practice of person-centered planning (O'Brien, O'Brien, & Mount, 1997, O'Brien & O'Brien, 1994), which provides people with disabilities, or anyone, an opportunity to gather a group of friends or colleagues together to help them create a vision for their future and develop a plan to achieve it. Tia keeps her person-centered plan posted in her office and sometimes consults it when making an important decision, as well as checking-in with the group who helped her develop it. Heidi discussed how important it is for her to have information provided to her in "plain language" when making an important decision, which she described as being clear without putting her down or making her "feel like a baby."

When these self-advocates want assistance in making a choice, it matters greatly to them who is providing such assistance. Most of them wanted support from someone who knew them well. For instance, for Joe this was his DSP, whom he had known for 2 years and always had an "open-door policy" (meaning they could talk about anything). For Katie it was her sister, whom she trusted greatly and had selected as her primary paid support person. Also important was seeking advice from professionals who had specialized knowledge, such as talking with doctors when making decisions about their healthcare. When selecting services, Heidi appreciated receiving support from a case manager who knew, and could explain clearly, what all her options were.

The self-advocates also talked about support that was not helpful when making choices and decisions. This included Joe, who said he would immediately replace a doctor who did not take the time to listen to his questions and clearly explain options to him, and Dan, who wanted to become his own guardian and noted that "I want to get married, but my guardians won't let me ... because they believe we're not ready ... I don't like that because they're not in the relationship!" Hunter and Holly decided not to select a representative payee to help them with their finances when they learned that "she could not even maintain a budget for herself."

What Works: Recommendations for Systems Change

Each of the self-advocates we interviewed had unique life goals, strengths, and support needs. While the level and amount of support preferred by each person varied, all agreed on some strategies to expand choice-making opportunities for people with disabilities. They posed suggestions for parents, schools, DSPs, case managers, government systems, and their colleagues with disabilities.

Recommendations for Families

> If you are a parent or a guardian or whatever, at least give them the opportunity to make that decision and give them the chance to experience it. If they don't fail, they don't learn.

The self-advocates we interviewed believed strongly that people need to be allowed to take risks, fail, and feel the consequences in order to be better prepared for the future. As noted above, many self-advocates felt that their parents or guardians were overprotective and recommended that families encourage their sons and daughters to make meaningful choices and take risks that seemed reasonable. Tia summed this up well in the quote above.

The dilemma faced by many families is finding the balance between protecting their family member with disabilities and allowing them to make choices that include some element of risk. Karen Sanders (2006) wrote extensively about the role of lowered expectations and overprotection in taking away normal growth opportunities from children and youth with disabilities. These include depriving the child of opportunities to learn to self-advocate and be independent, causing social isolation and leading to lowered self-esteem and self-confidence (Sanders, 2006). Shogren and Turnbull (2006) recommended an approach similar to that of Hunter's grandmother, who started by offering opportunities to make smaller choices (e.g., which shirt to wear or what to eat for breakfast), before offering more meaningful choices (e.g., having input on the contents of his individualized education plan). It was interesting that Heidi could not recall her parents allowing her to make many choices as a child, then struggled when faced with the major decisions she needed to make after high school, and had a breakdown that caused her to spend time in an institution. Katie also struggled in making choices about appropriate housemates as a young adult after growing up in an environment that provided ample opportunities for her to make choices, but that lacked in consistently providing nurturing and guidance. The approach taken by Hunter's grandmother allowed him many opportunities to make progressively larger choices and decisions in an environment that provides some structure and guidance.

Recommendations for Schools and Educators

> Schools are important places for people to learn to make meaningful choices and they teach students how to advocate.

As reflected in the quote above, Hunter and Holly believe that schools need to be more "student driven" and cater to the individual needs of each student. They advocate for students leading their IEP meetings, saying: "students should be able to describe their goals and what they need to succeed." Hunter further observes that: "the students will need to learn how to advocate for themselves going forward and the school is one of the earliest places to make meaningful choices." This aligns well with Joe's opinion that teachers need to listen carefully to their students and understand that each one has unique preferences and needs.

There were also recommendations about the content that schools should be sharing. For example, Dan suggests that schools provide opportunities for students to explore and practice social situations and activities while discussing openly and honestly their potential outcomes. He believes subjects that need to be addressed include sex, relationships, gambling, and drugs. While Cliff agrees with these suggestions, he offers another insight in calling for early education of the rights students with intellectual and developmental disabilities have. He suggests teaching students about the ADA and IDEA, observing that: "We cannot expect students to request their accommodations if they do not know that such supports exist." Once we begin to get students acclimated to making choices, they can have the experience to make better choices in the future.

These recommendations challenge educators and school systems to make significant changes, but there are many tools and practices available to help. For example, Agran, Blanchard, and Wehmeyer (2000) introduced the Self-Determined Learning Model of Instruction, which engages students to choose areas in which they want to learn, using a combination of goal setting, self-regulation, and problem-solving skills, with guidance and instruction from their teachers, to achieve their learning goals. In addition, multiple evidence-based curricula have been developed to teach students with disabilities, including students with intellectual and developmental disabilities, the skills and knowledge necessary to lead their IEP meetings (Cease-Cook, Test, & Scroggins, 2013; Wehmeyer & Lawrence, 1995; Woods, Sylvester, & Martin, 2010), and research has shown that the use of social skill training groups and social narratives are effective ways to support students on the autism spectrum in the acquisition of social skills (Tse, Strulovitch, Tagalakis, Meng, & Fombonne, 2007; Whittenburg, Ham, & McDonough, 2016).

Recommendations for Direct Support Professionals

> Go out to a coffee shop once a week or once a month and talk it out, talk like friends.

The self-advocates also provided recommendations for the DSPs who support them. Whether daily or intermittently, many people with disabilities rely on some level of support from others in a variety of life areas, such as maintaining personal health and hygiene, managing finances, or accessing community resources. This support may either add to or detract from a person's sense of feeling "in control," depending on how it is delivered. Joe's quote above refers to his belief that DSPs can facilitate opportunities and support people to make choices simply by being a trusted friend.

Although the number of evidence-based practices to guide DSPs in this area is limited, Joe's ideas are echoed and expanded on in the Code of Ethics of the National Alliance for Direct Support Professionals in the United States (2016), which stated that the role of DSPs includes seeking to understand the people they support "in the context of their personal history, their social and family networks, and their hopes and dreams for the future" and honoring their "choices, preferences, abilities and opinions…" (p.7). Similarly, the Australasian Code of Ethics for DSPs (McVilly and Newell, 2007) stated that: "Direct Support Professionals must support informed decisions made by clients……even where they personally disagree with those decisions or there is an element of risk involved" (p.20). Joe recommended that DSPs take time to get to know each person they support, seeing the individual as "a person, not just a job," and sharing new ideas "openly and honestly." However, two-sided conversations can be difficult when people are not able to articulate clearly what their desires and preferences are, so DSPs need to be creative in their expressive and receptive language. Heidi expresses her concern regarding this scenario, stating: "If I were more disabled, they would walk all over me."

Recommendations for Case Managers

> People can be a little creative without losing their license … think outside the box!

In the United States, many people with disabilities receive assistance to locate and coordinate supports from a case manager, and the self-advocates had several suggestions to improve their practice. For example, Heidi's quote above refers to her preference for case managers who are creative in providing and seeking supports, rather than being bound to traditional options offered through government systems.

On a similar note, Hunter and Holly were concerned about how the issue of marriage is addressed by case managers, urging that it never be discouraged.

The self-advocates also discussed the need for respect in the relationship between case managers and the people they support, seeing it as "a two-way street." Hunter and Holly believe that case managers need to be quick to respond and have more direct contact with the people they serve, allowing nothing to be "lost in translation" and ensuring "timely resolutions" when they are having problems. Katie valued an environment where everyone is "open and able to learn from each other" and added her belief that service providers must "listen more to the people they support, and not assume they have 'all the right answers.'"

A few innovations in case management and service delivery in the United States have created new options in how people coordinate their supports and receive case management services. For example, in some states, people with intellectual and developmental disabilities have the option of receiving a cash allotment to arrange community-based supports in lieu of choosing from a menu of traditional service options (e.g., living in a group residence or working in a sheltered employment setting). Such a shift changes the role of case managers to "support brokers" who must call on the kind of creativity Heidi appreciates in arranging new kinds of natural supports based on each person's preferences and life goals. Traditionally, case managers have either worked for the same entities that fund the services available to people with intellectual and developmental disabilities (i.e., state or local government) or the agencies who provide them with services (Moseley, 2004). Moseley (2004) noted the conflicts of interest that are bound to occur as those in the case management role balance the preferences of the person receiving services with the interest of the agencies who pay their salaries. Increasingly, self-advocates have the option of selecting their own case manager, including people who work outside the system (Amado, 2008). This can include parents, other trusted family members or friends, a person who independently contracts their services, or even the person him/herself. Given training and support, this option can allow self-advocates to place the kind of expectations Hunter, Holly, and others allude to with regard to their case managers and replace those who fail to meet the standard.

Recommendations for People with Disabilities

> I hung out with self-advocates who helped guide me to make the right choices….

These words from Katie expressed a strong belief in the benefits of taking part in self-advocacy activities. She—along with Joe, Tia, and Cliff—continues to work to grow the self-advocacy movement and feels the opportunity to be involved will help their peers in taking greater control of choices and decisions in their lives. The research literature supports this belief, demonstrating that as people with intellectual and developmental disabilities become involved in the disability civil rights movement, they benefit from meeting and working together with people who have similar disabilities. For example, in a study of leaders in self-advocacy activities, Caldwell (2010) found that being involved in self-advocacy activities helped people find new role models among their peers and learn new ways to resist disability-based oppression from others. Ryan and Griffiths (2015) characterized this change in perception of disability as a change in self-concept. Their successes counteracted earlier messages people received through being bullied by non-disabled peers while in school and overprotective parents and family members who sometimes stifled opportunities for personal growth. Finding success in their efforts is helpful to members of self-advocacy groups in gaining self-confidence and raising self-esteem. Katie's story of the transformation she experienced after joining a self-advocacy group and meeting new role models and Tia's newfound understanding of discrimination provide powerful examples of this, as do the positive changes in government policies regarding services for people with disabilities that Cliff takes pride in and feels partially responsible for, and the leadership development and even professional employment options created by Katie, Tia, Cliff, and Joe.

Recommendations for Government Systems

On a national level, Dan believes that government policies should be more supportive of people with disabilities. He calls for more affordable healthcare and increasing the availability of resources via outreach centers. Other self-advocates mentioned the need for legislation to increase the pay for DSPs, recognizing the importance of a consistent, reliable, and highly trained workforce that can grow to meet future demand.

While these are lofty goals, actions taken through the self-advocacy movement over the past few decades have made many positive changes in health, education, and home and community-based services received by all persons with disabilities in the United States (Ryan & Griffiths, 2015). For example, Cliff takes pride in being invited by Senator Edward Kennedy to testify before the United States Congress in 1973. In his testimony, Cliff urged the senators to broaden the definition of people included under the Developmental Disability Rights Act and assure people with disabilities were always at the table when policy decisions were being considered that could affect their lives. As a result of such advocacy by Cliff and others with intellectual and developmental disabilities, rules around providing home and community-based services in the United States now recognize the basic right to live self-determined lives, and self-advocates are routinely involved in policy discussions. As seasoned self-advocates like Heidi and Katie discuss problems they see in the service system (e.g., low DSP wages), they are quick to say "it's time to go to the state capitol and tell the legislators what we think." As a young self-advocate, Dan is gaining confidence and learning to believe his efforts can make a difference.

A common theme among the self-advocates was never to give up. Each person stated that at times it can be difficult to get the support you want, but it is worth it; you must persevere. Hunter and Holly offer this encouragement: "There is no struggle we can't overcome, be patient. Don't expect self-advocacy skills to be present all the time; that is where supports come in. Don't forget about the ability to overcome and do not allow the system to block you."

Conclusion

The stories and examples the self-advocates shared demonstrated the natural yearning to have control over the choices in one's life and illustrated how those choices helped people express their independence and individuality. In Katie's first unstable living situation away from home, we saw a young woman longing to experience the wider world beyond her childhood home for the first time. Cliff's condo was the result of a man wanting a place for himself to call home. Holly holds down a job to support herself and her family, while Hunter speaks at professional conferences and the two navigate married life together. Tia is a visual person who uses pictures and maps as props in her office. Heidi rides the bus to get from point A to point B, along with multitudes of other people in her community. Dan is a quirky guy who loves his job, loves to write, and would love for him and his girlfriend to get married.

The most striking and important theme was that it was impossible for these self-advocates to talk about their experiences making valued choices without also talking about the barriers they faced and necessity of developing strong self-advocacy skills. Despite unique circumstances surrounding each of these self-advocates, all of them found ways to make their voices heard in their own ways. Dan, for instance, advocates for himself through writing, some of which has been published. Katie, Tia, and Cliff have all found professional employment as leaders of the self-advocacy movement. Heidi advocates for others through volunteer work.

At the end of the day, we are all human. With the right kind of support from our families, our communities, and each other, we are all capable of making choices and decisions that will shape us into the best versions of ourselves.

References

Abery, B. H., Olson, M. R., Poetz, C. L., & Smith, J. G. (2019). Self-determination and self-advocacy: It's my life. In A. S. Hewitt & K. M. Nye-Lengerman (Eds.), *A community life: Community living and participation for individuals with intellectual and developmental disabilities* (pp. 117–140). Washington, DC: American Association on Intellectual and Developmental Disabilities.

Agran, M., Blanchard, C., & Wehmeyer, M. L. (2000). Promoting transition goals and self-determination through student self-directed learning: The self-determined leaning model of instruction. *Education and Training in Mental Retardation and Developmental Disabilities, 35*(4), 351–364.

Amado, A. N. (2008). Innovative models and best practices in case management and support coordination. *Policy Research Brief, 19*(1), 1–11.

Caldwell, J. (2010). Leadership development of individuals with developmental disabilities in the self-advocacy movement. *Journal of Intellectual Disability Research, 54*(11), 1004–1014.

Cease-Cook, J., Test, D.W., & Scroggins, L. (2013). Effects of the CD-Rom version of the self-advocacy strategy on quality of contributions in IEP meetings of high school students with intellectual disability. *Education and Training in Autism and Developmental Disabilities, 48*(2), 258–268.

McVilly, K., & Newell, C. (Eds.). (2007). *Australasian code of ethics for direct support professionals*. Melbourne, VIC: ASSID.

Moseley, C. (July, 2004). *Support brokerage issues in self-directed services*. Alexandria, VA: National Association of State Directors of Developmental Disabilities Services.

National Alliance for Direct Support Professionals. (2016). *NADSP code of ethics*. Albany, NY: National Alliance for Direct Support Professionals.

O'Brien, J, & O'Brien, C. L. (1994). Unfolding Capacity: People with disabilities and their allies building better futures together. Lithonia, Georgia: Responsive Systems Associates.

O'Brien, C. L., O'Brien, J., & Mount, B. (1997). Perspectives: Person-centered planning has arrived…or has it?" *Mental Retardation, 35*(6), 480–484.

Ryan, T. G., & Griffiths, S. (2015). Self-advocacy and its impact for adults with developmental disabilities. *Australian Journal of Adult Learning, 55*(1), 31–53.

Sanders, K. Y. (2006). Overprotection and lowered expectations of persons with disabilities: The unforeseen consequences. *Work, 27*, 181–188.

Shogren, K. A., & Turnbull, A. P. (2006). Promoting self-determination in young children with disabilities: The critical role of families. *Infants & Young Children, 19*(4), 338–352.

Tse, J., Strulovitch, J., Tagalakis, V., Meng, L., & Fombonne, E. (2007). Social skills training for adolescents with Asperger syndrome and high-functioning autism. *Journal of Autism and Developmental Disorders, 37*, 1960–1968.

Wehmeyer, M. L., & Lawrence, M. (1995). Whose future is it anyway? Promoting student involvement in transition planning. *Career Development for Exceptional Individuals, 18*(2), 69–83.

Whittenburg, H., Ham, W., & McDonough, J. (2016). *Research brief #3: Social narratives*. Richmond, VA: Virginia Commonwealth University Departments of Health, and Physical Medicine and Rehabilitation.

Woods, L L. Sylvester, L. & Martin, J.E. (2010) Student-Directed Transition Planning: Increasing Student Knowledge and Self-Efficacy in the Transition Planning Process. *Career Development for Exceptional Individuals, 33*(2) 106–114.

Part II
Policies, Practices and Systems that Affect Choice

Choice Within the Israeli Welfare State: Lessons Learned from Legal Capacity and Housing Services

Roni Holler, Shirli Werner, Yotam Tolub, and Miriam Pomerantz

This chapter examines the way that the choices of Israeli adults with intellectual disabilities are shaped by different disability laws and other state policies in two domains: legal capacity and housing services. In Israel, legal capacity issues are regulated by the 1962 Legal Capacity and Guardianship Law, which has recently been amended to provide preference for supported decision-making alternatives over guardianship. We show how prior to the amendment the law and its practice infringed on individuals' right to freedom and autonomy, especially given the extensive use of plenary guardianship and lack of meaningful supervision and regulations. An additional concern is related to the limited consideration given to the individuals' voice in guardianship appointment processes. The new amendment moved the Israeli legal capacity system a major step away from this guardianship regime. This positive change is currently very much on paper with several concerns and challenges still in need of being addressed.

With regard to housing services, we first focus on the process through which services are provided to adults with intellectual disabilities and the role assigned to service users in the process. We then describe the current housing solutions available in Israel, from the most common, large congregate facilities to community apartments and family homes. Finally, we show how each of these living schemes affects the individuals' right to choice in their daily lives. We conclude by providing

R. Holler · S. Werner (✉)
Paul Baerwald School of Social Work and Social Welfare, Hebrew University of Jerusalem, Jerusalem, Israel
e-mail: shirli.werner@mail.huji.ac.il

Y. Tolub
Bizchut – The Israel Human Rights Center for People with Disabilities, Jerusalem, Israel

M. Pomerantz
Paul Baerwald School of Social Work and the Faculty of Law, Hebrew University of Jerusalem, Jerusalem, Israel

© Springer Nature Switzerland AG 2020
R. J. Stancliffe et al. (eds.), *Choice, Preference, and Disability*, Positive Psychology and Disability Series, https://doi.org/10.1007/978-3-030-35683-5_5

several recommendations that represent initial steps in overcoming some of the aforementioned challenges within the two fields.

Introduction

The freedom to choose is inherent to modern, democratic society. However, as with many fundamental rights, choice has rarely been allocated on equal terms, with people with disabilities being a prime example. Usually perceived as lacking the required reason and capabilities, people with disabilities, especially those with intellectual disabilities, have been frequently denied the right to choose. An increasing body of knowledge has shown that compared to able-bodied individuals, individuals with disabilities, including those with intellectual disability, have fewer choices and exercise less self-determination in both minor and major life decisions (Wehmeyer & Abery, 2013).

Assuming that social policy is a key determinant of peoples' choices and informed by a relational, positive, and multifaceted understanding of choice, this chapter demonstrates how the Israeli welfare state has (or has not) promoted the realization of choice among people with intellectual disability. In what follows, we provide a definition and conceptualization of choice. Next, we review the Israeli welfare system with regard to people with intellectual disability. We then examine how the choices of Israeli people with intellectual disability are shaped by different disability laws and other state policies in two specific domains: legal capacity and housing services. Our analyses are based on secondary literature, unpublished research, laws and regulations, as well as interviews with key stakeholders. Note that both empirical and administrative data in the two fields are extremely scant. Where available, these are also employed in the analyses.

What Is Choice?

Choice is not a straightforward, consensual concept. Seen from multiple and often contradictory ideological perspectives including neoliberalism, consumerism, empowerment, the new public management tradition, and social perspective of disability, choice is a matter of ongoing debate. In understanding choice, scholars, policymakers, professionals, and laypeople have relied on different disciplines, including psychology, social policy, sociology, education, and philosophy. With this complexity in mind, this section defines choice and discusses some of its key features and controversies.

Choice is "making unforced selection of a preferred alternative from two or more options" (Stancliffe, 2001, p. 92). This conceptualization stresses three essential elements: the availability of (at least two) options, the freedom involved, and the act of choosing (compared to passive acceptance). Emphasizing the latter, and taking a psychological perspective, Beresford and Sloper (2008) view choice as "the outcome of a process which involves assessment and judgement; that is, the evaluation of different options and making a decision about which option to choose" (p. 2). Moreover, the available alternatives "should have some positive value; hence, a 'choice' between something which is definitely desired and something which is definitely not desired is not a true choice" (p. 2).

Choice as a Relational Construct

Liberal theories understand choice as individuals' ability to evaluate their situation independently. However, drawing on feminist ideas, the disability movement and disability studies scholars criticize this (neo-)liberal notion of choice, arguing that viewing independence as the primary value of personhood neglects other core values such as trust, caring, and interdependence. Moreover, while the common liberal view perceives self-reliance to be a prerequisite for autonomy and choice, both the feminist and the disability movement view relatedness and interconnectedness not as their antitheses, but as their prerequisites (Ells, 2001; Nedelsky, 1989). It is through our relationships with others in a supportive environment, it is argued, that we acquire the necessary skills and confidence for choice (Lotan & Ells, 2010).

Furthermore, by viewing rationality, individualism, and independence as preconditions for choice and by stressing that choice can and should be realized in the absence of interference by others, the liberal tradition has historically excluded from the right to autonomy people who need substantial support in the decision-making process, especially those with intellectual disability. Lastly, understanding choice and autonomy as an individual enterprise leads to blaming and depreciating those who fail to achieve the liberal ideal of autonomy (Davy, 2015).

Following these critiques, in this chapter, we employ a relational understanding of choice that challenges the dependence/independence dichotomy and recognizes that all humans are interdependent (Leece & Peace 2010). This account of choice speaks substantially to the experience of people with intellectual disability who "are often able to make decisions for themselves, but not necessarily on their own" (Davy, 2015, p. 140).

Choice in Practice

For choice to be meaningful, it should be realized in practice. Hence, an important conceptual distinction is that between negative and positive freedom of choice. Negative freedom of choice refers to the absence of any restraint that prevents a person from choosing, while positive freedom of choice refers to available resources in order to realize choices, without which choice would remain an empty concept. For example, if the state does not interfere with decisions of individuals with intellectual disability to live in the community, but does not make sure they have sufficient material, educational, and emotional resources to exercise their choice, we can say that while their negative freedom to choice has not been violated, their positive freedom has (Boyle, 2008; Stainton, 2002). Since a narrow, negative notion of choice runs the risk of obscuring fundamental inequalities (Fyson & Cromby, 2013), this chapter relies on a positive notion of choice and views it not only as a civil or political but also as a socioeconomic right (Carney, 2017).

Relatedly, for choice to be practical, the individual must also have some familiarity with the available options. This leads us to two other related features of choice. First is the ability to imagine available options and access to information about them. People with intellectual disability may not be able to imagine a wide range of possibilities mainly due to limited past experience (e.g., growing up in institution could result in difficulty imagining an alternative way of life). Second, they may have restricted access to information resulting in limited familiarity with the available options (Björnsdóttir, Stefánsdóttir & Stefánsdóttir., 2015; Shogren, Wehmeyer, Lassmann & Forber-Pratt, 2017). Importantly, and as elaborated below, these two difficulties are not mainly a result of personal deficiency, but rather of social barriers.

Another issue relates to the spheres of life in which choice is to be realized. Here too, we take a broad view of choice and argue that it does not have to be based on consumerist discourse and logic. This citizenship understanding of choice implies that choice does not have to be realized in a market-style mechanism (Glendinning, 2008) and that it can be embedded in all fabrics of citizens' life and not only those related to their role as consumers. Prime examples are the right to choose where to work or whether to vote in an election (Rabiee & Glendinning, 2010).

Social Services for People with Intellectual Disabilities in Israel

Services for people with intellectual disability in Israel are mainly under the responsibility of the Ministry of Social Affairs and Social Services. In 2016, close to 35,000 individuals with intellectual disability were documented by the ministry (Shalom, Ben Simchon & Goren, 2017). The ministry's responsibility can be traced back to the 1960s, when the Service for the Retarded was established (1962) and the Care for People with Mental Retardation Law (1969) was passed (Hovav & Ramot, 1998).[1] According to this law, every person suspected of having intellectual disability is mandatorily requested to undergo examination by a multi-professional diagnostic committee that determines their condition, treatment, and service needs, including the need for appointing a guardian,[2] and recommended housing and

---

[1] Welfare services for people with intellectual disability were provided by the ministry before the 1960s. However, the establishment of the service and enactment of the law expanded services dramatically.

[2] The committee's decisions over guardianship are not anchored in law; only recently, following a public critique, has the ministry instructed the committee to avoid taking such decisions. As of yet, it is too early to ascertain if and to what extent this recommendation is followed.

community services (e.g., employment, health, education, and leisure) (Care for People with Mental Retardation Law, 1969). Very few changes have been made in the law since its enactment. One of the more noteworthy was the 2000 amendment, which states that any person recognized by the committee as having intellectual disability is entitled to services from the ministry and calls for priority to community services (Amendment to the Care for People with Mental Retardation Law, 2000).

Another important milestone is the 1998 Equal Rights for People with Disabilities Law. Inspired by the landmark Americans with Disabilities Act of 1990, it entitles people with disabilities to equal rights in all aspects of life without discrimination, as well as the accommodations required for that purpose. Although the first drafts of the law granted people with disabilities the right to community services, in its final form, and due to financial and ideological considerations, the law was narrowed to focus mainly on employment and accessibility rights (Kanter, 2012).

Legal Capacity

In a modern democracy, a key manifestation of choice is *legal capacity*, that is, the right to be recognized as a full person before the law on an equal basis. Legal capacity includes legal agency – the right to make legal decisions for oneself (Flynn & Arstein Kerslake, 2014). Traditionally, based on atomistic, individualistic, and rationalist conceptions of the self, legal capacity has been contingent upon *mental capacity*. This coupling of legal and mental capacity has led to the appointment of guardians to decide for people assessed or even only assumed as lacking the skills to do so (Glen, 2012). Among people with disabilities, those with intellectual disability have been highly prone to this kind of substitute decision-making practice. As elaborated below, this practice raises many concerns with regard to choice, leading the UN Convention on the Rights of Persons with Disabilities (CRPD, 2006) to view legal capacity as an unconditional right and to urge member states to replace guardianship with other, less restrictive alternatives, including supported decision-making (SDM).

In Israel, legal and mental capacity issues are approached via the 1962 Legal Capacity and Guardianship Law (hereinafter: Capacity Law) that has undergone major reform in 2016. As evident from the review below, the reform has taken Israel a step forward in supporting people with intellectual disability to realize their personhood and choice. Yet, there are still unresolved questions and challenges.

The Israeli Capacity Law Before the 2016 Reform

The Capacity Law declares that "every person is capable of preforming legal acts"; however, it also restricts this right by stating "unless such capability has been revoked or restricted by law or judgment of a court" (Article 2). Accordingly, a guardian may be appointed for persons "unable to look after their own affairs"

(Article 33). In order to take care of such a person, the court gives the guardian the duty and power to make different legal decisions on behalf of the individual (Ben David, 2015).

Reviewing the law through the prism of freedom of choice raises substantial concerns, some of which are unique to the Israeli experience. These concerns touch on the nature of guardianship, the appointment procedure, and the supervision of guardians. As for its nature, guardianship has far-reaching effects on the individual's right to freedom and autonomy. Under this practice, a guardian makes the most important decisions of the individual's life, and the individual is no longer considered as having legal status but rather is "owned" by her guardian and must comply with her decision (Ben David, 2015; Doron, 2010).

Compared to other Western countries, this direct infringement on the individual's autonomy is further extended in Israel. First, although the law states that the authority of guardians should be limited to issues specified by the court, in the great majority of cases, a plenary guardian is provided with power over a wide range of decisions including the individual's assets, health, body, and personhood (Barel, Doron & Strier, 2015). Second, legal capacity is not static and depends on sociocultural factors (Flynn & Arstein-Kerslake, 2014). For example, while most people do not need to prove legal capacity to enter a romantic relationship, living in an institutional setting where such relationships are limited, or even prohibited, leads to situations where their realization depends on legal agency. As elaborated below, social forces in Israel, primarily housing arrangements, limit the lives of individuals with intellectual disability in many different ways. In this kind of geographic exclusionary regime (Soffer, Koreh & Rimmerman, 2017), the lack of legal capacity has even harsher implications. Third, the law provides little in the way of clear guidelines regarding the boundaries of this practice. For example, third parties often ask the guardian's permission for the individual with intellectual disability to use services or to allow them to perform various acts (e.g., participate in leisure activities or research), although the law itself does not require such permissions. This is often due to legal ignorance and fear of noncompliance. Whatever the reason, this de facto extension of the power entrusted with the guardian leads to "civil death," whereby the individual is no longer entitled to participate in the community without the guardian's involvement (Dinnerstein, 2012).

Another key concern relates to the guardianship appointment procedure, which in the case of people with intellectual disability is frequently the default practice without any prior substantial discussion regarding the appointment and with little weight placed on the individual's preference. This taken-for-granted procedure usually starts prior to age 18, when the diagnostic committee makes its recommendations. Further, many social services, including housing services, require guardianship before serving individuals with intellectual disability (Kanter & Tolub, 2017; Ministry of Labor, Social Affairs and Social Services [MOLSA], *Guardianship*, n.d. a). At all these initial stages of the appointment procedure, guardianship is framed by the various stakeholders as inevitable and universal.

Based on the recommendation of the diagnostic committee, parents (usually) initiate the appointment of a guardian with the help of a municipal social worker.

The social worker writes a report that should be based on opinions of professionals familiar with the individual (e.g., teacher, physician), her family, and her own. A letter of recommendation is also provided by a psychiatrist or the family physician who meets with the individual and advises on the individuals' status, ability to take care of their own needs, need for guardianship, and ability to understand the meaning of guardianship appointment. The social worker's and physician's report are submitted to the family court that decides on the appointment of a guardian (MOLSA, *Guardianship*, n.d. a).

Although the law required the court to hear the person's stand before ruling, in practice, this is often not the case, and only individuals deemed capable of understanding the issue and stating their opinion are given this right. Based on random sampling of court files, an Israeli study found that a medical certificate attesting that the individual was unable to express her view was included in 95.2% of cases (Doron, 2004). Similarly, in only about 10% of cases was such a hearing conducted (Tolub & Shlomai, in press). This situation is exacerbated by the lack of state-provided legal representation, leaving most individuals with intellectual disability without legal support in protecting their rights and representing their preferences (Doron, 2004). Moreover, the wishes of individuals with intellectual disability and their family, even when heard by the social worker before writing her report, are also mediated by her. This communication runs the risk of biasing or misrepresenting information. Further, the law does not clarify how much weight should be placed on the individual's wishes within this report or within the judge's decision, such as when the individual refuses guardianship or a specific guardian. Finally, even when the individuals' voice is heard, they are usually not given any real alternatives. On one hand, there was the threat of being subjected to guardianship and losing one's legal capacity. On the other hand, given that before the reform SDM alternatives were not recognized by the Israeli legal system, there was a threat of being left with no formal and recognized support to enable people to exercise their legal capacity.

Although not specific to intellectual disability, in approximately 85% of cases, the appointed guardian is a family member, while in the remaining 15%, the guardian is employed by a legal guardianship corporation (https://brookdale.jdc.org.il/regulating-guardianship/). Once a guardian has been appointed, another concern has to do with how the Israeli legal and welfare systems ensure that guardians, whether family members or corporation's employees, act not only for the (presumed) benefit of the individual but also according to their will and preferences. This involves three key issues. First, as stated by the State Comptroller repeatedly throughout the years, is the state's supervision of guardians (e.g., State Comptroller, 2012). An illustrative example for this "regulatory deficit" (Levi-Faur, Gidron, & Moshell, 2015) is the fact that in 2017, less than half the guardians have submitted the required annual report (Derech, Rotler & Tolub, 2018). Second, supervision is limited to financial and property issues, leaving important issues such as personal matters unsupervised (State Comptroller, 2012). Third, these financial requirements focus on protecting the person's "best interests" rather than her choice. In fact, prior to the reform, the only reference in the law to the individual's will required the guardians to hear the individuals' opinion "as long as they are capable of understanding the issues at stake and their opinions can be understood" (Article 36 of the Legal Capacity and Guardianship Law, 1962). Lastly, very few resources have been invested in supporting guardians, especially family members, in fulfilling their task and particularly their ability to understand and represent the choices of the individual with a disability.

The Amended Law and Its Implications for Choice

Given the above criticisms and thanks to the combined efforts of civil society organizations, led by Bizchut: The Israel Human Rights Center for People with Disabililties, an amendment was enacted to the Legal Capacity Law in March 2016 (Kanter & Tolub, 2017; Tolub & Shlomai, in press). The amendment included several significant progressive changes, which refer to the nature of guardianship, the guardians' appointment procedure, and the extent of their use. These changes moved the Israeli legal capacity system a major step away from the previous guardianship regime to a new "support paradigm" (Series, 2015), in which support is provided in order to enable people with disabilities to exercise their legal capacity on an equal basis with other citizens. However, these positive changes still exist only on paper, and as detailed below, they too raise important concerns and challenges (Kanter & Tolub, 2017; Soffer et al., 2017(.

A key change is that the law adopts the "necessity" and "last resort" principles by stating that guardianship must only be used if it is necessary in order to protect the person's interests, rights, and needs and only after considering other, less restrictive, options. Moreover, the amendment obligates judges both to limit the term of guardianship appointments and to restrict the authority of guardians to specific areas of need (e.g., medical, personal, or property issues).

Alternatives to guardianship, first and foremost SDM, are now recognized as legitimate legal practices.[3] The aim is for SDM to allow persons with intellectual disability to make their own choices about their life while getting support from others who can explain the issues, interpret the individuals' words and behaviors, and understand their preferences, desires, and choices (Blanck & Martinis, 2015; Devi, 2013; Dinnerstein, 2012; Shogren et al., 2017). This is designed to help people with diverse needs to exercise their right to legal capacity. In accordance with Article 12 of the Convention on the Rights of Persons with Disabilities (CRPD, 2006) and its relational understanding of decision-making and choice, the underlying rationale is that support and relationships are not a threat but often major facilitators of legal capacity and choice, particularly for people with intellectual disability (Series, 2015; Browning, Bigby & Douglas, 2014).

---

[3] Another key alternative recognized by the new amendment is enduring powers of attorney, which are not within the scope of this chapter.

Another set of changes touches on the proper conduct of guardians. Most importantly, the amendment states that their decision-making should be guided by the wishes of the individual subjected to guardianship. When these are impossible to determine, or when individuals are not in a condition to understand the issue involved, the guardian is obliged to act in accordance with their will as expressed prior to their current condition or in accordance with their past actions. The only reservation is in cases where the guardian has reason to believe that deciding according to the individual's explicit or implicit wishes may cause real harm. Relatedly, the new amendment provides people under guardianship with several key rights, from receiving information from the guardian, through providing free legal representation in medical decisions, to securing the rights to independence and privacy.

These changes seem to hold real promise for the freedom of choice of people with intellectual disability, particularly in challenging the previous automatic resorting to guardianship. The amendment, however, is not without flaws.

First, although appointing a guardian has been restricted, and although the new changes (potentially) challenge the automatic appointment procedure, it has not been repealed and consequently it is yet unclear to what extent, if at all, judges and social workers will embrace this change and limit their use of guardianship. This concern is exacerbated by the fact that despite the demand by organizations that represent persons with disabilities, the new amendment does not include the individual's will as a *crucial* factor in the appointment decision, leaving this decision based entirely on professional discretion. Added to this is the fact that the reform does not touch upon the practice of social workers and the way they should integrate an individual's will into their assessments of decision-making capacity. As Browning et al. (2014) rightly remind us, the SDM regime requires these assessments to include the support provided to the person; without this interdependent redefinition of mental capacity, "the full potential of the concept will not be realized" (p. 41). Further, the law still does not mandate that the individual involved appear in the legal proceeding, nor does it require or subsidize their legal representation. All these not only violate the freedom of choice of people with intellectual disability but run the risk that the restriction on using guardianship will remain a dead letter.

An additional set of concerns has to do with the proper conduct of guardians. According to the new amendment, the wishes of the individual should be the primary guiding principle in the guardians' decisions. However, studies in other countries have highlighted the difficulty in making decisions that are based solely on the wishes of the individual. Specifically, studies have shown that in making decisions, some carers also employ their own views on wider social norms, their own values, or what they perceive as the individual's wishes (Dunn, Clare, & Holland, 2009; Williams et al., 2012). Given the above-mentioned "regulatory deficit" of the Israeli legal and welfare systems, the fact the supervision is limited to financial and property issues, and the low level of support for guardians in fulfilling their tasks, it is questionable to what extent this progressive change will not be only on paper.

Other concerns deal with the proper implementation of SDM. First, although the amendment gives legal standing to supporters, due to budgetary constraints, the amendment and its current guiding principles[4] do not say anything about their funding. Hence, people whose family has limited means or who do not want to rely on their family will hardly be able to benefit from SDM in practice. The result is that if given the opportunity to do so at all, many individuals with intellectual disability will be forced to "choose" between making it on their own or to be subjected to guardianship.

A second concern is related to the quality of supporters. According to the new guidelines, supporters are required to take part in a formal training course that should cover such issues as social perspectives of disability. These trainings, however, are relatively short term, target nonrelatives, and do not provide field training. Further, these trainings only just began, and there is yet no available data on their utility or efficacy. Relatedly, the current regulations do not offer any kind of substantial, formal training for the person asking for support. A recent pilot study found that this kind of training is helpful in understanding the new SDM tool (Holler, Werner, Lester-Keidar, Wasser & Ronen, 2017). More broadly, most of the international research on SDM has adopted normative or policy analysis methodologies, while systematic, empirical evidence on what really works and how is scarce, posing a real challenge to the development of proper training and supervision for supporters (Arstein-Kerslake, Watson, Browning, Martinis & Blanck, 2017; Bigby et al., 2017; Shogren et al., 2017).

A final concern regarding the implementation of SDM is in how third parties (e.g., physicians, banks) will embrace this new tool. These third parties, as well as the public, may continue questioning the ability of individuals with intellectual disability to understand and exercise choice. This questioning may also be fueled by fear that in situations involving risk, they might be at blame for decisions made. Thus, "old" guardianship alternatives may be required, or at least the permission of the individual's relative, before providing services to the individual.

Housing Support Services

An additional and central field of social policy with significant repercussions for choice is housing support services. In this section, we focus on the process through which housing services are approved and how they affect the freedom of choice of service users with intellectual disability.

---

[4] At the time of writing, although the law mandates regulations, these have not yet been promulgated.

Procedures for Obtaining Housing Services and Their Implications for Choice

Housing services for people with intellectual disability in Israel are provided through the Care for People with Mental Retardation Law (1969). Once an individual is diagnosed with intellectual disability, the diagnostic committee recommends the type of housing service that meets their needs. This recommendation is made based upon information provided to the committee by the family and the social worker as well as upon a series of assessments made by professionals from the committee regarding the individuals' level of intellectual disability, capacities, and preferences.

While originally the law did not grant any statutory right to housing services, since 2000, they are provided as rights. Moreover, as part of public demand for deinstitutionalization, the 2000 amendment obligates the diagnostic committee to give priority to community-based services (Amendment to the Care for People with Mental Retardation Law, 1969, 2000; Kanter, 2012). Nevertheless, this deinstitutionalization reform is still in relatively early stages. As shown below, most people who receive housing services still live in institution-like settings.

After the diagnostic committee selects the type of housing support, a local placement committee provides the individual and his family with two to three concrete alternatives. These alternatives are based on a range of considerations, including the individual's cultural background, perceived needs, availability, and proximity. Next, the individual and his family (guardian) are invited to visit each setting, participate in an admission committee, and select the setting that best fits their wishes and needs.

This procedure raises some major concerns regarding the realization of choice. First and most directly, while the diagnostic committee is obliged to hear the individual and his guardian and consider their wishes, neither the law nor ministerial regulations clearly specify how much weight should be placed on these wishes. This flaw is even more significant given that in practice, the decision over the type of housing support is guided not only by the individual's needs but also, and perhaps mainly, by the availability of services and resources. This leaves little room for the individual's preferences, especially when these differ from those of professionals. No less problematic are cases where the individual's preferences differ from those of the family. The fact that many family members are also appointed as guardians gives rise to situations in which the guardian's wishes receive priority, and these are often wrongly considered as representing those of the individual with intellectual disability.

The role of the local placement committee is even more problematic as this committee is not anchored in law, but ministerial regulations. Although these regulations empower the committee to meet with the individual and her family, this is not mandated. Thus, in reality, many committees never see or hear the future resident before determining placement alternatives, and even if they do, as with the diagnostic committee, regulations do not specify state how much weight should be placed on individual's wishes.

Another procedural flaw concerns the relational nature of choice. Even if the individual's voice is heard and their wishes taken into account, in order for choice to be exercised, service users may still need support in imagining and understanding the available alternatives and in making sure their voice is properly articulated and encouraged. This support is even more important for individuals who are nonverbal or of lower functioning, for those who have lived in institutions for years without gaining firsthand knowledge about community-based services, and in situations in which this wish diverges from that of other stakeholders, including the family. In Israel, a key potential player in providing this support is the municipal social worker. Although little is known about the actual exercise of this responsibility, the large caseloads of municipal social workers are a barrier to establishing high-quality relationships with clients (Krumer-Nevo & Barak, 2007) and prioritizing what are perceived by policymakers as nonurgent tasks.

Similar difficulties arise when individuals wish to move from one housing setting to another. While the diagnostic committee is legally required to convene every 3 years, it usually only meets on demand (Lef & Rivkin, 2015). Thus, much responsibility is placed on the residential social worker who is (theoretically) responsible for helping individuals understand their right for re-diagnosis, available living arrangements, and potential impact on their lives, initiating the procedure and making sure their voices and wishes are articulated and encouraged. Here too, little is known about the actual exercise of this responsibility. However, the inherent tension between the social workers' obligation to residents and to service providers places many social workers in a conflict of interests (Lev & Ayalon, 2015). The growing privatization of housing services (Madhala-Brik & Gal, 2016) only exacerbates this dilemma.

An additional problem is that the placement committee typically provides few options. This problem is exacerbated given that residential settings in Israel are unequally distributed among regions, cities, and neighborhoods (Rimmerman, 2017; Yogev, Yogev & Man, 2012). According to a yet unpublished study by the authors, some families even relocate in order to use services provided elsewhere. In many other cases, the individual and her family choose not to make use of any of the options offered by the placement committee (Ben Ari, 2016; Klarman, 2004). This may be related to preference for a different type of housing than that selected by the diagnostic committee or discontent with specific options offered. Importantly, this refusal also implies that the decision to stay and live within the family home, as most people with intellectual disability do (see next section), is not necessarily the result of real choice.

The options offered by the placement committee are further limited by the monopoly of a relatively few number of providers within the Israeli assisted living market, leaving little room for "shopping." For example, 93% of the ministry's payments to residential settings in 2015 were made to only 10% of the providers (Madala-Brik & Gal, 2016).

Housing Alternatives

A persistent finding in the choice literature is that the type of housing, including its level of segregation and size, is a key predictor of choice opportunities for people with intellectual disability. In particular, a substantial body of research indicates that smaller, community-based settings generally provide more opportunities for choice than larger, congregate facilities (Kozma, Mansell, & Beadle-Brown, 2009).

In Israel, despite some recent deinstitutionalization efforts, residential services are still heavily institutional. Three kinds of institutional settings are available. The most common and problematic one is *meonot* (literally, "institutions"). Essentially, *meonot* are large-scale settings that meet Goffman's (1961) description of "total institutions" as breaking down the barriers ordinarily separating the three main spheres of life: living, working, and leisure. The 63 *meonot* in Israel vary widely in terms of population (e.g., age, religiosity, ethnicity, level of functioning); size (35–290 residents); and location (urban or rural, central or peripheral) (MOLSA, *Housing in a maon*, n.d. b). They are uniform, however, in their Goffmanite bureaucratic logic.

While *meonot* date back to the early years of statehood, during the 1970s, a new kind of institutional service – the hostel – has been established. Hostels are formally defined as housing between 12 and 34 residents (Shalom, Ben Simchon, & Goren, 2015). Unlike *meonot*, some of the services are provided in the community including leisure services and work settings.

The third and most recently developed type of institutional setting is called "branches." These settings house up to 24 residents and are located within the community. However, "branches" are not only larger than bona fide community settings but are also organizationally part of the *meonot*, with residents receiving most (if not all) of the medical, employment, and leisure services from the *meonot* (Rimmerman, 2017; Shalom et al., 2015). Similarly, the "branches" share their staff and other resources with the *meonot* with which they are affiliated.

Movement toward community settings, formally defined as housing up to six residents (Shalom et al., 2015), began in the 1980s. Known as community apartments, these settings are owned or leased by an agency (NGO or for-profit) and are supported by the agency's staff with varying degrees of intensity, according to the residents' needs. Residents are supposed to obtain many of their daily services from the community. Due to a recent change in the ministry's policy, in recent years, we have seen a slight rise in the number of people living in community apartments. Numerically speaking, however, this solution is still marginal, and this is especially true for people with greater needs.

Taken together, out of those living in supervised settings, 7319 (68.4%) live in *meonot* and their branches and 1924 (18%) in hostels, representing about 90% of the ministry's spending on residential services. Only 1456 (13.6%) live in community apartments (Shalom et al., 2017), representing only about 10% of the ministry's spending on such services (Information Retrieved from Personal communication, 2017). As elaborated below, most individuals with intellectual disability in Israel of all ages (68%) live at home. Although not enough data are available, it seems almost none of them live on their own or with roommates, but rather with parents or other family members. As we explained below, with regard to realizing choice, they too face many barriers.

Choice Within Meonot, *Hostels, and "Branches"*

Living in larger-scale institutions such as *meonot* poses many fundamental challenges for the realization of choice. Moreover, and as the experience of many European countries reveals (Mansell & Beadle-Brown, 2010; Mansell, Knapp, Beadle-Brown & Beecham, 2007), while being somewhat smaller in size and integrated in the fabric of community life, in practice, the organizational logic of small, modernized institutions such as hostels and "branches" is in many ways similar to *meonot* and Goffman's (1961) "total institution." Among other things, the care provided in these settings is characterized by depersonalization, rigid routines, block treatment, and social distance between staff and residents (Mansell & Beadle-Brown, 2010).

In this section, we will highlight some of the implications of these kinds of care settings with regard to choice. Note that some of these are a result of the organizational logic that characterizes institutions in general and do not reflect weaknesses in managing these settings. Others are unique to the Israeli scene and are exacerbated due to the ministry's policies and the management of the particular settings (e.g., Berenstein, 2011).

In order to manage everyday life, institutions serving many residents with diverse needs tend to enforce uniform norms and strict daily routines. Israeli residents at institutions, especially *meonot*, are provided specific times for activities, regular eating times and a fixed diet, regular sleeping hours, and participation in shared leisure activities. Residents are also expected to go to work each morning (usually within a sheltered workshop), even after retirement age (Lerner, 2008; Schwartz, 2003). Norms that are uniformly enforced require a high level of discipline. Residents are usually expected to conform to various rules that are not applied to people without intellectual disability. In Israel, these include, for example, strict visiting hours, limited freedom of movement within and outside the institution, and limited opportunities for communication with the outside world, including access to digital media.

In addition, most institutional services, including health and leisure services, are provided in-house, or at least in a one-size-fits-all model. In this kind of block treatment, the individual lacks control over service design and is denied the right to obtain supports within the community. This is even more so within institutions located far from the community. In some cases, the individual cannot even choose between the few alternatives available.

An additional key domain of choice relates to selecting the specific room an individual occupies and his or her roommates. Due to budget and space considerations, most rooms in institutions are shared between two to three roommates, and the choice of roommates is not theirs to make. Relatedly, living with a romantic partner is usually not a real option. More generally, privacy is a rare commodity. Living in a shared room, sharing a bathroom, having limited private space, being exposed to constant professional gaze, and forced to share information regarding your medical and psychological condition all lead to loss of privacy. This limits choice in various subtle and not-so-subtle ways, perhaps the most critical of which is the difficulty forming and maintaining intimate relationships and engaging in sexual activities (Hollomotz & The Speakup Committee, 2009).

Staff, especially direct care workers, are also highly influential in the realization of choice. As Goffman (1961) reminds us, total institutions tend to create social distance and a stratified social hierarchy between staff and residents. Within these unequal power relations, little room is left for residents to exercise choice and control over their lives. The restriction of choice by staff members is not, however, (only) a straightforward result of the institutional logic, but also stems from various policy and management variables, including staff working conditions, quality of training, and formal and informal guidelines and policies (Finlay, Walton & Antaki, 2008).

Specifically, several features of the Israeli residential care system have negative repercussions for choice. First, direct care workers in institutional settings come from low socioeconomic backgrounds and possess few academic qualifications. They are not paid well and work in very high-demand and stressful environments with low staff-to-resident ratios (Zakash & Gilad, 2010). Although employers rank trained direct support workers higher in their professional performance, including their ability to effectively support people with intellectual disability to make choices (Barlev & Rivkin, 2016), most direct care workers are undertrained. While the ministry offers formal training, only approximately 30% of all residential care workers receive it (Barlev & Rivkin, 2016). This is because training is not mandatory, requires the employers' permission and recommendation, is offered only to veteran workers with more than 11 years of education, and is usually paid for by workers themselves.

The performance of residential services reflects weaknesses in government regulation. Such services are primarily regulated by the outdated Supervision of Institutional Residences Law of 1965. Both the law and its regulation lack real enforcement mechanisms. More importantly, both focus almost entirely on setting health, safety, and hygiene standards at the expense of more subtle care issues, including choice. Geared toward protection rather than empowerment, the regulatory system is further weakened due to its other features including very limited attention to service users' input in the auditing process, inspectors' high work load, lack of clarity in defining the role and guidelines of inspectors, and lack of an independent ombudsman (Lahat & Talit, 2015; Rimon-Greenspan, 2014). In the absence of effective regulatory arrangements, and in a heavily privatized market, the performance of residential settings with respect to choice and related issues is at risk of being quite poor (Berenstein, 2011).

Choice in Community-Based Apartments

Studies in countries where the deinstitutionalization reform has already material-ized repeatedly show that compared to larger, congregate settings, more personal-ized, smaller, community-based services tend to provide their residents with more opportunities for choice and control (Kozma et al., 2009; Stancliffe et al., 2011). The relatively few studies conducted in Israel also indicate that residents of smaller settings report greater control of various decisions in their lives, such as the food they eat, their home styling, when to be visited by family and friends, the daily schedule, and what to do with their money (Berenstein, 2011).

Nevertheless, as the experience of other countries shows, living in community-based settings does not guarantee that the institutional mindset has vanished and that high levels of choice-making is realized (James, Harvey, & Mitchell, 2018; Kozma et al., 2009). In Israel, this is due both to the nature of the community apart-ment services and the way these services are designed, operated, and regulated.

One key concern is that although apartment and services are provided within the community, ownership and responsibility remain with the service provider. This leads to risk for the infringement of choice with respect to various issues, including how many residents will live in a room, who will be the room- and housemates, when and where to go for vacation, and more. It should also be noted that most agencies are privately run and are funded according to the number of residents they support, while not required by the ministry to provide services according to the individuals' wishes.

The weak regulatory system described above also plays a key role. Based on an outdated piece of legislation focused on protection rather than empowerment, this regulation is doubly irrelevant to monitoring a rights-based community housing. Lastly, here too, lack of training and low working conditions for the staff run the risk of providing low-quality care, with insufficient attention to residents' choice opportunities.

Choice Within the Family Home

As suggested above, most individuals with intellectual disability in Israel remain at home, usually with their parents or other family members. Although the family home is considered by the ministry to be the most preferable and community-based setting, allowing for the greatest degree of autonomy, a closer look reveals that in practice this living arrangement is associated with major choice-related concerns, mainly due to poor policy design.

The state provides various community-based services to those living in their own homes or with family, including (usually sheltered) employment, day settings, leisure services, and respite care. These, however, are not anchored in law but in ministry regulations, based on discretionary decisions, offer little (and in many cases no) alternatives from which to choose, and are standardized in nature. Moreover, these services include little in-home support. The ministry also offers some individuals personal assistance, but this is limited to 30 hours a month for up to 6 months. Further, unlike many Western countries, the Israeli welfare state does not operate any nationwide personal budget scheme allowing individuals with intellectual disability to control and select services according to their needs (Rimmerman, 2017). It also does not subsidize supported living – an arrangement in which individuals with intellectual disability live on their own or with roommates of their choice, in housing they own or rent, while receiving in-home support from providers who do not control the accommodation (Mansell & Beadle-Brown, 2010). All in all, the ministry devotes only about 16% of its housing budget to the majority of individuals with intellectual disability who live at home (Shalom et al., 2017).[5]

It is also important to acknowledge that the cost of living in Israel is very high, and this applies primarily to rental prices. Although individuals with intellectual disability are entitled to government subsidies, these fall far short of their expenses. Thus, without the family's support, such individuals cannot rent an apartment in the private market.

The described state of affairs affects choice in several ways. Due to the limited in-home support and lack of state's subsidies for supported living, individuals with intellectual disability do not have a real option to live on their own or with their partners, as most adults usually prefer. Research from other countries has also acknowledged that living in countries with particularly high costs of living potentially reduces choice opportunities for people with intellectual disability (Houseworth, Ticha & Stancliffe, 2018). Combined with the fact that the option of community apartments is also very limited, this means that the decision to live with family members is usually made due to lack of more attractive alternatives. Note also that the option of living with the family is not one that is equally available to all, as it depends on the family having adequate financial and other resources. Individuals whose families lack these resources are often forced into institutional settings (Nasser, Sachs, & Sa'ar, 2017).

The low level of state support provided to people with disabilities requires the individual to be heavily dependent on parents and other family members for support, which can lead to these individuals exercising undue control over the individual's daily life. Finally, lacking any nationwide personal budget scheme means that service users have little control over the services they utilize.

---

[5] The above information is processed from the data on page 389. The rest of the budget is designated to other functions such as diagnosing.

Conclusions

In this chapter, we sought to better understand how Israeli social policies impact upon the freedom of choice of individuals with intellectual disability. By taking a relational, positive, social, and multifaceted understanding of choice and focusing on two key policy domains – legal capacity and housing – our analysis highlights the decisive role of these policies in shaping opportunities for choice. Taken together, this analysis points to the vast gap between Articles 12 and 19 of the CRPD (2006) and the freedom of choice provided to people with intellectual disability in Israel.

Within the legal capacity realm, we have shown how guardianship limits individuals' right to freedom and autonomy. This restriction is exacerbated due to massive use of plenary guardianship and the lack of clear boundaries with regard to guardians' authority. Another infringement of the individual's right to freedom lies in the process of appointing a guardian, in which the individual's voice is not only rarely heard, but guardianship itself is perceived and framed by professionals as the only possible solution for people with intellectual disability. The recent reform, and the establishment of SDM as a legal tool, surely carries vast potential for transforming this guardianship regime and for bringing about greater choice. However, as we have shown, several concerns must be addressed in order for this new policy not to become "another tick box exercise" (Arstein-Kerslake et al., 2017, "The Danger Zone" para. 2) with little meaningful change in the lives of people with disabilities.

In relation to housing services, our analyses highlight how choices of individuals with intellectual disability are limited at many points in the process via which housing is provided, from the diagnostic committee, through the local placement committee and in everyday decisions within specific settings. The main drawback relates to the way the individual is heard at various stages of this process – if at all. Most Israeli individuals with intellectual disability who live outside the home live in institutional settings. Within such settings, choices are highly restricted given that uniform norms are enforced and that most services are provided strictly within the institution. While smaller, community-based apartments provide residents with more opportunities for choice and control, they too suffer from flaws. Finally, although most individuals with intellectual disability still live within the family home, our findings point to the coercive elements found in this kind of setting as well.

The two policy domains discussed above are closely related. For example, having the right to full legal capacity is a necessary (albeit not sufficient) condition for deciding where, with whom, and how to live. Conversely, while the lack of in-home support and personal budgeting acts as a barrier for those wishing to live by themselves, this barrier is also greatly influential with regard to supporting people with intellectual disability in decision-making.

Before discussing our recommendations, several limitations of our analysis need to be considered. Despite being central to shaping the opportunities for choice in peoples' life, neither legal capacity policy nor housing policy is sufficient to enable people with intellectual disability to realize their freedom of choice on an equal basis with others. Additional policies not discussed here, such as self-determination interventions in school, disability benefits, and contract and criminal law are important as well. In addition, similar to some European countries (e.g., Germany and Austria), when it comes to legal capacity, policy, and housing services for people with intellectual disability, systematic and robust empirical and administrative data are extremely scant in Israel.

What Works?

In this last section, we would like to provide several recommendations in an attempt to overcome the abovementioned challenges. The Ministry of Social Affairs and Social Services and the Ministry of Justice need to provide knowledge and training to social workers, judges, and other helping professionals on the legal amendment that in theory supports the rights of people with intellectual disability to choice. This is necessary in order to challenge the long-lasting tendency of these professionals to embrace guardianship as the default solution for people with intellectual disability. Moving away from the guardianship regime also requires the Israeli welfare state to make sure that no one is left behind and support in exercising legal capacity is provided according to need.

Development of proper training and effective regulation over supporters is needed so that SDM does not in itself become a guise for exploitation and manipulation. This will be a challenge given that the SDM is a new policy tool that has hitherto rarely been implemented and more rarely studied. Thus, it will be useful for Israeli policymakers to learn from recent international developments and models (e.g., Bigby et al., 2017; Douglas, Bigby, Knox & Browning, 2015; Shogren, Wehmeyer, Uyanik, & Heidrich, 2017).

Full and effective implementation of all the above recommendations may enable Israel to reach the next point in the transition toward a support paradigm. Although the changes made so far in Israeli law allowed for massive steps forward toward the realization of CRPD's Article 12, the mental and legal capacity nexus has remained intact and, accordingly, left guardianship as a legitimate, if not default legal, alternative. In order for Israel to realize the vision of Article 12, legal capacity must be treated as an unconditional right. Among other things, this will require Israel to decouple mental and legal capacity and reduce the prevalence of all forms of substituted decision-making, including that of guardianship.

Even more than in the legal capacity field, Israel still has a long way to go to realize the CRPD in relation to housing. A first major step toward that end is for the Ministry of Social Affairs and Social Services to determine a deadline by which all forms of institutions will close. Although an expert committee has already made that recommendation (Blanck et al., 2011), it was not followed.

We also call for the provision of living alternatives other than in out-of-home placements. This includes developing a generous personal budgeting scheme. In order for these types of living arrangement to become a real alternative for people with intellectual disability, high rental costs in Israel will need to be taken into consideration. Several attempts have recently been made to translate the rights to community living and personal budgeting into the Equal Rights Law, and efforts must be made to realize that vision (Blanck et al., 2011; Magor, Sandler-Lef, Stern, & Tolub, 2017; Proposed Amendment for the Equal Rights Law [Community Housing and Personal Budget], 2016).

Finally, it is important to acknowledge that laws reflect attitudes and perceptions. At the basis of the overuse of guardianship and institutional living lie social perceptions that do not recognize people with disabilities (especially those with intellectual disability) as having equal rights, including the right to choice. Changing this perspective requires many steps, from education through affecting public and academic discourse. At the policy level, the first step would be to replace the outdated Care for People with Mental Retardation Law with new legislation more in line with the right-based perspectives of disability and the CRPD (2006). The right to choice, autonomy, and control must be placed at the center of the new law and the services provided thereunder.

References

Amendment to the Care for People with Mental Retardation Act, 2000.

Arstein-Kerslake, A., Watson, J., Browning, M., Martinis, J., & Blanck, P. (2017). Future directions in supported decision-making. *Disability Studies Quarterly, 37*(1). https://doi.org/10.18061/dsq.v37i1.5070.

Barel, M., Doron, I., & Strier, R. (2015). Guardianship: A critical review. *Social Security, 96*, 55–85. [Hebrew].

Barlev, L., & Rivkin, D. (2016). *Certification of caregivers for people with intellectual and developmental disabilities in out-of-home housing accommodations: Evaluation study.* Jerusalem, Israel: Myers-JDC-Brookdale Institute. Retrieved from http://www.kshalem.org.il/uploads/pdf/article_2418_1465394059.pdf [Hebrew].

Ben Ari, O. (2016). Placement: Transition from family home to a housing framework. In N. B. Dor, N. Cohen, & A. Shemesh (Eds.), *A portfolio of services and programs for treating a person with intellectual and developmental disabilities.* Jerusalem, Israel: Ministry of Labor, Social Affairs and Social Services. [Hebrew]. Retrieved from http://www.kshalem.org.il/uploads/pdf/article_5011_1469687904.pdf

Ben David, M. (2015). *Guardianship: Law and practice.* Srigim-Li On, Israel: Nevo. [Hebrew].

Berenstein, L. (2011). *The relationship between the perception of quality of life within people with mental retardation and their housing accommodation* (Master's thesis). Retrieved from http://www.kshalem.org.il/uploads/pdf/article_3346_1383763146.pdf [Hebrew].

Beresford, B., & Sloper, P. (2008). *Understanding the dynamics of decision-making and choice: A scoping study of key psychological theories to inform the design and analysis of the panel study.* York, UK: Social Policy Research Unit, University of York.

Bigby, C., Douglas, J., Carney, T., Then, S., Wiesel, I., & Smith, E. (2017). Delivering decision making support to people with cognitive disability: What has been learned from pilot programs in Australia from 2010 to 2015. *Australian Journal of Social Issues, 52*(3), 222–240. https://doi.org/10.1002/ajs4.19

Björnsdóttir, K., Stefánsdóttir, G. V., & Stefánsdóttir, Á. (2015). 'It's my life': Autonomy and people with intellectual disabilities. *Journal of Intellectual Disabilities, 19*(1), 5–21. https://doi.org/10.1177/1744629514564691

Blanck, P., Haverman, M., Levy, J., Quinn, G., Rimmerman, A., & Soffer, M. (2011). *Integrated community living for people with intellectual disabilities (intellectual disability) in Israel: Final report of an international committee of experts. Submitted to the Israeli Ministry of Social Affairs and Social Services.* Retrieved from http://bizchut.org.il/he/wp-content/uploads/2016/06/Report-final-version-October-31-2011.pdf

Blanck, P., & Martinis, J. G. (2015). "The right to make choices": The national resource center for supported decision-making. *Inclusion, 3*(1), 24–33. https://doi.org/10.1352/2326-6988-3.1.24

Boyle, G. (2008). Autonomy in long-term care: A need, a right or a luxury? *Disability & Society, 23*(4), 299–310. https://doi.org/10.1080/09687590802038795

Browning, M., Bigby, C., & Douglas, J. (2014). Supported decision making: Understanding how its conceptual link to legal capacity is influencing the development of practice. *Research and Practice in Intellectual and Developmental Disabilities, 1*(1), 34–45. https://doi.org/10.1080/23297018.2014.902726

Care for People with Mental Retardation Act, 1969.

Carney, T. (2017). Prioritising supported decision-making: Running on empty or a basis for glacial-to-steady progress? *Laws, 6*(4), 18. https://doi.org/10.3390/laws6040018

Davy, L. (2015). Philosophical inclusive design: Intellectual disability and the limits of individual autonomy in moral and political theory. *Hypatia, 30*(1), 132–148. https://doi.org/10.1111/hypa.12119

Derech, R., Rotler, R., & Tolub, Y. (2018). *Shadow report #1: Implementation of the UN Convention on the Rights of People with Disabilities in Israel.* Israel: The Civil Forum for the Advancement of the UN Convention on the Rights of People with Disabilities. Retreived from: https://law-clinics.biu.ac.il/files/lawclinique/shared/mnh_-_hdvkh_hsvpy_8.7.18.pdf [Hebrew].

Devi, N. (2013). Supported decision-making and personal autonomy for persons with intellectual disabilities: Article 12 of the UN Convention on the Rights of Persons with Disabilities. *Journal of Law, Medicine & Ethics, 41*(4), 792–806. https://doi.org/10.1111/jlme.12090

Dinnerstein, R. (2012). Implementing legal capacity under article 12 of the UN Convention on the Rights of Persons with Disabilities: The difficult road from guardianship to supported decision-making. *Human Rights Brief, 19*(2), 8–12. Retrieved from http://digitalcommons.wcl.american.edu/cgi/viewcontent.cgi?article=1816&context=hrbrief

Doron, I. (2004). Aging in the shadow of the law. *Journal of Aging & Social Policy, 16*(4), 59–77. https://doi.org/10.1300/j031v16n04_04

Doron, I. (2010). *Law, justice and old age* (2nd ed.). Jerusalem, Israel: JDC-Eshel. [Hebrew].

Douglas, J., Bigby, C., Knox, L., & Browning, M. (2015). Factors that underpin the delivery of effective decision-making support for people with cognitive disability. *Research and Practice in Intellectual and Developmental Disabilities, 2*(1), 37–44. https://doi.org/10.1080/23297018.2015.1036769

Dunn, M., Clare, J., & Holland, A. (2009). Living a life like ours': Supported workers' accounts of substitute decision-making in residential care homes for adults with intellectual disabilities. *Journal of Intellectual Disabilities Research, 54*, 144–160.

Ells, C. (2001). Lessons about autonomy from the experience of disability. *Social Theory and Practice, 27*(4), 599–615. Retrieved from http://www.jstor.org/stable/23559192

Finlay, W. M. L., Walton, C., & Antaki, C. (2008). Promoting choice and control in residential services for people with learning disabilities. *Disability & Society, 23*(4), 349–360. https://doi.org/10.1080/09687590802038860

Flynn, E., & Arstein-Kerslake, A. (2014). Legislating personhood: Realising the right to support in exercising legal capacity. *International Journal of Law in Context, 10*(1), 81–104. https://doi.org/10.1017/s1744552313000384

Fyson, R., & Cromby, J. (2013). Human rights and intellectual disabilities in an era of 'choice'. *Journal of Intellectual Disability Research, 57*(12), 1164–1172. https://doi.org/10.1111/j.1365-2788.2012.01641.x

Glen, K. B. (2012). Changing paradigms: Mental capacity, legal capacity, guardianship and beyond. *Columbia Human Rights Law Review, 44*, 93. Retrieved from https://heinonline.org/HOL/Page?handle=hein.journals/colhr44&div=7&g_sent=1&casa_token=&collection=journals

Glendinning, C. (2008). Increasing choice and control for older and disabled people: A critical review of new developments in England. *Social Policy & Administration, 42*(5), 451–469. https://doi.org/10.1111/j.1467-9515.2008.00617.x

Goffman, E. (1961). *Asylums: Essays on the social situation of mental patients and other inmates.* New York, NY: Anchor Books.

Holler, R., Werner, S., Lester-Keidar, E., Wesser, O., & Ronen, D. (2017). *Supported decision-making courses: Study report.* Jeusalem, Israel: Bizchut. [Hebrew].

Hollomotz, A., & The Speakup Committee. (2009). 'May we please have sex tonight?': People with learning difficulties pursuing privacy in residential group settings. *British Journal of Learning Disabilities, 37*(2), 91–97. https://doi.org/10.1111/j.1468-3156.2008.00512.x

Houseworth, J., Stancliffe, R.J., & Tichá, R. (2018). Association of state-level and individual-level factors with choice making of individuals with intellectual and developmental disabilities. *Research in Developmental Disabilities, 83*, 77–90. https://doi.org/10.1016/j.ridd.2018.08.008

Hovav, M., & Ramot, A. (1998). The development of welfare services for the mentally handicapped in Israel. *Social Security: Special English Edition, 5*, 142–162.

James, E., Harvey, M., & Mitchell, R. (2018). An inquiry by social workers into evening routines in community living settings for adults with learning disabilities. *Social Work in Action, 30*(1), 19–32. https://doi.org/10.1080/09503153.2017.1342791

Kanter, A. (2012). There's no place like home: The right to live in the community for people with disabilities, under international law and the domestic laws of the United States and Israel. *Israel Law Review, 45*(2), 181–233. https://doi.org/10.1017/s0021223712000015

Kanter, A. S., & Tolub, Y. (2017). The fight for personhood, legal capacity, and equal recognition under law for people with disabilities in Israel and beyond. *Cardozo Law Review, 39*, 557–610.

Klarman, C. (2004). *Implementation of the decisions of the division's diagnostic committees for the treatment of mentally retarded persons: How it relates to the characteristics of the social worker and the characteristics of the person with mental retardation and his family* (Master's thesis). Retrieved from http://www.kshalem.org.il/uploads/pdf/article_3039_1383081440.pdf [Hebrew].

Kozma, A., Mansell, J., & Beadle-Brown, J. (2009). Outcomes in different residential settings for people with intellectual disability: A systematic review. *American Journal of Intellectual Disabilities, 114*(3), 193–222. https://doi.org/10.1352/1944-7558-114.3.193

Krumer-Nevo, M., & Barak, A. (2007). Service users and personal social services in Israel: Are we ready to hear what clients want to tell us? *Journal of Social Service Research, 34*(1), 27–42. https://doi.org/10.1300/J079v34n01_03

Lahat, L., & Talit, G. (2015). Regulation of personal social services: The Israeli experience. *Social Policy Administration, 49*(3), 335–355. https://doi.org/10.1111/spol.12076

Leece, J., & Peace, S. (2010). Developing new understandings of independence and autonomy in the personalised relationship. *British Journal of Social Work, 40*(6), 1847–1865. https://doi.org/10.1093/bjsw/bcp105

Lef, Y., & Rivkin, D. (2015). *People with developmental and intellectual disabilities who are under the Ministry of Welfare: Survey in Haifa and the northern district.* Jerusalem, Israel: Myers-JDC-Brookdale Institute. Retrieved from https://brookdale.jdc.org.il/wp-content/uploads/2018/01/693-15_Hebrew-report.pdf [Hebrew].

Legal Capacity and Guardianship Law, 1962.

Lerner, N. (2008). *Land of limited opportunities: The right of people with intellectual disabilities to live in the community.* Jerusalem, Israel: Bizchut. Retrieved from http://bizchut.org.il/he/wp-content/uploads/2011/07/thelandofthelimitedop.pdf [Hebrew].

Lev, S., & Ayalon, L. (2015). Running between the raindrops: The obligation dilemma of the social worker in the nursing home. *Health & Social Work, 40*(1), 10–18. https://doi.org/10.1093/hsw/hlu036

Levi-Faur, D., Gidron, N., & Moshell, S. (2015). The regulatory deficit of the privatization era. In I. Galnoor, A. Paz-Fuchs, & N. Zion (Eds.), *Privatization policy in Israel: State responsibility and the boundaries between the public 26 and the private sector* (pp. 439–479). Jerusalem, Israel: The van Leer Institute. [Hebrew].

Lotan, G., & Ells, C. (2010). Adults with intellectual and developmental disabilities and participation in decision making: Ethical considerations for professional–client practice. *Intellectual and Developmental Disabilities, 48*(2), 112–125. https://doi.org/10.1352/1934-9556-48.2.112

Madhala-Brik, S., & Gal, J. (2016). Outsourcing welfare services: Trends and changes. In A. Weiss (Ed.), *The state of affairs in Israel report: Society, economy and policy* (pp. 353–387). Jerusalem, Israel: Taub Center. [Hebrew].

Magor, Z., Sandler-Lef, A., Stern, E., & Tolub, Y. (2017). *Person-centered service for people with disabilities: A summary of a year of learning and international conferences. February and September 2016.* Jerusalem, Israel: JDC-Eshel. Retrieved from https://www.dmag.co.il/pub/jdc/ServiceOrientedPerson/files/assets/common/downloads/publication.pdf [Hebrew].

Mansell, J., & Beadle-Brown, J. (2010). Deinstitutionalisation and community living: Position statement of the comparative policy and practice special interest research group of the international association for the scientific study of intellectual disabilities. *Journal of Intellectual Disability Research, 54*(2), 104–112. https://doi.org/10.1111/j.1365-2788.2009.01239.x

Mansell, J., Knapp, M., Beadle-Brown, J., & Beecham, J. (2007). *Deinstitutionalisation and community living – Out-comes and costs: Report of a European Study. Volume 2: Main Report.* Canterbury, UK: Tizard Centre, University of Kent.

Ministry of Labor, Social Affairs and Social Services [MOLSA]. (n.d.-a). *Guardianship: The procedure of appointment.* Retrieved from http://www.molsa.gov.il/Populations/Disabilities/MentalRetardation/IntellectualDisabilities/Guardianship/Pages/GuardianshipOver18.aspx [Hebrew].

Ministry of Labor, Social Affairs and Social Services [MOLSA]. (n.d.-b). *Housing in a maon – Boarding school.* Retrieved from http://www.molsa.gov.il/Populations/Disabilities/MentalRetardation/Housing/Pages/Boarding.aspx [Hebrew].

Nasser, K., Sachs, D., & Sa'ar, A. (2017). A necessary evil: Residential placement of people with intellectual disability among the Palestinian minority in Israel. *Research in Developmental Disabilities, 60*, 115–124. https://doi.org/10.1016/j.ridd.2016.11.018

Nedelsky, J. (1989). Reconceiving autonomy: Sources, thoughts and possibilities. *Yale Journal of Law & Feminism, 1*(1), 7–36. Retrieved from http://digitalcommons.law.yale.edu/yjlf/vol1/iss1/5

Proposed Amendment for the Equal Rights Law (Community Housing and Personal Budget), 2016.

Rabiee, P., & Glendinning, G. C. (2010). Choice: What, when and why? Exploring the importance of choice to disabled people. *Disability & Society, 25*(7), 827–839. https://doi.org/10.1080/09687599.2010.520896

Rimmerman, A. (2017). *Disability and community living policies.* Cambridge, UK: Cambridge University Press.

Rimon-Greenspan, H. (2014). *Mechanisms for the protection of people with disabilities in housing and institutions.* Jerusalem, Israel: Bizchut. [Hebrew].

Schwartz, C. (2003). Self-appraised lifestyle satisfaction of persons with intellectual disability: The impact of personal characteristics and community residential facilities. *Journal of Intellectual and Developmental Disability, 28*(3), 227–240. https://doi.org/10.1080/13668250310001150991

Series, L. (2015). Relationships, autonomy and legal capacity: Mental capacity and support paradigms. *International Journal of Law and Psychiatry, 40*, 80–91. https://doi.org/10.1016/j.ijlp.2015.04.010

Shalom, G., Ben-Simchon, M., & Goren, H. (2015). Chapter 6, Part A: People with intellectual and developmental disabilities. In Y. Tzeva (Ed.), *Review of social services 2014* (pp. 545–585). Jerusalem, Israel: Ministry of Labor, Social Affairs and Social Services. [Hebrew].

Shalom, G., Ben-Simchon, M., & Goren, H. (2017). Chapter 6, Part A: People with intellectual and developmental disabilities. In Y. Tzeva (Ed.), *Review of social services 2016* (pp. 377–404). Jerusalem, Israel: Ministry of Labor, Social Affairs and Social Services. [Hebrew].

Shogren, K. A., Wehmeyer, M. L., Lassmann, H., & Forber-Pratt, A. (2017). Supported decision making: A synthesis of the literature across intellectual disability, mental health, and aging. *Education and Training in Autism and Developmental Disabilities, 52*(2), 144–157. Retrieved from https://search.proquest.com/docview/1900043396?accountid=14546

Shogren, K. A., Wehmeyer, M. L., Uyanik, H., & Heidrich, M. (2017). Development of supported decision making inventory system. *Journal of Intellectual and Developmental Disability, 55*(6), 432–439. https://doi.org/10.1352/1934-9556-55.6.432

Soffer, M., Koreh, M., & Rimmerman, A. (2017). Politics of geographic exclusion: Deinstitutionalization, hegemony and persons with intellectual disability in Israel. *Disability & Society, 32*(8), 1180–1198. https://doi.org/10.1080/09687599.2017.1344825

Stainton, T. (2002). Taking rights structurally: Disability, rights and social worker responses to direct payments. *British Journal of Social Work, 32*(6), 751–763. https://doi.org/10.1093/bjsw/32.6.751

Stancliffe, R. J. (2001). Living with support in the community: Predictors of choice and self-determination. *Mental Retardation and Developmental Disabilities Research Reviews, 7*(2), 91–98. https://doi.org/10.1002/mrdd.1013

Stancliffe, R. J., Lakin, K. C., Larson, S., Engler, J., Taub, S., & Fortune, J. (2011). Choice of living arrangements. *Journal of Intellectual Disability Research, 55*(8), 746–762. https://doi.org/10.1111/j.1365-2788.2010.01336.x

State Comptroller. (2012). Supervision of guardians. In *Annual Report 62* (pp. 813–851). Jerusalem, Israel: Ministry of Justice. [Hebrew].

Supervision of Institutional Residences Law, 1965.

Tolub, Y., & Shlomai, O. (in press). 'Not in therapy': The shift from therapy-centered language to a language of autonomy and human rights in the appointment procedure of a guardian for a person; following the enactment of the Legal Capacity and Guardianship Law (Amendment number 18), 2016. *Bar-Ilan Law Studies.*

UN General Assembly, *Convention on the Rights of Persons with Disabilities and Optional Protocol*, U.N Doc. A/RES/61/106 (2006, December 13). Available from: http://www.un.org/disabilities/documents/convention/convoptprot-e.pdf

Wehmeyer, M. L., & Abery, B. H. (2013). Self-determination and choice. *Intellectual and Developmental Disabilities, 51*(5), 399–411. https://doi.org/10.1352/1934-9556-51.5.399

Williams, V., Boyle, G., Jepson, M., Swift, P., Williamson, T., & Heslop, P. (2012). *Making best interests decisions: People and processes*. London, UK: Mental Health Foundation.

Yogev, O., Yogev, T., & Man, Y. (2012). The Standards Testing Committee for the location of residential housing in the community. Ministry of Social Affairs: Israel. Retrieved from: https://www.molsa.gov.il/Focus/Documents/%D7%93%D7%95%D7%97%20%D7%95%D7%A2%D7%93%D7%AA%20%D7%94%D7%91%D7%93%D7%99%D7%A7%D7%94.pdf. [Hebrew]

Zakash, D., & Gilad, N. (2010). *Direct caregivers' perceptions of the quality of work environment and the task of feeding in nursing institutions for people with cognitive disabilities*. Haifa, Israel: Haifa University. Retrieved from http://www.kshalem.org.il/uploads/pdf/article_6183_1381859210.pdf [Hebrew].

Choices, Preferences, and Disability: A View from Central and Eastern Europe

Renáta Tichá, Olha Telna, Jan Šiška, Dušan Klapko, and Laurie Kincade

Introduction

This chapter will highlight the influences of macrosystem factors (society, governments, systems) on the evolution of empowerment and choice making of people with disabilities in Eastern societies, with specific examples from the Czech Republic and Ukraine. A comparison will be made to Western historical understandings of self-determination. A case will be made for the role of social capital, communication, advocacy, and self-advocacy in the development of self-determination and the importance of using such tools to balance power at the macrosystem level. Specifically it will be argued that social capital, effective communication, advocacy, and self-advocacy have the potential to increase self-determination, including meaningful and effective choice making and preference expression, for people in general and those with disabilities in particular in any society (macrosystem). By doing so, people with disabilities can become equal members of society and experience lives of freedom, rights, and dignity as already afforded to them on paper by existing international and national laws and policies.

R. Tichá (✉) · L. Kincade
University of Minnesota, Minneapolis, MN, USA
e-mail: tich0018@umn.edu

O. Telna
Kharkiv Academy for Humanitarian and Pedagogical Studies, Kharkiv, Ukraine

J. Šiška
Charles University, Prague, Czech Republic

D. Klapko
Masaryk University, Brno, Czech Republic

© Springer Nature Switzerland AG 2020
R. J. Stancliffe et al. (eds.), *Choice, Preference, and Disability*, Positive
Psychology and Disability Series, https://doi.org/10.1007/978-3-030-35683-5_6

East and West

Based on different historical and developmental trajectories, Western and Eastern societies have viewed individuals as having more or less free will to express their preferences and make their own choices in life. This divide that is influenced by modernization and economic development is often referred to as the Global North and Global South, with an additional recent reference to the Global East (Müller, 2018). Western societies have placed significant value on the power and freedom of the individual, often attributed to placing emphasis on free will, self-determination, and sense of responsibility (Lynn-Jones, 1998; Allik & Realo, 2004; Hao, 2015). Western societies have tended to constrain the power of their governments in people's lives (Lynn-Jones, 1998). From the perspective of social theory, coming from the work of Max Weber, Western societies have been built on shared norms and values and an approach to governance based on consensus among individuals, while Eastern societies for many years adopted ideas of Karl Marx on the dominance of certain social groups and the inevitable conflict as an agent of rapid social change (Melichar, 2016). Eastern societies have tended to emphasize the power of governments and ideological convictions for large numbers of people or collectivism (Kemmelmeier, Burnstein, Krumov, & Genkova, 2003; Allik & Realo, 2004).

Allik and Realo (2004) posit that an increase in individualism, independence, heightened respect for human rights, and mutual trust are related to modernization and more prosperous societies. According to Leake (2012), self-determination in the traditional sense is largely an outcome of Western, more prosperous societies. Having choice and control are among the critical aspects of the Western concept of self-determination (Wehmeyer, 2004; Wemeyer & Abery, 2013).

In Western societies, families of people with disabilities and people with disabilities themselves have been able to exercise choice making, which led to the initiation of civil rights movements rooted in the belief that each individual has their own "unalienable rights" (Fleischer & Zames, 2001; Shapiro, 1993) as granted by the US constitution. In Eastern societies, individual rights have not been emphasized and exercised with such spirit of advocacy until quite recently with the initiation and adoption of the United Nations Convention on the Rights of Persons with Disabilities (UN CRPD, 2006) and local legislations and policies that emphasize the right of people with disabilities to education and inclusion. As a result, it has not been until recently that families and people with disabilities in Eastern countries have begun to express their preferences and make choices about their lives, including in education, employment, and other areas, to assume the position of equal members of society.

Post-Soviet countries, located largely in Eastern but also in Central Europe, share several socio-political characteristics, including stigma, social isolation and low public awareness of people with disabilities, lack of reliable data on people with disabilities, and continued placement of people with disabilities in institutions due to the lack of services available in the community (Gevorgianiene & Sumskiene, 2017). Despite the signing and ratification of the CRPD and developing their own legislation, changes at the governmental level have not reached people with disabilities and their families. The authors argue that the slow change to supporting the rights of people with disabilities is due to the long-lasting legacy of post-Soviet values and influence that left people with disabilities and their families largely excluded from society.

Leotti, Iyengar, and Ochsner (2010) argue that making choices during one's day and across the life span provides people with a sense of control over the environment. Through the choices we make, we express our preferences, which in turn reinforces our perception of control and self-efficacy. If we lose this ability to make choices, we are also likely to lose our sense of control over our lives. Having choices and thus feeling in control in our environment has been shown to have a positive impact on the lives of people with and without disabilities (Leotti et al., 2010; Tichá et al., 2012). Research has demonstrated that when choice is taken away from both children and adults, it negatively affects their emotional, cognitive, and behavioral responses and may lead them to having external locus of control and learned helplessness (Leotti et al., 2010). According to the social learning psychologist Julian Rotter, locus of control refers to the manner with which we attribute having control to either our personal (internal) or other environmental (external) factors. Learned helplessness is a psychological concept that dates back to the 1970s and Martin Seligman. Learned helplessness is a state that results from situation uncontrollability and can lead to negative emotional, cognitive, and motivational outcomes (Mohanty, Pradhan, & Jena, 2015). One can argue that as a result of the historical developments of societies and the impact on their citizens, people in Eastern societies have likely developed an external locus of control that has over time led to learned helplessness in many. In fact, research does support this argument. Testé (2017) highlighted the influence of cultural norms on the expression of beliefs of control, citing cross-cultural studies that found that people in more collectivistic Eastern societies were more likely to have an external locus of control than members of more individualistic Western societies. Testé (2017) expanded on this research to demonstrate that people in societies with more external locus of control (Eastern societies) tend to dehumanize others (see them as less human) than societies with internal locus of control.

Models of Human Development and Disability

People with and without disabilities live their lives within the context of their societies, communities, families, and friends. Moving away from the *medical model* of disability, the development of a person with or without disability has in progressive societies been more recently conceptualized as an interaction between the individual and their social context and broader environment. In the medical model, the capacities and opportunities of an individual were defined and determined by their disability or medical condition. In fact, defectology, a deficit-focused approach to people with disabilities, originated in Russia under the guidance of the Russian psychologist Lev Vygotsky who lived on brink of the nineteenth and twentieth centuries. In 1925, Vygotsky played a key role in establishing a lab in Moscow for the study of abnormal child development that became the Institute of Defectology in 1929 (Grigorenko, 1998). Defect and defectology are terms still used today in less developed parts of Russia and other Eastern European countries. The medical model has been detrimental to many people with disabilities both in Western and still up to now in Eastern societies by placing children and adults in institutions, away from their family members and others, without a provision of appropriate supports to live as part of a society.

In a *social model*, the quality of life of a person with a disability is conceptualized as an interdependence between an individual and the way family, friends, community, and society respond to the person's needs and dreams. This model is built on the perspective that the extent to which a person with a disability feels included and welcomed depends on the attitudes and perceptions of those around them. If a child with a disability is born in an educated and affluent family and a community and society that believe that every human being should be afforded the right to live their lives to the fullest potential, his or her life will most likely be different from a child born into circumstances that do not afford such opportunities. Opportunities for development are closely related not only to the resources available within the society, community, and family but also to the values that society places on a single individual and their human and civil rights (Bricout, Porterfield, Fisher, & Howard, 2004). Practically, if a child is valued for their strengths and talents and is afforded the needed supports and services, she or he would ultimately be able to make similar choices as a child without a disability.

The *transactional model* of development and disability emphasizes the interaction between the individual and the resources and values in societies. For example, it tackles the questions of how does the education setting of the child affect their opportunity for employment and how does the social service system prepare parents and their child for the transition from school to adult life in the community (Bricout et al., 2004)? These questions will be answered based on the approach to self-determination in each society as described in the above paragraphs. Because of the difference in the values Western and Eastern societies place on an individual's contributions to society's success and progress, there are different resources dedicated to services and supports for children, youth, and adults with disabilities. In the transactional model, the availability and quality of societal resources and type of values affect the development of an individual with a disability and their ability to contribute to society and quality life. Resources include opportunities for different types of medical care, social interactions and relationships, educational approaches, and employment opportunities.

Bronfenbrenner (1994) in his ecological model ties the different models of development into one system. Bronfenbrenner's ecological theory is a framework that can be used to conceptualize how individual development is influenced by multiple interconnected environmental systems (Bronfenbrenner, 1994). Bronfenbrenner highlighted the importance of studying individual development through analyzing the environments in which people are embedded and the interactions between people and their environments. Described by Bronfenbrenner (1977), the following systems in which individuals are embedded include:

1. Microsystem: the interaction between the person and immediate settings within which they are embedded (e.g., family, school, etc.);
2. Mesosystem: the interaction between two microsystems (e.g., home-school collaboration);
3. Exosystem: the interaction between the developing person and another setting that does not contain the individual (e.g., how the work environment of a parent influences their child); and
4. Macrosystem: refers to the cultural environment of the individual, including economic, social, education, legal, political, and historical systems in which the individual is embedded. The macrosystem can include explicitly defined laws, regulations, and rules; however, typically, the cultural environment also includes a variety of unwritten, informal customs, values, attitudes, beliefs, and norms. These societal attitudes and beliefs toward a group of people significantly impact other systems (e.g., schools, home-life) and the daily interactions people have within those environments. For example, if a society believes parents should hold the burden of raising their child with a disability, the government will likely not provide the necessary resources to support that family.

To reflect on the models of disability described above, one can see that the medical model focuses on the individual as a carrier of disability or a defect with limited consideration of aspects of the environment or the connections within it. The social model focuses on the different microsystems in a person's life, including family, friends, teachers, etc. The transactional model examines the relationships between different microsystems (mesosystem) and how these affect the individual. Bronfenbrenner's ecological model adds the macrosystem, thus taking into account societal and cultural laws, regulations, rules, as well as attitudes, values, and norms. Although all aspects of the ecological model are viewed as important, the focus of this chapter is on how macrosystems impact choices and preferences of individuals with disabilities in Eastern and Western societies.

Advocacy and Self-advocacy

There is another model of disability that is closely connected with the concept of self-determination and builds on the social and transactional models, the human rights model of disability. This model coincides with the adoption of the CRPD in 2006. According to Degener (2014, 2016), CRPD is the first universal human rights tool that states that people with disabilities are entitled to their rights regardless of their type and level of disability. In this model of disability, every person, regardless of their ability or disability, is afforded human dignity and equality as opposed to charity. This approach views disability not as an inherent condition, but rather as a social construct created when a person's disability interacts with environmental barriers. The human rights model provides people with disabilities and their advocates legal support in challenging discrimination based on disability. Strnadova and Evans (2015), in their article on autonomy of older women with intellectual disability (ID), point out that one of the leading principles of the CRPD is "respect for inherent dignity, individual autonomy including the freedom to make one's own choices, and independence of persons" (Article 3).

One could argue that the human rights model transcends the other models of disability in that it goes beyond describing the situation in an individual with a disability is operating by placing the power, responsibility, and locus of control back on the person and calls on the systems within which the individual lives and interacts to act in accordance to the international law.

Social Capital

The social and transactional models of disability are closely connected to the concept of social capital, which can be understood as the extent to which an individual is connected to others (e.g., friends, colleagues, etc.) and the degree which relationships are reciprocal and based on mutual trust (Allik & Realo, 2004). The definition of social capital very much resembles Bronfenbrenner's micro- and mesosystems.

Even though not a new idea, in recent years, the concept of social capital has been highlighted as a potential powerful strategy to better the lives of people, including those with disabilities. Condeluci, Ledbetter, Ortman, Fromknecht, and DeGries (2008) make a direct connection between social capital and the ecological model. Condeluci et al. (2008) argue that social capital has an impact on the micro (family, friends), meso (community or organization), and/or macro (city, state, or nation) levels. According to Condeluci, there are three types of resources that constitute social capital: instrumental (e.g., help with taking care of a pet), emotional (e.g., talking about a problem with a friend), and informational (e.g., information about job openings). Access to social capital has been linked to many benefits, including improved health, behavioral, educational, and vocational outcomes (Condeluci et al., 2008). Thus, he proposes that without changing the culture in such a way that people with disabilities become an integral part of diverse social networks, there will not be significant improvement in their lives.

Walker et al. (2011) differentiated between two types of social capital: bonding and bridging. Bonding social capital refers to relationships with others who have similar psychosocial characteristics and interests and engage in similar activities. Bridging social capital, in contrast, is based on relationships with people who have different characteristics, skills, perspectives, and involvement in other activities in order to achieve an apparently unattainable goal or result. Bridging can also occur at an organizational level when two or more organizations collaborate to be more effective. Walker et al. (2011) argue that a lack of social capital for people with disabilities has led to different barriers to full societal inclusion. Social capital can have a direct impact on one's ability to access and participate in inclusive environments by utilizing their opportunities and choices. Individuals with social capital have the resources, capacity, and supports to achieve greater inclusion and a better quality of life by experiencing a more emotionally satisfying lifestyle, exercising more diverse choices, and having greater autonomy in decision making, i.e., greater self-determination.

Research has shown that there is a positive relationship between more individualistic societies (mostly Western or the global North, including the many states of the USA as well as Canada, Sweden, the Netherlands, Denmark, etc.) and higher social capital compared to more collectivistic cultures (mostly to the East or the global South, including Slovenia, Romania, or Argentina). In addition, countries with higher social capital tend to view independence, personal time, personal accomplishments, and freedom to choose one's own goals as important (Allik & Realo, 2004). Social capital is important for people in achieving their goals (e.g., getting a job). About half of us get a job as a result of personal communication, recommendation, or mentoring. Social capital is critical for people with disabilities. Successful transition programs typically place greater emphasis on relationship building and connections between the person and school with the community in addition to vocational training (Leake, 2012).

The importance of social capital has been highlighted in social-ecological models of self-determination (Walker et al., 2011; Abery & Stancliffe, 2003) in the form of formal (teachers and specialists) and informal social supports – microsystems (friends and family), the relationship between the individuals and these social groups. For example, Strnadova and Evans (2015) in their study on autonomy of older women with ID in the Czech Republic and Australia identified environmental factors in the form of limited social networks and limiting behavior of significant others (e.g., parents) in the lives of older people with ID as important environmental factors related to autonomy. Available social capital was related to the living situation of the women. When the women in the study moved away from institutions or from their parents to more independent settings, they experienced greater autonomy and happiness.

Self-determination

Even though self-determination had been defined in the West by well-known theorists and researchers in special education and disability from the perspective of an individual who is the one in control and empowered, having free will or agency (Wehmeyer, 2004) over those things in life that matter to them (Abery & Stancliffe, 2003; Wehmeyer & Abery, 2013), there have emerged definitions connected more closely to the collectivist paradigm. Leake (2012) notices that even in Western societies when people talk about their experiences of making their choices and achieving their goals, they typically acknowledge others who helped them along the way. They also often talk about these relationships as being reciprocal. These social factors or social capital however tends to stay in the background as contextual information, rather than being the focus of the self-determined actions. The above-cited theorists and researchers in self-determination in the USA do mention the importance of interdependence and shared decision making, especially for people with more significant disabilities. Abery and Stancliffe (2003) in their social-ecological model of self-determination get the closest to positing that social capital is essential for all of us to be as self-determined as possible. They do so by focusing on the importance of the environment in their model of self-determination through the lens of ecological theory (Bronfenbrenner, 1994). In their model of self-determination, Abery and Stancliffe (2003) view different microsystems (peers, family, friends, school, services), mesosystems (the way microsystems are interconnected), and the exosystem (an outer layer that may affect the individual indirectly, e.g., parents' work situation) as essential for a person to be truly self-determined. Wehmeyer and Abery (2013) specifically emphasize the need for studying self-determination within the context of relationships. In addition, unlike many other models of self-determination, they also take into account the macrosystem in the form of societal institutions, laws, rules, expectations, attitudes, and values.

Abery (2013) extended the notion of social capital as a key factor in self-determination and quality of life of people with disabilities, discussing the importance of a linguistic relationship to a community of language speakers. Abery (2013) references Abery and Stancliffe's ecological model of self-determination and concludes that a linguistic relationship provides a connection between the individual and his or her macrosystem or shared culture. Without sharing a common set of normative linguistic or communication practices and therefore common culture and without establishing a link between those practices and the linguistic understanding and expression, self-determination does not exist. Abery (2013) emphasizes that linguistic communication and relationships make us human, form our histories, and connect us with our macrosystems.

The Impact of Macrosystems on Self-determination

The impact of macrosystems on self-determination, including choice making, for people with disabilities has not been thoroughly studied thus far. Macrosystems that represent larger systemic governmental, historic, and cultural structures have often been interpreted in terms of the values that are assigned to individuals and groups within a society. In the context of this chapter, macrosystems in Western and Eastern countries have assigned different values or powers to individuals vs. groups of individuals, and certain groups of individuals have been traditionally marginalized. It is the basic tenet of social dominance theory (Sidanius et al., 2004) that societies create group-based hierarchies that have led to different types of group-based oppressions. According to social dominance theory, group-based oppression is a result of both institutional and individual discrimination and the interaction between them. In the context of macrosystems, the focus here is on the influence of social institutions (e.g., schools, organized religions, governments), often led by powerful individuals, on unequal allocation of resources (e.g., wealth, power, education, or health care), to those who belong to dominant and privileged groups, while leaving less desirable activities and outcomes (e.g., dangerous and underpaid work, lack of or low-quality education and health care) to less powerful groups. Social dominance theory considers institutional discrimination as one of the key factors in creating and sustaining systems of group-based hierarchy, thus creating an imbalance of power. In the context of the post-Soviet legacy, group-based hierarchies with maximum power at the top can be easily viewed as manifestations of the macrosystem's influence on marginalized groups, including people with disabilities.

Young (2012) discusses the oppression of certain groups within macrosystems. She refers to groups of individuals who share similar experiences in relation to macrosystems (e.g., women, Roma, people with disabilities, etc.) as "structural social groups." In her view, people behave according to the relationship of the group with which they identify to their macrosystems. She believes that an equalizing factor between those in power or in charge of macrosystem operations and groups of individuals who experience marginalization (including people with disabilities) is participatory decision making based on reciprocal communication and mutual understanding as well as local autonomy. These interactions need to transcend the individual and happen at the level of the structural social groups in order to lead to equal relationships.

Leake and Skouge (2012) in their preamble to the special issue on self-determination as a social construct highlight the importance of culture and cultural values in defining self-determination. This perspective has been supported by multiple researchers, including Frankland, Turnbull, Wehmeyer, and Blackmountain (2004) when studying self-determination in the Navajo culture, Lee and Wehmeyer (2004) in their work on self-determination in the Korean education context, and Gevorgianiene and Sumskiene (2017) in their investigation of the rights of persons with intellectual disabilities in post-Soviet countries. Shogren (2011) in her review of 10 articles on self-determination and culture concluded that culture is an important factor in the way people view and practice self-determination. She also concluded that cultural identity is a multifaceted construct that interacts with the value systems of family and child. She recommended that self-determination goals are shaped based on the child and family's values and culture.

The Czech Republic and Ukraine

The Czech Republic and Ukraine are presented here not only from first-account perspectives of the authors but also as a representation of two countries of different geographical locations, histories, and cultures that have a post-Soviet legacy. The Czech Republic is a relatively small country in Central Europe that has been a Soviet satellite communist country until 1989. It now has a democratically elected government, is considered a developed country, is part of the European Union, and has flourished economically. It is a peaceful country with a very high percentage of people who are atheists. Ukraine is the largest European country located in Eastern Europe. It was part of the Soviet Union until its independence in 1991. Even though Ukraine has made a lot of progress since that time and now has a democratically elected government, it is still considered a developing country largely due to its slow economic development and an ongoing political and military dispute with Russia. The majority of people in Ukraine consider themselves Christian. Both countries are of Slavic heritage and have over the centuries experienced high and low points in their sovereignty. Both have been occupied not only by the Soviet Union but throughout history by other countries in their regions as well.

The Czech Context for Choice Making and Preferences for People with Disabilities Article 19 of UNCRPD gives people with disabilities the right to a home in the community like everyone else, choice over their living situation, and support for full inclusion and participation in the community. The Czech Republic ratified the CRPD in 2009. Article 19 breaks down the right to live and be included and participate in the community on an equal basis with others into three elements. Each is equally applicable to all persons with disabilities, irrespective of the type or severity of their impairment: choice, support, and availability of community services and facilities (Council of Europe Commissioner for Human Rights, 2012).

In this chapter, we analyze these elements from a macrosystem perspective. We argue that the macrosystem influences choices people with disabilities make on a daily basis as well as over the life course. We assert that there is a relationship between state ideologies in countries of the former communist bloc and systematic institutionalization that restricts options for community-based services and choice and limits empowerment of persons with disabilities living during the so-called socialist regime and the first two decades after the regime change in 1989.

After the Second World War, Czechoslovakia (Czechoslovakia split into the Czech Republic and Slovakia in 1993) became part of the so-called Eastern Bloc. Education and care for people with disabilities were built upon the Russian concept of defectology. Social policy was centralized and bureaucratized. Welfare work could only take place under the strict control of the central government. The legislation on social welfare only consisted of one type of service, so-called institutional care for persons with disabilities, which was further divided into institutional care disaggregated by disability type, sex, and age. As a result, persons with disabilities and particularly those with intellectual disability were placed in a highly segregated network of institutional care facilities. The residents were positioned into a role of passive recipients of static long-term care. Regime in institutions was further reinforced by fixed daily routines ignoring individual needs and preferences of residents. The state did not offer to families any alternative other than placing a family member with disability into institutional care (Čámský, Sembdner, & Krutilová, 2011). In addition, residential care facilities were situated in rural localities with fewer local inhabitants, far from residents' family members and friends. Residents were considered as objects of the system, not as active agents, whose wishes and needs must be addressed when planning of support and delivery.

Finally, people who had limitations in promoting their legitimate interests were not adequately protected from being harmed by others, whether by misconduct of public authorities or by inadequate provision of social services (The Chamber of Deputies, Czech Republic, 2005).

The political and economic changes that happened in the country after the collapse of the communist regime in 1989 also affected public policy. Despite the fact that institutional care as a model was systematically challenged by parent organizations, NGOs, and international agencies based on human rights principles, this model continued. Desirable changes toward empowerment of service users and community-based services were often questioned by management of "traditional" institutions, which frequently linked quality of services to physical environment and equipment rather than to factors, such as support in decision making and/or application of person-centered planning (Čámský et al., 2011).

Even though statistics on people with ID in the Czech Republic are of limited accuracy and are not collected across all relevant sectors, the 1998 National Plan reported a total of 1.2 million persons with disability (11% of the population). According to the Czech Statistical Office in 2008, there were 106,699 or 1% of people with ID in the country (Šiška & Beadle-Brown, 2011). Based on the limited national and international data estimates, the majority of persons with ID in the Czech Republic remain institutionalized (Vann & Šiška, 2006).

Adoption of the new legislative framework based on the CRPD in social services was slow compared to the relatively fast transformation in financial and business sectors. The Social Services Act came into force only in 2006 (Šiška & Beadle-Brown, 2011). The act gave new rights to service users who now are legally empowered to make decisions about the kind of care, extensions to it, or the place of delivery. The new legislation aimed at diverting social services from "provision focused" to "person centered" based on the rights of service users, such as the right to self-determination and the right to make decisions on where to live. Some positive progress was demonstrated, for example, a decrease in the number of persons with disabilities living in large residential institutions. Similarly, data show that the number of those who use community-based services for such personal assistance rose from 1422 in 2007 to 7182 in 2013, which is a fivefold increase (FRA, 2017).

Nevertheless, some discrepancies between predicted expectations (policy) and reality (practice) can be observed. In particular, opportunity to exercise one's right to make a decision on one's place of living and on who provides support is far from reality for many. Life trajectories of persons with disabilities are often guided by what is available, rather than by what an individual prefers. In addition, negative attitudes, low awareness, and low expectations were seen as key barriers faced by persons with disabilities as well as the availability and flexibility of support services (Šiška, Beadle-Brown, Káňová, & Šumníková, 2018). Limited community-based services particularly in more rural locations created additional demands that increased placement in institutional care facilities (Šiška, 2010). Central government admits that the higher demand of people with disabilities and their families for placement in traditional institutions does not indicate a better quality of services provided in institutions. Such demand is primarily caused by the lack of community-based services (Ministry of Labour and Social Affairs, 2006).

Deinstitutionalization remains far from satisfactory (Ministry of Labour and Social Affairs, 2015). Social exclusion of persons with disabilities was further addressed by the Constitutional Court in 2018, when the court confirmed the right to accessible and appropriate social care services. The right to a dignified and independent life without social exclusion is a general social right of citizens, and the regional governments are obliged to ensure this right for people with disabilities (Constitutional Court Findings, file no. I. ÚS 2637/17). This case law on right of persons with disabilities to community living is a significant accomplishment which might have a potential to become an agent of change of deinstitutionalization processes.

The key reasons for gaps in deinstitutionalization can be classified into several areas, including political will and political reluctance. Both are influenced by the political climate. The political climate has changed significantly during the last two decades in the Czech Republic, with unstable political will and support for deinstitutionalization. Another critical barrier is the financial cost of shifting toward community-based services, which discourage those who have political power and who are responsible for social services to support this process. As regional governments are founders of social care facilities, they are often reticent to change (Rabová, 2018).

In principle, service users and their families have a choice over where to live, but there remain significant limitations. Political reluctance is one of the significant barriers to progress toward translating policy into practice. As a result, people with disabilities have limited opportunities to make choices related to where they live and who provides their supports. Deinstitutionalization and the movement toward choice making and preferences in community settings for people with disabilities must therefore gain momentum at both the governmental and ground levels to assure alignment with Article 19 of the CRPD.

The Ukrainian Context for Choice Making and Preferences for People with Disabilities According to official statistics, in Ukraine, about 2.8 million persons (6.1% of the total population) are reported to have a disability (Ukrinform, 2016). However, this number does not include the 1.5% of people with temporary disabilities and 30 to 50 percent of elderly people whose disability emerged due to aging (Ukrayinska Pravda, 2014). Also, in Ukraine, conditions such as dyslexia and attention deficit hyperactivity disorder (ADHD) are not considered to be disabilities, which adds approximately 30 percent or 151 thousand of children with disabilities (Ukrinform, 2016). Parents often choose not to disclose their child's disability by not registering with the local medical and/or social services in an attempt to avoid stigma and prejudice that are still common in the Ukrainian society, which also does not help getting accurate statistics.

The National Statistics Bureau of Ukraine in its annual reports does not effectively document the access of people with disabilities to community living, inclusive education, labor market, or economic activity. However, the report provides evidence for Ukrainians with disabilities living with their "healthy" relatives, as it is more socially accepted and less expensive for the system than providing the necessary support to ensure social and economic inclusion of individuals with disabilities who live independently. That said, according to Gevorgianiene and Sumskiene (2017), in 2012, there were still 151 institutions with 30,000 residents in Ukraine. Children and adults with more severe disabilities tend to be the ones who live in institutions and tend not to have access to education or the community. Independent living is more common among young people with disabilities who prefer to study, live, and/or work in big cities as there are fewer supports in rural areas (CRPD Concluding observation Ukraine, 2015). This is due to the architectural and financial inaccessibility of 99% of buildings in Ukraine (excluding schools and hospitals, most of which are partly accessible, e.g., have street ramps and wide front doors) as well as due to the negative attitudes toward people with disabilities and their desire to be independent (Ukrainian Helsinki Human Rights Union, 2015). For example, young persons who are blind or utilize a wheelchair often face discrimination when trying to rent an apartment. Common reasons for refusals include the ideas that the presence of a disability may cause property damage or lead to physical trauma of the tenants with disabilities (Senishyn, 2016).

In the field of education and employment, the situation is somewhat different; more people with disabilities can access local schools (but not universities) and get involved in paid work. Research has indicated that Ukraine has a wide network of community-based services and very active NGOs, many times led by parents of children with disabilities (Gevorgianiene & Sumskiene (2017). According to the Ministry of Education and Science of Ukraine, during the past 3 years, the number of special educational settings and boarding schools for disabled children decreased by 5.1% (Ministerstvo Osvity i Nauky Ukrayiny, 2018). But that hardly means that all students with disabilities who had attended those educational settings now go to the local schools because in the same 3 years there was a 22.4% increase in number of local rehabilitation centers for children with severe developmental disabilities (Ministerstvo Osvity i Nauky Ukrayiny, 2018). The Ministry of Education also reports that a law on inclusive education passed in 2017 has been highly effective, stating that the number of students with disabilities attending "inclusive schools" has grown by 53.6% (1460 persons) compared to 2015 (Ministerstvo Osvity i Nauky Ukrayiny, 2018). These figures show how preferable inclusive or special education is for parents of children with disabilities, but children with disabilities are rarely involved in decision making about their educational placements (Ukrainian Helsinki Human Rights Union, 2015).

The employment rates for persons with disabilities are also increasing. Almost 35.8% of the Ukrainians with disabilities aged 16 to 60 are reported to be employed with the exception of people with more extensive support needs who are less likely to be employed, with only 13% reporting employment (Sylantyeva, 2018). Moreover, Ukrainian enterprises tend to involve people with disabilities mainly into "employment on paper" when the person is reported to be working but instead receives a small amount of money as a compensation for their name being used. In doing so, these employers can avoid paying the "disability unemployment tax" to the state (CRPD Concluding Observation Ukraine, 2015).

As a former Soviet Union state, Ukraine has inherited the totalitarian approach to policy making regarding people with disabilities. In the Soviet Union, where the vast majority of citizens used to live on the edge of poverty (Phillips, 2002), the systems of special medical treatment, special education, and special access to goods and services have been provided for all medically certified people with disabilities. However, access to special facilities was limited depending on the disability category. In the Soviet Union, some people with disabilities received more supports than people from other social groups, thus sometimes appearing to have certain advantages and privileges. At the same time, the communist regime provided the strictest policy of institutionalization, which meant no preferences or choices were provided to people with disabilities about their supports and services. No person with a physical and/or mental disability had an access to either inclusive education or employment. The government subsidized a wide range of "special" institutions where most people with disabilities were kept from birth till death (McCagg & Siegelbaum, 1989). Furthermore, people with disabilities, as a social group, existed outside of mainstream society. That is, a network of closed communities specific to various disabilities was established by the government. In each region of the country, there were special schools and factories as well as institutions created separately for people who were blind or deaf or had physical disabilities or mental illness (Tobis, 2000). At this point in time, the system of special care does not exist in policy any longer. However, in every region of Ukraine, one can still find special schools and special factories where persons with disabilities receive education and employment.

After the collapse of the Soviet Union, the Ukrainian economy suffered a range of setbacks and is currently the second weakest economy in Eastern Europe (Sen Nag, 2017). Several political crises, such as the annex of the Crimean peninsula by Russia in 2014 and the war in the East of the country, have led to greater instability of the state and increased poverty of its people. Under these circumstances, persons with disabilities, whose income is usually lower and expenditure higher (due to their disability), tend to face double oppression and stay "invisible" in society (Yanchenko, 2016).

Ukraine is generally rated as a disability-unfriendly country (Ukrayinska Pravda, 2014) as most of the public environments are totally inaccessible for people with mobility, hearing, and/or visual impairments, and therefore, a significant number of persons with disabilities (especially those with severe mobility and psychiatric conditions) rarely go out of their homes (Yanchenko, 2016). Houses, city streets, public transport, and infrastructure lack accessibility. Even newly built ramps (mostly at the state hospitals and social services) are often poorly constructed and dangerous for wheelchair users (Makarenko, 2015). Most theaters, museums, supermarkets, schools, universities, and other public buildings have no installed elevators even in the big cities.

Moreover, according to the State Statistics Service report, in 2016, Ukrainians spent almost a half of their income (49.8%) to buy food, while in the EU, the monthly food expenditure is only 12.3% for an average household (Shapran, 2017). If you add the cost of utilities and rent, there is almost nothing to spend on clothes, rest, and leisure. Therefore, most Ukrainians are not involved in sports activities, tourism, or museum and theater going. Even going out for a meal is a "rare pleasure" for the vast majority of population. Consequently, financial deprivation and inaccessible public environments and social stigma leave few choices for people with disabilities in Ukraine, whose main focus is on securing their everyday living needs, including food, rent, and utilities. However, disability frequently leads to additional costs related to medical care, rehabilitation, and special equipment. The state is responsible for providing a person with disability with all the necessary medical and social services, rehabilitation aids, and juridical advice (The law of Ukraine "About bases of social security of disabled people in Ukraine," 1991), but the procedure of getting any kind of assistance from the government is usually so complicated and time consuming that many people with disabilities prefer either to get no supports or to cover all the required expenses themselves. Only recently have younger people with disabilities who have grown up in an independent Ukraine gained higher education, got jobs, and had opportunities to experience life abroad in the EU, the UK, the USA, or Canada.

The younger generation of people with disabilities in Ukraine challenge social stigmas. They prefer not to see their disability as a "personal tragedy" or "medical problem" as disability tended to be understood in the Soviet Union (Phillips, 2002). They prefer to live active lives, just as their peers in the Western countries, and try to make the Ukrainian society more inclusive and disability-friendly. Due to the significantly lower (compared to the Western countries) social benefits, the only way to do this is establishing many different NGOs and public initiatives, as well as participating in the Paralympic and other disability movements.

Recently, there have been several notable initiatives focused on disability issues in Ukraine, including Dostupno.ua and Fight for Right. Dostupno.ua is an initiative held by a group of wheelchair users who test various public places all over the country to verify if they are accessible for people with disabilities. The main goal of the project is to show that people who use a wheelchair can visit the same places as people with no mobility impairments. The initiative also is intended to encourage policy-makers and businesses to change their attitudes toward people with disabilities and make public environments more accessible and disability-friendly (en. Hromadske.ua, 2016). "Owners of cafes don't know how to behave because they don't see them [people with disabilities]. When we come and ask to change something, they don't understand why," says Margo Hontar, co-founder of Dostupno.ua (en.hromadske.ua, 2016). Though the initiative just started in December of 2015, it has achieved some visible success; some owners of public places are consulting with the Dostupno.ua about how to make their business (often a café or restaurant) accessible for people with disabilities (en.hromadske.ua, 2016).

The Fight for Right is a campaign organized by people with visual disabilities who want to educate society about how disability does not imply limitation. "That's the society, that creates limits," says Julia Sachuk, coordinator of the project (dd.ua, 2017). "We can do everything all others do, and are just like everybody else," she adds (dd.ua, 2017). Since August 2016, when the Fight for Right started, its activists have engaged in a number of "extreme" activities: diving, skiing, riding a quadri-cycle, jumping with a chute, and cycling through almost half of the country on tandems (dd.ua, 2017). Sachuk states that people with disabilities who engage in these activities are not always met with understanding, but they work to navigate around barriers. "The only problem was with a chuting station," says the activist, "they said, the law prohibits to jump if you're blind, even with an instructor" (dd.ua, 2017). But this prohibition could not stop Julia and her friends; through the social network, they established a private chuting club that agreed to organize the jumping session for people with visual disabilities.

These are only two examples of many projects undertaken by young activists with disabilities in Ukraine to advocate for independent living, self-respect, and making a change. It is worth mentioning, however, that disability activism, in the social model sense, is mainly accessible to Ukrainians who have access to higher education, a good job, and experiences in Western societies (either as a student, or as a visiting scholar, or as a tourist). Those with no experiences like these, who represent the vast majority of the disabled population (The Disabled World, 2017), are often not prepared to assert their human rights, but instead have to focus on surviving and meeting their basic daily needs.

Inclusion in Ukraine is now quite formalized. Maryna Poroshenko, the former president's wife, is very engaged in inclusion initiatives. It is very popular to talk about inclusion at all levels; there are now "inclusive books," "inclusive exhibitions and concerts," "inclusive music," and "inclusive photography." These inclusion activities are typically organized only for people with certain types of disabilities, e.g., for people who are blind, deaf, or with cerebral palsy – never all together. There is a lot of talk about these issues on TV and social media, and consequently, people start to think and sometimes try to behave in a more appropriate way when meeting a person with disability in a public environment. Another positive result is that peo-ple with disabilities gradually have started to be heard and consulted with. This is, however, true only for those who have higher education, a good job, and a high social status (e.g., a chairman of a public organization of people with disabilities, a university professor, or a person with disability who works for an international agency).

In summary, Ukrainians with disabilities tend to fall into two groups: those who have access to opportunities that enable them to make choices and engage in advo-cacy activities and those who are still heavily influenced by the Soviet perception of disability (i.e., the medical model) and choose to receive a small pension from the state ($50 to $70 monthly, depending on the type of disability) to meet their basic needs. The second group rarely engages in the community. There are some notable initiatives at the macrosystem level that are beginning to positively affect public's awareness. These initiatives, however, have not reached many organizations, includ-ing universities, or individuals with disabilities, especially outside of the Ukrainian capital, Kyiv.

What Works: Potential Solutions to Enhancing Choice-Making Opportunities and Preference Expression in Post-soviet Societies

This chapter highlighted the influence of macrosystem factors on choices and preferences of people with disabilities, given the unique histories, cultures, laws, and power dynamics of post-Soviet societies. Even though much work remains to be done in Western societies to enhance choice making and support the development of self-determination of people with disabilities, there is even more that needs to occur structurally and socially in post-Soviet countries to assure that laws and policies are not merely words on paper.

When discussing potential solutions for enhancing opportunities and capacities for choice making and preference expression of people with disabilities in Eastern countries, we conceptualize such solutions in two main ways: (1) making changes at the macrosystem level by addressing inequalities between groups of individuals who have power and those who experience any level of neglect or discrimination and (2) fostering social capital for people with disabilities to be able to develop and nurture mutual relationships, and communicate and advocate effectively with individuals within their own but also other networks. Advocacy and self-advocacy permeate both approaches. Advocating within social networks to reach local and national systems and governments has led to many desired changes in the West.

Leake (2012) points out that in a review of self-determination curricula, Karvonen et al. (2004) found that social relationship building was a missing component of many existing self-determination curricula. Existing curricula tend to be competency/skills based and often do not sufficiently examine the transfer of these skills to real-life situations (Stancliffe, 2001). Relationship building is more complex and useful than developing social skills divorced from real-life application. Leake (2012) advocates for "supported friendships," an important component of person-centered planning for people with intellectual and developmental disabilities. In this approach, friends, family members, advocates, and service providers work with the person with a disability toward their goals as their support social network.

Walker et al. (2011) make a case for a social-ecological model of self-determination as one that can effectively capture the reciprocal environmental and personal factors required to effectively design and evaluate interventions to promote self-determination. Social-ecological models have multiple advantages over medical and other deficit-based models. In social-ecological approaches, interventions are designed not only to enhance the capacity of the person but also to minimize environmental barriers.

Walker et al. (2011) propose that a social-ecological approach that emphasizes social capital and social inclusion provides the best model for facilitating self-determination by (a) facilitating experiences and enhanced opportunities that promote self-determination, (b) supporting the creation of social networks that result in social capital and that promote formal and informal relationships between the individual and microsystems, (c) empowering people to direct their own learning or supports, and (d) advocating for policies and practices that emphasize the fundamental human right of all people to exercise their free will in ways meaningful to them. Some of the examples of strategies proposed include promoting choice-making opportunities, enabling access through universal design, educating family members and professionals on how to best support self-determination in individuals with disabilities, designing funding systems that support choice and control, and promoting inclusion in school, community, and employment.

Condeluci et al. (2008) noted: "It is amazing that, as of this writing, there has been no major study or effort, either at the university or foundation level, that has scientifically studied social capital and disability" (p. 137). Leake (2012) calls on funders and researchers to develop this important line of work that can support the next generation of people with disabilities in experiencing better opportunities for choice making, self-determination, and social inclusion.

We would add that the newest line of research in self-determination and choice making is one that crosses cultures and continents, one that breaks glass ceilings for people with disabilities, regardless of what macrosystem they happen to be born in. In order to do that, in addition to building social capital of people with disabilities, including effective communication within and between various social networks, there is a need to recognize that every person has an inherent value manifested as possessing civil and human rights. In order to uphold those rights, there is a need for advocacy that family members and people with disabilities in Western societies have practiced for many years to achieve remarkable goals. Advocacy that builds on the rights and on social capital of people with disabilities has the potential to result in successfully enforcing the laws on inclusion that governments in the Czech Republic and Ukraine and other Central and Eastern European countries have adopted or developed within their cultural contexts. Increased social relationships and networks as well as active voice of people with disabilities have the potential to change macrosystems by equalizing access to resources, including information, services, education, jobs, and ultimately power. In concrete terms, the legislation that has been adopted in the Czech Republic and Ukraine, but whose effects are not yet reaching individuals with disabilities, represents a macrosystem that is still holding onto its power. In contrast, in the USA, the Americans with Disabilities Act (ADA) of 1990 was a culmination of people's voices and organized advocacy efforts being heard that led to the policies to eliminate attitudinal, communication, transportation, policy, and physical barriers for people with disabilities to participate in society. This law, however, was preceded by decades of discrimination, institutionalization, family burden, and struggles to find one's courage and voice for protests, marches, and demonstrations that resulted in many important policies and laws to support the rights of people with disabilities to live in society to the fullest extent possible.

In conclusion, systems and governments of not only post-Soviet countries but any country that values democratic principles should keep asking themselves: "Are we treating all our citizens as equal partners in democracy? Is power distributed fairly to all our citizens, regardless of their personal and social characteristics and affiliations? And in the words of Václav Havel (1986), the Czech dissident, president, and advocate for the "power of the powerless," we should ask ourselves: "Are we living in truth?"

References

Abery, B. H., & Stancliffe, R. J. (2003). A tripartite-ecological theory of self-determination. In M. L. Wehmeyer, B. H. Abery, D. E. Mithaug, & R. J. Stancliffe (Eds.), *Theory in self-determination: Foundations for educational practice* (pp. 43–78). Springfield, IL: Charles C. Thomas.

Abery, T. (2013). *Self-determination and language.* Unpublished manuscript. Minneapolis, MN: University of Minnesota.

About Bases of Social Security of Disabled People in Ukraine. (1991). No. 875-XII. Retrieved from http://cis-legislation.com/document.fwx?rgn=15901

Allik, J., & Realo, A. (2004). Individualism-collectivism and social capital. *Journal of Cross-Cultural Psychology, 35,* 29–49. Retrieved from https://doi.org/10.1177/0022022103260381.

Bricout, J. C., Porterfield, S. L., Fisher, C. M., & Howard, M. O. (2004). Linking models of disability for children with developmental disabilities. *Journal of Social Work in Disability & Rehabilitation, 3,* 45–67.

Bronfenbrenner, U. (1977). Toward an experimental ecology of human development. *American Psychologist,* 513–531. Retrieved from https://pdfs.semanticscholar.org/a857/783a2bfc8aef8c93c200b3c635549237b434.pdf

Bronfenbrenner, U. (1994). Ecological models of human development. In T. Husen & T. N. Postlethwaite (Eds.), *International encyclopedia of education* (Vol. 3, 2nd ed., pp. 1643–1647). Oxford, England: Pergamon Press/Elsevier Science.

Čámský, P., Sembdner, J., & Krutilová, D. (2011). *Social services in the Czech Republic in theory and practice.* Prague, Czech Republic: Portál.

Condeluci, A., Ledbetter, M. G., Ortman, D., Fromknecht, J., & DeGries, M. (2008). Social capital; A view from the field. *Journal of Vocational Rehabilitation, 29,* 133–139.

Constitutional Court Findings, file no. I. ÚS 2637/17, Czech Republic.

Council of Europe Commissioner for Human Rights. (2012). *The right of people with disabilities to live independently and be included in the community.* Retrieved from https://www.coe.int/t/commissioner/source/prems/RightsToLiveInCommunity-GBR.pdf

CRPD Concluding Observation Ukraine. (2015). *Alternative report on implementation of the Convention on the Rights of Disabled Persons.* Retrieved from http://tbinternet.ohchr.org/_layouts/treatybodyexternal/Download.aspx?symbolno=INT%2fCRPD%2fNHS%2fUKR%2f21337&Lang=ru

DD.ua. (2017, February 17). *Drayv u borotbi za svoyi prava abo yak nezryachi lyudi pidkoryuyut stihiyi* [Drive in fighting for rights or how people with visual disabilities conquer the world]. Retrieved from https://dt.ua/personalities/drayv-u-borotbi-za-svoyi-prava-abo-yak-nezryachi-lyudi-pidkoryuyut-stihiyi-_.html

Degener, T. (2014). A human rights model of disability. In P. Blanck & E. Flynn (Eds.), *Routledge handbook of disability law and human rights* (pp. 31–49). London, UK: Routledge.

Degener, T. (2016). Disability in a human rights context. *Laws, 5,* 35. https://doi.org/10.3390/laws5030035

Disabled World (2017). *The Crisis in Ukraine and People with Disabilities.* Retrived from https://www.disabled-world.com/editorials/political/ukraine.php

Fleischer, D. Z., & Zames, F. (2001). *The disability rights movement: From charity to confrontation.* Philadelphia, PA: Temple University Press.

FRA. (2017). *From institutions to community living Part III: outcomes for persons with disabilities.* Retrieved from https://fra.europa.eu/en/publication/2017/independent-living-outcomes

Frankland, H. C., Turnbull, A. P., Wehmeyer, M. L., & Blackmountain, L. (2004). An exploration of the self-determination construct and disability as it relates to the Dine (Navajo) culture. *Education and Training in Developmental Disabilities, 39,* 191–205.

Gevorgianiene, V., & Sumskiene, E. (2017). P.S. for post-Soviet: A glimpse to a life of persons with intellectual disabilities. *Journal of Intellectual Disabilities, 21,* 235–247.

Grigorenko, E. L. (1998). Russian "Defectology": Anticipating perestroika in the field. *Journal of Learning Disabilities, 31,* 193–207.

Hao, S. (2015). *An analysis of American individualism culture.* Retrieved from https://haosuy-awen.wordpress.com/2015/02/19/an-analysis-of-american-individualism-culture/

Havel, V. (1986). *Living in truth.* Boston, MA: Faber & Faber.

Hromadske.ua. (2016). *Making Ukraine more accessible for disabled people.* Retrieved from https://en.hromadske.ua/posts/making_ukraine_more_accessible_for_disabled_people

Karvonen, M., Test, D. W., Wood, W. M., Browder, D., & Algozzine, B. (2004). Putting Self-Determination into Practice. *Exceptional Children, 71*(1), 23–41.

Kemmelmeier, M., Burnstein, E., Krumov, K., & Genkova, P. (2003). Individualism, collectivism, and authoritarianism in seven societies. *Journal of Cross-Cultural Psychology, 34*, 304–322.

Leake, D. (2012). Self-determination requires social capital, not just skills and knowledge. *Review of Disability Studies on Self-Determination, 8*, 1–10.

Leake, D., & Skouge, J. (2012). Introduction to the special issue: Self-determination as a social construct: Cross-cultural considerations. *Review of Disability Studies, 8*, 5–10.

Lee, S. H., & Wehmeyer, M. L. (2004). A review of the Korean literature related to self-determination: Future directions and practices for promoting the self-determination of students with disabilities. *Korean Journal of Special Education, 38*, 369–390.

Leotti, L. A., Iyengar, S. S., & Ochsner, K. N. (2010). Born to choose: The origins and value of the need for control. *Trends in Cognitive Science, 14*, 457–463.

Lynn-Jones, S. M. (1998). *Why the United States should spread democracy. Discussion Paper.* Belfer Center for Science and International Affairs, Harvard Kennedy School. Retrieved from https://www.belfercenter.org/publication/why-united-states-should-spread-democracy

Makarenko, O. (2015). *Grassroot efforts attempt to budge Ukraine's soviet attitude to disability.* Retrieved from http://euromaidanpress.com/2015/12/04/will-returning-war-veterans-budge-ukraines-soviet-attitude-to-disability/

McCagg, W. O., & Siegelbaum, L. (1989). *The disabled in the Soviet Union: Past and present, theory and practice.* Pittsburgh, PA: University of Pittsburgh Press.

Melichar, B. (2016). Karl Marx versus Max Weber: The forefathers' heritage as a social history constant. *The Central European Journal of Social Sciences and Humanities, 24*, 87–97.

Ministerstvo Osvity i Nauky Ukrayiny. (2018). *Statystychni dani* [Statistical data]. Retrieved from https://mon.gov.ua/ua/statistichni-dani

Ministry of Labour and Social Affairs, Czech Republic. (2006). *Koncepce podpory transformace pobytových sociálních služeb 2007–2013* [The Conception for Support of Transformation of Social Services]. Retrieved from https://www.databaze-strategie.cz/cz/mpsv/strategie/koncepce-podpory-transformace-pobytovych-socialnich-sluzeb-2007-2013?typ=struktura

Ministry of Labour and Social Affairs, Czech Republic. (2015). *Strategie rozvoje sociálních služeb na období 2015–2025* [Strategy for Development of Social Services for the Period 2016—2025]. Retrieved from https://www.mpsv.cz/cs/29623

Mohanty, A., Pradhan, R. K., & Jena, L. K. (2015). Learned helplessness and socialization: A reflective analysis. *Psychology, 6*, 885–895.

Müller, M. (2018). In Search of the Global East: Thinking between North and South. *Geopolitics*, 1–22. https://doi.org/10.1080/14650045.2018.1477757.

Phillips, S. D. (2002). *Living in a "parallel world": Disability in post-soviet Ukraine.* Retrieved from http://digitalcommons.ilr.cornell.edu/gladnetcollect/444/

Rabová, L. (2018). *Transformation of social services for people with disabilities in the context of deinstitutionalization* (Master's thesis). Retrieved from https://is.muni.cz/th/l112b/DP_Gatnarova.pdf

Sen Nag, O. (2017). *Poorest countries in Europe.* Retrieved from https://www.worldatlas.com/articles/the-poorest-countries-in-europe.html

Senishyn, O. (2016). *Dvoye zakhohanyh nezriachyh u Lvovi otrimuyut vidmovi vid orendo-dawtsiw zhytla* [A couple of blind lovers gets refusals from landlords in Lviv]. Retrieved from https://zaxid.net/dvoye_zakohanih_nezryachih_u_lvovi_otrimuyut_vidmovi_vid_oren-dodavtsiv_zhitla_n1409986?fbclid=IwAR1ZxQxm9kQ1_uO3AjRjxdfVJLrkIyaZ9Nzn_Vq5CwL9XX3XccZOg1Z0PGE

Shapiro, J. P. (1993). *No pity: People with disabilities forging a new civil rights movement.* New York, NY: Three Rivers Press.

Shapran V. (2017). *How many are eating Ukrainians.* Retrieved from https://intmassmedia.com/2017/08/16/how-many-are-eating-ukrainians/

Shogren, K. A. (2011). Culture and self-determination: A synthesis of the literature and directions for future research and practice. *Career Development for Exceptional Individuals, 34*, 115–127. https://doi.org/10.1177/0885728811398271

Sidanius, J., Pratto, F., van Laar, C., & Levin, S. (2004). Social dominance theory: Its agenda and method. *Political Psychology, 25*(6), 845–880.

Šiška, J. (2010). *Fundamental rights situation of persons with mental health problems and persons with intellectual disabilities: Desk report Czech Republic.* Retrieved from https://www.academia.edu/3443097/Fundamental_Rights_situation_of_persons_with_mental_health_problems_and_persons_with_intellectual_disabilities_desk_report_Czech_Republic

Šiška, J., & Beadle-Brown, J. (2011). Developments in deinstitutionalization and community living in the Czech Republic. *Journal of Policy and Practice in Intellectual Disabilities, 8*, 125–133. https://doi.org/10.1111/j.1741-1130.2011.00298.x

Šiška, J., Beadle-Brown, J., Káňová, Š., & Šumníková, P. (2018). Social inclusion through community living: Current situation, advances and gaps in policy, practice and research. *Social Inclusion, 6*, 94–109. https://doi.org/10.17645/si.v6i1.1211

Stancliffe, R. J. (2001). Living with support in the community predictors of choice and self-determination. *Mental Retardation and Developmental Disabilities Research Reviews, 7*, 91–98.

Strnadova, I., & Evans, D. (2015). Older women with intellectual disabilities: Overcoming barriers to autonomy. *Journal of Policy and Practice in Intellectual Disabilities, 12*, 12–19.

Sylantyeva, I. (2018). *Osvita ta pratsevlashtuvannia osib z invalidnistiu v Ukrayini: Yakoyu ye realna statystka?* [Education and employment of people with disabilities in Ukraine: What are the real statistics?] [Blog post]. Retrieved from https://www.obozrevatel.com/ukr/society/osvita-ta-pratsevlashtuvannya-osib-z-invalidnistyu-v-ukraini-yakoyu-e-realna-statistika.htm

Testé, B. (2017). Control beliefs and dehumanization: Targets with an internal locus of control are perceived as being more human than external targets. *Swiss Journal of Psychology, 76*, 81–86.

The Chamber of Deputies, Czech Republic. (2005). *Důvodová zpráva k návrhu zákona o sociálních službách* [Justification report for a proposed law on social services]. Retrieved from https://www.google.com/search?q=duvodova-zprava-zakon-o-socialnich-sluzbach-05-2005&rlz=1C1GGRV_enGE751AM751&oq=duvodova-zprava-zakon-o-socialnich-sluzbach-05-2005&aqs=chrome..69i57.346j0j9&sourceid=chrome&ie=UTF-8

Tichá, R., Lakin, K. C., Larson, S. A., Stancliffe, R. J., Taub, S., Engler, J., ... Moseley, C. (2012). Correlates of everyday choice and support-related choice for 8,892 randomly sampled adults with intellectual and developmental disabilities in 19 states. *Intellectual and Developmental Disabilities, 50*, 486–504.

Tobis, D. (2000). *Moving from residential institutions to community-based social services in Central and Eastern Europe and the former Soviet Union.* Washington, D.C.: World Bank.

Ukrainian Helsinki Human Rights Union. (2015). *Human rights in Ukraine: The first half of 2015.* Retrieved from http://helsinki.org.ua/files/docs/1442348382.pdf

Ukrayinska Pravda. (2014). *Ukrainian city for all or only for the elect?* Retrieved from https://en.wikipedia.org/wiki/Disability_in_Ukraine#cite_ref-UPDiU21814_2-0,

Ukrinform. (2016). *Sogodni v Ukraini I sviti Den ludej z obmezenimi fizicnimi mozlivostami* [Today Ukraine and the world celebrate the Day of People with Limited Physical Abilities]. Retrieved from https://www.ukrinform.ua/rubric-society/2132617-sogodni-v-ukraini-i-sviti-den-ludej-z-obmezenimi-fizicnimi-mozlivostami.html

United Nations. (2006). *Convention on the rights of persons with disabilities and optional protocol.* New York, NY: United Nations.

Vann, B. H., & Šiška, J. (2006). From 'cage beds' to inclusion: The long road for individuals with intellectual disability in the Czech Republic. *Disability & Society, 21*, 425–439.

Walker, H. M., Calkins, C., Wehmeyer, M. L., Walker, L., Bacon, A., Palmer, S. B., ... Johnson, D. R. (2011). A social-ecological approach to promote self-determination. *Exceptionality, 19*, 6–18. https://doi.org/10.1080/09362835.2011.537220

Wehmeyer, M. L. (2004). Self-determination and the empowerment of people with disabilities. *American Rehabilitation, 28*, 22–29.

Wehmeyer, M. L., & Abery, B. (2013). Self-determination and choice. *Intellectual and Developmental Disabilities, 51*, 399–411. https://doi.org/10.1352/1934-9556-51.5.399

Yanchenko, K. (2016). *Invisible but exist: Ukrainian people with disabilities struggle not to be marginalized.* Retrieved from http://euromaidanpress.com/2016/09/28/invisible-but-exist-ukrainian-people-with-disabilities-struggle-not-to-be-marginalized/#arvlbdata

Young, I. M. (2012). *Justice and the politics of difference.* Princeton, NJ: Princeton University Press.

Choice, Control and Individual Funding: The Australian National Disability Insurance Scheme

Carmel Laragy and Karen R. Fisher

Introduction

Australia's new National Disability Insurance Scheme (NDIS) is radically changing how disability services and supports are provided. Legislation underpinning the NDIS gives people with disability choice and control when it says they have:

> …the same right as other members of Australian society to be able to determine their own best interests, including the right to exercise choice and control, and to engage as equal partners in decisions that will affect their lives, to the full extent of their capacity. (Commonwealth of Australia, 2013, S4.8)

The principles promoted in the NDIS legislation are closely aligned to those of self-determination discussed in other chapters of this book. This chapter reviews evidence from three key NDIS documents showing the extent to which NDIS participants have choice and control over the use of their allocated funding. These three documents have different perspectives and report different findings. While there is agreement on the NDIS principles, implementing the principles is complex and challenging. This chapter does not focus on the many people with disability ineligible for funding packages, although their exclusion is a serious concern because many people are missing out on services as state- and territory-based agencies close and resources are transferred to the national NDIS.

This chapter briefly reviews evidence that supports the introduction of self-directed individual funding packages used by the NDIS, it describes the new scheme and it considers who is included and excluded. The three sources that provide data to review the scheme are the Council of Australian Government's

C. Laragy (✉)
School of Social and Political Sciences, The University of Melbourne,
Melbourne, VIC, Australia
e-mail: carmel.laragy@unimelb.edu.au

K. R. Fisher
Social Policy Research Centre, UNSW, Sydney, NSW, Australia

© Springer Nature Switzerland AG 2020
R. J. Stancliffe et al. (eds.), *Choice, Preference, and Disability*, Positive
Psychology and Disability Series, https://doi.org/10.1007/978-3-030-35683-5_7

(COAG, 2018) NDIS quarterly report; the Australian Government's Joint Standing Committee on the NDIS (Australian Government Joint Standing Committee on the National Disability Insurance Scheme, 2018) that examined the transition from previous state- and territory-based disability services to the NDIS; and the independent evaluation of the NDIS trials commissioned by the Government and conducted by Mavromaras, Moskos, Mahuteau, and Isherwood (2018) from Flinders University. Findings from these reports are reviewed using a framework presented by Professor Beresford et al. (2011) from the Centre for Citizen Participation at Brunel University, London. This identifies factors they found to contribute to choice and control in an individual funding environment.

Evidence Supporting the NDIS

Findings from Australian and international studies show that self-directed individual funding packages can result in better outcomes compared to block-funded services for people with disability when certain conditions are met. People need adequate funding, information and support to make informed decisions, creative support from coordinators and other professionals, administrative support as required, welcoming communities and appropriate services to purchase (Laragy, 2018; Laragy, Fisher, Purcal, & Jenkinson, 2015).

In the United States, *Cash and Counseling* program recipients were able to self-direct their individual funding. The program was extensively evaluated by Mahoney and his team in large-scale studies across many states, sometimes using randomised control groups. They provided convincing evidence of the effectiveness of the program compared to traditional block-funded supports. Their research publications include Mahoney, Wieler Fishman, Doty, and Squillace (2007); Norstrand, Mahoney, Loughlin, and Simon-Rusinowitz (2009); O'Keeffe (2009); and Harry et al. (2017). Their positive findings were supported by another US study that interviewed administrators from 34 of the 42 states that give people with developmental disabilities the opportunity to self-direct their supports (DeCarlo, Bogenschutz, Hall-Lande, & Hewitt, 2018). This study found that participants had increased opportunities for self-determination and improved relationships with support staff. They also identified challenges that have been noted in other studies. In particular, case managers and coordinators need to change their practice to become less controlling and share decision-making with participants.

Further evidence of the effectiveness of self-directed individual funding programs comes from the United Kingdom (Glendinning et al., 2008). A randomised control study compared the outcomes of 500 participants using 'Individualised Budgets' with those of 500 people receiving traditional block-funded support services who had no opportunity to self-direct. Those with 'Individualised Budgets' could choose the level of administrative management they wanted to undertake. The findings were generally positive, although the interviews were conducted only a few months after the program commenced and many findings were speculative rather than reports of actual outcomes. Despite the limitations of this study, it contributed to an encouraging environment for the development of the NDIS.

NDIS Background

Australian's Productivity Commission reviewed national disability services in 2011 (Productivity Commission, 2011). This is an independent research and advisory body funded by the Australian Government that reports on economic, social and environmental issues. The review produced a critical report that described the disability service system as '...underfunded, unfair, fragmented, and inefficient' (2011, p. 2). It concluded that the previous disability support 'system' was unsustainable on multiple grounds. Problems identified included:

- A lack of adequate resources and services.
- Services focusing on people in crisis that distracted from early intervention and better long-term planning.
- People with similar levels of functionality receiving different levels of support depending on their location, timing or the origin of their disability—this was called the 'lottery' of services.
- Service provision was dependent on the vagaries of annual budgets which did not allow people with disability to make long-term plans or be guaranteed lifetime supports.
- Some communities were particularly disadvantaged, for example, people in regional and remote areas, Indigenous people and people from a non-English speaking background.
- People with disability were told they must fit into existing programs rather than programs being designed to meet their needs.
- Service providers used outdated models that stifled innovation and flexibility.
- Overall, people with disability were treated paternalistically, had limited choice of service provider and had little control of what happened to them.

The Productivity Commission recommended that the NDIS be established on competitive market and insurance principles. Their aim was to replace state- and territory-based block-funded disability services, that tended to be rigid and rule bound, with an innovative and responsive system using an open, competitive market model; opportunities for people to self-direct their individual allocations if preferred; and investment in early intervention to reduce lifelong expenditure. To achieve these aims, they proposed the NDIS with two parts. One would provide individual funding support packages, and the second would promote personal and community capacity building so that people with disability can be welcomed into the community and included in mainstream services.

A community grassroots campaign called Every Australian Counts (2018) supported the Productivity Commission's push for the NDIS. People with disability; families, carers and their friends and supporters; advocacy organisations; and the

National Disability and Carer Alliance consisting of peak organisations for disability services joined together to lobby for the introduction of the NDIS.

NDIS Beginnings

In 2013, the Australian Government commenced a 3-year NDIS trial of individual funding packages in selected parts of Australia, consistent with the Productivity Commission's recommendations and community pressures. After reviews and adjustments, the full NDIS rollout commenced in July 2016. When it is fully functional from 2019, the NDIS will support approximately 475,000 participants with individual funding packages (Productivity Commission, 2017). A notable difference between the NDIS and disability programs in many other western countries is that NDIS participants will not have access to block-funded disability services. They will use their allocated funds to purchase disability supports from disability or mainstream services.

The ambitious scale of Australia's NDIS can be gauged by comparing it with the US 'participant-directed long-term services and support programs (PD-LTSS)'. The United States, with a population of around 326 million people (Census Bureau, 2017), has approximately 750,000 people in 102 PD-LTSS programs (Sciegaj et al., 2016). These programs serve individuals of all ages and with all types of disabilities. The authors quoted figures from a national survey of publicly funded participant-directed programs conducted in 2010–2011. The US figures are comparatively low when compared to the 475,000 Australia NDIS participants aged up to 65 years from a population of 25 million people (Australian Bureau of Statistics (ABS), 2018). The NDIS is trying to establish consistent national policies and practices and provide equity across a vast geographical area while offering choice, control and flexibility. In contrast, the majority of US programs had less than 500 participants (Sciegaj et al., 2016). Additionally, there were design and policy differences in terms of who was allowed to self-direct their funds; how funding could be spent; whether a financial management service (FMS) was required to manage payment to support workers, taxes and accounts; whether family members could be employed; and whether participants could determine pay rates of support workers. The NDIS is grappling with all these issues as it rolls out nationally.

The NDIS was partly funded by a 0.5% increase in the national Medicare levy (Parliament of Australia, 2013). This levy is a tax that funds universal health care and provides increased funding for disability supports. The NDIS redirects government funds away from state and territory block-funded disability service providers to individual funding packages (COAG, 2018). This radical redesign of disability services is occurring on a scale that arguably has not been attempted in other countries. The NDIS does not pay for income support, day-to-day living costs or informal supports already available from family and friends or for services already provided by health and education departments.

Political factors hastened the introduction of the NDIS before it was fully designed. A Labour Government enacted the NDIS legislation (Commonwealth of Australia, 2013) and commenced the NDIS trial of individual funding packages before facing a national election in 2013 where it was defeated, as had been widely predicted. The following year, an independent review of the NDIS acknowledged its remarkable achievement in overcoming obstacles and commencing the trial in a short space of time (Whalan, Acton, & Harmer, 2014). This review also likened the NDIS to 'building the plane while flying', and 'the Agency is like a plane that took off before it had been fully built and is being completed while it is in the air' (2014, p. 7). The 'Agency' mentioned is the National Disability Insurance Agency (NDIA) which administers the NDIS. The NDIA commenced implementing this complex system change before the NDIS was fully designed, and it has continued to evolve over the past 5 years.

The community capacity building component of the NDIS is called *Information, Linkages and Capacity Building* (ILC), and it is slowly being rolled out across the states (National Disability Insurance Scheme (NDIS), 2018b). When fully operational, it is intended to benefit all people with disability, including the 90% who are ineligible for individual packages. Community organisations can apply for two types of ILC grants:

 (i) Personal capacity building—these projects aim to increase the skills, resources and confidence of people with disability and their families to participate in community activities alongside other community members.
 (ii) Community capacity building—these projects work to support mainstream services and community organisations to become more inclusive of people with disability.

The NDIS Quality and Safeguarding Framework, which has the task of ensuring standards are met and safeguards are in place, was only introduced in 2018 (Australian Government, Department of Social Services, 2018). While the NDIS's premature beginning has caused considerable frustration, it might never have commenced had it been delayed until planning was completed.

Eligibility for Individual Support Packages

The NDIS has strict eligibility criteria for individual support packages. The NDIS Act specifies eligibility as having a permanent impairment, substantially reduced psychosocial or other functional capacity, an impairment that affects capacity for social and economic participation and a need for lifetime support under the NDIS (Commonwealth of Australia, 2013, S24.1). People assessed as eligible have a legal entitlement to supports and allocations are not capped.

Over 4.3 million Australian citizens aged 16–65 years have a disability (Australian Bureau of Statistics (ABS), 2015). This number far exceeds the 475,000 NDIS individual support package available (Productivity Commission, 2017). This gap is a serious concern. It means that 90% of people with disability will have to rely on mainstream services because state-based services are closing as their resources are being transferred to the NDIS. Further, people who acquire impairments from the age of 65 years are ineligible for the NDIS and they have to apply for aged care support.

Planning

People who are assessed as eligible for the NDIS have a formal planning meeting. This consists of a planning conversation/meeting with an NDIS representative to discuss the person's life situation, current supports, aspirations and goals for the future. Initially the NDIS discouraged family members, advocates and current service providers from attending these meetings with the intention of giving the people with disability an opportunity to express their wishes to the NDIS planner. This strategy was soon abandoned because the plans developed often lacked context and were impractical. The NDIA now contracts selected service provider organisations to employ *Local Area Coordinators* (LACs) to provide pre-planning support to people with disability and their families and carer. The importance of pre-planning is now widely recognised by service providers and peer support groups who meet with the person before the formal NDIS planning or review meeting to define goals and strategies (Australian Government Joint Standing Committee on the National Disability Insurance Scheme, 2018). The planning and review meetings produce an agreed plan within itemised categories, and costs have to be approved by a senior NDIA staff member before it is funded. The three documents reviewed in this chapter show that these procedures are often highly bureaucratic and disempowering for the people with disability and are being reviewed.

The Commonwealth of Australia (2013) says that people's goals should determine their funding and supports. They should receive 'reasonable and necessary' supports to maximise their independence, live independently and be included in the community as fully participating citizens in mainstream activities and employment. The person's goals documented in their plan, not the type and severity of a person's impairments, are supposed to determine their funding and the supports provided. Two people with similar types and severity of impairment may have different goals. One person may want to pursue education and a professional career, while another may want more family and community connections. There is no formula that prescribes 'reasonable and necessary supports'; they are supposed to be determined by the person's goals. In practice, NDIA staff and representatives make subjective assessments that determine funding allocations.

If participants are dissatisfied with the approved plan, they can appeal to higher levels within the NDIA and subsequently to the Administrative Appeals Tribunal (Administrative Appeals Tribunal (AAT), 2018a). The AAT provides independent reviews of decisions made by Australian Government agencies. Disability advocacy services are funded by government to support NDIS participants who are dissatisfied with their plan or the decision that they are ineligible. The appeal process is cumbersome and slow, and the NDIA often settles before formal AAT hearings. The AAT's concerns about the NDIS are discussed later in this chapter.

After the plan and budget are endorsed by the NDIA, participants choose a management strategy. They can self-direct their allocated funds, sometimes with the assistance of a nominee; their plan can be managed by a registered plan management provider; or the plan can be managed by the NDIA (National Disability Insurance Scheme (NDIS), 2018a). When the NDIA manages a plan, all supports must be purchased from a NDIS-registered provider. Those who self-direct their funds or use a registered plan management provider can decide to purchase from a disability service provider or the open market, as long as the items come within the remit of their goals and plan. Plans and outcomes achieved are reviewed annually, biennially or when circumstances change.

Method

Three key documents regarding the NDIS are reviewed in this chapter and provide evidence of the extent to which the NDIS offers participants choice and control. One is the Council of Australian Governments report (COAG, 2018) which presents the Government's statistics and reports high satisfaction levels; the second is the Australian Government Joint Standing Committee on the National Disability Insurance Scheme (2018) which held public hearings and received submissions during 2017; and the third is the independent evaluation conducted by Mavromaras et al. (2018) from the National Institute of Labour Studies at Flinders University in Adelaide. The reports focus on the NDIS and its procedures. They only give brief mention to the dissatisfaction and frustrations felt by those who were not accepted into the scheme.

The COAG data (2018) were collected by the NDIS. An NDIA engagement team member contacted 98% of participants or their families/carers in 2016–2017 after they received their initial plan to establish baseline data. A satisfaction questionnaire was administered at repeated points in time and the findings compared, and the latest survey included questions about short-term outcomes. The outcomes questionnaire used a framework that looked at outcomes in four life stages. These baseline data will be compared with subsequent surveys. The overall satisfaction ratings given were calculated by averaging the satisfaction ratings of each participant surveyed. Responses were recorded anonymously, and some participants chose not to complete the survey.

The Joint Standing Committee conducted 8 public hearings across the nation and received 82 submissions from individuals and organisations about the NDIS during 2017. The great majority of submissions and presentations were critical of the NDIS.

Mavromaras et al. (2018) evaluated the NDIS trial from 2014 to 2017. Data were collected at two points in time. The study looked at the impacts of the trial on people with disability, their families and carers, the disability sector and its workforce, mainstream providers and services, other stakeholders and the wider community. It also examined high-level processes which contributed to or impeded achieving positive outcomes. It compared trial groups receiving NDIS services and control groups with similar demographics receiving traditional block-funded services using both qualitative and quantitative methods. Quantitative survey data were collected from over 3,000 NDIS participants and 2,000 of their family members and carers. The control group survey data came from about two-thirds of these numbers. Interviews were conducted with over 60 NDIS participants and families and carers. Surveys and interviews were conducted twice, with fewer responses in the second wave of data collection.

Findings from the three reports are reviewed using a framework developed by Professor Beresford et al. (2011) from the Centre for Citizen Participation at Brunel University, London. The framework was developed using evidence from a 4-year national study that identified factors that contributed to people having choice and control over their disability supports and their lives in individual funding programs. They took a user-controlled, participatory, rights-based approach involving a consortium of organisations and stakeholders and identified key factors that contribute to service recipients having choice and control. While the UK context is different from the Australian NDIS, the factors Beresford et al. identified as important for promoting choice and control provide a useful framework for reviewing the NDIS findings. The key factors are as follows:

(i) Funding—having adequate funding is the most important factor identified.
(ii) Workforce—skilled, well-trained and well-supported workers who received adequate pay and recognition are essential.
(iii) Accessible support—information, advice, support and advocacy are needed to negotiate the social care system.
(iv) Access to mainstream services—all services and systems such as transport and education need to be made accessible to enable independent living.
(v) Informal care—family and friends are important and they need information and capacity building to support service users maximise their independence.
(vi) Institutionalism and occupational practice—organisations need to overcome barriers that often arise which increase bureaucratisation and avoid having a preoccupation with negative risk expressed in terms of 'safeguarding' and maintaining 'health and safety'; and workers need to be affirming and respectful and have positive attitudes and good listening and communication skills to provide positive experiences.

Findings

The findings from the COAG (2018) report, the Australian Government Joint Standing Committee on the National Disability Insurance Scheme (2018) report and the Mavromaras et al. (2018) evaluation are presented below. Findings explicitly about choice and control are presented first, and additional findings are presented under the headings Beresford et al. (2011) identified as contributing to choice and control in individual funding programs. The three reports do not include outcomes from the community capacity building part of the NDIS called *Linkages and Capacity Building* (ILC) (National Disability Insurance Scheme (NDIS), 2018b) because this only commenced in 2017 and data are not yet available.

The COAG report shows there were 148,953 active participants with an approved NDIS plan in March 2018. Twenty-nine per cent of participants recorded autism as their primary disability, and a further 29% recorded intellectual disability as their primary disability. Psychosocial disability was the next most frequent disability at 7%. However, the proportion of people with psychosocial disability was only half that expected based on population demographics, suggesting that many who are eligible are not accessing the scheme (National Disability Insurance Scheme (NDIS), 2017). Other disabilities were recorded as 5% or lower. The COAG report noted that the proportion of disability types may change when the scheme is fully rolled out because the initial trials in different areas targeted specific age groups and specific types of disability.

Choice and Control

In the COAG and the Mavromaras et al. reports, the majority of NDIS respondents reported high satisfaction levels regarding the extent of their choice and control, and they considered that they had reasonable and necessary supports. Some NDIS participants were dissatisfied with their level of choice and control, and a small number felt they were worse off. The data are complex in that satisfaction levels varied across different participant groups and sometimes varied within one group using different methods and at different points in time. This chapter tries to capture these differences while also presenting an overall picture. The Mavromaras et al. evaluation report provides comparisons with previous support, which is useful when assessing the impact of the NDIS. The Joint Standing Committee gave an opportunity for people to express their grievances, and the resultant report mostly documents deficiencies in NDIS practices and processes.

The COAG report presents a predominately positive picture of the NDIS. Approximately 65% of NDIS participants aged 15 years and over reported that the scheme gave them increased choice and control. While choice and control had increased, most people wanted more. Seventy-three per cent of participants 25 years and older wanted more choice and control, especially to engage with social activities. This group had a low level of community and social activities, with only 26% having a paid job and only 36% being actively involved in a community, cultural or religious group during the previous 12 months.

The COAG report also recorded improvements in other life areas for NDIS participants. Seventy-two per cent of participants reported increased assistance with daily living activities; 61% had more social, community and civic participation;

46% thought the NDIS helped them know their rights and advocate effectively; 82% of family/carers thought the NDIS had increased their child's ability to communicate, and 90% reported that the scheme assisted their child's development and facilitated access to specialist services.

The Standing Committee Report documented a wide range of concerns about the transition from state- and territory-based disability services to the NDIS and made 26 recommendations for change. All the recommendations served to increase participants' choice and control, although the report was not framed around these concepts. Key issues that impacted negatively on choice and control are noted below.

The Mavromaras et al. independent evaluation of the NDIS trial identified positive characteristics and outcomes as well as issues to be addressed, especially workforce issues. Overall, the report was quite positive considering the disruption and uncertainties they identified. They reported that the majority of participants and their families and carers thought they had more choice and control in the NDIS than was previously available; and statistics showed they had more choice and control than people in a control group. The small proportion of participants who self-directed their package was particularly pleased with the greater choice and flexibility they had over the services they purchased. Interestingly, NDIS participants tended to give more positive responses the longer they were in the scheme. These improvements were thought to result from people becoming familiar with the NDIS and its processes and language. Over time, they were more likely to change service providers and request additional types of supports and more flexibility in the timing, location and provision of their supports. In contrast to the NDIS participants, a quarter of families and carers reported that their choice and control declined the longer they were in the scheme, and the reason for this was not clear.

The Mavromaras et al. evaluation found that satisfaction with the amount of choice and control available varied according to disability type, the age of participants, whether a family carer or recipient responded and where people lived. There was more choice in urban areas because more service providers were available; and family carers of an adult participant reported more choice and control than those caring for children. NDIS participants with a mental/psychosocial disability gave the lowest rating to having choice and control. As reported by COAG, while the NDIS gave participants more choice and control, the majority of people still wanted more.

Factors identified in the three reports that contributed to increased choice and control are listed below under the headings Beresford et al. (2011) identified.

Funding

According to the COAG report, the NDIS has managed within its budget in each of the 5 years of its operation. This is despite less people exiting the scheme than expected and higher than expected package costs. The detailed participant data the NDIA collects includes costs and outcomes. These data are compared with the earlier estimates and 'actuarial monitoring occurs continuously and allows management to put in place strategies as required' (COAG, 2018, p. 60). While the strategies used to contain costs are not specified by COAG, the Administrative Appeals Tribunal (AAT) (2018a, 2018b) provides evidence that allocations for individual budgets are being cut and people are not receiving reasonable and necessary support.

The Mavromaras et al. evaluation found there was a lack of transparency as to how NDIS planning decisions were made and funds were allocated. There was variability across plans and across trial sites for participants with the same type of disability and needs. Some participants were not told why funding was refused after it had been discussed in planning meetings or why funding for items was cut which had been given previously.

COAG reported on the underutilisation of allocated funds. They found that only 64% of funds allocated were utilised in 2013–2014, 75% in 2014–2015, 75% in 2015–2016 and 66% in 2016–2017. The proportion of funds utilised dropped in 2016–2017 because the scheme expanded during that year and approximately two-thirds of the participants were on their first plan. Typically people utilise less of their allocated funds in their first year when they take some time to become familiar with the NDIS rules, decide which supports best suit their needs and goals and source appropriate services and supports.

The Joint Standing Committee noted that there is a serious funding shortfall for the *Information, Linkages and Capacity Building Program (ILC)* program and it does not have sufficient funds to achieve its objectives. The ILC program is intended to assist all people with disability, not just those eligible for the NDIS support. The Committee also noted there are boundary issues and funding disputes between the NDIA and other national and state and territory departments such as health, aged care, education, transport, housing and justice. These are leading to reduced access to services for both NDIS participants and people with disability not eligible for an NDIS package.

Workforce

The Mavromaras et al. evaluation provided an extensive review of the NDIS workforce and discussed the importance of having a viable workforce for NDIS participants so they can exercise choice and control. After acknowledging the profound impact the NDIS is having on the workforce, the evaluation found:

- The number of support worker positions increased, although there were concerns about increased casualisation of positions.
- The disability sector, including support workers, initially had a positive view of the NDIS. However, this view darkened during the trial.
- New roles typically had lower rates of pay and skill levels than those before the NDIS. This led to concerns about the de-professionalisation of the disability workforce and lower quality service provision.

- Concerns grew regarding the financial viability of service providers and the security of support worker positions.
- NDIA staff implementing the NDIS expressed concerns about high work pressures detracting from their work standards. These included planners with overly high administrative burdens, *Local Area Coordinators* not having time to promote community engagement and *Plan Support Coordinators* struggling to undertake both plan implementation and community engagement.
- Respondents across all interview groups wanted NDIA staff to be trained to increase their understanding of disability types and associated needs.
- The full impact of the NDIS on employment in the disability sector will take time to be realised.

Concerns expressed to the Joint Standing Committee about workforce shortages are largely captured in the above list. The National Disability Services, the peak body for service providers, was particularly concerned about the profile of the future disability workforce. These concerns are discussed below.

Accessible Support

The Joint Standing Committee reported on 'thin markets' in rural and remote areas that did not have necessary services and supports. People impacted the most were those with complex needs, those involved in the criminal justice system, those from culturally and linguistically diverse (CALD) backgrounds and Aboriginal and Torres Strait Islanders. The service gaps were accentuated by the closure of state and territory programs before a market for NDIS services was developed. COAG reported that new services were being established as the NDIS business model intended, and there was a 19% increase in the number of active approved NDIS providers in the quarter finishing in March 2018, with 43% of these being individual sole traders. However, this increase was not keeping up with demand.

The hourly rate for services set by the NDIA was thought to be too low to incentivise market development, especially in rural and remotes areas (COAG, 2018; Australian Government Joint Standing Committee on the National Disability Insurance Scheme, 2018). The rate set and the quantum of funds allocated limited participants' choice and control. While the NDIS-independent pricing review conducted by McKinsey and Company (2018) was less critical of current funding levels, it forecasts future workforce shortages and recommended price increases.

The NDIS received high numbers of complaints about people with disability not having necessary information, advice, support and advocacy to work with the scheme (COAG, 2018). Of the 13,223 complaints received about the NDIA, 31% concerned timeliness, 19% individual needs, 8% reasonable and necessary supports and 6% unclear information. Of the 692 complaints received about services, 24% were about the supports being provided, 15% about service delivery, 14% about staff conduct and 14% about provider processes.

On a more positive note, the Mavromaras et al. evaluation found that NDIS participants needed intensive support initially, and this reduced over time as they became familiar with processes and better able to exercise choice and control. However, people with intellectual disability, complex support needs and some others continued to need ongoing support to achieve positive outcomes. The evaluation identified a need for more advocacy and better advice and assistance around planning and plan implementation to improve choice and control for all NDIS participants, especially as the NDIS guidelines kept changing.

Access to Mainstream Services

The NDIS facilitates access to mainstream services using three processes. NDIS participants use individual funding packages to pay for mainstream services; the NDIS liaises with schools and medical and other services to coordinate services; and the NDIS allocates *Information Linkages and Capacity Building* (ILC) grants to build the capacity of people with disability to access services and mainstream services and the wider community to welcome all people with disability.

The COAG reported that approximately 90% of participants with an active plan approved after 1 July 2016 had accessed mainstream supports. They were predominantly accessing supports for health and well-being, lifelong learning and daily activities. However, COAG did not know the extent of this involvement.

The Joint Standing Committee noted that the *Information, Linkages and Capacity Building Program (ILC)* program is responsible for connecting people with disability to their communities and to appropriate disability, community and mainstream supports. However, this important feature of the scheme was underfunded, and they held grave concerns that people with disability will not gain access to mainstream services.

Informal Care

The importance of family and friends to NDIS participants is acknowledged in the three reports. The COAG data showed that the majority of parents and carers of children had positive experiences in the NDIS. Around 63% of families and carers of children reported that the NDIS had improved the level of support for their family, and 66% to 69% reported that the NDIS had improved their ability/capacity to help their child develop and learn and had improved their access to services, programs and activities in the community.

The Standing Committee heard that families and carers were important in planning and review meetings to provide a broad picture of the NDIS participants' needs and preferences.

The Mavromaras et al. evaluation reported a mix of positive and negative impacts of the NDIS on families and carers. Many were able to exercise better choice and control, and a small number were able to take breaks from their caring role. However, many wanted the NDIS plans and reviews to place more focus on the person in the context of their family and have less individual focus and some still struggled to have time away from their support role.

Institutionalism and Occupational Practices

Institutionalism is defined as organisations having bureaucratic barriers and a focus on risk aversion expressed in terms of 'safeguarding' and maintaining 'health and safety'. The Mavromaras et al. evaluation examined cultural change as services transitioned to the NDIS and reported that overall, despite some exceptions, there was a slow but steady improvement as services became more flexible. The entry of new competitors in the NDIS market was thought to be a contributing factor. While service providers initially viewed the NDIS in a positive light, over time they faced problems with inadequate NDIS pricing, and they became more fearful of their financial sustainability.

The Joint Standing Committee received many complaints of negative NDIS experiences. For example, the scheme was slow to enrol people, and in September 2017 there were over 34,500 eligible people waiting; and there were delays in plan approvals, plan activations and access to services. The Committee received evidence of inconsistent funding packages being granted to NDIS participants across all jurisdictions, with some participants who had similar conditions and similar support needs receiving vastly different plans and funding. The difference was often attributed to planners lacking the necessary knowledge, expertise and experience to work with people with disability.

Despite the many problems reported about planning processes, COAG reported that the overall satisfaction with the NDIS planning was high. Eighty-four per cent of participants surveyed rated their satisfaction with the NDIS planning process as either good or very good. Further, over 90% of participants 'Agreed' or 'Strongly Agreed' that their planner listened to them and that they had enough time to tell their story; and 71% said that they understood what was in their plan. However, these positive ratings have to be tempered by the number of complaints made. Dissatisfied NDIS participants first appeal within the NDIA, and if still dissatisfied they appeal to the Administrative Appeals Tribunal (AAT). COAG reported that 6% of NDIS participant had lodged a complaint and 0.29% proceeded to an AAT appeal. One of these appeals, which resulted in a scathing assessment of the NDIA, is discussed below.

Discussion

The reports produced by (COAG, 2018) and Mavromaras et al. (2018) generally painted a positive picture of the NDIS in terms of providing the majority of NDIS participants with increased choice and control. More people than ever before were receiving disability support, and they had more choice and control to use these individual funding packages flexibly to purchase supports and services from the open market as well as from the disability sector. The two studies also identified various shortcomings and noted that some people were missing out. The Standing Committee report focused on NDIS failings. The mix of positive and negative findings reported are mirrored in almost every report on the NDIS. One such report was the Warr et al. (2017) study conducted by the University of Melbourne. They interviewed 42 NDIS participants and 16 parents or adult children of NDIS participants in the Barwon trial site in the early days of the scheme. Many respondents reported positive experiences with the NDIS, including increased funding to access services and resources and reduced waiting lists for services. They also identified issues that limited participant's choice and control. These were (i) insufficient services and resources to help people navigate the client-driven market system; (ii) service providers not being flexible and innovative; (iii) people in rural areas having limited options and funding being consumed in travelling expenses; (iv) unspent funding, sometimes because no services were available, being withdrawn because NDIS planners assumed the supports were unnecessary; and (v) people with fluctuating disabilities, including people with psychosocial disability, not allowed to purchase services, equipment and support on an ad hoc basis as required to meet their episodic needs.

The University of Sydney and Community Mental Health Australia (2018) studied the choices the NDIS gives to people with psychosocial disability and concluded that they are missing out. They found that the NDIA is failing to engage appropriately with people experiencing psychosocial disability, that existing services are closing because funding is being diverted to the NDIS and that solutions being implemented are poorly coordinated and funded. They proposed solutions for each of the problems identified. These included maintaining existing services until the NDIS can offer appropriate supports, providing better information, giving specific support for Aboriginal and Torres Strait Islander people, providing person-centred supports for the application process, planning and review meetings and training NDIS staff regarding psychosocial disability.

To give the NDIA their due, they have taken a number of steps to respond to negative feedback. Their report titled *Improving the NDIS Participant and Provider Experience* (National Disability Insurance Scheme (NDIS), 2018c) outlines steps they are taking to overcome NDIS shortcomings and maximise participant choice and control, especially for the most vulnerable and marginalised. The steps are as follows:

- Replacing phone interviews with face-to-face planning and review meetings

- Providing information that is clear, consistent and available in accessible formats such as easy English, braille and languages other than English
- Providing a consistent point of contact with an NDIS staff member or representative
- Making more connections with health, education and transport services to promote greater community inclusion and a sense of belonging
- Improving the NDIS web portal and tools for easier use by people with disability and providers (National Disability Insurance Scheme (NDIS), 2018c, p. 4)

The NDIS also created the *Quality and Safeguards Commission* in 2018 (National Disability Insurance Scheme (NDIS), 2018d). This is an independent agency which will regulate the NDIS market, handle complaints about the quality and safety of NDIS supports and services, provide national consistency, promote safety and quality services, resolve problems and identify areas for improvement. The aims are laudable and it remains to be seen if this is achievable.

The NDIS needs to be recognised for its achievements developing and implementing the NDIS across this vast nation in just 5 years and its willingness to respond to criticisms. The reports revealed how challenging it is to develop communication, planning, coordination and support systems and supply an expanding workforce which is attuned to the NDIS principles, especially in rural and remote areas.

The biggest threat to the NDIS appears to be inadequate funding. The NDIS has to manage within its budget allocated by the Australian Government. Being a government body, the NDIA cannot make public statements criticising the Government's allocation, and it is subject to government constraints on total staff numbers. A 0.5% Medicare levy funded the initial stages of the NDIS in 2013. In 2017 the Australian Government announced a further 0.5% increase in the Medicare levy to ensure ongoing funding to take effect in 2019 (Australian Broadcasting Commission (ABC), 2018). However, this decision was reversed in 2018 and additional funds have to come from general revenue. Consequently NDIS funding is subject to the vacillating economic conditions of the day, leaving the NDIS in a potentially precarious financial position.

With some exceptions, most problems identified in the reports reviewed can be linked to budgetary restraints and cost-cutting measures, the exceptions being the need for planners with appropriate knowledge, skills and experience and NDIS processes that are attuned to the episodic nature of psychosocial disability.

The Administrative Appeals Tribunal (Administrative Appeals Tribunal (AAT), 2018a, 2018b) provides evidence of the dire impact of NDIS cost-cutting measures. The Deputy President of the AAT heard an appeal by a young woman who was dissatisfied with the amount allocated to her in her NDIS plan. Before the appeal was heard, the NDIA produced a second and a third plan, both providing less than the first. Appeal hearings are supposed to be low cost and accessible and held 'in a casual setting and focus on open conversation and participation' (Administrative Appeals Tribunal (AAT), 2018b). However, this appeal hearing had protracted legal arguments because the NDIA challenged the authority of the AAT to hear an appeal when a second and third plan had been put into effect. It is hard to see any reason for the NDIA's pursuit of this matter with the AAT other than to contain costs. The Deputy President of the AAT gave a stinging rebuke to the NDIA in his judgement, and amongst a string of comments he accused the NDIA of being '… bloody-minded by …enacting a new plan while a subsisting plan is being reviewed by the Tribunal…; decision-making … slow and difficult to interpret…; [the young woman's experience] is far from being an isolated one…; the steps … not always … timely and transparent' (2018, S24 & S30). Clearly the AAT Deputy President thought the NDIA's efforts to reduce the young woman's allocation were 'bloody minded' and not in her best interests.

The NDIS sets pay rates for contracted planners, coordinators and support workers. These are set at a low level commensurate with people having low qualifications (Cortis, Macdonald, Davidson, & Bentham, 2017; National Disability Services, 2018). Consequently, skilled and experienced staff who expect higher wages are discouraged from working for the NDIS, and NDIS participants have reduced opportunities to select the staff they want. This restricts the choices available to all participants and impacts negatively on those with complex needs who require experienced staff. Additionally, workers employed on these low rates have precarious working conditions.

COAG reported that 'actuarial monitoring occurs continuously and allows management to put in place strategies as required' to contain costs (2018, p. 60). This includes setting pay rates for NDIS services and supports, individual allocations in support packages and *Information, Linkages and Capacity Building* grants. Mavromaras et al. (2018) found that some individual allocations had been reduced in the second wave of planned and participants were given no explanation for this. Also, there are procedural changes that cut costs, such as the frequency of reviews changing from annual to biennial and planning meetings changing from face-to-face to telephone interviews.

There are tensions for the NDIA when managing within its budget and paying sustainable wages to retain a skilled workforce. The disability workforce profile produced by the National Disability Services (2018), the peak body for service providers, shows that the disability workforce is growing at 9% per year, which is faster than other areas. However, this growth has been in casualised and part-time positions, while full-time and permanent positions declined. The initial evidence suggests that the sector is losing highly skilled and well-motivated workers and substituting them with casualised and part-time workers who will have high turnover, low morale and inconsistent standards. While it is too early to know how the workforce situation will play out, we do know there is likely to be a workforce shortage as the NDIS participant numbers increase.

The NDIA commissioned the McKinsey and Company (2018) *Independent Pricing Review* to consider whether the current NDIS pricing strategy and rates of pay will create a sustainable disability market. McKinsey found the NDIS pricing structure did not create the necessary incentives for future market growth and there are likely to be future shortages of workers when the NDIS is fully operational. McKinsey recommended price increases to make service providers sustainable and to attract necessary therapists and support workers. Even if the NDIA wants to comply with the McKinsey report recommendations, it is hamstrung by the budget allocated to them. It seems likely they will cut or contain individual funding allocations and continue to underfund the *Information Linkages and Capacity Building* (ILC) program to stay within their budget.

Evidence from the three reports reviewed and other studies led to the conclusion that the NDIS needs adequate funding for it to achieve its aims of giving people with disability more choice and control. Although money alone will not make this complex national system work effectively, insufficient funding will limit its potential.

The possibility of fraud and exploitation is an additional factor the NDIS is considering and established a new Fraud Taskforce in July 2018 (National Disability Insurance Scheme (NDIS), 2018e). The Australian vocational training area stands as a warning to the NDIS because services were privatised and unscrupulous providers used loopholes to exploit vulnerable service users (Miller & Hayward, 2017). While the new *Quality and Safeguards Commission* in 2018 (National Disability Insurance Scheme (NDIS), 2018d) is charged with regulating the NDIS market and ensuring safety, every part of the NDIS will need to be attuned to possible scams and systemic exploitation.

A review of individual funding programs in Australia prior to the NDIS identified factors that give people with disability greater choice (Purcal, Fisher, & Laragy, 2014). Key factors are who holds the allocated funds and where support can be purchased. People who self-directed their allocated funds and purchased from the open market had maximum choice. People needed quality standards, supported decision-making, access to information and access to community services and supports to maximise their choices. The review also found that insufficient funds and a shortage of support to purchase, especially in regional areas, constrained choices.

The importance of access to information has been identified in a number of individual funding studies (Laragy, David, & Moran, 2016). People need information that is (i) accessible and diverse in format, mode, source and location; (ii) personalised and targeted; (iii) accurate, consistent and timely; (iv) from a trusted source; (v) independent; (vi) culturally appropriate; (vii) actively promoted to 'hard to reach' groups and (viii) gender appropriate.

What Would Promote Choice and Control in the NDIS?

The factors identified in this chapter that promote choice and control align well with the categories Beresford et al. (2011) presented. These provide a helpful guide for further developing the NDIS.

Adequate funding for the national NDIS scheme is needed. Individual funding packages need to be sufficient to give people with disability choice and control and to employ support workers with the necessary skills and experience. NDIS price items need to be set high enough to encourage the development of an NDIS market. The *Information Linkages and Capacity Building* (ILC) program needs more funding to fulfil its mission in supporting all people with disability to access, and be welcomed by, mainstream services.

Adequate funding is necessary to promote the recruitment of a skilled, responsive and flexible workforce. While qualified therapists and allied health workers will be needed, not every NDIS participant wants qualified support workers. Some participants prefer to recruit and train their own unqualified support workers, especially people who self-directed their funds. As the number of qualified workers is not going to meet the estimated demand, having the option to employ unqualified workers will ease workforce pressures. However, strategies to ensure service quality and avoid exploitation are needed.

The NDIS is providing support to more people with disability than ever before. However, it has a long way to go to reach out to all people with a disability. Those who are articulate are benefiting, often with support from their family and carers. However, the most isolated, marginalised and disadvantaged are missing out. Much needs to be done to give equal access to Aboriginal and Torres Strait Islander people, other ethnic groups, people with psychosocial disability, low socioeconomic groups and people in rural and remote communities. All people with disability need information to make informed decisions. More efforts are needed to provide information in accessible formats to everyone.

The *Information Linkages and Capacity Building* (ILC) arm of the NDIS only commenced in 2017. This is funding projects that facilitate independence and give better access to mainstream services and opportunities. If adequate funding is provided, the ILC program will possibly facilitate the NDIS vision. However, the current funding limitations are a major concern.

Informal carers are a cornerstone of the support system for many people with disability. Although they were often excluded by the NDIS initially, their contribution has been increasingly appreciated. Assessment processes plus planning and review meetings have increasingly included family and friends. In the future, they need to have a valued place where they can support the person with disability while ensuring that the person's choices are paramount.

The radical over hall of the disability sector by the NDIS has strived to overcome institutionalisation and organisational structures in disability segregated services. These previously offered a limited range of services and staff were often patronising and assumed control. The NDIS is trying to create a competitive disability market that will give people with disability choice and control. Professional staff are learning to change their occupational practice to share control with people with disability. However, unlearning professional assumptions of being the expert who makes decisions for others is slow and difficult, and the evidence suggests that there is some way to go.

As is often quoted, the NDIS is a once-in-a-lifetime opportunity for people with disability. It needs to be funded, nurtured and evaluated to ensure it reaches its potential.

References

Administrative Appeals Tribunal (AAT). (2018a). Website: http://www.aat.gov.au

Administrative Appeals Tribunal (AAT). (2018b). *National Disability Insurance Scheme Division, File Number(s): 2016/3237 and 2017/6358, Re: FFVQ.* Website: http://www.austlii.edu.au/cgi-bin/viewdoc/au/cases/cth/AATA/2018/1968.html

Australian Broadcasting Commission (ABC). (2018). Website: http://www.abc.net.au/news/2018-04-25/medicare-levy-increase-to-fund-ndis-scrapped/9696746

Australian Bureau of Statistics (ABS). (2015). *Disability, ageing and carers, Australia: First results, 2015.* Canberra: Australian Bureau of Statistics (ABS). Website: http://www.abs.gov.au/AUSSTATS/abs@.nsf/0/56C41FE7A67110C8CA257FA3001D080B?Opendocument

Australian Bureau of Statistics (ABS). (2018). *Australia's population to reach 25 million.* Website: http://www.abs.gov.au/ausstats/abs%40.nsf/mediareleasesbyCatalogue/C3315F52F6219DE9CA2582E1001BC66A?OpenDocument

Australian Government, Department of Social Services. (2018). *NDIS quality and safeguarding framework.* Website: https://www.dss.gov.au/disability-and-carers/programs-services/for-people-with-disability/ndis-quality-and-safeguarding-framework

Australian Government Joint Standing Committee on the National Disability Insurance Scheme. (2018). *Transitional Arrangements for the NDIS.* Canberra: Australian Government Joint Standing Committee on the National Disability Insurance Scheme. Website: https://www.aph.gov.au/Parliamentary_Business/Committees/Joint/National_Disability_Insurance_Scheme/Transition

Beresford, P., Fleming, J., Glynn, M., Bewley, C., Croft, S., Branfield, F., & Postle, K. (2011). *Supporting People: Towards a person-centred approach.* Bristol: The Policy Press.

Census Bureau. (2017). *Population estimates, July 1, 2017.* Website: https://www.census.gov/quickfacts/fact/table/US/PST045217

Commonwealth of Australia. (2013). *National Disability Insurance Scheme Act 2013.* Website: https://www.legislation.gov.au/Details/C2013A00020

Cortis, N., Macdonald, F., Davidson, B., & Bentham, E. (2017). *Reasonable, necessary and valued: Pricing disability services for quality support and decent jobs.* Health Services Union, Australian Services Union, and United Voice. Sydney. Website: https://www.sprc.unsw.edu.au/media/SPRCFile/NDIS_Pricing_Report.pdf

Council of Australian Governments (COAG). (2018). *National Disability Insurance Scheme COAG 2018 Disability reform council quarterly report March.* Canberra: Council of Australian Governments (COAG). Website: https://www.ndis.gov.au/medias/documents/report-q3-y5-pdf/Report-to-the-COAG-Disability-Reform-Council-for-Q3-of-Y5.pdf

DeCarlo, M. P., Bogenschutz, M. D., Hall-Lande, J. A., & Hewitt, A. S. (2018). Implementation of self-directed supports for people with intellectual and developmental disabilities in the United States. *Journal of Disability Policy Studies.* Advance online publication. https://doi.org/10.1177/1044207318790061

Every Australian Counts. (2018). Website: http://www.everyaustraliancounts.com.au/

Glendinning, C., Challis, D., Fernández, J.-L., Jacobs, S., Jones, K., Knapp, M., … Wilberforce, M. (2008). *Evaluation of the Individual Budgets pilot programme final report.* York, Social Policy Research Centre: University of York.

Harry, M. L., MacDonald, L., McLuckie, A., Battista, C., Mahoney, E. K., & Mahoney, K. J. (2017). Long-term experiences in cash and counseling for young adults with intellectual disabilities: Familial programme representative descriptions. *Journal of Applied Research in Intellectual Disabilities, 30*(4), 573–583.

Laragy, C. (2018). Flexible person-centred funding models. In P. Ramcharan & S. Thompson (Eds.), *Community services of the future: An evidence review* (pp. 10–16). Melbourne: Futures Social Services Institute (FSSI). Website: https://vcoss.org.au/wp-content/uploads/2018/02/Community-services-of-the-future-FSSI-2018-FINAL.pdf

Laragy, C., David, C., & Moran, N. (2016). A framework for providing information in individualised funding programmes. *Qualitative Social Work, 15*(2), 190–208.

Laragy, C., Fisher, K. R., Purcal, C., & Jenkinson, S. (2015). Australia's individualised disability funding packages: When do they provide greater choice and opportunity? *Asian Social Work and Policy Review, 9*, 282–292.

Mahoney, K. J., Wieler Fishman, N., Doty, P., & Squillace, M. (2007). The future of Cash & Counseling: The framers' view. *Health Services Research, 42*(1), 550–566.

Mavromaras, K., Moskos, M., Mahuteau, S., & Isherwood, L. (2018). *Evaluation of the NDIS, final report*. Adelaide: National Institute of Labour Studies, Flinders University. Website: https://www.dss.gov.au/disability-and-carers/programs-services/for-people-with-disability/national-disability-insurance-scheme/ndis-evaluation-consolidated-report

McKinsey & Company. (2018). *Independent pricing review, National Disability Insurance Scheme*. Website: https://www.ndis.gov.au/medias/documents/ipr-final-report-mckinsey/20180213-IPR-FinalReport.pdf

Miller, P., & Hayward, D. (2017). Social policy 'generosity' at a time of fiscal austerity: The strange case of Australia's National Disability Insurance Scheme. *Critical Social Policy, 37*(1), 128–147.

National Disability Insurance Scheme (NDIS). (2017). *Key data on psychosocial disability and the NDIS as at 31 March 2017*. Website: https://www.ndis.gov.au/medias/documents/hda/h2c/8804425367582/Attachment-A-Key-Data-on-NDIS-and-Psychosocial-Disability.pdf

National Disability Insurance Scheme (NDIS). (2018a). *Planning*. Website: https://www.ndis.gov.au/operational-guideline/planning/managing-funding-supports

National Disability Insurance Scheme (NDIS). (2018b). *Information, Linkages and Capacity Building (ILC)*. Website: https://www.ndis.gov.au/communities/ilc-home.html

National Disability Insurance Scheme (NDIS). (2018c). *Improving the NDIS participant and provider experience*. Website: https://www.ndis.gov.au/medias/documents/pathway-review-report/Report-NDIS-Pathway-Review.pdf

National Disability Insurance Scheme (NDIS). (2018d). *Quality and Safeguards Commission*. Website: https://www.ndiscommission.gov.au/

National Disability Insurance Scheme (NDIS). (2018e). *NDIS Fraud Taskforce*. Website: https://formerministers.dss.gov.au/18064/ndis-fraud-taskforce-established-to-tackle-crime/

National Disability Services. (2018). *Australian disability workforce report February 2018*. Sydney. Website: https://www.nds.org.au/policy/australian-disability-workforce-report-second-edition-highlights-workforce-risks1

Norstrand, J., Mahoney, K. J., Loughlin, D., & Simon-Rusinowitz, L. (2009). *What impact does the ability to purchase goods and services have on participants in Cash & Counseling programs?* Boston: National Resource Center for Participant-Directed Services, Boston College.

O'Keeffe, J. (2009). *Implementing self-direction programs with flexible individual budgets: Lessons learned from the Cash and Counseling replication states*. Princeton, NJ: National Resource Center for Participant-Directed Services. Website: http://www.nasuad.org/sites/nasuad/files/hcbs/files/153/7636/CC_Replication_Report_final.pdf

Parliament of Australia. (2013). *A short history of increases to the Medicare levy*. Website: https://www.aph.gov.au/About_Parliament/Parliamentary_Departments/Parliamentary_Library/FlagPost/2013/May/A_short_history_of_increases_to_the_Medicare_levy

Productivity Commission. (2011). *Disability care and support, inquiry report, No. 54*. Website: http://www.pc.gov.au/projects/inquiry/disability-support/report

Productivity Commission. (2017). *National Disability Insurance Scheme (NDIS) costs: Study report*. Canberra: Website: https://www.pc.gov.au/inquiries/completed/ndis-costs/report/ndis-costs.pdf

Purcal, C., Fisher, K. R., & Laragy, C. (2014). Analysing choice in Australian individual funding disability policies. *Australian Journal of Public Administration, 73*(1), 88–102.

Sciegaj, M., Mahoney, K. J., Schwartz, A. J., Simon-Rusinowitz, L., Selkow, I., & Loughlin, D. M. (2016). An inventory of publicly funded participant-directed long-term services and supports programs in the United States. *Journal of Disability Policy Studies, 26*(4), 245–251.

University of Sydney, & Community Mental Health Australia. (2018). *Mind the gap: The National Disability Insurance Scheme and psychosocial disability. Final report: Stakeholder identified gaps and solutions.* Sydney. Website: http://sydney.edu.au/health-sciences/documents/mind-the-gap.pdf

Warr, D., Dickinson, H., Olney, S., Hargrave, J., Karanikolas, A., Kasidis, V., Katsikis, G., Ozge, J., Peters, D. & Wheeler, J. (2017). *Choice, control and the NDIS.* Melbourne Social Equity Institute, University of Melbourne. Website: http://socialequity.unimelb.edu.au/news/news-archive/choice-control-and-the-ndis-report

Whalan, J., Acton, P., & Harmer, J. (2014). *A review of the capabilities of the National Disability Insurance Agency.* Website: https://www.ndis.gov.au/html/sites/default/files/documents/capability_review_2014_3.pdf

Preference, Choice, and Self-Determination in the Healthcare Context

Brian H. Abery and Lynda L. Anderson

Healthcare and Disability

In the 2010 US census, 54 million Americans had disabilities, representing about 19% of the noninstitutionalized population (U.S. Census Bureau, 2010). Although people with disabilities make up a relatively small percent of the US population, they account for 47% of total medical expenditures. The number of people in the USA and across the globe living with disabilities will grow substantially in the next 35 years, primarily because of the aging of the population (Iezzoni, 2011). At least partly due to this demographic trend, the management of chronic illness and disability has received increased attention over the past few decades, as have the healthcare disparities that exist between people with disabilities and the remainder of the population.

Chronic health conditions among people with disabilities as well as in the general population pose a significant strain on the healthcare systems worldwide. As many as 87% of people with a disability report having at least one chronic condition (Kinne, Patrick, & Doyle, 2004). Relative to the general population, people with disabilities face unique risks for poor health outcomes and experience higher rates of co-occurring chronic conditions than do people in the general population. This is especially true for people with intellectual and developmental disabilities (Anderson et al., 2013).

In this chapter, we review the health disparities experienced by people with disabilities in the USA and the history of how the country's healthcare system has responded to members of this segment of the population. The literature related to choice and control in the healthcare domain will subsequently be reviewed with a focus on both the personal capacities supportive of preference and choice in this

B. H. Abery (✉) · L. L. Anderson
Institute on Community Integration, University of Minnesota, Minneapolis, MN, USA
e-mail: abery001@umn.edu

© Springer Nature Switzerland AG 2020
R. J. Stancliffe et al. (eds.), *Choice, Preference, and Disability*, Positive Psychology and Disability Series, https://doi.org/10.1007/978-3-030-35683-5_8

area and the ecological factors at play. In the concluding section of the chapter, processes and tools for supporting healthcare choice, control, and self-determination for people with disabilities will be reviewed.

Health Disparities and Disability

Healthy People 2020 outlines the health goals in the USA for the coming decade. One of the overarching goals was to eliminate health disparities. The US Office of Disease Prevention and Health Promotion (ODPHP) (2014) defines health disparities as "[a] particular type of health difference that is closely linked with social, economic, and/or environmental disadvantage" (http://www.healthypeople. gov/2020/about/foundation-health-measures/Disparities).

Social determinants of health play a powerful role in understanding health disparities. They include individual behavior and genetics, but also environmental factors, including socioeconomic status, literacy, poverty, discrimination, and public policy (ODPHP, 2014). People with disabilities experience many of the social determinants associated with health disparities, including poverty and discrimination. Krahn and Fox (2014) identified disability in and of itself and the learning history that goes along with it as risk factors that have the potential to limit an individual's choice and control and, in turn, the quality of health outcomes experienced. In the 2001–2005 National Health Interview Surveys, people with disabilities were more likely to smoke or be obese and less likely to be physically active, all factors associated with increased health risk (Iezzoni, 2011). Despite these risk factors, people with disabilities were significantly less likely to report that their healthcare providers had discussed their health-related behavioral issues with them during office visits. The 2006 Medical Expenditure Panel Survey (MEPS) data showed the same pattern of lack of access to quality care and poorer health outcomes, despite medical expenses for people with disabilities being 4.3 times higher than for the general population (Reichard, Stolze, & Fox, 2011). In their review of recent studies focused on this issue, Krahn, Walker, and Correa-De-Araujo (2015) concluded that these health disparities, most of which are avoidable, are not primarily caused by the person's underlying disability, but by system-level factors.

Lack of access to high-quality healthcare for people with disabilities and severely limited choice and control over healthcare result from a variety of factors. These include challenges related to communication barriers, negative attitudes toward disability held by healthcare providers, limited skill sets possessed by healthcare personnel to effectively interact with patients with disabilities, the lack of training healthcare providers receive in this area, and a funding system that provides lower levels of reimbursement for services delivered to people using public versus private healthcare insurance (Reichard & Turnbull III, 2004). Because of these factors, people with disabilities, especially people with intellectual and developmental disabilities, too often do not receive more than cursory physical examinations, experience providers directing communication at caregivers rather than the patient, are rarely involved in decision-making about treatment, and experience difficulties making appointments (Larson, Anderson, & Doljanac, 2005) Misdiagnoses, over-medication, and, at the extreme, avoidable deaths are too common (Ward, Nichols, & Freedman, 2010). These experiences, although prevalent in the USA, are even more frequent and intense in many international contexts, making not only the exercise of preference and choice a near impossibility but access to healthcare of any quality extremely difficult (Blair, 2012; Welyczko, 2018).

In the USA, physicians, nursing staff, and other healthcare personnel report multiple challenges to providing effective healthcare to people with disabilities. Low levels of responsiveness to the unique healthcare needs of this population starts quite early in the careers of providers. Brown, Graham, Richeson, Wu, and McDermott (2010), for example, found that medical students exhibited poorer performance caring for patients with intellectual disability compared to others in tasks varying from taking a medical history, conducting physical exams, and ordering laboratory tests, reflecting the lack of disability training in most medical programs. Most adults with disabilities also rely on Medicaid-funded insurance programs that have notoriously poor provider reimbursement levels, further decreasing access to care (Birenbaum, 2009).

The lack of experience of most healthcare personnel in the USA in working with people with disabilities is directly reflected at a policy level in the clinical guidelines and subsequent care. Mizen, Maclie, Cooper, and Melville (2012) found that most clinical guidelines fail to address people with disabilities as being at high risk for secondary health conditions despite research indicating high prevalence of these health-related challenges. They also noted that policy development committees at federal and state agencies and managed care organizations often failed to include people with disabilities on groups developing guidelines for the provision of care (Mizen et al., 2012). Guidance that could be available for healthcare providers on appropriate screening and treatment for people with disabilities is therefore missing.

The resulting health disparities experienced by people with disabilities include high rates of chronic conditions. People with disabilities are 14–16 times more likely than the general population to report at least 1 chronic condition, and nearly a quarter report more than one chronic condition (Vogel et al., 2007). Relative to the general population, people with intellectual and developmental disabilities face unique risks for poor health outcomes (Anderson et al., 2013), experiencing both decreased life expectancy and greater rates of co-occurring conditions (Scepters et al., 2005). Further, they are more likely to develop health problems and have a greater probability of experiencing chronic conditions (Reichard et al., 2011; Tyler, Schramm, Karafa, Tang, & Jain, 2010).

History of Preference, Choice, and Control for People with Disabilities in Healthcare

As people with disabilities in the USA have moved from institutions into the community, attitudes toward members of this group as well as the frameworks used to provide supports and services have changed dramatically. In both the education and social services realms, disability has become progressively conceptualized as an aspect of diversity, and a basic human rights perspective based on the concept of equity has gained support. As a result, the manner in which services provided has increasingly become person-centered with opportunities for the expression of preference, choice-making, and self-determination emphasized. Despite a multitude of societal changes that have taken place over this period, much less transformation with respect to disability has occurred within medicine. Remaining grounded in an individualist perspective, the focus in healthcare remains on disability being conceptualized as pathology and as a problem inherent in the individual (Brandt & Pope, 1997).

The ICF framework (World Health Organization [WHO], 2001) and its focus on participation have potentially important implications for opportunities related to the expression of preference and the exercise of choice within the healthcare context. The framework shares several concepts with health-related behavioral change theories, making it a useful tool for the development of health interventions for people with disabilities (Ravesloot et al., 2011). Personal control, for example, is conceptualized as an important component of participation (Heinemann et al., 2013). Participation in healthcare decision-making in turn has been found to be related to the quality of the patient-provider relationship, leading to enhanced knowledge and understanding with respect to one's condition (Eldh, Ekman, & Ehnfors, 2010).

In 2006 the United Nations Convention on Rights of Persons with Disabilities (United Nations [UN], 2006) declared the "right of persons with disabilities to the enjoyment of the highest attainable standard of health without discrimination on the basis of disability." Article 25 of the CRPD states that persons with disabilities have the right to the same range, quality, and standard of free or affordable healthcare as provided to other persons; health services that are specific to their disabilities; high-quality care based on informed consent; and the provision of health insurance that is both affordable and provided in a fair and reasonable manner (UN, 2006). This framework is driving changes to the delivery of healthcare services to people with disabilities around the world.

Self-Determination

Self-determination, as we operationalize it, refers to individuals exercising the degree of choice and control they desire over those areas of life they define as important (Abery, Olson, Poetz, & Smith, 2019; Abery & Stancliffe, 2003). The construct includes, but is not limited to, an individual's causal agency (Shogren, Wehmeyer, Palmer, Rifenbark, & Little, 2015). Rather, it focuses on the goodness-of-fit people experience between desired and actual levels of personal control in those areas of life they consider important. Although related to personal control, self-determination is more complex in that it takes into consideration the fact that people desire varying degrees of control over different areas of life often opting to share decision-making with others. Within the healthcare context, for example, few people desire to have complete control over their healthcare decision-making. Instead they wish to share decision-making authority with trusted others who, within this context, typically include medical personnel. It also reflects the fact that to experience self-determination, the expression of preferences as well as the exercise of control need to be in areas of life that a person deems important and sees the value of making choices and decisions.

The exercise of self-determination does not take place in isolation, but rather within an individual's ecosystem. It can be conceptualized in terms of transactions between the person and their environment – a process, the foundation of which is embedded relationships. Drawing on the work of Bronfenbrenner (1992) and Garbarino (2017), Abery and colleagues (Abery et al., 2019) acknowledge the importance of a person's self-determination competencies. These capacities, however, are viewed as supportive though not necessary for self-determination. Contextual factors associated with a multilevel ecosystem must also be considered.

Self-determination, choice, and preference with healthcare can therefore be viewed as being exercised within the context of the healthcare environment and the relationships a person establishes with and within it (Abery et al., 2019). These can be relationships with individuals (e.g., a physician, nurse) or systems, whether they be small (e.g., specific clinic, etc.) or large (a state human services system). Different relationships offer different opportunities for the expression of preference and choice.

Choice and Control Within the Healthcare System

The healthcare system in the USA is complex, fragmented, and sometimes overly restrictive in terms of program eligibility. It leaves many people with disabilities with little to no healthcare coverage. Others experience cost-sharing burdens that not only prevent them from being able to express preferences and exercise desired levels of choice and control but result in their being unable to afford wellness visits, medication, and/or long-term care (National Council on Disability, 2007). One by-product of this fragmented system is that contact with healthcare providers is all too often characterized by series of trips to the emergency room after relatively simple-to-treat problems become significantly more complicated (Lunsky et al., 2012). Receiving healthcare supports in an environment in which it is unlikely that one will be interacting with the same medical personnel on each visit (e.g., an emergency department) limits the development of relationships that increase an appreciation for patient preferences and the exercise of choice and control on the part of those receiving services.

To engage in choice-making, one must first have opportunities to make choices – or more specifically have more than one option from which to choose. Unfortunately, this is often not the case for people with disabilities, as healthcare systems in most countries provide far fewer opportunities for choice for individuals with disabilities than the general population (Al-Abdulwahab & Al-Gain, 2003; Werner, 2012). For the most part, this difference has nothing to do with a person's capacity, or lack thereof, to express preferences and make choices but, rather, is a result of system-level factors and policies, one of which centers on how healthcare providers are reimbursed for their services.

Healthcare reimbursement for people with disabilities in the USA Healthcare for a large portion of people with disabilities in the USA is financed partially or fully through the Center for Medicaid and Medicare Services (CMS), a federally funded public insurance program. The reliance of most people with disabilities on public insurance serves to decrease access to care, as well as opportunities for choice and respect for preferences because of low reimbursement rates paid to providers (Anderson et al., 2013). Primary care private practices are usually paid on a fee-for-service basis and are paid far less for wellness and immediate care services (e.g., providing medications and lifestyle counseling) than specialists are reimbursed for procedural and imaging services (Bodenheimer, Berenson, & Rudolf, 2007).

Almost a decade ago, the results of the Medicare Payment Advisory Commission beneficiary survey found that 28% of beneficiaries reported problems finding a primary care physician. This represented a 17% increase from 2006 and has risen even more in the subsequent decade (Medicare Payment Advisory Commission, 2009). Poor reimbursement rates and rising operating costs have forced a growing number of physicians to accept fewer or no Medicare and Medicaid patients (Anderson et al., 2013), a trend that has increased in recent years (Bodenheimer & Pham, 2010).

In a study of Medicare and Medicaid users, Higgins, Shugrue, Ruiz, and Robison (2015) asked beneficiaries about their healthcare. Participants reported a wide range of experiences in provider choice, with many users indicating that they changed their doctors quite often. This was, however, *not* by choice in most instances. Groups strongly asserted that provider choice is extremely limited for Medicaid and Medicaid beneficiaries because so many providers refuse to take their insurance. Most participants indicated that the doctors available to them had to be selected from a limited list and that these healthcare professionals often canceled appointments when reimbursements were delayed. A significant number reported being turned away by providers who no longer were accepting Medicare or Medicaid, even those who had seen their primary care physicians for many years. Given the current approach to healthcare financing in the USA, it is not difficult to understand why many people with disabilities feel unwelcomed in healthcare settings and perceive their role as passive recipients of care (Ryan, Patrick, Deci, & Williams, 2008).

Enhancing the Delivery of Healthcare to People with Disabilities

Most efforts focused on increasing the responsiveness of the healthcare system, including respect for patient preferences and choice, have failed to include people with disabilities (Mizen et al., 2012). Research in this area undertaken with people with disabilities, however, does show considerable promise. The most effective of these efforts have focused on educating persons with disabilities to take a more active role in their health and healthcare and attempted to integrate healthcare systems in a manner that people with disabilities experience improved access to both the system and healthcare personnel.

Among members of the general population, studies of healthcare approaches supporting patient choice and control have found these factors to be strong predictors of (1) better health outcomes, (2) increased access to and satisfaction with care, (3) lower healthcare costs, and (4) higher levels of patient activation (Carman et al., 2013; Hibbard & Greene, 2013; McMillan et al., 2013). A meta-analysis of datasets that used a self-determination theory framework in healthcare or health promotion studies found that supporting patient autonomy improved self-regulation and perceived control, which ultimately improved physical and mental health (Ng et al., 2012). The approaches taken in these initiatives would likely benefit a large percentage of people with disabilities.

Patient activation Patient activation refers to the ability of an individual to practice health-promoting behaviors; manage chronic conditions; obtain health-related information and communicate with health providers; and choose quality providers (Hibbard & Greene, 2013). High activation has been shown to improve several health-related outcomes, including increased use of preventive care, fewer episodes of hospitalizations and emergency department visits, and overall lower healthcare costs (Greene, Hibbard, Sacks, Overton, & Parrotta, 2015; Hibbard & Greene, 2013). Higher patient activation has also been positively associated with symptom management, higher levels of hope, and lower emotional discomfort in people with schizophrenia (Kukla, Salyers, & Lysaker, 2013).

Self-efficacy and health behavior change In social cognitive theory, perceived self-efficacy is viewed as influencing motivation and action both directly and indirectly and is a key factor in behavior change (Bandura, 1977). In this model, perceived control is required for behavioral action. Both behavior and outcome expectancy are considered key factors in health behavior change. The value one places on health is also an important predictor of health behavior change (Wallston & Wallston, 1982). Bandura (2004) posited that there is a reciprocal relationship between self-efficacy and goals, outcome expectations, and perceived barriers and supports. The balance of these factors influences motivation to make health behavior change. Having high self-efficacy is associated with higher goals and greater commitment.

Bandura (2004) also noted that health is a social matter and not solely an individual problem. Environmental and social structures are just as important in health behavior change. This is a critical component to understanding health behavioral change for adults with disability. Family members and paid caregivers often make day-to-day decisions about diet and activities, leaving little opportunity for people with disabilities, and especially people with intellectual and developmental disabilities, to engage in health-promoting behavior even when they desire to do so (Bodde, Seo, & Frey, 2009).

Supporting Preference, Choice, and Self-Determination in the Healthcare Context

Supporting the exercise of preference, choice, and self-determination within healthcare is not a simple task. Unlike those areas of life in which people with disabilities can be supported to exercise greater control through the development of additional personal capacities, the exercise of choice and control within healthcare is limited by system-level factors. Skills, knowledge, and attitudes/beliefs supportive of choice and control are a necessary, but not sufficient, ingredient for significant positive change in the exercise of self-determination to take place within this facet of life. Rather, one must take an ecological perspective (Bronfenbrenner, 1992; Garbarino, 2017) to support change in this area. The positive side of this approach is that it is not contingent upon people with disabilities needing to learn new skills and develop additional capacities but rather focuses on the healthcare system making accommodations and providing adaptations.

To effectively support choice and control, the healthcare system must actively engage people with disabilities in health awareness, self-advocacy, health literacy, and health promotion activities to enable them to participate in, if not direct, their own healthcare (Marks & Heller, 2003). People with disabilities are often unable to represent their own health concerns due to a lack of understanding of how healthcare systems work. Healthcare delivery systems must therefore develop and integrate effective networks of primary care providers and other health professionals that can positively impact health outcomes for people with disabilities.

Systems Change

Bechtel and Ness (2010) noted that what patients most value in their healthcare interactions is a whole person approach that includes a physician taking the time to get to know the patient; a patient-provider relationship based on shared decision-making, trust, and respect; provision of the supports people need to effectively self-manage their health concerns; and communication and coordination. Although Betchel and Ness' work did not primarily focus on people with disabilities, their results clearly represent what most, if not all, people are seeking from their healthcare systems.

In its joint position statement on health and mental healthcare, the American Association on Intellectual and Developmental Disability (AAIDD) and The Arc of the United States noted that although many people encounter difficulty in finding affordable, high-quality healthcare, people with intellectual and developmental disabilities face additional barriers when attempting to access health services. One target for systems change identified by AAIDD and The Arc focused on the creation of standards of care for people with disabilities and models of care provision that take their unique needs into account. These organizations contend that such standards should account for the unique healthcare needs of people with disabilities, integrate concepts of self-direction and self-determination, and reflect the need for and benefits of person-centeredness. One approach that includes most of these recommendations is the patient-centered medical home.

The Patient-Centered Medical Home Model A medical home is a clinical setting that serves as a central resource for a patient's ongoing medical care providing healthcare services in a patient-centered manner. Patient-centered care puts the individual at the center of care (Moore, 2008) and combines comprehensive primary care, coordination of services, patient empowerment, and direct involvement in healthcare decision-making (American Academy of Family Physicians, 2007). Evidence emerging from a number of studies (e.g., Davies et al., 2009; Sumsion & Lencucha, 2007) indicates that patients value an approach to care in which they are able to develop a relationship with their provider and be involved in healthcare decision-making. Evaluations of PCMHs for people with disabilities have shown that both adult patients and parents of pediatric patients who utilize PCMHs are highly satisfied with their care and view provider-patient interactions as empowering (Reid et al., 2010; Solberg, Asche, Fontaine, Flottemesch, & Anderson, 2011; Weedon, Carbone, Bilder, O'Brien, & Dorius, 2012).

The PCMH framework has the potential to enhance opportunities for preference and informed choice-making for people with disabilities. Unlike contacts with emergent care staff, patients using PCMHs establish ongoing relationships with a primary care provider. As a result, these healthcare professionals are much more likely to understand the preferences, values, communication style, and concerns of the patients they serve than an emergent care specialist. Within the PCMH context, patients are also accessing providers who have an explicit focus on patient-centered care and care coordination. As Abery and colleagues have suggested (2019), self-determination is exercised with the context of relationships. The establishment of relationships with a primary care provider and ancillary healthcare staff that include support to navigate the healthcare system has the potential to significantly enhance support for preference and choice-making in a number of ways. As a patient-centered approach, the PCMH model also explicitly supports patient empowerment and active membership in the multidisciplinary team.

Although related to patient activation, patient empowerment is a more proactive concept. It reflects patients' self-determination and their capacity to make autonomous decisions (Aujoulat, Marcolongo, Bonadiman, & Deccache, 2008). Within the context of a stable relationship with a care provider in which knowledge is communicated in an understandable and meaningful way, patients are more likely to develop confidence in their ability to make *informed* choices about their health (Ludman et al., 2013). Research also suggests that with confidence, patients are empowered to act in a more self-determined manner communicating more assertively and effectively with providers, when expressing their health concerns and preferences (Chen, Mortensen, & Bloodworth, 2014), seeking more health information, and taking charge of their care (Aujoulat et al., 2008; Aujoulat, d'Hoore, & Deccache, 2007).

The development of community-based PCMHs that offer access to person-centered care for people with disabilities has been a slow process, but innovative programs are in place. In Colorado Springs, Colorado, for example, the Developmental Disabilities Health Center (DDHC) was developed to provide multidisciplinary, fully integrated healthcare to adults with intellectual disability (https://www.peakvista.org/locations/ddhc). The DDHC provides primary healthcare, behavioral health, and psychiatric services, as well as referrals to specialty care. It has done several things specifically designed to make healthcare more person-centered. Appointments with patients with disabilities are lengthened to provide time for both relationship building and effective communication; lighting is adapted to provide accommodations for people with sensory issues; examination rooms are enlarged to allow for multiple people an individual might desire to accompany them; and equipment was selected with the needs of people with physical disabilities in mind. Even more important than the physical setting is that healthcare personnel, from receptionists to nursing staff and physicians, have received training with respect to disabilities.

Healthcare Provider Training

A patient-centered medical home is of little value if the healthcare personnel providing services are not accessible, fail to understand people with disabilities, and show little respect for their right to be involved in their healthcare decision-making. Unfortunately, a large percentage of people with disabilities have difficulties communicating their needs and advocating for themselves in what are often extremely complex healthcare systems. People with disabilities are likely to require longer periods of time to process questions, need to frequently ask for clarification, and tend to be reluctant to ask questions or advocate for themselves. In today's world of managed care, however, this is often not available (Yarnall et al., 2009).

Within this context, people with disabilities report frequently experiencing insensitive staff and communication barriers with healthcare providers (Reichard & Turnbull III, 2004). Physicians themselves report their own lack of training on how to effectively treat people with disabilities, inadequate exposure to and discomfort with members of this group, and lack of time to adequately deliver healthcare services to them (Reichard & Turnbull III, 2004).

Over the years, medical education programs have shown variable curricular emphasis on disability. There currently exist few standards in this area, and there are no national expectations that healthcare professionals receive disability education. In spite of this lack of training, most people with disabilities look to general practitioners for their medical care. This situation is slowly changing for the better. Some US medical and nursing schools are beginning to offer disability-focused content, typically in psychology, psychiatry, or pediatrics programs. *The Alliance for Disability in Health Care, Inc.* (http://www.adhce.org/), a not-for-profit organization of medical and nursing school faculty and other healthcare educators, is now working to integrate disability-related content and experiences into all healthcare training programs. The Alliance serves as a clearinghouse of information on the disability training of healthcare staff and has taken a major step forward in developing competencies for healthcare professionals who desire to work with people with disabilities.

The AAIDD (2006) and The Arc of the United States (2013) have noted that people with intellectual and developmental disabilities may have difficulties communicating their needs and making healthcare decisions without support. Healthcare education therefore needs to develop and formalize training that emphasizes respect, communication skills, relationship building, and the concepts of shared and/or supported decision-making. Though potentially able to enhance the healthcare outcomes of all patients, training in these areas is critical for providers of healthcare services to people with disabilities. This education must ensure that physicians and nurses develop the professional competencies to understand their patients and learn what healthcare issues are troubling them, communicate diagnoses and recommendations in a respectful and clear manner, and grasp the basic right of people with disabilities to self-determination. This training will need to include both didactic coursework to familiarize healthcare personnel with a wide variety of disabilities and ongoing face-to-face interactions with people with disability from all walks of life in addition to the "standard patient" clinical training.

Shared and Supported Decision-Making

Shared decision-making is a process in which a patient and their healthcare provider share information to come to a consensus about a treatment plan (Charles, Gafni, & Whelan, 1997). Recent federal and state policies are supportive of this approach, including the Affordable Care Act, which calls for the broad application of shared decision-making as a way to improve care quality and patient experience. The approach is an essential element in Medicare's Shared Savings and Accountable Care Organization programs (CMS, 2011). In addition, legislation enacted in the State of Washington where a number of shared decision-making pilot projects are taking place implies that shared decision-making meets legal standards for informed consent (Kuehn, 2009). The increased interest shown by policy makers in shared decision-making is not unique to the USA. Härter, van der Weijden, and Elwyn (2011) found policy-related activities in 13 countries designed to support patient engagement in healthcare decision-making.

Increased interest in shared decision-making is closely related to initial research studies that indicate lower overall medical costs (Veroff, Marr, & Wennberg, 2013). Additional studies have found that patients who participate in shared decision-making exhibit an enhanced understanding of healthcare choices and, as a result, receive treatment that is better aligned with their preferences (Stacey et al., 2011). In a meta-analysis of shared decision-making and health outcomes, Durand et al. (2014) found that it significantly improved health outcomes for disadvantaged populations, including people with disabilities and limited literacy.

A shared decision-making process for people with cognitive disabilities may include a team of supporters in addition to the individual, such as family and caregivers. The level of involvement of the person with a disability will depend on personal capacities and characteristics. However, even people with more significant disabilities can contribute to the decision-making process through their life stories that can help the team understand what they value (Sullivan & Heng, 2018). People with intellectual and developmental disabilities can be supported in the shared decision-making process through a structured, planned approach that includes identifying the decision/choice to be made, asking questions that need to be answered, identifying who needs to be a part of the decision, and the best process for supporting the person with a disability to participate (Lotan & Ells, 2010).

Supported decision-making Some people with disabilities will be unable to take part in shared healthcare decision-making in the absence of a significant amount of support. One approach to facilitate preference, choice, and control for them is supported decision-making (SDM) (Blanck & Martinis, 2015). Although there are multiple approaches to SDM, it generally occurs when people use trusted friends, family members, or advocates to help them understand their situations and choices so they can make their own informed decisions (Campanella, 2015; Dinerstein, 2012).

At its core, supported decision-making is a highly interpersonal process in which the healthcare provider, person with a disability, and his or her trusted supporter(s) collaborate to share the best available information with which to make informed choices. These choices are based upon the individual's preferences. Supported decision-making is person-centered, relying on not just a provider's clinical expertise but his/her relationship with the person with a disability and their support team (Alston et al., 2012).

One simple strategy to support shared and supported decision-making is to ensure that people with disabilities are provided with the option of using a health passport. Health passports are portable documents that communicate information about medical history, medications, healthcare preferences, and other information that can be useful for healthcare providers to make appropriate diagnoses and to provide treatments. Health passports may increase both the healthcare self-determination and health literacy skills of people with disabilities (McNaughton, Balandin, Kennedy, & Sandmel, 2010). They also improve communication between providers and patients about health problems, are effective tools in emergent care, and support improved health-related knowledge (Heifetz & Lunsky, 2018; Nguyen, Lennox, & Ware, 2014).

Supporting Health Education and Literacy

Limited health literacy has been associated with health disparities for some time now (Institute of Medicine, 2009) and is related to low levels of patient choice and control. Improved health education and literacy is therefore a critical component for people with disabilities to exercise control over their health and manage chronic conditions (WHO, 2001). Communication and literacy building approaches that increase access to information can improve decision-making and lead to more informed choices. To make informed choices about their healthcare, people need access to information regarding their own health, the healthcare system, and the coverage under which they are insured (Wolf et al., 2009). Access to and understanding of this information may present challenges for specific groups of people especially people with intellectual and developmental disabilities.

A number of strategies can effectively increase the level of access to health-related information, including the use of the principles of universal design. For people with intellectual disability and limited literacy skills, for example, pictorial manuals and handbooks have been demonstrated to be effective in teaching health-related skills (Feldman, 2004). Other researchers have demonstrated that pictorial adaptations of mainstream educational materials can increase understanding in this area (Glazemakers & Deboutte, 2013).

Photographs as a communication tool are also a strategy to support health literacy among people with disabilities. Anderson (2019) found that adults with intellectual disability could successfully use photographs to support their health-related behavior. Although the use of illustrations, photographs, and iconic imagery can enhance understanding of health information, people with disabilities also need access to culturally appropriate health information regarding the availability services and how to access them in a complex system. This is an area where it would likely be helpful for patients, especially patients with disabilities, to have someone to help them navigate the system.

Over the last decade, researchers have explored the use of technology as a health literacy and education tool for people with a variety of disabilities. Technology in healthcare broadly refers to the combined use of information and communication technologies and health monitoring devices and covers a wide variety of technologies such as internal (implants for monitoring physiological signals), devices integrated into clothes (wearable technologies), and smart house technologies. Ptomey et al. (2015) employed tablet computers to support young adults with intellectual and developmental disabilities to monitor their own food intake and exercise in a successful weight loss program. In a similar vein, Naslund, Aschbrenner, Barre, and Bartels (2015) supported lifestyle interventions targeting weight loss, exercise, and community access among persons with serious psychiatric disabilities enrolled in a weight loss program through the use of wearable activity monitoring devices (e.g., Fitbits and iPhone).

Medical needs can also be monitored through devices such as the Medtronic (www.medtronic.com), which allows doctors to monitor patients with disabilities in their homes. This information is sent electronically to the health network, and clinicians can then monitor the information and make any necessary medical decisions. Wessel (2019) has developed and is testing a system that uses the web or cable systems to which persons with disabilities are connected to support management of chronic healthcare conditions through activity reminders, monitoring of activities of daily living, and the dispensing and appropriate use of medication. The system can be set up to collect diagnostic information and through Bluetooth technology directly send this information to a person's health provider so that steps can be taken to provide the necessary prevention and care.

Care Coordination and Navigation

A critical factor to consider in supporting healthcare choice and control is the extent to which each of these is of an "informed nature." If one is not aware of possible alternatives for care, potential side effects, and costs, it's impossible to adequately articulate one's preferences, make informed choices, or exercise self-determination. Given the complexity of healthcare, consumers must possess a sophisticated set of skills in order to effectively understand the options available to them and benefit from the services to which they have access. For a variety of reasons, this is a challenge to people with disabilities that impact cognitive capacities. Care coordination and navigation are two strategies that are being tried to support healthcare-related decision-making and ensure that it is of an informed nature.

Care coordination and navigation organize patient care activities to facilitate the appropriate delivery of healthcare services (Council on Children with Disabilities Medical Home Implementation Project Advisory Committee, 2014, e1452). They are processes that link people with disabilities with appropriate services and resources in a coordinated effort to achieve good health. Care coordinators proactively communicate with the people they serve on a regular basis using a proactive approach to detect social or medical problems before a person experiences crisis. In the USA, care coordination is among the six national priority areas targeted for improvement by the National Quality Strategy (National Priorities Partnership., 2011). It is intended as a method of information gathering and sharing, barrier reduction, and advocacy for patients bridging gaps in the services they receive and empowering them to make good healthcare choices.

Care coordinators are typically healthcare staff specially trained for coordination responsibilities and drawn from social workers and nursing staff (Darnell, 2007). Care navigation, while originally undertaken by healthcare professionals, is increasingly being led by patients with past experiences with similar conditions. Both approaches are intended to reduce barriers, enhance patient empowerment through information sharing, and bridge service gaps.

Adults with disabilities generally desire to play an active part in managing their health. Two critical roles that Baumbusch, Phinney, and Baumbusch (2014) have identified for care coordinators in this area are *helping patients understand the nature of their health-related problems* and *supporting patients to navigate the healthcare system.* The first role entails clear communication focused on plain language and ensuring that healthcare staff respond to patient questions in a manner the person can understand. The second theme focuses on strategies developed jointly by the patients and their physicians to manage health needs.

In recent years, a number of states have established care coordination organizations to better coordinate care for persons with disabilities. These organizations take the best features of the medical home model and add intensive social service supports (Palsbo, Mastal, & O'Donnell, 2006). A hallmark of care coordination is that healthcare professionals function as teams, using either integrated or collaborative models to actively engage patients in healthcare decision-making providing them with the information they need to make informed choices.

Given the potential of care coordination and navigation to enhance respect for preferences, choice, and decision-making within the healthcare context, it is surprising that more research has not studied its impact on choice and control within healthcare. That which has been undertaken, however, makes a good case for the use of this approach. McAllister et al. (2018) found that care coordination facilitated goal identification and progress, reduce unmet needs, and increased feelings of empowerment. Working with families, Sheftall et al. (2019) found that parents of patients with disabilities were quite satisfied with the care coordination they received and that the healthcare staff serving in this role spent a good deal of time advocating for the person with a disability served. Ruggiano, Shtompel, and Evardsson (2015) found that, when provided with care coordination supports, older adults with disabilities were significantly more likely to make decisions about services, interventions, and providers. In one study that did attempt to directly determine the impact of choice and control on the experience of people with disabilities within the healthcare context, Anderson and Abery (2016) found that patient access to care coordination and care navigation supports enhanced self-determination experienced with respect to their health and healthcare, as well as increased satisfaction with healthcare services. Increased self-determination was directly related to greater opportunities for choice and decision-making.

Conclusion

As a result of a variety of system-level factors, people with disabilities face numerous health inequities that lead to health disparities. In addition to poorer health outcomes, people all too often also experience less choice and control within the healthcare context and encounter a lack of respect for their preferences. One approach to improving both of these outcomes is to focus on supporting persons with disabilities to develop the knowledge, skills, and attitudes necessary to more effectively advocate for themselves with physicians, nursing staff, benefits administrators, and other healthcare personnel. This is the approach taken in programs designed to enhance patient empowerment, activation, health literacy, and self-efficacy. On the basis of the research reviewed in this chapter, it can be concluded that this strategy does make a positive difference for a good number of people with disabilities.

An alternative approach to enhancing choice, control, and self-determination within the context of interest is to make changes that support easier access to healthcare systems and ensure that providers possess the knowledge, skills, and capacities to support all individuals exercising greater self-determination. Research evidence suggests that this is more likely to happen when healthcare is delivered within the context of person-centered medical home model that provides care coordination to patients and is staffed by personnel who are well trained to support persons with disabilities to maintain their health and wellness. Improving the patient-provider relationship with a focus on enhancing understanding of disability, mutual respect, effective communication, and shared or supported decision-making has the potential to both enhance choice in the healthcare context and improve health-related decisions and outcomes.

Working within this framework, educational interventions aimed at enhancing the self-determination capacities of individuals with disabilities can be conceptualized as complimentary to efforts designed to ensure that the system is more user-friendly and accommodations are made for patients with disabilities in a manner that both empowers them and protects their basic human rights. Further research and the development and testing of interventions such as these are needed to learn more about what approaches are most efficacious for which people and develop best practices for healthcare providers.

References

Abery, B. H., Olson, M. R., Poetz, C. L., & Smith, J. G. (2019). Self-determination and self-advocacy: It's my life. In A. S. Hewitt & K. M. Nye-Langerman (Eds.), *Community living and participation for people with intellectual and developmental disabilities* (pp. 117–140). Washington, D.C.: American Association on Intellectual and Developmental Disabilities.

Abery, B. H., & Stancliffe, R. J. (2003). A tripartite ecological theory of self-determination. In M. L. Wehmeyer, B. H. Abery, D. Mithaug, & R. J. Stancliffe (Eds.), *Theory in self-determination: Foundations for educational practice* (pp. 43–78). Springfield, IL: Charles C. Thomas Publishing.

Al-Abdulwahab, S. S., & Al-Gain, S. I. (2003). Attitudes of Saudi Arabian health care professionals towards people with physical disabilities. *Asia Pacific Disability Rehabilitation Journal, 14*(1), 63–70.

Alston, C., Paget, L., Halvorson, G., Novelli, B., Guest, J., et al. (2012). *Communicating with patients on health care evidence*. Washington, D.C.: Institute of Medicine Sep. (Discussion Paper). Available from: http://www.iom.edu/~/media/Files/Perspectives-Files/2012/Discussion-Papers/VSRT-Evidence.pdf

American Academy of Family Physicians. (2007). *Joint principles of the patient-centered medical home*. Washington, D.C.:. Patient-Centered Primary Care Collaborative; 2007: American Academy of Pediatrics, American College of Physicians, and American Osteopathic Association.

American Association on Intellectual and Developmental Disabilities. (2006). *Declaration on health parity for persons with intellectual and developmental disabilities*. Washington, D.C.: American Association on Intellectual and Developmental Disabilities.

Anderson, L. L., & Abery, B. H. (2016). *The impact of care coordination and navigation on the health care self-determination of persons with physical disabilities*. Technical Report #2, Minneapolis, MN: University of Minnesota, Institute on Community Integration.

Anderson, L. L., Humphries, K., McDermott, S., Marks, B., Sisirak, J., & Larson, S. (2013). The state of the science of health and wellness for adults with intellectual and developmental disabilities. *Intellectual and Developmental Disabilities, 51*(5), 385–398.

Anderson, MapelLentz, Hallas-Muchow & Gulaid (2019). In A.S. Hewitt & K.M. Nye-Lengerman (Eds.), Community living and participation for people with intellectual and developmental disabilities. Washington D.C.: American association on intellectual and developmental disabilities.

Aujoulat, I., d'Hoore, W., & Deccache, A. (2007). Patient empowerment in theory and practice: Polysemy or cacophony? *Patient Education and Counseling, 66*(1), 13–20.

Aujoulat, I., Marcolongo, R., Bonadiman, L., & Deccache, A. (2008). Reconsidering patient empowerment in chronic illness: A critique of models of self-efficacy and bodily control. *Social Science & Medicine, 66*(5), 1228–1239.

Bandura, A. (1977). Self-efficacy: Toward a unifying theory of behavioral change. *Psychological Review, 84*(2), 191.

Bandura, A. (2004). Health promotion by social cognitive means. *Health Education & Behavior, 31*(2), 143–164.

Baumbusch, J., Phinney, A., & Baumbusch, S. (2014). Practising family medicine for adults with intellectual disabilities: Patient perspectives on helpful interactions. *Canadian Family Physician, 60*(7), e356–e361.

Bechtel, C., & Ness, D. L. (2010). If you build it, will they come? Designing truly patient-centered health care. *Health Affairs, 29*(5), 914–920.

Birenbaum, A. (2009). Left behind: Health services and people with severe disabilities. *Intellectual and Developmental Disabilities, 47*(1), 47–49.

Blair, J. (2012). Caring for people who have intellectual disabilities. *Emergency Nurse, 20*(6), 15–19.

Blanck, P., & Martinis, J. (2015). The right to make choice: The National Resource Center for Supported Decision Making. *Inclusion, 3*(1), 35–39.

Bodde, A. E., Seo, D. C., & Frey, G. (2009). Correlation between physical activity and self-rated health status of non-elderly adults with disabilities. *Preventive Medicine, 49*(6), 511–514.

Bodenheimer, T., Berenson, R. A., & Rudolf, P. (2007). The primary care–specialty income gap: Why it matters. *Annals of Internal Medicine, 146*, 301–306.

Bodenheimer, T., & Pham, H. H. (2010). Primary care: Current problems and proposed solutions. *Health Affairs, 29*(5), 799–805.

Brandt, E. N., & Pope, A. M. (1997). *Enabling America. Assessment of the role of rehabilitation science and engineering*. Washington, D.C.: National Academy Press.

Bronfenbrenner, U. (1992). *Ecological systems theory*. London, UK: Jessica Kingsley Publishers.

Brown, R. S., Graham, C. L., Richeson, N., Wu, J., & McDermott, S. (2010). Evaluation of medical student performance on objective structured clinical exams with standardized patients with and without disabilities. *Academic Medicine, 85*(11), 1766–1771.

Campanella, T. (2015). Supported decision-making in practice. *Inclusion, 3*(1), 35–39.

Carman, K. L., Dardess, P., Maurer, M., Sofaer, S., Adams, K., Bechtel, C., & Sweeney, J. (2013). Patient and family engagement: A framework for understanding the elements and developing interventions and policies. *Health Affairs, 32*(2), 223–231.

Centers for Medicare and Medicaid Services. (2011). Medicare program; Medicare shared savings: Accountable care organizations: Proposed rule. *Fed Register, 76*(57), 19527–19654. Available from: https://federalregister.gov/a/2011-7880

Charles, C., Gafni, A., & Whelan, T. (1997). Shared decision-making in the medical encounter: What does it mean? (or it takes at least two to tango). *Social Science & Medicine, 44*(5), 681–692.

Chen, J., Mortensen, K., & Bloodworth, R. (2014). Exploring contextual factors and patient activation: Evidence from a nationally representative sample of patients with depression. *Health Education & Behavior, 41*(6), 614–624.

Darnell, J. S. (2007). Patient navigation: A call to action. *Social Work, 52*(1), 81–84.

Davies, E., Shaller, D., Edgman-Levitan, S., Safran, D. G., Oftedahl, G., Sakowski, J., & Cleary, P. D. (2009). Evaluating the use of a modified CAHPS survey to support improvements in patient-centred care: Lessons from a quality improvement collaborative. *Health Expectations, 11*, 160–176.

Dinerstein, R. D. (2012). Implementing legal capacity under Article 12 of the UN Convention on the Rights of Persons with Disabilities: The difficult road from guardianship to supported decision-making. *Human Rights Brief, 19*(2), 8–12.

Durand, M. A., Carpenter, L., Dolan, H., Bravo, P., Mann, M., Bunn, F., & Elwyn, G. (2014). Do interventions designed to support shared decision-making reduce health inequalities? A systematic review and meta-analysis. *PLoS One, 9*(4), e94670.

Eldh, A. C., Ekman, I., & Ehnfors, M. (2010). A comparison of the concept of patient participation and patients' descriptions as related to healthcare definitions. *International Journal of Nursing Terminologies and Classifications, 21*(1), 21–32.

Feldman, M. A. (2004). Self-directed learning of child-care skills by parents with intellectual disabilities. *Infants & Young Children, 17*(1), 17–31.

Garbarino, J. (2017). *Children and families in the social environment: Modern applications of social work*. New York, NY: Routledge Publishing.

Glazemakers, I., & Deboutte, D. (2013). Modifying the 'Positive Parenting Program' for parents with intellectual disabilities. *Journal of Intellectual Disability Research, 57*(7), 616–626.

Greene, J., Hibbard, J. H., Sacks, R., Overton, V., & Parrotta, C. D. (2015). When patient activation levels change, health outcomes and costs change, too. *Health Affairs, 34*(3), 431–437.

Härter, M., van der Weijden, T., & Elwyn, G. (2011). Policy and practice developments in the implementation of shared decision making: An international perspective. *Zeitschrift für Evidenz, Fortbildung und Qualität im Gesundheitswesen, 105*(4), 229–233.

Heifetz, M., & Lunsky, Y. (2018). Implementation and evaluation of health passport communication tools in emergency departments. *Research in Developmental Disabilities, 72*, 23–32.

Heinemann, A. W., Magasi, S., Bode, R. K., Hammel, J., Whiteneck, G. G., Bogner, J., & Corrigan, J. D. (2013). Measuring enfranchisement: Importance of and control over participation by people with disabilities. *Archives of Physical Medicine and Rehabilitation, 94*(11), 2157–2165.

Hibbard, J. H., & Greene, J. (2013). What the evidence shows about patient activation: Better health outcomes and care experiences; fewer data on costs. *Health Affairs, 32*(2), 207–214.

Higgins, P. S., Shugrue, N., Ruiz, K., & Robison, J. (2015). Medicare and Medicaid users speak out about their health care: The real, the ideal, and how to get there. *Population Health Management, 18*(2), 123–130.

Iezzoni, L. I. (2011). Eliminating health and health care disparities among the growing population of people with disabilities. *Health Affairs, 30*(10), 1947–1954.

Institute of Medicine (2009). *Toward health equity and patient-centeredness: Integrating health literacy, disparities reduction and quality improvement: Workshop summary*. Washington, D.C.: National Academies Press.

Joint position statement of AAIDD and the Arc (2013). Autonomy, decision-making supports, and guardianship. https://www.aaidd.org/news-policy/policy/positionstatements/autonomy-decision-making-supports-and-guardianship.

Kinne, S., Patrick, D. L., & Doyle, D. L. (2004). Prevalence of secondary conditions among people with disabilities. *American Journal of Public Health, 94*(3), 443–445.

Krahn, G. L., & Fox, M. H. (2014). Health disparities of adults with intellectual disabilities: What do we know? What do we do? *Journal of Applied Research in Intellectual Disabilities, 27*(5), 431–446.

Krahn, G. L., Walker, D. K., & Correa-De-Araujo, R. (2015). Persons with disabilities as an unrecognized health disparity population. *American Journal of Public Health, 105*(S2), S198–S206.

Kuehn, B. (2009). States explore shared decision making. *JAMA, 301*(24), 2539–2541.

Kukla, M., Salyers, M. P., & Lysaker, P. H. (2013). Levels of patient activation among adults with schizophrenia: Associations with hope, symptoms, medication adherence, and recovery attitudes. *The Journal of Nervous and Mental Disease, 201*(4), 339–344.

Larson, S. A., Anderson, L., & Doljanac, R. (2005). Access to health care. In W. Nehring (Ed.), *Health promotion for persons with intellectual and developmental disabilities* (pp. 129–184). Washington, D.C.: American Association on Mental Retardation.

Lotan, G., & Ells, C. (2010). Adults with intellectual and developmental disabilities and participation in decision making: Ethical considerations for professional–client practice. *Intellectual and Developmental Disabilities, 48*(2), 112–125.

Ludman, E. J., Peterson, D., Katon, W. J., Lin, E. H., Von Korff, M., Ciechanowski, P., ... Gensichen, J. (2013). Improving confidence for self-care in patients with depression and chronic illnesses. *Behavioral Medicine, 39*(1), 1–6.

Lunsky, Y., Lin, E., Balogh, R., Klein-Geltink, J., Wilton, A. S., & Kurdyak, P. (2012). Emergency department visits and use of outpatient physician services by adults with developmental disability and psychiatric disorder. *Canadian Journal of Psychiatry, 57*, 601–607.

Marks, B., & Heller, T. (2003). Bridging the equity gap: Health promotion for adults with intellectual and developmental disabilities. *Nursing Clinics of North America, 38*, 205–228.

McAllister, J. W., McNally Keehn, R. B., Rodgers, R. O., Mpofu, P. M., Monahan, P., & Lock, T. (2018). Effects of a care coordination intervention with children with neurodevelopmental disabilities and their families. *Journal of Developmental & Behavioral Pediatrics, 39*(6), 471–480.

McMillan, S. S., Kendall, E., Sav, A., King, M. A., Whitty, J. A., Kelly, F., & Wheeler, A. J. (2013). Patient-centered approaches to health care: A systematic review of randomized controlled trials. *Medical Care Research and Review, 70*(6), 567–596.

McNaughton, D., Balandin, S., Kennedy, P., & Sandmel, T. (2010). Health transitions for youth with complex communication needs: The importance of health literacy and communication strategies. *Journal of Pediatric Rehabilitation Medicine, 3*(4), 311–318.

Medicare Payment Advisory Commission. (2009). *Report to the Congress: Medicare payment policy.* Washington, D.C.: MedPAC.

Mizen, L. A. M., Maclie, M. L., Cooper, S.-A., & Melville, C. A. (2012). Clinical guidelines contribute to the health inequities experienced by individuals with intellectual disabilities. *Implementation Science, 7*(42), 1–9.

Moore, M. (2008). What does patient-centered communication mean in Nepal? *Medical Education, 42*, 18–26.

Naslund, J. A., Aschbrenner, K. A., Barre, L. K., & Bartels, S. J. (2015). Feasibility of popular m-health technologies for activity tracking among individuals with serious mental illness. *Telemedicine and e-Health, 21*(3), 213–216.

National Council on Disability. (2007). *Issues in creating livable communities for people with disabilities: Proceedings of the panel.* Washington, D.C.: The Council.

National Priorities Partnership. (2011). *Input to the secretary of health and human services on priority for the National Quality Strategy.* Washington, D.C.: National Quality Forum.

Ng, J., Ntoumanis, N., Thøgersen-Ntoumani, C., Deci, E. L., Ryan, R. M., Duda, J. L., & Williams, G. C. (2012). Self-determination theory applied to health contexts: A meta-analysis. *Perspectives on Psychological Science, 7*(4), 325–340.

Nguyen, M., Lennox, N., & Ware, R. (2014). Hand-held health records for individuals with intellectual disability: A systematic review. *Journal of Intellectual Disability Research, 58*(12), 1172–1178.

Office of Disease Prevention and Health Promotion [ODPHP]. (2014). *Healthy people 2020: Disparities.* Retrieved from http://www.healthypeople.gov/2020/about/foundation-health-measures/Disparities on 2/5/15.

Palsbo, S. E., Mastal, M. F., & O'Donnell, L. T. (2006). Disability care coordination organizations: Improving health and function in people with disabilities. *Case Management, 11*(5), 255–264.

Ptomey, L. T., Sullivan, D. K., Lee, J., Goetz, J. R., Gibson, C., & Donnelly, J. E. (2015). The use of technology for delivering a weight loss program for adolescents with intellectual and developmental disabilities. *Journal of the Academy of Nutrition and Dietetics, 115*(1), 112–118.

Ravesloot, C., Ruggiero, C., Ipsen, C., Traci, M., Seekins, T., Boehm, T., & Rigles, B. (2011). Disability and health behavior change. *Disability and Health Journal, 4*(1), 19–23.

Reichard, A., Stolze, H., & Fox, M. H. (2011). Health disparities among adults with physical disabilities or cognitive limitations compared to individuals with no disabilities in the United States. *Disability and Health Journal, 4*, 59–67.

Reichard, A., & Turnbull, H. R., III. (2004). Perspectives of physicians, families, and case managers concerning access to health care by individuals with developmental disabilities. *Mental Retardation, 42*(3), 181–194.

Reid, R. J., Coleman, K., Johnson, E. A., Fishman, P. A., Hsu, C., Soman, M. P., ... Larson, E. B. (2010). The group health medical home at year two: Cost savings, higher patient satisfaction, and less burnout for providers. *Health Affairs, 29*, 835–843.

Ruggiano, N., Shtompel, N., & Evardsson, D. (2015). Engaging in coordination of health and disability services as described by older adults: Processes and influential factors. *The Gerontologist, 55*(6), 1015–1025.

Ryan, R. M., Patrick, H., Deci, E. L., & Williams, G. C. (2008). Facilitating health behavior change and its maintenance: Interventions based on self-determination theory. *The European Health Psychologist, 10*, 2–5.

Scepters, M., Keer, M., O'Hara, D., Bainbridge, D., Cooper, S.-A., Davism, R., & Wehmeyer, M. (2005). Reducing health disparity in people with intellectual disabilities: A report from the health issues special interest research group of the International Association of Intellectual Disability. *Journal of Policy and Practice in Intellectual Disabilities, 2*(3–4), 249–255.

Sheftall, A. H., Chisolm, D. J., Alexy, E. R., Chavez, L. J., Mangione-Smith, R. M., Ferrari, R. M., & Song, P. H. (2019). Satisfaction with care coordination for families of children with disabilities. *Journal of Pediatric Health Care, 33*(3), 255–262.

Shogren, K. A., Wehmeyer, M. L., Palmer, S. B., Rifenbark, G. G., & Little, T. D. (2015). Relationships between self-determination and post-school outcomes for youth with disabilities. *The Journal of Special Education, 48*(4), 256–267.

Solberg, L. I., Asche, S. E., Fontaine, P., Flottemesch, T. J., & Anderson, L. H. (2011). Trends in quality during medical home transformation. *Annals of Family Medicine, 9*(6), 515–521.

Stacey, D., Bennett, C. L., Barry, M. J., Col, N. F., Eden, K. B., Holmes-Rovner, M., ... Thomson, R. (2011). Decision aids for people facing health treatment or screening decisions. *Cochrane Database of Systematic Reviews*, (10), CD001431.

Sullivan, W. F., & Heng, J. (2018). Supporting adults with intellectual and developmental disabilities to participate in health care decision making. *Canadian Family Physician, 64*(Suppl 2), S32–S36.

Sumsion, T., & Lencucha, R. (2007). Balancing challenges and facilitating factors when implementing client-centered collaboration in a mental health setting. *British Journal of Occupational Therapy, 70*, 513–520.

Tyler, C. V., Schramm, S. C., Karafa, M., Tang, A. S., & Jain, A. K. (2010). Electronic health record analysis of the primary care of adults with intellectual and other developmental disabilities. *Journal of Policy and Practice in Intellectual Disabilities, 7*, 204–210.

U.S. Census Bureau. (2010). Facts for features: 20th anniversary of Americans with disabilities Act: July 26. Washington, D.C.: Census Bureau; 2010 May 26. Available from: http://www.census.gov/newsroom/releases/archives/facts_for_features_specialeditions/cb10-ff13.html

U.S. Office of Disease Prevention and Health Promotion (ODPHP). (n.d.). *Healthy people 2020.* http://www.healthypeople.gov/2020/about/foundation-health-measures/Disparities

United Nations [UN]. (2006). *Convention on the Rights of Persons with Disabilities.* Available from: http://www.un.org/disabilities/documents/convention/convention_accessible_pdf.pdf

Veroff, D., Marr, A., & Wennberg, D. E. (2013). Enhanced support for shared decision making reduced costs of care for patients with preference-sensitive conditions. *Health Affairs, 32*(2), 285–293.

Vogel, C., Shields, A. E., Lee, T. A., Gibson, T. B., Marder, W. D., Weiss, K. B., & Blumenthal, D. (2007). Multiple chronic conditions: Prevalence, health consequences, and implications for quality, care management, and costs. *Journal of General Internal Medicine, 22*(suppl. 3), 341–345.

Wallston, K. A., & Wallston, B. S. (1982). Who is responsible for your health: The construct of health locus of control. In G. S. Sanders & J. M. Suls (Eds.), *Social psychology of health and illness* (pp. 65–95). Hillsdale, NJ: Lawrence Erlbaum Associates.

Ward, R. L., Nichols, A. D., & Freedman, R. J. (2010). Uncovering health care inequalities among adults with intellectual and developmental disabilities. *Health & Social Work, 35*(4), 280–290.

Weedon, D., Carbone, P., Bilder, D., O'Brien, S., & Dorius, J. (2012). Building a person-centered medical home: Lessons from a program for people with developmental disabilities. *Journal of Health Care for the Poor and Underserved, 23*(4), 1600–1608.

Welyczko, N. (2018). Working with patients with long-term conditions and learning disabilities. *Journal of Kidney Care, 3*(4), 224–229.

Werner, S. (2012). Individuals with intellectual disabilities: A review of the literature on decision-making since the Convention on the Rights of People with Disabilities (CRPD). *Public Health Reviews, 34*(2), 14.

Wessel, P. (2019). *Supporting the independent living of persons with disabilities through the use of smart home technology.*. Unpublished concept paper. Minneapolis, MN: Genesis Institute.

Wolf, M. S., Wilson, E. A., Rapp, D. N., Waite, K. R., Bocchini, M. V., Davis, T. C., & Rudd, R. E. (2009). Literacy and learning in healthcare. *Pediatrics, 124*(Supplement 3), S275–S281.

World Health Organization [WHO]. (2001). *Health promotion: Report by the Secretariat.* Fifty-fourth World Health Assembly A54/8.

Yarnall, K. S., Østbye, T., Krause, K. M., Pollak, K. I., Gradison, M., & Michener, J. L. (Eds.). (2009). Family physicians as team leaders: "Time" to share the care. *Preventing Chronic Disease, 6*(2), 1–6.

Part III
Choice and Preference Across the Lifespan

The Development of Choice-Making and Implications for Promoting Choice and Autonomy for Children and Youth with Intellectual and Developmental Disabilities

Michael L. Wehmeyer and Karrie A. Shogren

Choice and autonomy are critical in healthy child and adolescent development. In developmental psychology, the term autonomy is frequently used to discuss developmental milestones pertaining to choice. In this chapter, we examine the development of choice-making and preferences and the relationship of these two constructs to the development of autonomy. Further, we examine the relative contribution of choice and autonomy to other important areas of development, including motivation, self-determination, and adolescent development, and then discuss how choice-making and preferences can be fostered in children and adolescents with intellectual and developmental disabilities.

You have read what is meant by choice throughout this text. At the simplest level, making a choice involves the selection of a preference from more than one option. But, of course, like most aspects of human behavior, there is more to "choice" than is evident at the surface level. According to psychologists who study choice and autonomy, there are three processes subsumed under the broader notion of choice. First, there is the degree to which a context affords someone the opportunity to choose. We see this all of the time in advertising and marketing. For example, for a single brand of toothpaste, a manufacturer advertises that they are providing "choice" because a consumer can purchase various sizes of toothpaste tubes (6.4 oz., 5.1 oz., or 3.5 oz.), singly or in a two pack, with or without whitener, with or without mouthwash, in gel or paste, flavored or not flavored, and on and on. In this case, "choice" means that the context (available versions of the same brand) provides you the opportunity to select that which best fits your preferences and needs. Second, there is the act of a person selecting from among two or more options. This is the

M. L. Wehmeyer (✉)
Beach Center on Disability, University of Kansas, Lawrence, KS, USA
e-mail: wehmeyer@ku.edu

K. A. Shogren
Kansas University Center on Developmental Disabilities,
University of Kansas, Lawrence, KS, USA

© Springer Nature Switzerland AG 2020
R. J. Stancliffe et al. (eds.), *Choice, Preference, and Disability*, Positive
Psychology and Disability Series, https://doi.org/10.1007/978-3-030-35683-5_9

physical act of choosing. This second meaning of choice depends upon the first: that is, you cannot make a choice unless the environment affords the opportunity to choose. The third element of choice that is studied is, to some degree, distinct from either of these physical elements of choosing. It is the perception of choice.

At this point, it is worth introducing ideas pertaining to autonomy as they relate to choosing. Autonomy is a term with many meanings and interpretations. In a comprehensive survey of autonomy in adolescent development, Soenens, Vansteenkiste, Petegem, Beyers, and Ryan (2018) noted that "autonomy is traditionally defined as independence or self-reliance; that is, the extent to which one behaves, decides, or thinks without relying on others" (p. 3). Soenens and colleagues refer to this understanding as reflecting *autonomy-as-independence*. The act of choosing – that is making a choice from various options – is closely associated with the notion of *autonomy-as-independence*.

But, there is a second way to understand autonomy that is more consistent with understandings associated with self-determination and intrinsic motivation, and that is *autonomy-as-volition*. The word volition is derived from the same Latin root as the word voluntary, and considering what the latter means assists with understanding the former. To volunteer is to do something in full expression of one's will; one volunteers one's time or money or expertise without coercion and willingly. Volition, in turn, refers to acting based upon one's will; acting volitionally means that you act on your own, based upon your own preferences and interests.

To act volitionally implies that you act deliberately and consciously based upon your preferences, interests, beliefs, and values, rather than being induced, coerced, or acting because someone else wants you to act in a certain way. When we think about autonomy-as-volition, what we're referring to is not necessarily acting independently but instead acting based upon our preferences and interests and, typically, in pursuit of goals that are of value to us and that enhance our quality of life. This is of particular importance for people with disabilities, who may need support (e.g., may not be able to do things independently) to perform preferred activities. So, if a person with a physical disability wants to prepare dinner, but requires assistance to get ingredients together, mix and stir recipe ingredients, put the dish into the oven, and so forth, it is not important that the person did not perform these tasks alone and without assistance (e.g., autonomy-as-independence) but that the person chose what to eat and the meal preparation process was carried out according to that person's preferences and desires (autonomy-as-volition).

Autonomy-as-volition results not only from the physical act of choosing, but from *the perceptions and beliefs* of someone that they are acting based upon their own preferences, interests, and values. Sometimes this involves acting independently, but often as not, it does not. Soenens et al. (2018) noted that autonomy-as-independence "is mainly about … how much adolescents depend on others and who is regulating a certain behavior or goal … in other words, it is mainly defined in interpersonal terms" while autonomy-as volition "is more about within-person concordance; that is, about the degree to which behaviors or goals are aligned with one's deeply held values, preferences, and interests" (p. 6). This becomes particularly important when considering the development of choice and of promoting choice among children and youth with intellectual and developmental disabilities in that because of physical, cognitive, or sensory support needs, they may not be able to "independently" perform a task or action. But, as long as that task or action is taken based upon the child or young person's preferences and interests, one can see it as volitional action.

Think about this in terms of child development. The traditional notion of development, particularly as children move into early adolescence, is that the development of "autonomy" involves young people acting independent of parental support and, often even, parental knowledge or permission. Adolescent development has historically been viewed through a lens of rebellion against parental (and societal) rules. Within an autonomy-as-volition framework, however, it is not whether the young person acts "independent" of parental authority but whether the young person's actions are based upon their preferences, interests, and values and not those of others, including parents. As long as the young person's actions are consistent with their own preferences, interests, and values, within the autonomy-as-volition frame, the degree to which the "rules" that governed or bracketed the action were set by parents or not becomes, more or less, irrelevant. Even when there is a conflict between parents and the young person, if that conflict involves a consideration and discussion of the young person's perspective, preferences, and views, even if the outcome is that parents disagree and set a boundary that opposes the action that the adolescent would prefer to take, such conflicts "may be adaptive for autonomy development in that they provide opportunities for different views to be expressed, understood, and perhaps changed" (Smetana, 2018, p. 63).

Interestingly, research in motivation has found that not all "choices" are equally motivating or, even, motivating at all. Take the situation in which you are in the grocery store and you are staring at an aisle of cereal boxes: there are dozens of brands, flavors, and sizes, some with and without marshmallows, widely varying in caloric content or fiber, and so on. In many cases, the cornucopia of "choices" seems not motivating but in fact overwhelming and unmotivating. You might think that one thing that makes this choice situation unmotivating is that the brand or type of cereal you choose is a trivial choice. But research has shown that it is not the actual significance of the choice that matters; in fact, even seemingly trivial choices can be motivating.

Nor is level of interest in the choice necessarily motivating. Research shows that motivation to perform uninteresting tasks can be enhanced by providing a choice. Patall and Hooper (2018) showed that allowing high school students to choose which (of two) homework assignments they would complete (both assignments covered the same topic and achieved the same objectives) improved students' autonomous motivation and their self-reported competence in completing the homework and, in fact, improved performance on the unit test covering the homework material when compared with the same outcomes for high school students in a yoked condition who completed the same homework assignment as one student in the experimental group. On the other hand, infusing choice into an already highly preferred action (e.g., do I want chocolate fudge brownie ice cream or butter pecan ice cream or a dip of both?) has little impact on motivation, since the task is already highly motivating (Soenens et al. 2018).

Now, returning to the previous discussion about the three meanings of choice (as a feature of the context, as the physical act of selecting an option, and as perceived choice), the aforementioned research has shown that it is not only the choice itself that influences positive outcomes like enhanced motivation and improved performance but the perception of choice. Patall and Hooper defined *perceived choice* as the "subjective experience of having opportunities to make choices, options to choose among, and the experience of freedom while choosing" (Patall & Hooper, 2018, p. 151). In their homework experiment discussed previously, Patall and her colleague collected data on students' perceptions of the degree to which they were provided choice opportunities by their teacher as well as their perceptions of the degree to which their teacher supported their autonomy. It turns out that the students' perceptions of their teachers' autonomy support was a stronger factor in their reports of intrinsic motivation and perceived competence as well as test performance in the class than simply the choice itself.

And, so, it is clear that providing choice opportunities leads to multiple, positive benefits for educating students. Patall and Hooper summarized it as such: "providing students with task-related choices leads to enhanced feelings of autonomy (volitional functioning), interest, enjoyment, and persistence on a task and to enhanced task value, effort, engagement, performances, subsequent learning, and perceived competence" (Patall & Hooper, 2018, p. 153).

So, as you can see, when we consider the development of choice and preference, we have to look at domains that go beyond the physical act of choosing or the availability of choice opportunities to explore the development of autonomy-as-volition and its role within choosing.

The Development of Choice and Autonomy-as-Volition

The development of choice and autonomy is, obviously, lifelong and involves multiple domains of development. In this section, we look at the development of choice and preferences and, in the second part, examine the development of autonomy-as-volition.

The Development of Choice and Preferences

So, what are the "developmental" elements of choice and preference? Most of the important developmental activities and milestones in this domain occur in early childhood and during the elementary years. At the level of choosing as a physical action, developmental research focuses on children's capacities to identify and communicate preferences. Once a child develops these capacities, the development of choice-making ability relies on the opportunities in a child's environments to make selections and experience the consequences of these choices; that is, that the context provides "choice." Later in development, older children and young adolescents begin to incorporate their choice-making abilities into the development of more complex skills, such as the development of decision-making skills, the process of which includes as a final step making a choice of a preferred alternative.

Human beings come to the world hardwired to express preferences. That is, research with infants documents that some preferences are, in fact, innate. A preference for sweet tasting foods, for example, is present for all infants at birth (Ventura & Mennella, 2011). More surprisingly, perhaps, infants less than 1-day old are already able to recognize facial features with very little exposure to faces and are able to identify the same face when presented in different sizes and orientations (Slater & Kirby, 1998). Moreover, infants are born with a "preference" for looking at faces over almost any other shape or image. Why is this important? Of course, infants looking at faces help bond infants to adults, and the quickly acquired "preference" for a familiar face ensures that infants recognize and are bonded to their mothers, who are not only a source of stimulation for all sorts of developmentally important actions but also a source of food. Thus, young children engage in rudimentary choice-making very early in life. Infants and young children often choose through eye gaze or pointing at one option instead of another. Between 15 and 18 months, young children can choose between two familiar objects upon request; by 2 years of age, a child can choose one object from a group of five upon request (Palmer, Wehmeyer, & Shogren, 2017).

So, the development of preferences involves a mix of innate biological capacities and the stimulation and opportunities available in the environment. The relative contributions of innate preferences and environmental stimulation and choice opportunities are not well understood. Why do some people become enthusiastic collectors and others have no interest in collecting? Why do some people become fanatical about sports and other people remain uninterested? The truth is, we do not know, but we do know that although there are innate biological elements to the development of preferences, passions, or interests, they cannot be expressed until the child has the opportunity to interact with various options and potential passions and interests. Preferences emerge, then, based on infants' interactions with individuals, objects, and the environment (Doll, Sands, Wehmeyer, & Palmer, 1996). That pattern is repeated throughout development. That is, children and then adolescents develop preferences as a function of their interaction with stimuli, activities, and opportunities.

Having a preference is only one part of making a choice, however. Choosing involves the *expression* of a preference, and, thus, the development of communication becomes important. During infancy, children learn to cry to get something they want (or reject something they don't want), smile socially to communicate that they are happy, or use eye gazes and initial vocalizations to express their preferences. By 10 months of age, infants can use their developing motor skills to express preferences by pointing, reaching toward a preferred object, and, eventually, moving toward an object. There is a developmental trend to the intentionality of these actions. Initially, an infant may point to an item to indicate they want it but without an understanding that by doing so they may actually get access to what they are pointing toward. They are communicating, essentially: I like that or want that. Eventually, though, they learn that the act of pointing serves not just as an expression of their preference but also a means to obtain that preferred object or activity. Once they learn that such communicative efforts can elicit the outcome they desire, they begin to use communication purposefully and intentionally to make choices. So, the cry of a hungry 1 year old has become not only an expression of an internal state (hunger) but also an attempt to get someone else to meet that need. By 1 year of age, most children have developed the skills for communicating a preference and making a selection from options. The development of language enhances the child's ability to communicate preferences.

The Development of Autonomy-as-Volition

We have discussed, to this point, the development of choice in the sense of the act of choosing, developing, and expressing preferences and interests. The development of perceived choice, or autonomy-as-volition, is certainly related to and contingent upon the development of these mechanisms of choosing and choice expression and, in fact, builds on the attainment of those developmental milestones through later childhood and adolescence. Research and theory in motivation, and specifically in the context of self-determination theory (Ryan & Deci, 2017), view autonomy as a basic, innate psychological need that motivates humans and energizes action, and the fulfillment of this basic need for autonomy contributes to greater well-being and life satisfaction. The development of perceived choice, then, relates to the increasing opportunities for children and adolescents to act in ways that enable them to fulfill this need for autonomy. Part of that developmental process involves young persons' interactions with their parents/family members, as has been discussed previously, as well as their peers. Causal agency theory, which was discussed in chapter "Self-Determination, Preference and Choice", provides a framework to identify the skills, abilities, and attitudes that people use to implement volitional and causal actions to satisfy their basic need for autonomy. There are a number of such skills, beliefs, and abilities that are foundational to the development of autonomy-as-volition during childhood, beginning with the development of choice-making skills discussed previously, as well as the development of problem-solving skills, self-regulation skills, and goal-setting and attainment skills. All of these enable young people to act based upon preferences, interests, beliefs, and values and, thus, facilitate the development of autonomy-as-volition.

First, though, we need to emphasize that the development of autonomy is closely associated with identity development. A comprehensive exploration of this developmental domain is beyond the scope of this text, but it is important to note that for one to become autonomous, in the autonomy-as-volition sense, one must have self-awareness and self-knowledge. In early childhood, this involves an initial understanding of oneself as separate from others, particularly caregivers. Young children begin to understand that their feelings may be different from those of others.

As children start elementary school, they are able to label and identify common feelings and to identify how one's feelings can change and can drive interests, preferences, and passions (Palmer et al., 2017). And, of course, identity development becomes a major focus of adolescence and is closely associated with the development of skills and abilities associated with acting as an agent in one's life. This, in turn, is directly linked to the development of problem-solving, self-regulation, and goal-setting and attainment skills, each of which is discussed in the following paragraphs.

In the context of development, *problem-solving* can be thought of as "what children do when they have a goal in mind but are encountering an obstacle to reaching the goal and do not know how to achieve it" (Landy, 2002. p. 474). Particularly in early childhood, most problems to be solved involve interactions with other people, including the problem of how to act with greater autonomy. Between 12 and 18 months, the actions of infants reflect increased "awareness of social demands, and the ability to initiate, maintain, and cease behavior to comply with caregivers' requests" (Geldhof, Fenn, & Finders, 2017, p. 225). By 2 years of age, children can exhibit self-control. The development of problem-solving includes, in part, the development of perspective taking, which emerges around 4 years of age as children begin to understand that their perspectives – their thoughts, motivations, interests, purposes – are different from those of others and not always aligned (Palmer et al., 2017). Another domain of importance in the early development of problem-solving skills involves the development of executive functioning skills. Within the context of early development, executive functioning can be "understood in age-related increases in complexity of rules children can formulate and use when solving problems" (Palmer et al., p. 77) and is associated with maturation and the development of cognitive skills that govern later self-regulation and goal-setting skills.

Inherent in the development of problem-solving is the development of domain- and means-specific beliefs. First, children develop the capacity to differentiate between and among domains; that is, they learn that different domains of functioning "have different challenges and require different skills" (Little, Snyder, & Wehmeyer, 2006, p. 397). They begin to learn that they can influence some outcomes by working hard and/or improving their ability and that other outcomes (winning the lottery!) are simply in the domain of luck and chance. In this context, they begin to understand their abilities, from self-descriptions of abilities that are inaccurate as a very young child to the capacity (in adolescence) to understand how their abilities compared with those of others. As these skills emerge, children begin to use self-evaluations to determine the efficacy of actions and to change course if need be (Palmer et al., 2017).

Self-regulation, in the context of this chapter, refers to the development of knowledge and abilities to regulate coping responses and choose actions that fulfill goals and lead to outcomes that are preferred. Again, elements of self-regulation are innate, and very young infants show the capacity to differentiate some aspects of behavior in response to changes in their environment. Children are, intrinsically, active and curious and are prone to investigate their environments and contexts. The more they are provided opportunities in those environments to explore, the more likely they will develop more complex responses to problems in the environment and, thus, enhance self-regulation skills. The development of self-regulation involves issues pertaining to temperament and the regulation of emotion. Emotional regulation, or the capacity to regulate one's feelings and expression of emotions in ways that enable one to achieve desired outcomes, becomes an important task of development (Geldhof et al., 2017). Another element in the development of self-regulation involves the development of executive functioning skills; as children mature, they develop inhibitory control (that is, the ability to refrain from acting on impulse or automatically so as to act in another way that is more adaptive with regard to achieving a goal), working memory abilities, increased attentional skills, and future-oriented, goal-directed skills (Geldhof et al., 2017). Development of inhibitory control is important for the development of autonomy-as-volition because adolescents must often defer gratification in order to reach a goal and obtain a preferred outcome. A young person might much rather play video games at night than practice a musical instrument, but if that young person knows that such practice will lead to a highly preferred activity, such as performing in an end-of-year school performance, the more immediately desired activity can be put aside.

Goal setting and attainment are also important to the development of autonomy-as-volition. Goals regulate one's action to achieve autonomy. The development of goal-setting and attainment skills begins early in development with infants' and young children's emergence of understandings of the relationship between someone who acts and the objective of that action. By 1 year of age, infants can determine the goal associated with an action and, by 4 years of age, identify goals if given a series of pictured actions. By 5 years of age, children can link goals and actions (Palmer et al., 2017). These understandings emerge at the same time as do understandings of causality (chance, effort, ability), as discussed previously. Research with late-elementary-aged students (third, fourth grade) indicates that they can begin to understand the basics of cause and effect in hypothesis testing. Future-oriented thinking is also important in that goals are inherently future focused. Future orientation and a related set of skills, planning and self-initiation, involve the "acquisition of skill sets that include anticipatory knowledge, problem definition, and strategy selection and improved metacognition and metarepresentation skills" (Geldhof et al., p. 91) that emerge through early and later adolescence.

We provide this broad overview of the development of choice (as choosing) and autonomy (as volition) to set the stage for better understanding how to promote these developmental outcomes for children and youth with intellectual and developmental disabilities. In the following section, we discuss "what works" in promoting the development of choice and autonomy of children and youth with intellectual and developmental disabilities.

What Works

Promoting choice and autonomy begins with promoting the act of choosing. Although some children with more extensive support needs may need systematic instruction on how to make choices (e.g., communicate one's preference), most instructional activities focus not on teaching choice-making but instead on providing "choice;" that is, providing opportunities for students to express their preferences and make choices throughout their daily school activities. For example, Brown et al. (1993) developed a model of choice diversity for embedding choice-making opportunities throughout the natural course of a student's day. The model delineates potential areas of choice within an activity. Students can choose instructional materials to complete an activity; choose among different activities that are intended to achieve the same learning goals; choose when, where, and with whom to engage in a learning activity; and choose when to end a particular activity or, even, whether to engage in the activity at all.

Adults can encourage a preschoolers' emergent understanding of the links between choice and later opportunities by revisiting the choices that have been made, helping the child identify consequences or outcomes of those choices, and discussing plans for similar choice opportunities in the future. The use of social stories is a means to do this instructionally that is frequently used in special education practice. For example, Barry and Burlew (2004) used social stories to teach choice-making skills to young children with autism, resulting in improvement in these skills. This process (that is, understanding of links between choice and later opportunities) also contributes to students' capacity to self-evaluate performance and will contribute to the emergence of self-regulation (Palmer et al., 2013).

Palmer et al. (2013) introduced the *Foundations for the Development of Self-Determination* model, which identified basic foundational skills for developing self-determination later in life. Keeping in mind that until they are, at least, young adolescents, children have neither the capacity nor opportunity to become "self-determined" (that is, they remain dependent upon others for most things), these foundational skills leading to later self-determination become, in essence, the building blocks for promoting choice and autonomy.

In addition to efforts to promote choosing, then, the Foundations model emphasizes the importance, in early childhood and elementary years, of opportunities to develop problem-solving, self-regulation, and engagement skills. Beginning with the first of these, the first step in any problem-solving process is to identify and explicate the problem. Adults can encourage children to identify problems they might have as they occur and work with students to articulate possible solutions. For example, when a piece of technology doesn't work in a classroom, it is not unusual for the teacher to simply think through possible solutions and try to fix the problem without saying anything. But, if the teacher speaks aloud to the class about what the problem is and talks through the possible solutions, the students in the class can become involved in solving the problem and begin to learn how the process works. The purpose of such instruction is not necessarily to have preschool children generate all possible solutions but to begin to think about generating alternative solutions. This, in turn, contributes to the development of self-regulation skills.

Engagement is an important aspect because, as mentioned previously, many problems that must be solved involve other people. Research identified by Palmer and colleagues found that promoting choice opportunities increases social interactions and peer engagement and task persistence. These, in turn, promote opportunities for young children to explore their environments and, in so doing, encounter and learn to solve problems in those environments.

Of course, for preschool- and elementary-aged children, adults will play a major role in promoting choice-making, problem-solving, self-regulation, and engagement. We have discussed the importance of providing choice and problem-solving opportunities in the promotion of these foundational skills. Palmer et al. (2013) identified two types of approaches for enhancing the foundational skills: "intentional and consistent adult cues to elicit choice, direct engagement, and promote self-regulation" and "environmental, material, or instructional accommodations to provide access to choices or settings that reduce distractions and are conducive to self-regulation" (pp. 42–43). These involve simple strategies such as those proposed by Brown et al. to infuse choice opportunities into instruction. Preschool and elementary classrooms are frequently structured to facilitate these types of activities through play centers or learning centers, as well as active, small-group instructional activities.

Palmer and Wehmeyer (2003) evaluated the impact of a model to promote self-regulated problem-solving and goal setting, the Self-Determined Learning Model of Instruction (about which more information will be provided next), for use with young children with intellectual and developmental disabilities. As described subsequently, the model supports teachers to teach students to engage in self-regulated problem-solving to set and attain goals that are based upon personal preferences, interests, and learning needs. Palmer and Wehmeyer found that children as young as 5 years of age could learn, with adequate supports and scaffolding, to set goals and work through the process to attain goals. Palmer and Wehmeyer (2002) adapted this instructional model for use by parents as a means to promote parenting styles that emphasize student choice and autonomy and teach problem-solving and goal-setting skills.

Choice-making continues to be an important activity as children get older, though less emphasis is placed on learning to make choices and more is placed on incorporating choice-making into more complex skills, decisions, or activities. For example, Cooper and Browder (1998) found that teaching young adults with intellectual disability to make choices improved outcomes of community-based instruction, and Watanabe and Sturmey (2003) found that promoting choice-making opportunities in vocational tasks for young adults with disabilities increased engagement in the activity. Choice-making and problem-solving skills become embedded in activities like social skills instruction (O'Reilly, Lancioni, & O'Kane, 2000), leisure and recreation decisions (Datillo & Hoge, 1999), and employment decision-making (Gumpel, Tappe, & Araki, 2000). A frequently identified practice to promote greater autonomy and self-determination has been adolescent involvement in education and transition planning, which emphasizes expressing preferences and making choices in the context of school and adult-life planning. A number of intervention programs have been shown to improve such student involvement, with the *Whose Future Is It Anyway?* program (Wehmeyer et al., 2004) having been validated with students with intellectual disability (Wehmeyer, Palmer, Lee, Williams-Diehm, & Shogren, 2011).

The intervention with the strongest evidence of positive impact to promote self-regulated problem-solving, goal setting, autonomy, and self-determination is the aforementioned Self-Determined Learning Model of Instruction (SDLMI; Shogren,

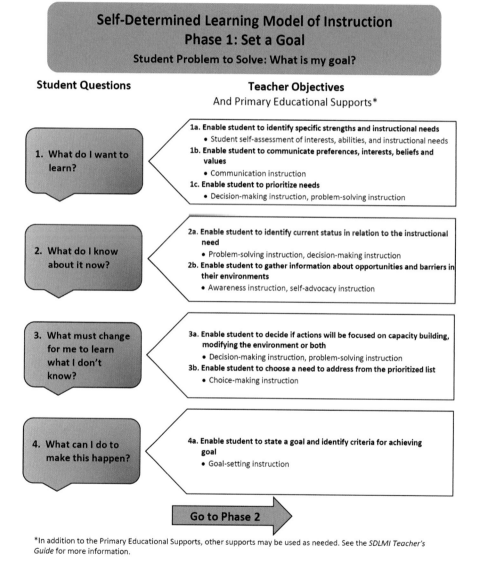

*In addition to the Primary Educational Supports, other supports may be used as needed. See the *SDLMI Teacher's Guide* for more information.

Fig. 1 Self-determined learning model of instruction phase 1. (From Shogren et al., 2017. © 2017 Kansas University Center on Developmental Disabilities. All rights reserved. Used with Permission)

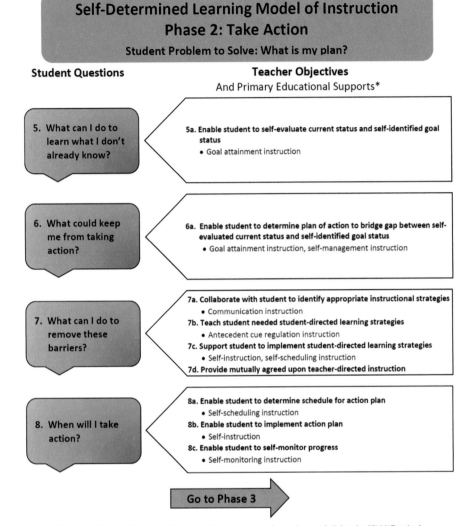

Fig. 2 Self-determined learning model of instruction phase 2. (From Shogren et al., 2017. © 2017 Kansas University Center on Developmental Disabilities. All rights reserved. Used with Permission)

Wehmeyer, Burke, & Palmer, 2017). The SDLMI is a model of instruction to enable teachers to teach students with and without disabilities to self-regulate problem-solving to set educationally relevant goals, design action plans to achieve those goals, and monitor progress toward those goals, adjusting the plan or goal as necessary. As depicted in the SDLMI Teacher's Guide (Shogren et al., 2017, available online at http://www.self-determination.org) and in Figs. 1, 2, and 3, the model

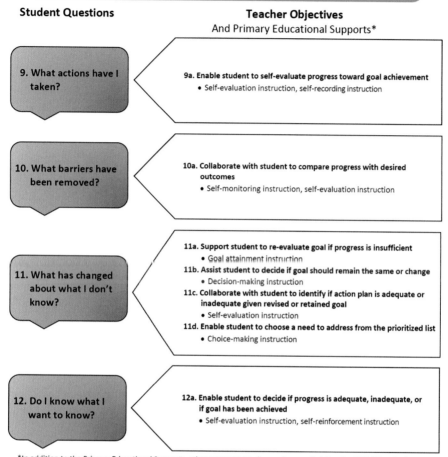

Self-Determined Learning Model of Instruction
Phase 3: Adjust Goal or Plan
Student Problem to Solve: What have I learned?

Student Questions

Teacher Objectives
And Primary Educational Supports*

9. What actions have I taken?

9a. Enable student to self-evaluate progress toward goal achievement
• Self-evaluation instruction, self-recording instruction

10. What barriers have been removed?

10a. Collaborate with student to compare progress with desired outcomes
• Self-monitoring instruction, self-evaluation instruction

11. What has changed about what I don't know?

11a. Support student to re-evaluate goal if progress is insufficient
• Goal attainment instruction
11b. Assist student to decide if goal should remain the same or change
• Decision-making instruction
11c. Collaborate with student to identify if action plan is adequate or inadequate given revised or retained goal
• Self-evaluation instruction
11d. Enable student to choose a need to address from the prioritized list
• Choice-making instruction

12. Do I know what I want to know?

12a. Enable student to decide if progress is adequate, inadequate, or if goal has been achieved
• Self-evaluation instruction, self-reinforcement instruction

*In addition to the Primary Educational Supports, other supports may be used as needed. See the *SDLMI Teacher's Guide* for more information.

Fig. 3 Self-determined learning model of instruction phase 3. (From Shogren et al., 2017. © 2017 Kansas University Center on Developmental Disabilities. All rights reserved. Used with Permission)

consists of three phases. Each phase has a problem for the student to solve (What is my goal? What is my plan? What have I learned?). The student solves the problem by answering a series of four questions that are unique to the focus of each phase but, in each phase, constitute a problem-solving sequence.

The first question in the first phase prompts students to identify their preferences, interests, strengths, and areas of instructional need pertaining to the goal topic, so the process is anchored in student choice. Further, the process promotes student autonomy-as-volition rather than simply autonomy-as-independence because the focus, particularly in the action planning phase, is on creating a plan that achieves the goal (which is based upon the student's preferences and interests) and not simply on the student doing things independently. The model includes teacher objectives and educational supports tied to each student question that provide information for teachers as to how to support students to answer each question.

There are a number of studies that have established the efficacy of the SDLMI to promote self-regulated problem-solving and goal-setting skills for students with intellectual and developmental disabilities as well as promote more positive self-determination and school and post-school outcomes (Lee, Wehmeyer, & Shogren, 2015; Shogren et al., 2019; Shogren, Palmer, Wehmeyer, Williams-Diehm, & Little, 2012; Wehmeyer et al., 2012). Further, Shogren, Plotner, Palmer, Wehmeyer, and Paek (2014) showed that teachers who implemented the SDLMI with their students showed higher levels of expectations for those students as a function of teaching self-regulated goal setting and attainment. The SDLMI is particularly useful to promote choice and autonomy, as it is a multicomponent intervention that enables teachers to teach students most of the skills important to the development of choice and autonomy, including self-regulation, problem-solving, and goal-setting skills. Further, as discussed previously, the model can be used (with additional scaffolding and supports) with younger children.

Too often, the development of choice and autonomy is taken for granted. That is, there are limited direct efforts to intervene to promote these outcomes. And yet, as has been discussed in this chapter, there are multiple ways in which these developmentally valuable outcomes can be addressed at home and in school and doing so promote more positive school and life outcomes.

References

Barry, L. M., & Burlew, S. B. (2004). Using social stories to teach choice and play skills to children with autism. *Focus on Autism and Other Developmental Disabilities, 19,* 45–51.

Brown, F., Belz, P., Corsi, L., & Wenig, B. (1993). Choice and diversity for people with severe disabilities. *Education and Training in Mental Retardation, 28,* 318–326.

Cooper, K. J., & Browder, D. M. (1998). Enhancing choice and participation for adults with severe disabilities in community-based instruction. *Journal of the Association for Persons with Severe Handicaps, 23,* 252–260.

Datillo, J., & Hoge, G. (1999). Effects of a leisure education program on youth with mental retardation. *Education and Training in Mental Retardation and Developmental Disabilities, 34,* 20–34.

Doll, E., Sands, D., Wehmeyer, M. L., & Palmer, S. (1996). Promoting the development and acquisition of self-determined behavior. In D. J. Sands & M. L. Wehmeyer (Eds.), *Self-determination across the life span: Independence and choice for people with disabilities* (pp. 65–90). Baltimore, MD: Paul H. Brookes.

Geldhof, G. J., Fenn, M. L., & Finders, J. K. (2017). A self-determination perspective on self-regulation across the life span. In M. L. Wehmeyer, K. A. Shogren, T. D. Little, & S. J. Lopez (Eds.), *Development of self-determination through the life-course* (pp. 221–236). New York, NY: Springer.

Gumpel, T. P., Tappe, P., & Araki, C. (2000). Comparison of social problem-solving abilities among adults with and without developmental disabilities. *Education and Training in Mental Retardation and Developmental Disabilities, 35*, 259–268.

Landy, S. (2002). *Pathways to competence: Encouraging healthy social and emotional development in young children.* Baltimore, MD: Paul H. Brookes Publishing.

Lee, S. H., Wehmeyer, M. L., & Shogren, K. A. (2015). The effect of instruction with the self-determined learning model of instruction on students with disabilities: A meta-analysis. *Education and Training in Autism and Developmental Disabilities, 50*(2), 237–247.

Little, T. D., Snyder, C. R., & Wehmeyer, M. (2006). The agentic self: On the nature and origins of personal agency across the lifespan. In D. K. Mroczek & T. D. Little (Eds.), *Handbook of personality development* (pp. 61–80). Mahwah, NJ: LEA.

O'Reilly, M. F., Lancioni, G. E., & O'Kane, N. (2000). Using a problem solving approach to teach social skills to workers with brain injuries in supported employment settings. *Journal of Vocational Rehabilitation, 14*, 187–194.

Palmer, S. B., Summers, J. A., Brotherson, M. J., Erwin, E. J., Maude, S. P., Stroup-Rentier, V., ... Haines, S. J. (2013). Foundations for self-determination in early childhood: An inclusive model for children with disabilities. *Topics in Early Childhood Special Education, 33*(1), 38–47.

Palmer, S. B., & Wehmeyer, M. L. (2002). *A parent's guide to the self-determined learning model for early elementary students.* Lawrence, Kansas: Beach Center on Disability, University of Kansas. Accessed online at https://beachcenter.lsi.ku.edu/sites/default/files/inline-files/Beach/parents-guide-to-sd.pdf

Palmer, S. B., & Wehmeyer, M. L. (2003). Promoting self-determination in early elementary school: Teaching self-regulated problem-solving and goal-setting skills. *Remedial and Special Education, 24*(2), 115–126.

Palmer, S. B., Wehmeyer, M. L., & Shogren, K. A. (2017). The development of self-determination during childhood. In M. L. Wehmeyer, K. A. Shogren, T. D. Little, & S. J. Lopez (Eds.), *Development of self-determination through the life-course* (pp. 71–88). New York, NY: Springer.

Patall, E. A., & Hooper, S. Y. (2018). The role of choice in understanding adolescent autonomy and academic functioning. In B. Soenens, M. Vansteenkiste, & S. Van Petegem (Eds.), *Autonomy in adolescent development: Toward conceptual clarity* (pp. 145–167). London, UK: Routledge.

Ryan, R., & Deci, E. (2017). *Self-determination theory: Basic psychological needs in motivation, development, and wellness.* New York, NY: Guilford.

Shogren, K., Palmer, S., Wehmeyer, M. L., Williams-Diehm, K., & Little, T. (2012). Effect of intervention with the self-determined learning model of instruction on access and goal attainment. *Remedial and Special Education, 33*(5), 320–330.

Shogren, K. A., Burke, K. M., Antosh, A., Wehmeyer, M. L., LaPlante, T., Shaw, L. A., & Raley, S. (2019). Impact of the self-Determined learning model of instruction on self-determination and goal attainment in adolescents with intellectual disability. *Journal of Disability Policy Studies, 30*(1), 22–34.

Shogren, K. A., Plotner, A. J., Palmer, S. B., Wehmeyer, M. L., & Paek, Y. (2014). Impact of the self-determined learning model of instruction on teacher perceptions of student capacity and opportunity for self-determination. *Education and Training in Autism and Developmental Disabilities, 49*(3), 440–448.

Shogren, K. A., Wehmeyer, M. L., Burke, K. M., & Palmer, S. B. (2017). *The self-determined learning model of instruction: Teacher's guide.* Lawrence, KS: Kansas University Center on Developmental Disabilities.

Slater, A., & Kirby, R. (1998). Innate and learned perceptual abilities in the newborn infant. *Experimental Brain Research, 123*, 90–94.

Smetana, J. G. (2018). The development of autonomy during adolescence: A social-cognitive domain theory view. In B. Soenens, M. Vansteenkiste, & S. V. Petegem (Eds.), *Autonomy in adolescent development: Towards conceptual clarity* (pp. 53–73). London, UK: Routledge.

Soenens, B., Vansteenkiste, M., Petegem, S. V., Beyers, W., & Ryan, R. (2018). How to solve the conundrum of adolescent autonomy? On the importance of distinguishing between independence and volitional functioning. In B. Soenens, M. Vansteenkiste, & S. V. Petegem (Eds.), *Autonomy in adolescent development: Towards conceptual clarity* (pp. 1–32). London, UK: Routledge.

Ventura, A. K., & Mennella, J. A. (2011). Innate and learned preferences for sweet taste during childhood. *Current Opinion in Clinical Nutrition & Metabolic Care, 4*(4), 379–384.

Watanabe, M., & Sturmey, P. (2003). The effect of choice-making opportunities during activity schedules on task engagement of adults with autism. *Journal of Autism and Developmental Disorders, 33*, 535–538.

Wehmeyer, M., Lawrence, M., Kelchner, K., Palmer, S., Garner, N., & Soukup, J. (2004). *Whose future is it anyway? A student-directed transition planning process* (2nd ed.). Lawrence, KS: Beach Center on Disability.

Wehmeyer, M. L., Palmer, S. B., Lee, Y., Williams-Diehm, K., & Shogren, K. A. (2011). A randomized-trial evaluation of the effect of whose future is it anyway? On self-determination. *Career Development for Exceptional Individuals, 34*(1), 45–56.

Wehmeyer, M. L., Shogren, K., Palmer, S., Williams-Diehm, K., Little, T., & Boulton, A. (2012). The impact of the self-determined learning model of instruction on student self-determination. *Exceptional Children, 78*(2), 135–153.

Preference Assessments, Choice, and Quality of Life for People with Significant Disabilities

Helen I. Cannella-Malone and Linsey M. Sabielny

Introduction

Within the context of daily life, people make a myriad of choices that can be inconsequential to life altering. For example, people choose what to wear, what to eat, and when and if to get out of bed in the morning. They also choose which bills to pay, who to engage with, or where or whether to work. Given this reality, one might assume, then, that all people have this same access to choice-making opportunities, yet people with significant disabilities have historically been given very limited, if any, opportunity to make everyday choices (Bambara & Koger, 1996; Coupe-O'Kane & Goldbart, 2018; Curryer, Stancliffe, Dew, & Wiese, 2018; Kearney, Bergan, & McKnight, 1998; Stancliffe & Abery, 1997; Stancliffe & Wehmeyer, 1995). Over the past several decades, the focus on provision of supports for people with significant disabilities has shifted from a focus on highly structured remedial programs (e.g., sheltered workshops) where limited opportunities for choice-making were provided to a focus on quality of life encompassing physical, material, social, and emotional well-being and self-determination (Kearney et al., 1998). Choice and choice availability are essential to quality of life, and structuring the environment in a way that makes choice-making opportunities more accessible has been demonstrated to be an effective means of increasing choice-making opportunities for people with significant disabilities (Cooper & Browder, 2001). For example, using picture schedules that can be individually arranged, so a student can choose the order of daily activities wherever possible, is a simple way to incorporate choice.

H. I. Cannella-Malone (✉)
The Ohio State University, Columbus, OH, USA
e-mail: malone.175@osu.edu

L. M. Sabielny
DePaul University, Chicago, IL, USA
e-mail: lsabieln@depaul.edu

© Springer Nature Switzerland AG 2020
R. J. Stancliffe et al. (eds.), *Choice, Preference, and Disability*, Positive
Psychology and Disability Series, https://doi.org/10.1007/978-3-030-35683-5_10

There is significant research demonstrating that preferences can be systematically identified for people with significant disabilities (c.f., Cannella, O'Reilly, & Lancioni, 2005; Lancioni, O'Reilly, & Emerson, 1996; Tullis et al., 2011). Moreover, once preferred stimuli are identified, these can be used to support and teach people with significant disabilities to make choices, resulting in increased autonomy and a higher quality of life.

In this chapter, we argue that preference assessments should be used to identify highly preferred stimuli, which can then be used within choice contexts to improve the quality of life for people with significant disabilities. We present this chapter in three parts. First, we will briefly describe the various preference assessments that have research support that can be used with people who, for whatever reason, cannot tell us what they prefer. Second, we will discuss how the results from preference assessments can be used not only to teach new skills but also to improve overall quality of life. Finally, we will discuss what works with respect to moving beyond knowing what a person prefers to using information gathered from preference assessments to provide meaningful, high-quality choices that can ultimately impact a person's quality of life.

Part I: Preference Assessments

There are generally four types of systematic preference assessments that have been used to identify the preferences of people with significant disabilities – single stimulus, paired choice (with and without eye gaze), multiple stimulus, and free operant – each with its advantages and disadvantages. Each person's unique communication needs and preferences should be carefully considered in determining which assessment may be appropriate for each individual. In this section, we will briefly describe how these assessments are conducted and discuss their primary advantages and disadvantages.

Single-Stimulus Preference Assessment The single-stimulus preference assessment was designed for people with significant disabilities who do not make a choice when presented with more than one stimulus (Pace, Ivancic, Edwards, Iwata, & Page, 1985). In this assessment, each trial (i.e., presentation of a single stimulus) includes only one stimulus, and the person is given an opportunity to engage (or not) with that stimulus. This assessment provides information about each stimulus individually, such as whether and how a person is engaged with the stimulus (e.g., did they touch the stimulus, push it away, or ignore it?), their affect (i.e., expression of pleasure or displeasure) when engaging with the stimulus (e.g., smiling, crying, turning away), and how long they engaged with the stimulus.

The primary advantage of using a single-stimulus assessment is that it allows access to information about stimuli that a person with significant disabilities might prefer, even though they do not make choices between multiple stimuli. Knowing these preferences provides educational and support teams information that they can use to begin teaching new skills, which could allow future use of more efficient preference assessment procedures. A primary disadvantage of this assessment is its inability to provide information about preference of a stimulus in relation to the other stimuli evaluated in the assessment or in the person's environment.

Paired Choice Preference Assessment In an attempt to define a procedure that would better differentiate preferred from non-preferred stimuli for people with significant disabilities, Fisher, Piazza, Bowman, Hagopian, Owens, and Slevin (1992) analyzed a forced-choice (i.e., paired choice) assessment wherein pairs of stimuli were presented, and the participants were required to select one of the two stimuli. Using the paired choice assessment, a group of stimuli are presented in pairs, with each stimulus paired with every other stimulus. Each pair is presented to the person, who gains access to one stimulus by choosing it from the pair. Once all pairs have been presented, a preference hierarchy can be generated by determining how often each stimulus was chosen.

A variation of this assessment allows people to make selections using eye gaze (Cannella-Malone, Sabielny, & Tullis, 2015); Fleming et al., 2010. The procedures are identical, but rather than physically reaching for a stimulus, selections are made through eye gaze. Using this selection method can be cumbersome for the individual, who may tire more quickly using only their eyes to communicate, and administrator, who has to pay particular attention to the positioning of the person with disabilities, has to carefully define what a selection will be (e.g., looking at a stimulus for 1 s or 3 s or 5 s), and will likely have to rely on some subjective judgment of where the person with disabilities is looking. Even with these challenges, using eye gaze as a selection method has been successful in identifying reinforcing stimuli for people who have the most significant intellectual and physical disabilities for whom engaging with the environment requires significant, specific, and systematic supports (e.g., Cannella-Malone, Schmidt, & Bumpus, 2018).

The paired stimulus procedure has the advantage of resulting in a preference hierarchy, wherein differentiation between preferred and non-preferred stimuli can be made. This information allows educational and support teams to use the most preferred stimuli strategically (e.g., when teaching a novel skill). One disadvantage of this assessment is the time it takes to complete (DeLeon & Iwata, 1996). However, if a person is not currently making choices from an array, this assessment will provide more information than the single-stimulus assessment.

Multiple Stimulus Assessments For people who make choices from an array of more than two stimuli, researchers have worked to further increase the efficiency of preference assessments (e.g., DeLeon & Iwata, 1996; Windsor, Piche, & Locke, 1994). Multiple stimulus assessments can be conducted more quickly than paired choice assessments and maintain the differentiation between more and less preferred stimuli. Two formats of multiple stimulus assessments have been researched: multiple stimulus with (MSW) and without replacement (MSWO). In both assessments, an array of stimuli is presented to a person with significant disabilities who is given the opportunity to select one of the stimuli and engage with it. In the MSW, the stimulus engaged with is replaced in the array and can be selected again in subsequent trials (Windsor et al. 1994). In the MSWO, once a stimulus is selected, it is not replaced in the array and cannot be selected again (DeLeon & Iwata, 1996).

As long as the person being assessed can choose from an array of stimuli, the primary advantage of the MSWO is that a preference hierarchy can be determined more quickly than with a paired choice assessment. The primary disadvantage of the MSW assessment is that a full hierarchy may not be identified, as it is possible to select the same stimulus for all trials in the assessment. As such, it is possible for only one preferred stimulus to be identified, even though several stimuli in the array might be preferred. Given this, it is generally recommended that the MSWO be used to assess the preferences of people with significant disabilities.

Free Operant Assessments In another effort to improve the efficiency of systematic preference assessments, researchers have explored free operant formats (e.g., Roane, Vollmer, Ringdahl, & Marcus, 1998; Sautter, LeBlanc, & Gillett, 2008). Within this format, a stimulus array is presented for a short period of time (e.g., 5 min), and the person being assessed is given noncontingent access to the entire array. During this assessment, the assessor monitors which stimuli the person engages with. Stimuli engaged with more are considered to be more preferred.

As with the single-stimulus assessment, it is not possible to gather information on the relative preference of one stimulus to another. However, the short duration of this assessment makes it a strong candidate for quickly identifying potentially reinforcing stimuli. For instructional and support teams, it is reasonable to consider using this assessment at the start of an instructional session to identify what a person might like to work for on a particular day without having to run a full assessment at the start of each set of instructional trials.

Some Thoughts on Choosing Stimuli to Include in an Assessment For each assessment described in this section, it is important to consider the extent to which the person has had experience with a given stimulus and how that might affect their interaction with it during the preference assessments. Including a novel stimulus might result in artificially higher or lower rates of responding for a variety of reasons (e.g., exciting new item, not knowing how to engage with it), and once the item becomes more familiar, rates might become more stable. A simple solution could include allowing time to sample all items before the preference assessment, so that there is sufficient time to see how each item is manipulated, how it works, and so on.

Part II: Using Preference Assessments to Improve Quality of Life

Conducting systematic preference assessments is a first step in identifying and using a hierarchy of preferences for people with significant disabilities. In this section, we will discuss ways in which preference assessment results can be used to inform practice and how this, in turn, improves quality of life.

Using Results to Inform Practice Just as a preference assessment is only as good as the stimuli included, the results are only as good as the extent to which they are used to inform practice. Informing practice can be accomplished by using preferred stimuli as reinforcers, incorporating preferred stimuli into leisure skills and/or hobbies, increasing motivation and "buy-in" through choice, and expanding the settings in which each of these is utilized.

Using Preferred Stimuli as Reinforcers Stimuli identified via preference assessments often function as reinforcers. Those that are identified as highly preferred tend to differentially reinforce behaviors at a higher rate and/or frequency than stimuli that have been identified as moderately or less preferred (Graff, Gibson, & Galiatsatos, 2006). These stimuli can, and should, be used during instruction to reinforce desired behaviors, whether they are academic or functional in nature. In addition, preferred stimuli can be used to reinforce behaviors that are just being learned (i.e., in acquisition) as well as to maintain already learned behaviors. To use a preferred stimulus as a reinforcer, the practitioner should provide the stimulus contingent upon a desired behavior. If the targeted behavior increases, the instructor has now identified a preferred stimulus that can *also* function as a reinforcer. It is important for the practitioner to remember guidelines for using reinforcers effectively, particularly focusing on using a variety of reinforcers as well as those that are of high quality (Wheeler & Richey, 2014). It is also important to note that not all preferred stimuli will become reinforcers, and practitioners should not assume that a preferred stimulus will function as one. This is not necessarily a problem, though, as preferred items can be incorporated into the environment, for example, as instructional materials or leisure activities.

Incorporating Preferred Stimuli into Leisure Activities Although it is useful for preferred stimuli to function as reinforcers, practitioners can utilize these stimuli even if they do not function as reinforcers. For example, preferred stimuli and activities can be incorporated into leisure skills and/or hobbies. How most people spend their free time (e.g., leisure, hobbies) is often focused on activities they enjoy. However, many people with significant disabilities may have restricted interests or limited opportunities to develop or build skills that would allow them to use free time in meaningful ways (Solish, Perry, & Minnes, 2010). Therefore, using stimuli or activities that have been identified as preferred via a preference assessment is an effective way to support people with significant disabilities to learn about and engage in activities that they enjoy. It should be noted, however, that it is not necessary to immediately be able to engage in preferred activities independently, and instead practitioners can use knowledge of preferences to support the person to engage in stimuli or activities more meaningfully. For example, in a study conducted by Cannella-Malone et al. (2016), the authors evaluated the preferences for a variety of leisure stimuli for young adults with significant disabilities. The results demonstrated that the participants initially indicated clear preferences for leisure activities that then shifted once instruction was provided on how to engage with the leisure materials. In other words, preference assessments are effective in identifying preferred stimuli, but instruction may be necessary for people with significant disabilities to make an informed choice on the stimuli with which they are truly interested in engaging. Practitioners, then, should use preferences to structure and guide environmental opportunities, but they should also continue to provide education and support, recognizing that preferences may change over time and that adjustments will need to be made accordingly.

Provision of Choice In addition to using the results of preference assessments to inform practice, providing opportunities to make choices is a powerful tool for any practitioner and a way to increase quality of life for people with significant disabilities. There are several studies that suggest that the provision of choice is unnecessary if the stimulus provided in a no-choice condition is highly preferred (e.g., Lerman et al., 1997; Romaniuk & Miltenberger, 2001; Vaughn & Horner, 1997). Although the results of these studies suggest that what is essential is the identification and provision of highly preferred stimuli, it is important to distinguish between preference and choice: choice is the mechanism through which an individual can express preferences. Although preference may remain stable over time (Zhou, Iwata, Goff, & Shore, 2001), choice is the mechanism through which an individual can express those preferences. For example, a person may always prefer basketball, regardless of the other options; or they may prefer basketball one day and football the next. Without the provision of choice, these preferences may be lost, reducing the person's autonomy and quality of life.

Although there is some evidence that identifying (and then providing) highly preferred stimuli is most important, there is also evidence available indicating that many people prefer the opportunity to make a choice over an opportunity in which the choice has been made for them. For example, if a person chooses to play basketball when given a variety of options (e.g., baseball, football), and then that same choice is automatically given at the next opportunity (i.e., basketball is chosen for you), the person is more likely to participate in the first context (i.e., choice) than in the second (i.e., no choice), even though the same activity was provided. In other words, even when an activity is "supposed" to be preferred and has been demonstrated to be preferred in the past (e.g., basketball), it may no longer be preferred if it is chosen for you. This isn't simply due to a change in preference; this is due to the power of choice. Research has indicated that people often demonstrate a preference for choice, in and of itself (Tiger, Hanley, & Hernandez, 2006; Schmidt, Hanley, & Layer, 2009), and that the opportunity to make a choice can be a preferred activity and may even function as a reinforcer, providing additional justification for providing choice-making opportunities.

Choice has also been linked to an increase in task engagement and decrease in challenging behavior, making it an ideal solution for a variety of behaviors and settings (e.g., Dunlap et al., 1994; Dyer, Dunlap, & Winterling, 1990; Powell & Nelson, 1997). By providing people with significant disabilities the opportunity to have a voice in sharing what they prefer and do not prefer, and to be provided with the opportunity to make choices, practitioners are empowering people across the lifespan to communicate and make decisions about their lives.

Expanding the Contexts for Preference Assessments Preference assessments can also be used to identify a wide variety of preferences across various settings.

Traditionally, preference assessments have been used to identify preferences for edibles and tangibles/activities, which were then used to reinforce desired behaviors during instruction or during behavior management. However, over the past several years, preference assessments have not only improved in method of delivery and implementation, but their scope has been broadened in terms of the type of stimuli and settings being evaluated. For example, preference assessments have successfully been used to identify work preferences, preferred jobs, and community-based reinforcers (e.g., Almeida, Allen, Maguire, & Maguire, 2018; Horrocks & Morgan, 2009; Reid, Parsons, & Green, 1998; Reid, Parsons, Towery, Lattimore, Green, & Brackett, 2007) for people with significant disabilities. For example, Horrocks and Morgan (2009) compared the use of two different preference assessment delivery systems (i.e., video-based paired stimulus, traditional MSWO) to identify the preferred jobs for three people with significant disabilities. The authors found that both assessments were equally effective in identifying highly preferred activities, with both assessments identifying the same highest preference job for all three participants, even though the video-based assessment did not provide contingent access to the stimuli upon selection. This demonstrates the flexibility with which preference assessments can be conducted, including delivery method, setting, and materials.

Improving Quality of Life Choice and preference are not only used to inform practice, but they can also be used to improve the quality of life for people with significant disabilities. We will identify some key ways in which choice and preference can have a significant impact on a person's well-being and can provide an avenue for learning about the person and how they can result in exposure that increases opportunities for the person.

Research indicates that teaching students to participate in activities such as hobbies (e.g., puzzles, art projects, music) or work tasks (e.g., clerical, food and beverage preparation, lawn care) can have positive social and emotional effects, such as an increase in activity level and social interactions (Jerome, Frantino, & Sturmey, 2007). As previously discussed, preference assessments are an effective method for identifying leisure activities and work preferences for people with significant disabilities, and the opportunity to make a choice has been linked with increases in task engagement and decreases in challenging behavior. Taken together, the effects of using preferred stimuli and opportunities to make choices in practice can have a significant impact on the well-being of a given individual. Winking, O'Reilly, and Moon (1993) found that workers with significant disabilities were much more likely to enjoy their work if the tasks involved in their job matched their work preferences.

An additional way that assessing a person's preferences and providing choices can enhance quality of life is by providing a means for others to get to know them better. By providing a person with significant disabilities an opportunity to make a choice and to demonstrate preferences, the practitioner is given more information about that person. The person is provided the opportunity to "say" something about themselves – that they prefer ice cream over doughnuts and would much rather listen to pop music than classical. This gives the practitioner an opportunity to "listen" to the person where they might not otherwise have done so or known *how* to do so.

Previous research has indicated that practitioners often choose common items, overlook idiosyncratic items, and/or identify the incorrect reinforcer nearly 50% of the time when attempting to identify preferred stimuli (Cannella-Malone, Sabielny, Jimenez, & Miller, 2013). In addition, although it may be an efficient method for identifying stimuli to *include* in a preference assessment, practitioner opinion alone is not sufficient for identifying stimuli that will likely be preferred or function as a reinforcer (Reid et al., 2007). Given the number of unknowns, it makes far more sense to have the person "speak" for themselves, by giving them opportunities to make choices throughout their day.

As previously mentioned, research has demonstrated that preferences can shift once a person has been taught how to engage in or with a specific activity (Cannella-Malone et al., 2016). This is especially relevant for people with significant disabilities, who may have restricted and/or limited interests because of a lack of exposure to opportunities to learn and experience an array of activities. By teaching a person with significant disabilities how to engage in leisure skills that are of interest to them, that person's preferences will likely shift to preferring that activity over one to which they have not had exposure. By doing this, a practitioner can continue to increase a person's skill repertoire. Instead of limiting a person to what is in their immediate environment and/or assumed to be typical for other people with significant disabilities, identifying stimuli through a preference assessment allows practitioners to expose them to stimuli or activities that they may never otherwise come in contact with. In addition, this person is now more fully equipped to engage with other people and environments due to the variety of experiences they have been exposed. If this had not been the case, and a person's opportunity to make choices or indicate their own preferences had been limited, practitioners are essentially forcing their choices. For example, if a person is never given the opportunity to choose or engage in photography, they might never learn that they enjoy it or that they are good at it, which limits their ability to socialize with others who enjoy photography, attend photography events, or pursue a career in photography. The more people with significant disabilities can be exposed to choices, the wider their world and their opportunities become.

Part III: High-Quality Choices: What Works

The Need to Provide High-Quality Choices As noted above, choice is the mechanism through which a person with a significant disability can express their preference at a specific point in time. Through the identification of highly preferred stimuli and activities, and the provision of choice around these activities, doors can be opened for people with significant disabilities that might otherwise have remained permanently closed. For example, if one assumes that a person with a significant disability is not able to work outside of a sheltered workshop setting, they will never have the opportunity to engage in community employment. If, however, one was to conduct an MSWO assessment to identify work preferences, steps could be taken to systematically teach the preferred job skills, identify a potential job site in the community, and provide the person with significant disabilities the opportunity to engage in that job in the community. Without question, this is hard work for all involved. However, the potential long-term benefits are also well worth the effort.

One reason that incorporating choice-making opportunities into the daily routine of a person with significant disabilities can be so impactful is because of the myriad opportunities available for utilizing preferences and choices. Finding little ways throughout the day to incorporate choice and preference can go a long way to communicate to the person with significant disabilities that the practitioner is listening, that they value the person's input, and that they are dedicated to building that person's self-advocacy. For example, as a means for increasing autonomy, preferences related to self-care (e.g., dressing, shaving, diet, positioning) can be identified by providing a person with significant disabilities the opportunity to make choices in these contexts. Such small choices can change the way a person interacts with the environment and the people around them, because they are expected to engage (i.e., given the choice) and reinforced for engaging (i.e., by choosing what they are going to wear and actively engaging with their service provider).

Providing choices to people with significant disabilities can be distinctly different from providing choices to other populations. As we have previously discussed, we make innumerable choices every day of our lives, some of which seem tiny and inconsequential and some of which seem overwhelming or even daunting. Regardless, we make those decisions. People with disabilities, especially those with significant disabilities, often have those decisions made for them. Consider that, for some people, it may be difficult to start making choices if they have never been given the opportunity previously. It may, in fact, even be a skill deficit that needs to be directly taught or could serve as a trigger for challenging behavior. It is okay, and recommended, to start small. Practitioners should consider ways in which they can start offering choices, such as which route their client would like to take to the cafeteria or whether their student wants to hang their art project at the top of the board or at the bottom. During snacks and meals, practitioners can offer available options, limiting the array to two or three to start and then opening it up to the whole snack cabinet or cafeteria once the person with significant disabilities has become comfortable and confident that their environment will support them in making choices. Opportunities to make choices can even be a large part of educational programming, such as having students choose their own superhero power to describe how it works (i.e., science), what they want to do with it (i.e., English language arts), and the impact this superhero will have on their community (i.e., social studies). It could even be expanded to include how the person with significant disabilities is developing and presenting their superhero idea (e.g., drawing, choosing from preselected pictures, presentation via vocal-output device). But it can also be as simple as having the student choose between a red marker and a blue marker when coloring in their superhero mask.

Identifying Preference Is Simply a Starting Point For a person with significant disabilities, systematically identifying stimuli and activities that they prefer is an essential first step in increasing that person's autonomy and helping them share their identity with the people around them. Relationships are built around learning what other people enjoy, finding commonalities and differences, and learning about new and different things through experience. For people with significant disabilities, opportunities to engage in this way might be limited due to the severity of their disability and assumptions made about what they can and cannot do. Families, educational teams, community-based service providers, and researchers, among others, must all work to systematically identify the preferences of people with significant disabilities and work diligently to use that information to expand their worlds.

Systematically identifying preferences is a key first step, but we all must work to use that information in meaningful and consistent ways, by using the identified stimuli as reinforcers when teaching, providing access to preferred activities during leisure times, and considering preferences for work or activities when considering what the day of a person with significant disabilities might look like. Each of these considerations can be enhanced through the consistent and frequent provision of choices. We all make choices all of the time, and the quality of our lives varies depending on the choices we make. People with significant disabilities should be given the same opportunities to make choices and impact the quality of their lives as well.

References

Almeida, D. A., Allen, R., Maguire, R. W., & Maguire, K. (2018). Identifying community-based reinforcers of adults with autism and related disabilities. *Journal of Behavioral Education, 27*, 375–394. https://doi.org/10.1007/s10864-018-9295-x

Bambara, L. M., & Koger, F. (1996). *Opportunities for daily choice making*. Washington, D.C.: American Association on Mental Retardation.

Cannella, H. I., O'Reilly, M. F., & Lancioni, G. (2005). Choice and preference assessment research with people with severe to profound developmental disabilities: A review of the literature. *Research in Developmental Disabilities, 26*, 1–15. https://doi.org/10.1016/j.ridd.2004.01.006

Cannella-Malone, H. I., Miller, O., Schaefer, J. M., Jimenez, E. D., Page, E. J., & Sabielny, L. M. (2016). Using video prompting to teach leisure skills to students with significant disabilities. *Exceptional Children, 82*, 463–478. https://doi.org/10.1177/0014402915598778

Cannella-Malone, H. I., Sabielny, L. M., Jimenez, E. D., & Miller, M. M. (2013). Pick one!: Conducting preference assessments with students with significant disabilities. *Teaching Exceptional Children, 45*, 16–23.

Cannella-Malone, H. I., Sabielny, L. M., & Tullis, C. A. (2015). Using eye gaze to identify reinforcers for individuals with severe multiple disabilities. *Journal of Applied Behavior Analysis, 48*, 680–684. https://doi.org/10.1002/jaba.231

Cannella-Malone, H. I., Schmidt, E. K., & Bumpus, E. C. (2018). Assessing preference using eye gaze technology for individuals with significant intellectual and physical disabilities. *Advances in Neurodevelopmental Disorders, 2*, 300–309. https://doi.org/10.1007/s41252-018-0072-6

Cooper, K. J., & Browder, D. M. (2001). Preparing staff to enhance active participation of adults with severe disabilities by offering choice and prompting performance during a community purchasing activity. *Research in Developmental Disabilities, 22*, 1–20.

Coupe-O'Kane, J., & Goldbart, J. (2018). *Whose choice?: Contentious issues for those working with people with learning difficulties*. New York, NY: Routledge.

Curryer, B., Stancliffe, R. J., Dew, A., & Wiese, M. Y. (2018). Choice and control within family relationships: The lived experience of adults with intellectual disability. *Intellectual and Developmental Disabilities, 56*, 188–201. https://doi.org/10.1352/1934-9556-56.3.188

DeLeon, I. G., & Iwata, B. A. (1996). Evaluation of a multiple-stimulus presentation format for assessing reinforcer preferences. *Journal of Applied Behavior Analysis, 29*, 519–533. https://doi.org/10.1901/jaba.1996.29-519

Dunlap, G., dePerczel, M., Clarke, S., Wilson, D., Wright, S., White, R., & Gomez, A. (1994). Choice making to promote adaptive behaviors for students with emotional and behavioral challenges. *Journal of Applied Behavior Analysis, 27*, 505–518. https://doi.org/10.1901/jaba.1994.27-505

Dyer, K., Dunlap, G., & Winterling, V. (1990). The effects of choice making on the problem behaviors of students with severe handicaps. *Journal of Applied Behavior Analysis, 23*, 515–524. https://doi.org/10.1901/jaba.1990.23-515

Fisher, W., Piazza, C. C., Bowman, L. G., Hagopian, L. P., Owens, J. G., & Slevin, I. (1992). A comparison of two approaches for identifying reinforcers for persons with severe and profound disabilities. *Journal of Applied Behavior Analysis, 25*, 491–498. https://doi.org/10.1901/jaba.1992.25-491

Fleming, C. V., Wheeler, G. M., Cannella-Malone, H. I., Basbagill, A. R., Chung, Y. C., & Graham Day, K. (2010). An evaluation of the use of eye gaze to measure preference of individuals with severe physical and developmental disabilities. *Developmental Neurorehabilitation, 13*, 266–275. https://doi.org/10.3109/17518421003705706

Graff, R. B., Gibson, L., & Galiatsatos, G. T. (2006). The impact of high- and low-preference stimuli on vocational and academic performances of youths with severe disabilities. *Journal of Applied Behavior Analysis, 39*, 131–135. https://doi.org/10.1901/jaba.2006.32-05

Horrocks, E. L., & Morgan, R. L. (2009). Comparison of a video-based assessment and a multiple stimulus assessment to identify preferred jobs for individuals with significant intellectual disabilities. *Research in Developmental Disabilities, 30*, 902–909. https://doi.org/10.1016/j.ridd.2009.01.003

Jerome, J., Frantino, E. P., & Sturmey, P. (2007). The effects of errorless learning and backward chaining on the acquisition of internet skills in adults with developmental disabilities. *Journal of Applied Behavior Analysis, 40*, 185–189. https://doi.org/10.1901/jaba.2007.41-06

Kearney, C. A., Bergan, K. P., & McKnight, T. (1998). Choice availability and persons with mental retardation: A longitudinal and regression analysis. *Journal of Developmental and Physical Disabilities, 20*, 291–305.

Lancioni, G. E., O'Reilly, M. F., & Emerson, E. (1996). A review of choice research with people with severe and profound developmental disabilities. *Research in Developmental Disabilities, 17*, 391–411. https://doi.org/10.1016/0891-4222(96)00025-X

Lerman, D. C., Iwata, B. A., Rainville, B., Adelinis, J. D., Crosland, K., & Kogan, J. (1997). Effects of reinforcement choice on task responding in individuals with developmental disabilities. *Journal of Applied Behavior Analysis, 30*, 411–422. https://doi.org/10.1901/jaba.1997.30-411

Pace, G. M., Ivancic, M. T., Edwards, G. L., Iwata, B. A., & Page, T. J. (1985). Assessment of stimulus preference and reinforcer value with profoundly retarded individuals. *Journal of Applied Behavior Analysis, 18*, 249–255. https://doi.org/10.1901/jaba.1985.18-249

Powell, S., & Nelson, B. (1997). Effects of choosing academic assignments on a student with attention deficit hyperactivity disorder. *Journal of Applied Behavior Analysis, 30*, 181–183. https://doi.org/10.1901/jaba.1997.30-181

Reid, D. H., Parsons, M. B., & Green, C. W. (1998). Identifying work preferences among individuals with severe multiple disabilities prior to beginning supported work. *Journal of Applied Behavior Analysis, 31*, 281–285. https://doi.org/10.1901/jaba.1998.31-281

Reid, D. H., Parsons, M. B., Towery, D., Lattimore, L. P., Green, C. W., & Brackett, L. (2007). Identifying work preferences among supported workers with severe disabilities. Efficiency and accuracy of a preference assessment protocol. *Behavioral Interventions, 22*, 279–296. https://doi.org/10.1080/07317110902895226

Roane, H. S., Vollmer, T. R., Ringdahl, J. E., & Marcus, B. A. (1998). Evaluation of a brief stimulus preference assessment. *Journal of Applied Behavior Analysis, 31*, 605–620. https://doi.org/10.1901/jaba.1998.31-605

Romaniuk, C., & Miltenberger, R. G. (2001). The influence of preference and choice of activity on problem behavior. *Journal of Positive Behavior Interventions, 3*, 152–159. https://doi.org/10.1177/109830070100300303

Sautter, R. A., LeBlanc, L. A., & Gillett, J. N. (2008). Using free operant preference assessments to select toys for free play between children with autism and siblings. *Research in Autism Spectrum Disorders, 2*, 17–27. https://doi.org/10.1016/j.rasd.2007.02.001

Schmidt, A. C., Hanley, G. P., & Layer, S. A. (2009). A further analysis of the value of choice: Controlling for illusory discriminative stimuli and evaluating the effects of less preferred items. *Journal of Applied Behavior Analysis, 42*, 711–716. https://doi.org/10.1901/jaba.2009.42-711

Solish, A., Perry, A., & Minnes, P. (2010). Participation of children with and without disabilities in social, recreational and leisure activities. *Journal of Applied Research in Intellectual Disabilities, 23*, 226–236. https://doi.org/10.1111/j.1468-3148.2009.00525.x

Stancliffe, R., & Wehmeyer, M. L. (1995). Variability in the availability of choice to adults with mental retardation. *Journal of Vocational Rehabilitation, 5*, 319–328.

Stancliffe, R. J., & Abery, B. H. (1997). Longitudinal study of deinstitutionalization and the exercise of choice. *Mental Retardation, 35*, 159–169. https://doi.org/10.1352/0047-6765(1997)035<0159:LSODAT>2.0.CO;2

Tiger, J. H., Hanley, G. P., & Hernandez, E. (2006). An evaluation of the value of choice with preschool children. *Journal of Applied Behavior Analysis, 39*, 1–16. https://doi.org/10.1901/jaba.2006.158-04

Tullis, C. A., Cannella-Malone, H. I., Basbagill, A. R., Yeager, A., Fleming, C. V., Payne, D., & Wu, P. (2011). A review of the choice and preference assessment literature for individuals with severe to profound disabilities. *Education and Training in Autism and Developmental Disabilities, 46*, 576–595.

Vaughn, B. J., & Horner, R. H. (1997). Identifying instructional tasks that occasion problem behaviors and assessing the effects of student versus teacher choice among these tasks. *Journal of Applied Behavior Analysis, 30*, 299–312. https://doi.org/10.1901/jaba.1997.30-299

Wheeler, J. J., & Richey, D. D. (2014). *Behavior management: Principles and practices of positive behavior supports* (3rd ed.). Upper Saddle River, NJ: Pearson.

Windsor, J., Piche, L. M., & Locke, P. A. (1994). Preference testing: A comparison of two presentation methods. *Research in Developmental Disabilities, 15*, 439–455.

Winking, D. L., O'Reilly, B., & Moon, M. S. (1993). Preference: The missing link in the job match process for individuals without functional communication skills. *Journal of Vocational Rehabilitation, 3*, 27–42. https://doi.org/10.3233/JVR-1993-3305

Zhou, L., Iwata, B. A., Goff, G. A., & Shore, B. A. (2001). Longitudinal analysis of leisure-item preferences. *Journal of Applied Behavior Analysis, 34*, 179–184. https://doi.org/10.1901/jaba.2001.34-179

Choices and Transition from School to Adult Life: Experiences in China

Tianxi Xu, Juan Tang, Yuan Zhou, and Wenwei Ouyang

Introduction

Choice and self-determination for people with disabilities have been discussed and practiced in the special education and disability field since 1972 (Nirje, 1972; Stancliffe, 2001). Making informed choices often results in enhanced self-determination. Research exploring self-determination and its promotion ranges across different age groups and different disability types (Wehmeyer & Palmer, 2003). Researchers have identified self-determination as an important skill that correlated with improved post-school success for students with disabilities (Ju, Zeng, & Landmark, 2017; Test et al., 2009; Wehmeyer & Palmer, 2003). For example, Wehmeyer and Palmer (2003) found that self-determination skills in high school were significant predictors of adult outcomes in different life domains including employment, post-school education, financial independence, and independent living. Similarly, Test et al. (2009) found that self-determination is an evidence-based predictor of post-school success for students with disabilities. The contents and constructs of self-determination theories have been explored in different cultures across the world, such as in the United States (Shogren, 2013; Wehmeyer, 2005), Korea (Seo, 2014), Japan (Ohtake & Wehmeyer, 2004), Spain (Mumbardó-Adam, Guàrdia-Olmos, & Giné, 2018), and Italy (Ginevra et al., 2013). Researchers in those countries found that self-determination behaviors and skills are significant in enhancing positive adult outcomes for students with disabilities; however, the perceptions and expressions of self-determination in various cultures can differ (Ginevra et al., 2013).

T. Xu (✉)
Central China Normal University, Wuhan, China
e-mail: tianxi.xu@mail.ccnu.edu.cn

J. Tang
The University of Newcastle, Callaghan, NSW, Australia

Y. Zhou · W. Ouyang
Shenzhen Yuanping Special Education School, Shenzhen, China

© Springer Nature Switzerland AG 2020
R. J. Stancliffe et al. (eds.), *Choice, Preference, and Disability*, Positive
Psychology and Disability Series, https://doi.org/10.1007/978-3-030-35683-5_11

We begin this chapter with an introduction to self-determination and choice-making, followed by an overview of special education and school to adult transition for students with disabilities in China and a literature review on self-determination related to people with disabilities in China. We examine and analyze post-school outcomes achieved by school leavers who exited from Shenzhen Yuanping Special Education School in the last 5 years. Finally, we provide recommendations for future research and practice to promote choice-making and self-determination for Chinese school leavers with disabilities.

Choice and Self-Determination

Efforts to promote choice-making and self-determination have been recognized as promising predictors of valued post-school transition outcomes for people with disabilities (Stafford, 2005; Wehmeyer & Abery, 2013). Stancliffe canvassed the literature on choice in the disability field and proposed that choice refers to "making an unforced selection of a preferred alternative from two or more options" (Stancliffe, 2001, p. 92). The definition implies the provision of at least two alternatives and an active selection based on the individual's preference. It is evident that choice-making opportunities and skills are important for major transitions and for quality of life for people with disabilities (Smyth & Bell, 2006). The functional theory of self-determination regards self-determination as an essential component of the process of individualization and personal development (Wehmeyer & Abery, 2013). Researchers reviewed the meanings of self-determination from the psychoeducational perspective, the ecological perspective, and the sociopolitical perspective in the literature and concluded that communication competence, personal characteristics, self-determination competencies, and environmental variables were predictors of different levels of choice and self-determination (Stancliffe, 2001). The exploration of various self-determination definitions and related concepts indicates that free volition, choice, and control represent the important essence of the term. However, compared to their typically developing peers, people with disabilities usually have fewer opportunities to make choices, express preferences, take risks, deal with responsibilities, and exercise control over their lives and environment (Harris, 2003). They therefore may lack confidence in making choices. Nonetheless, choice-making and self-determination should be promoted for people with disabilities to help them achieve the desired post-school transition outcomes.

Special Education and Post-school Transition in China

Special education in China has progressed rapidly in the last two decades; the improvement of special education quality and the enhancement of quality of life for people with disabilities and their families have become the subject of much recent attention and have led to resource reallocation in China. In recent years, secondary school education and transition to adulthood have become priorities in the field of special education and services for students with disabilities (Central People's Government of China, 2017; General Office of the State Council of People's Republic of China, 2014). However, transition from school to adulthood for students with disabilities in China is in an early stage of development that requires action from different stakeholders (Xu, Dempsey, & Foreman, 2014). An overview of special education and transition education and services is presented below.

Special Education in China

About 2000 years ago, ancient Chinese classics documented that people in China were encouraged to assist and support those with disability, mainly because of the influence of Confucianism (Shen, McCabe, & Chi, 2008; Yang & Wang, 1994). Nevertheless, special education developed very slowly before 1978 due to the unstable political situation and restricted resources (Deng, Poon-McBrayer, & Farnsworth, 2001; Ellsworth & Zhang, 2007). The development of special education in China began to flourish after 1979, especially after the "opening and reform." With the enactment of the Compulsory Education Law in 1986, China began to pay more attention to the equal rights for individuals with disabilities. Governments at all levels began to set up schools and classes to address the educational needs of children with disability, and the school attendance rate of students with disability increased dramatically (Deng et al., 2001). Since then, universal 9-year compulsory education has been implemented in China.

According to annual statistics of the Ministry of Education in the People's Republic of China (PRC), by 2017 there were 24,093 special education classes operated in 2107 special education schools in China and 623 special education classes in regular schools, with 578,826 students with special needs enrolled. About 52.6% of the students with special needs are learning in regular schools (including students learning in regular classes in regular schools and 623 special education classes in regular schools across the country) (Ministry of Education of the People's Republic of China, 2013, 2018). The reauthorization of the Compulsory Education Law in 2006 and the Regulation on the Education for People with Disabilities (2017 revision) were vitally important for securing education rights and other necessary support for students with special needs. For example, the reauthorized Compulsory Education Law of 2006 has five clauses addressing special education provisions, which promote the zero-reject principle for students with disabilities, stipulate increased funding for students with disabilities and their teachers, and specify necessary classroom facilities and resources for the education of students with special needs (Wang & Feng, 2014). After years of commitment, learning in regular classes and attached special education classes in regular schools have become a main component of the special education system in China. Special education schools continue to be a significant component of the system, which is supplemented by home visiting services, family education, and community education (Ministry of Education of the People's Republic of China, 2013). Although more and more students with disabilities are enrolling in regular schools, special education schools in China continue to play an essential role in supporting school-aged students with disabilities. Special education schools in many cities also serve as special education resource centers, and teachers from special education schools are itinerant teachers for those who are learning in regular schools or learning at home due to health or transportation issues.

Transition Education and Services in China

As documents record, in 1912 priority was assigned to vocational education and general knowledge instruction for Chinese people with disabilities for the first time, when Jian Zhang became the first Chinese citizen to launch a special education school for students with hearing or vision impairment in China (Deng et al., 2001). However, legislation rarely mentioned vocational education and employment rights for people with disability until the revised Constitution (National People's Congress of the People's Republic of China, 1982), which mandated that the state and society should provide assistance in gaining work for people with hearing, vision, and other impairments. Likewise, the Vocational Education Law (National People's Congress of the People's Republic of China, 1996) and the Law of the Protection of Disabled Persons (China Disabled Persons' Federation, 2008) required that vocational education and support should be provided and working rights should be ensured for people with disability.

The Regulation on the Education for People with Disabilities (2017 revision) stipulates that further education and higher education institutes should not reject students due to disabilities as long as they meet the entry requirements. The recently released Annual Statistical Bulletin regarding the development of programs for people with disabilities in China states that 8466 students with special needs were enrolled in 112 secondary classes (equivalent to year 10–12 in Australia) in special education schools and 12,968 students with special needs were enrolled in 132 junior vocational schools (these schools focus on vocational skills development for students with special needs, the enrolment duration is often 4 years, and students need to complete year 9 to be enrolled in these schools) across the country (China Disabled Persons' Federation, 2018). In regard to higher education for students with disabilities, students with hearing or vision impairment who desire to further their study attend the special college entrance examination each year and have opportunities to study in colleges or universities.

Despite increased commitment to vocational education and higher education, Chinese adults with disability are usually restricted to a few occupations. For instance, individuals with intellectual disability usually work in restaurants and hotels as cleaners or service assistants or do repetitive sorting and assembling jobs, handcrafts, and gardening (Lai, Li, & Meng, 2013; Zhao, 2011). Centralized employment, the quota scheme, and self-employment are the three main forms of employment for people with disability in China. *Centralized employment* refers to employment in various welfare enterprises, in work-rehabilitation organizations, and for people with vision impairments in massage therapy centers. Most or all of the workers in these centralized employment settings have a disability or multiple disabilities. Welfare enterprises are special manufacturers, which are funded by the government and mainly employ people with disability. *The quota scheme* is stipulated by the Regulations on the Employment of Persons with Disabilities in China of 2007, which requires all mainstream employers in China to employ people with disabilities at a proportion of more than 1.5%. The specific percentage may vary and be determined by local government according to the actual conditions. Employment policies in China have been gradually transferred from a segregated to an inclusive approach (Huang, Guo, & Bricout, 2008; Liao & Lai, 2010). More and more service providers and employers are involved in the quota scheme for people with intellectual disability (Du, Li, & Lei, 2013).

Based on the sixth national census and the second national sampling census of people with disability in China, there were approximately 85 million people with disabilities in China by the end of 2010, within which the number of persons with intellectual disability was 5.68 million and the number of persons with vision impairment and hearing impairment was 12.63 and 20.54 million, respectively (China Disabled Persons' Federation, 2012). Statistics indicate that, from 2007 to 2012, people with intellectual disability experienced much more difficulty in gaining employment than their peers with other types of disabilities, even though more vocational training and guidance opportunities were available to them. For example, the Chinese Labor Market Developmental Report (Lai et al., 2013) revealed that between 2007 and 2012, the employment rate for persons with intellectual disability decreased from 52.8% to 38.4%, whereas the percentage of persons with intellectual disability who received vocational training and guidance services increased from 25.2% in 2007 to 46.6% in 2012. However, the employment rates for persons with hearing impairment and vision impairment during the period were stable (around 50%), although less than 21% of persons with sensory impairments received vocational training and guidance services between 2007 and 2012. These employment rates are somewhat positive but remain far lower than the overall employment rate of 67.9% for adults in China (National Bureau of Statistics, 2018), indicating that there is still room for further improvement in employment outcomes for people with disabilities.

These data signify that more attention should be paid to post-school transition services, especially for people with intellectual disability. Transition is a critical period when young people with disability have an important opportunity to join the mainstream labor force. Western researchers found that self-determination is an important indicator for post-school success for individuals with disabilities (Ju et al., 2017; Shogren, Wehmeyer, Palmer, Rifenbark, & Little, 2013), while the Chinese literature has not investigated the relationship between choice-making or self-determination and post-school transition for students with disabilities, although there are a few empirical studies on school to adulthood transition in China (Xu et al., 2014; Xu, Dempsey, & Foreman, 2016).

Choice and Self-Determination in China

Unlike the decades of exploration elsewhere in the world, studies of self-determination in the disability field did not appear in the Chinese literature until 2005 (Bao & Zhang, 2005). The significance of self-determination in achieving desired outcomes for students with disabilities has gradually gained currency in China in recent years (Xu, 2016); however, special education teachers and parents usually regard self-determination literally as "make one's own choices/decisions" (Wang, 2018). Since its emergence in the Chinese literature, several researchers have reviewed theoretical models of self-determination in the United States and reflected the aspirations of those models for special education and disability services in the Chinese context (Xu & Zhang, 2010; Zhang & Bao, 2005). Researchers and practitioners have also explored effective interventions and family support strategies to develop self-determination competencies for persons with intellectual disabilities (He, 2015).

In addition, based on the translation and modification of the AIR Self-Determination Scale (Wolman, Campeau, DuBois, Mithaug, & Stolarski, 1994), researchers have investigated self-determination among Chinese teenagers with hearing impairment, vision impairment, physical impairment, and autism. Teenagers with physical impairment usually have limited opportunities to self-determine, and they usually have a low or mid-level of self-determination (Zhang, 2017). Unlike their peers with physical disabilities, teenagers with vision impairment usually do better on self-determination (Leng, 2016). The severity of autism and the placement options for teenagers with autism are significantly correlated to their performance on self-determination (Gao, 2016). In addition, researchers found that thematic instruction was an effective practice in the development of self-determination for students with intellectual disability (Li, 2008). This approach involves selecting and highlighting themes such as making choices and controlling emotions through multiple instruction units or courses.

With regard to the theoretical framework of self-determination, policies in the special education and disability field rarely mention self-determination. Indeed, the term has not yet been systematically and legitimately defined in China, which makes it challenging for it to take root in the Chinese context (Wang, 2018). However, in recent years, with the emphasis on the "inclusion" and "support" paradigms for students with disabilities in China, the 2016 National Curriculum Standard for Schools for Students with intellectual disability clearly lists most of the self-determination skills. This recent development indicates that there may be a favorable circumstance to facilitate self-determination for students with intellectual disability (Wang, 2018). Researchers have proposed several strategies, such as the provision of self-determination opportunities and the promotion of the concept of self-determination locally, to enable systematic cultivation of self-determination (Wang, 2018; Xu, 2016). Some Chinese academics and practitioners have recognized the importance of self-determination, but with a long history influenced by the Confucian thoughts, and the collectivism-orientated culture, China will find its own way to promote the concept of self-determination and to identify effective tactics to help individuals with intellectual disability to gain relevant self-determination skills.

Choice and Post-school Outcomes in Shenzhen

The broad choice options in post-school transition that students with disabilities in China have are similar to elsewhere, including employment, tertiary education, and community living. As noted previously, students with sensory impairments often have access to tertiary education, and it is relatively easier for them to be employed (typically doing massage jobs) after completing high school. However, students with intellectual disability usually have very limited access to tertiary education and are often confined to segregated settings doing repetitive and nonfunctional job tasks (Xu et al., 2016).

In the authors' experience, post-school outcomes are closely related to the local community's level of economic development. For those better-resourced areas, students with disabilities usually have more choices of further education and employment opportunities. For example, most of the poorer areas do not provide any secondary or vocational education programs for students with disabilities once they have completed the compulsory 9-year education; however, students in better-resourced schools usually have access to continuing public education after finishing year 9. Moreover, students can choose different vocational courses and different internship placements within these vocational education programs. Students with disabilities in those regions or schools are more likely to achieve supported employment in the mainstream labor market as there are wider choices of job opportunities. Shenzhen is one of the best-resourced cities in China, and Shenzhen Yuanping Special Education School is one of the largest comprehensive public schools in China. The school enrolls local residents with disabilities and provides education and employment training services for students from years 1 to 12, with the last 3 years focusing on life skills training, vocational education, and employment services. Currently, there are 988 students with disabilities enrolled in the school, with 218 of the 988 students enrolling in high school program (Years 10–12). From September 2018, with the release of the Second Special Education Promotion Plan in Shenzhen, all students have access to the high school program in Yuanping School for 3 years after completing year 9 if they desire to continue to study. However, before the release of the Second Special Education Promotion Plan, students who completed year 9 had to meet several requirements, and only those students with medium or low support needs had access to the high school program. Therefore, the annual intake was approximately 30 students for the high school program.

Within the high school program, students can choose to focus on either academic study or vocational training. Students who focus on academic study in high school can choose to sit the China University Entrance Examination in the second semester of year 12 to attempt to gain access to a tertiary education program. Those students who select vocational education and training as their focus in high school receive intensive vocational skills training and learn other relevant skills such as social skills and independent living skills for 3 years before seeking employment. Post-school outcomes of school leavers who exited from Shenzhen Yuanping Special Education School in the last 5 years are analyzed below. Thereafter, the situations of two school leavers with disabilities who have obtained different post-school outcomes when they graduated from Yuanping will be described to demonstrate how they exercised choice to achieve those outcomes.

Analysis of the Five-Year Post-school Outcomes

Post-school outcome data for school leavers with disabilities, including students with intellectual disability, autism, cerebral palsy, and hearing impairment, were collected when students exited school. Students in Yuanping Special Education School usually transition to employment, tertiary education, community living, and other training programs when they complete their high school (year 12). This chapter categorizes post-school outcomes into four groups:

1. *Supported employment*, a personalized model for supporting people with disabilities to secure and retain paid employment in the mainstream labor market. Vocational education teachers from Yuanping Special Education School provide most support to their students and graduates, coworkers at the job site also provide certain support, and social workers and job coaches hired by the China Disabled Persons Federation in Shenzhen sometimes may provide support for graduates from Yuanping Special Education School's high school program as well.
2. *Adult service center*, graduates in this group will receive further vocational education services in the center organized by the China Disabled Persons Federation in Shenzhen. Participants do not receive any wages and they can generally stay in the center for maximum 3 years.
3. *Auxiliary employment*, a new type of employment that was approved by the China Disabled Persons Federation and other relevant departments in 2015. It aims to provide working-age people with disabilities with centralized employment in a setting where most or all of the workers have disabilities. This form of employment is especially intended for those with intellectual, mental, or severe physical disabilities who intend to work but have challenges achieving employment in the competitive mainstream labor market. Auxiliary employment is more flexible regarding work time, intensity, and payment, relative to the employment situation of workers without disability.
4. *Other exits*, including further education, returning home, and moving to another city (domestic and overseas) after graduation.

Table 1 summarizes the post-school outcomes that have been achieved by students who graduated from year 12 from Yuanping Special Education School between 2013 and 2017. As the table demonstrates, most students with disabilities achieved either supported employment or auxiliary employment following graduation. It is worth pointing out that Yuanping Special Education School started to expand its enrollment number for students in year 7 in 2011; therefore, in 2014 the number of students who completed year 9 increased, and the number of graduates from the high school program increased to 52 accordingly in 2017.

In order to compare the differences in the post-school outcomes achieved by students with different disabilities, we categorized graduates over the 5 years into four groups: students with (a) hearing impairment, (b) intellectual disability, (c) autism, and (d) other disability. As Table 2 demonstrates, more than half of the graduates between 2013 and 2017 had intellectual disability, and the number of graduates with hearing impairment and autism was each less than 20% of the total number of graduates over the 5 years.

As the two tables show, graduates with different types of disability achieved varying post-school outcomes from 2013 to 2017. To be specific, the majority of the graduates with hearing impairment successfully obtained a job in the open labor market (supported employment) at graduation; however, only around a third of the graduates with intellectual disability were able to achieve supported employment and 22% auxiliary employment. For graduates with autism, only 15% achieved supported employment, whereas slightly more than 50% were placed in auxiliary employment settings. To sum up, based on 5-year data on post-school outcomes achieved by graduates from Shenzhen Yuanping Special Education School, we found that more students with hearing impairment gain supported employment when compared to their peers with intellectual disability, autism, or other disabilities. In addition, the fact that one-third of students with intellectual disability attained supported employment shows that, in Shenzhen, this outcome is not only desirable but is also achievable.

The data reported in Tables 1 and 2 provide a valuable start for analyzing employment outcomes of students with a disability. However, these two tables only present the overall employment outcomes achieved by high school program graduates by different disability categories from 2013 to 2017. It is difficult to identify potential factors that may have influenced the employment outcomes, and it is not possible for the authors to draw reliable conclusions about which strategies are effective in enhancing students' choice-making skills and in achieving better post-school outcomes. Therefore, other information will be needed on employment outcomes (e.g.,

Table 1 Post-school outcomes achieved by students from Yuanping Special School between 2013 and 2017

Year	Supported employment	Adult service center	Auxiliary employment	Other exits	Total
2013	12 (44%)	5 (19%)	2 (7%)	8 (30%)	27 (100%)
2014	12 (40%)	9 (30%)	6 (20%)	3 (10%)	30 (100%)
2015	9 (33%)	11 (41%)	3 (11%)	4 (15%)	27 (100%)
2016	14 (41%)	7 (21%)	9 (26%)	4 (12%)	34 (100%)
2017	21 (40%)	10 (19%)	19 (37%)	2 (4%)	52 (100%)
Total	68 (40%)	42 (25%)	39 (23%)	21 (12%)	170 (100%)

Table 2 Post-school outcomes achieved by students from Yuanping Special School between 2013 and 2017 by students' disability type

Disability type	Supported employment	Adult service center	Auxiliary employment	Other exits	Total
Hearing impairment	27 (87%)	0 (0%)	1 (3%)	3 (10%)	31 (100%)
Intellectual disability	30 (32%)	35 (37%)	21 (22%)	9 (9%)	95 (100%)
Autism	4 (15%)	4 (15%)	14 (52%)	5 (18%)	27 (100%)
Other disability	7 (41%)	3 (18%)	3 (18%)	4 (23%)	17 (100%)
Total	68 (40%)	42 (25%)	39 (23%)	21 (12%)	170 (100%)

Note: "Other disability" includes cerebral palsy, speech disorder, and multiple disabilities

work hours, wages, type of job, job tenure), support processes (e.g., the type and amount of support at work), and training inputs (e.g., the nature and amount of vocational training), to better understand what kind of training and support is effective in leading to better employment and other important post-school outcomes.

In order to obtain a better understanding about how students with intellectual disability go through the process of achieving anticipated outcomes, the authors report follow-up information about two graduates who achieved different post-school outcomes to examine their choices and self-determination experiences in the process of transition to employment.

Two Post-school Transition Cases

Graduate 1 Angel (pseudonym) works in the staff restaurant in a major international hotel in Shenzhen. She has been working in the hotel since 2011 when she graduated from Yuanping Special Education School's vocational education program, where she did her year 10 to 12. The following three paragraphs are provided, respectively, by Angel, her employer, and her former vocational education teachers at Yuanping Special Education School.

My Learning Experience (Angel's Own Story)

My name is Angel. I was born in August 1992. I am a woman with intellectual disability. I studied in Liyuan Primary School and then Hongling Middle School before enrolling in year 8 at Yuanping Special Education School. After enrolling in Yuanping, I performed well in my academic work. Yuanping provided me with a variety of course options and internship opportunities. I selected what I was interested in and completed several vocational courses at school, including office clerk,

Chinese knotting handicraft art, and making artificial flowers using silk stockings. I also attended bowling classes in the school because I really like it. I participated in several bowling competitions at the national and international Special Olympic Games and have won several prizes.

About a year before I graduated, my teacher asked me whether I would like to gain some work experience in a major international hotel in Shenzhen. I was interested in working in a hotel and attended an informal interview with a senior manager from the hotel. About 3 weeks after the interview, I started my work experience in the hotel's Engineering Department as a secretary assistant. My teacher from Yuanping and my supervisor at the hotel taught me the required skills such as typing and designing tables using Microsoft Word. My teachers visited me every day in the first 2 weeks. After 2 months of experience, I could manage most of the tasks as a secretary assistant, although I sometimes may need help from my supervisor and colleagues. All of them were very friendly and are always ready to help me. I liked the working environment in the hotel. I liked my colleagues and enjoyed my stay there. I learned a lot. When I finished my work experience, my supervisor invited me to work in the hotel's Kitchen Team when I graduated from Yuanping. I was very excited, because my family and I wished for me to work there. Hence, I started to work at the Hotel when I graduated from Yuanping, and I now work in the hotel's staff restaurant.

I have been going to exercise lessons at the *Happy Women's School* for more than 2 years, where I learned to how to develop a beautiful physique. I also learn classical dancing to keep my posture. I sometimes attend etiquette and floriculture classes to make my life colorful. I am working very hard at making progress in my appearance and manners. I try to be an elegant lady and to become more and more beautiful.

Our Bowling Champion (Edited Extract from the Hotel's Internal Newsletter)

On 10th of July 2015, Angel, Commis 2 from our hotel's staff restaurant took part in the ninth "National Special Olympics Day" competition organized by Guangdong Province, and successfully won a gold medal in the bowling competition. Angel graduated from Yuanping Special Education School that partnered with our hotel in the EMBRACE Project. Angel joined us in 2011 and became a member of the Kitchen Team in our staff restaurant. She was often recognized by our internal guests because of her hospitality service. She is talented at playing bowling, and she has won plenty of medals in many bowling competitions, from national games to world games. She won one gold medal and two bronze medals in the World Special Olympics Games in 2007 which were held in Shanghai when she was 15 years old. Congratulations to Angel!

A Star in Vocational Education (By Angel's Vocational Education Teachers at Yuanping Special Education School)

Like all other students in the vocational education program in Yuanping Special Education School, Angel and her family participated in the program entrance assessment that identified her interests, hobbies, skills, desires, and support needs. Information about her family's expectations for Angel was also collected. Then an individualized employment plan was developed together with Angel and her family. Within the plan, we decided which courses Angel would study and which work experiences Angel would have. After 3 years of study, she has been employed by a major international hotel in Shenzhen as a regular employee in the staff restaurant for 7 years. During her stay with us in the vocational program, we provided both in-school simulated and on-site work experiences for her. She and her classmates are entitled to choose which simulated courses and workplace experiences to go to. Based on her interests and desires, apart from the academic courses and life skills courses she had to attend, she chose several vocational courses to explore her vocational interests, including Chinese knots, Microsoft computer software skills, and operation of print machines. She also participated in different bowling games and has won many medals. In the last year of her study, Angel and several of her classmates did their internships in a major international hotel in Shenzhen. Because of Angel's excellent record in office work skills, she was placed in the Engineering Department as a secretary assistant. After 2 months of unpaid internship, Angel learned most of the work-related skills and maintained a good relationship with her coworkers and supervisors. Based on her pleasant experience in the hotel, she applied for another position in the hotel when it became available and became a regular paid employee in the staff restaurant, packing and distributing food for the staff of the hotel. At the time of writing, Angel has been working in the hotel's staff restaurant for 7 years. She has also established her family, and she was married and has a baby now. In her spare time, she keeps on participating in bowling, and from 2016 she started to attend exercise and etiquette classes twice a month and posts her updates occasionally on social media platforms.

Graduate 2 Will (pseudonym) is a young man with a speech disorder and mild intellectual disability. He was born in November 1996. Will started to study in Yuanping Special Education School in September 2004. He performed very well in school and won several prizes. He enrolled in the vocational education program (year 10–12) from September 2013 to June 2016. During the 3-year program, he studied courses such as literacy, mathematics, and social adaptation. He also chose to learn some vocational skills including Chinese cooking and how to use Office software based on his strengths and interests. For example, having completed those courses, he knows how to develop a table using Excel, how to edit a document using Word, how to make slides using PowerPoint, and how to trim videos.

In year 12, he did his internship in a property appraisal company, and his job responsibilities included data entry and document organization. At the beginning of his internship, he was reluctant to communicate with other people and struggled with the work procedures. He worked very hard to overcome those barriers, and with the on-site support of vocational teachers from Yuanping, Will gradually learned how to complete the job and successfully graduated from Yuanping. However, the appraisal company did not offer him a job after he finished his work experience there. In June 2016, Will was offered with a cleaning job in a local community when he graduated. However, Will's parents were not happy with the job and did not accept the offer. Instead, Will's parents encouraged him to enroll in a 2-year community college program in digital media design and development, so that he could find a "good" job. He graduated from the college with a diploma in July 2018, and his parents found a job for him, working at a local sports center as a data administrator.

From these two graduates' experiences, we find that parents and school teachers have a great influence on persons with disabilities when they make their educational and vocational choices. For example, the individual's choices and decisions about which vocational courses to take or which work experience to complete were usually influenced by or even decided by parents and teachers. Some degree of teacher and parental involvement is to be expected for students of this age, irrespective of disability. However, it is important for individuals with disabilities to develop their own choice-making and self-determination skills and to have real opportunities to exercise these skills. Students with more experience of making choices in different settings may become more independent and better-informed decision-makers in adulthood. Therefore, parents and teachers need to be careful when presenting individuals with opportunities to make choices, not to be over-involved in "proxying" and making choices *for* their child or student.

In addition, the quality of support system and the inclusiveness of the community play an important role in facilitating each individual's choice-making. From *the employer's newsletter*, it seems that the Hotel acknowledged the diversity of their workforce and respected the achievements that each employee obtains. This situation, together with the support or her work colleagues, may be an important factor in Angel's choice to begin work and to continue to work successfully with the hotel. Meanwhile, it is evident that a well-operated collaboration between school and the enterprise is an advantage for school leavers to make informed choices and to achieve meaningful post-school outcomes. Another critical message arising from these cases is that individuals with disabilities have the ability to make important choices, and to become self-determined, as we can see from Angel's case and her wish to be an elegant and beautiful lady. She chooses to attend relevant classes or programs to assist her to achieve those goals.

In contrast to Angel's experience, Will was very passive in making his own choices, whereas his parents made most decisions for him. As we can imagine, when presented with the same course options, the same work experience opportunities, and the same work placement options, who made the final decision and how this final decision was made really matter. It may be easier and faster for parents and teachers to make choices for their child or student; however, in these circumstances, the student will learn little about informed choice-making but may instead learn that his or her views are not important.

Implications for Future Research and Practice

Choice-making and self-determination are important elements as individuals transition to adulthood. From the research discussed and situations of the two graduates, we know that persons with disabilities are able to make informed choices and should be provided with opportunities to do so. Therefore, transformation of the prevailing mindset is important for family members, teachers, and the public, especially in the Chinese context where choice-making and self-determination are relatively new concepts. We would encourage more research on local theoretical frameworks for choice and self-determination and simultaneously on the investigation of effective strategies that Chinese parents, teachers, and other stakeholders can use to facilitate choice-making and self-determination of individuals with disabilities. Likewise, in the practice domain, we recommend providing more opportunities for individuals to make their own choices and embedding choice-making into daily activities, as this will generate enhanced self-determination which in turn should lead to positive post-school transition outcomes. Meanwhile, it would be worthwhile investigating experiences of choice-making and self-determination to facilitate the exploration about China's own way of promoting the concept of self-determination in the Chinese context.

References

Bao, Z., & Zhang, X. (2005). Self-determination learning theory and it's intervention model. *Chinese Journal of Special Education, 6*, 41–45.

Central People's Government of China. (2017). *Announcement about the distribution of the second round of special education enhancement plan 2017–2020 endorsed by the Ministry of Education and other departments*. Retrieved from http://www.gov.cn/xinwen/2017-07/28/content_5214071.htm

China Disabled Persons' Federation. (2008). *Law of the People's Republic of China on the protection of disabled persons*. Retrieved from http://temp.cdpj.cn/bzfxg/2008-04/25/content_10515.htm

China Disabled Persons' Federation. (2012). *The total number of population with disabilities in China by the end of 2010*. Retrieved from http://www.cdpf.org.cn/sjzx/cjrgk/201206/t20120626_387581.shtml

China Disabled Persons' Federation. (2018). *2017 statistical bulletin on the development of programs for people with disabilities*. Retrieved from http://www.cdpf.org.cn/zcwj/zxwj/201804/t20180426_625574.shtml

Deng, M., Poon-McBrayer, K. F., & Farnsworth, E. B. (2001). The development of special education in China: A sociocultural review. *Remedial and Special Education, 22*(5), 288–298. https://doi.org/10.1177/074193250102200504

Du, L., Li, L., & Lei, J. (2013). The development of supported employment in the US and its implications for China. *Chinese Journal of Special Education*, (9), 14–19.

Ellsworth, N. J., & Zhang, C. (2007). Progress and challenges in China's special education development: Observations, reflections, and recommendations. *Remedial and Special Education, 28*(1), 58–64. https://doi.org/10.1177/07419325070280010601

Gao, Y. (2016). *The study on current ability and influencing factors of self-determination for adolescent with autism spectrum disorder.*. (Master of Education). Chongqing, China: Chongqing Normal University.

General Office of the State Council of People's Republic of China. (2014). *Special education promotion plan (2014–2016)*. Retrieved from http://www.gov.cn/zwgk/2014-01/20/content_2570527.htm

Ginevra, M. C., Nota, L., Soresi, S., Shogren, K. A., Wehmeyer, M. L., & Little, T. D. (2013). A cross-cultural comparison of the self-determination construct in Italian and American adolescents. *International Journal of Adolescence and Youth, 20*(4), 501–517. https://doi.org/10.1080/02673843.2013.808159

Harris, J. (2003). Time to make up your mind: Why choosing is difficult. *British Journal of Learning Disabilities, 31*(1), 3–8. https://doi.org/10.1046/j.1468-3156.2003.00181.x

He, M. (2015). Research on the educational intervention strategies that promotes self-determination skills for students with intellectual disability. *A Journal of Modern Special Education, 7–8*, 83–84.

Huang, J., Guo, B., & Bricout, J. C. (2008). From concentration to dispersion: The shift in policy approach to disability employment in China. *Journal of Disability Policy Studies, 20*(1), 46–54. https://doi.org/10.1177/1044207308325008

Ju, S., Zeng, W., & Landmark, L. J. (2017). Self-determination and academic success of students with disabilities in postsecondary education: A review. *Journal of Disability Policy Studies, 28*(3), 180–189. https://doi.org/10.1177/1044207317739402

Lai, D., Li, C. a., & Meng, D. (2013). *Chinese labor market developmental report: Employment for persons with disabilities in the process of building a moderately prosperous society in all respects*. Beijing, China: Beijing Normal University Press.

Leng, X. (2016). *Research on ability situation and influencing factors of self-determination for teenagers with visual impairment*. (Master of Education). Chongqing, China: Chongqing Normal University.

Li, D. (2008). *Research on promoting students' abilities of self-determination in the process of individualized education program*. (Master of Education). Chongqing, China: Chongqing Normal University.

Liao, J., & Lai, D. (2010). The construction of disability employment service system: The transition from segmentation to integration. *Population and Development, 16*(6), 84–87,96.

Ministry of Education of the People's Republic of China. (2013). *Special education in China made substantial progress*. Retrieved from http://www.moe.gov.cn/publicfiles/business/htmlfiles/moe/s7455/201307/154095.html

Ministry of Education of the People's Republic of China. (2018). *Basic statistics of special education*. Retrieved from http://www.moe.gov.cn/s78/A03/moe_560/jytjsj_2017/qg/201808/t20180808_344707.html

Mumbardo-Adam, C., Guardia-Olmos, J., & Gine, C. (2018). Assessing self-determination in youth with and without disabilities: The Spanish version of the AIR self-determination scale. *Psicothema, 30*(2), 238–243. https://doi.org/10.7334/psicothema2017.349

National Bureau of Statistics. (2018). *2017 statistical bulletin on national economy and social development in China*. Retrieved from http://www.stats.gov.cn/tjsj/zxfb/201802/t20180228_1585631.html

National People's Congress of the People's Republic of China. (1982). *Constitution of the People's Republic of China*. Retrieved from http://www.npc.gov.cn/englishnpc/Constitution/node_2830.htm

National People's Congress of the People's Republic of China. (1996). *Vocational education law of the People's Republic of China*. Retrieved from http://www.gov.cn/banshi/2005-05/25/content_928.htm

Nirje, B. (1972). The right to self-determination. In W. Wolfensberger (Ed.), *The principle of normalization in human services* (1st ed., pp. 176–193). Toronto, Canada: National Institute on Mental Retardation.

Ohtake, Y., & Wehmeyer, M. (2004). Applying the self-determination theory to Japanese special education contexts: A four-step model. *Journal of Policy and Practice in Intellectual Disabilities, 1*(3/4), 169–178.

Seo, H. (2014). Promoting the self-determination of elementary and secondary students with disabilities: Perspectives of general and special educators in Korea. *Education and Training in Autism and Developmental Disabilities, 249*(2), 277–289.

Shen, Q., McCabe, H., & Chi, Z. (2008). Disability education in the People's Republic of China: Tradition, reform and outlook. In S. L. Gabel & S. Danforth (Eds.), *Disability and the politics of education: An international reader* (pp. 177–199). New York, NY: Peter Lang.

Shogren, K. (2013). A social-ecological analysis of the self-determination literature. *Intellectual and Developmental Disabilities, 51*(6), 495–511. https://doi.org/10.1352/1934-9556-51.6.496

Shogren, K. A., Wehmeyer, M. L., Palmer, S. B., Rifenbark, G. G., & Little, T. D. (2013). Relationships between self-determination and postschool outcomes for youth with disabilities. *The Journal of Special Education, 48*(4), 256–267. https://doi.org/10.1177/0022466913489733

Smyth, C., & Bell, D. (2006). From biscuits to boyfriends: The ramifications of choice for people with learning disabilities. *British Journal of Learning Disabilities, 34*(4), 227–236. https://doi.org/10.1111/j.1468-3156.2006.00402.x

Stafford, A. (2005). Choice making: A strategy for students with severe disabilities. *Teaching Exceptional Children, 37*(6), 12–17. https://doi.org/10.1177/004005990503700602

Stancliffe, R. (2001). Living with support in the community: Predictors of choice and self-determination. *Mental Retardation and Developmental Disabilities Research Reviews, 7,* 91–98.

Test, D., Mazzotti, V., Mustian, A., Fowler, C., Kortering, L., & Kohler, P. (2009). Evidence-based secondary transition predictors for improving postschool outcomes for students with disabilities. *Career Development for Exceptional Individuals, 32*(3), 160–181. https://doi.org/10.1177/0885728809346960

Wang, S. (2018). Local interpretation and realization of self-determination by students with intellectual disabilities. *Chinese Journal of Special Education, 6,* 29–34.

Wang, M., & Feng, Y. (2014). Special education today in China. In A. Rotatori, J. Bakken, S. Burkhardt, F. Obiakor, & U. Sharma (Eds.), *Special education international perspectives: Practices across the globe* (pp. 663–668). Bingley, UK: Emerald Group Publishing Ltd..

Wehmeyer, M. (2005). Self-determination and individuals with severe disabilities: Re-examining meanings and misinterpretations. *Research and Practice for Persons with Severe Disabilities, 30*(3), 113–120.

Wehmeyer, M., & Abery, B. (2013). Self-determination and choice. *Intellectual and Developmental Disabilities, 51*(5), 399–411. https://doi.org/10.1352/1934-9556-51.5.399

Wehmeyer, M., & Palmer, S. (2003). Adult outcomes for students with cognitive disabilities three years after high school: The impact of self-determination. *Education and Training in Developmental Disabilities, 38*(2), 131–144.

Wolman, J., Campeau, P., DuBois, P., Mithaug, D., & Stolarski, V. (1994). *AIR self-determination scale and user guide.* Retrieved from http://www.ou.edu/zarrow/AIR%20User%20Guide.pdf

Xu, S. (2016). Research on self-determination for people with disabilities and its implication for education. *Journal of Chongqing Normal University (Philosophy and Social Science), 2,* 84–91.

Xu, S., & Zhang, F. (2010). Research on self-determination for people with disabilities in the US and its implications. *Psychological Science, 33*(1), 235–237.

Xu, T., Dempsey, I., & Foreman, P. (2014). Views of Chinese parents and transition teachers on school-to-work transition services for adolescents with intellectual disability: A qualitative study. *Journal of Intellectual & Developmental Disability, 39*(4), 342–352. https://doi.org/10.3109/13668250.2014.947920

Xu, T., Dempsey, I., & Foreman, P. (2016). Validating Kohler's Taxonomy of Transition Programming for adolescents with intellectual disability in the Chinese context. *Research in Developmental Disabilities, 48,* 242–252. https://doi.org/10.1016/j.ridd.2015.11.013

Yang, H., & Wang, H. (1994). Special education in China. *The Journal of Special Education, 28*(1), 93–105. https://doi.org/10.1177/002246699402800107

Zhang, Y. (2017). *The study on current situation and influencing factors of self-determination for adolescent with physical disorder..* (Master of Education). Chongqing, China: Chongqing Normal University.

Zhang, X., & Bao, Z. (2005). A review on the research about self-determination. *Chinese Journal of Special Education, 9*, 78–81.

Zhao, X. (2011). An investigation report on the current primary vocational education for children with intellectual disability in urban areas in China. *Chinese Journal of Special Education, 1*, 25–32.

Employment Opportunities for People with Intellectual Disabilities

Jan Tøssebro and Terje Olsen

Introduction

This chapter addresses a phase in the life course where one is expected to work; greater still, it is a moral obligation. The German sociologist Kohli (1985, 2007) suggests that in modern western societies, employment structures peoples' life span into three fixed stages: the preparatory, the active, and the retirement phases – where active refers to activity in the labour market. His point is worth noting because it demonstrates how deeply rooted employment is in our lives and societies. Solvang (1993) has argued that employment 'is the core factor connecting the individual and society and is a main aspect of the role as citizen' (p. 7, our translation). One might add that it is the primary valued adult role, and being excluded from this role has a range of social consequences.

Employment opportunities for people with disabilities are, however, limited, and the employment rates are far below the wider population. This applies internationally and to all OECD countries (OECD, 2010). In these countries, the disability employment rates are typically 25–40% below that of the population. People with disabilities are, however, a very heterogeneous group with different labour market opportunities depending on among other issues type of impairment, education level, and age of onset of impairment (Tøssebro & Wik, 2015). Research reviews consistently show that the employment rates are particularly low among people with intellectual disabilities or mental health problems (Greve, 2009; Parmenter, 2011; Verdonshot, de Witte, Reichrath, Buntix, & Curs, 2009). Even though labour markets and support systems differ between countries, the extremely marginal position

J. Tøssebro (✉)
Norwegian University of Science and Technology (NTNU), Trondheim, Norway
e-mail: jan.tossebro@ntnu.no

T. Olsen
Fafo Institute for Labour and Social Research, Oslo, Norway

© Springer Nature Switzerland AG 2020
R. J. Stancliffe et al. (eds.), *Choice, Preference, and Disability*, Positive Psychology and Disability Series, https://doi.org/10.1007/978-3-030-35683-5_12

of people with intellectual disabilities appears to apply across the board (Bush & Tassé, 2017; Butterworth, Hiersteiner, Engler, Bershadsky, & Bradley, 2015; Hedley et al., 2017; McConkey, Kelly, Craig, & Keogh, 2017). People with intellectual disabilities are reported to have three to four times lower employment rates than non-disabled people, and, if employed, they are much more likely to be in segregated settings than people with other types of impairments (Verdonshot et al., 2009).

In this chapter, we discuss the opportunities and choices regarding employment for this group of particularly marginalised people in the labour market. Such a discussion could be conducted rather simplistically: People with intellectual disabilities are likely to be excluded from the open labour market, have few choices, and are in general exempted from the normative duty to work. However, in order to understand their situation in greater depth, one needs to address details in their labour market position, the role of active labour market supports, their subjective perceptions, the strategies they use in order to cope with the situation, how social norms affect their narratives about employment, and so on. In short, there is a need for both detail and contextualisation.

Before moving on, however, we should add that one issue is omitted. When discussing choice and employment in the general population, one tends to distinguish between choice *of* occupation (the type of work you do) and choice *in* the occupation (self-determination at work). This chapter will mainly address the former issue, since the main theme in policy and the scientific literature on employment and intellectual disabilities is the limited opportunities in the labour market.

The Context of the Employment of People with Intellectual Disabilities

In Fig. 1, we have suggested a model for the analysis of the employment situation of people with intellectual disabilities. We will obviously not be able to do full justice to the complexity of the model in this chapter but rather provide a set of thoughts and then relate this to experiences and coping strategies of people themselves. We have placed the experiences and coping strategies of individuals in the centre, a centre that is strongly affected by the surrounding contextual circles. It is important to note that the experiences and coping strategies are not just about how people make sense of and adapt to their situation but also that there is agency. This agency is especially important for the interpretation of choice and self-determination.

Generally speaking, we will argue that the inner individual circle is affected by four types of societal or normative contexts. The first is the social meaning of work. This is about the importance of work in modern societies and the position of employment as *the* valued social role in the active phase of the life course. We do, however, need to dig somewhat deeper into this than simply stating the importance of work. The literature on the psychological, social, and health consequences of unemployment among the general population has pointed to a number of functions that

Fig. 1 A contextual model of the employment situation of people with intellectual disabilities

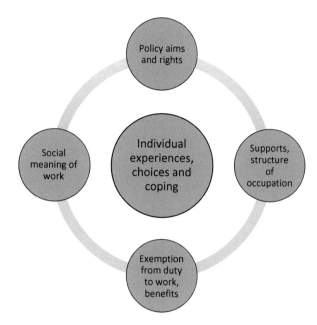

employment has for the individual and his/her role in society. There is, furthermore, a need to look into the concept of work. This needs to be explored as contextual information for the understanding of the employment situation of people with intellectual disabilities.

Second is the context of policy aims and rights. The point here is evident on both the national and international level. The *right* to employment is included in international human rights conventions such as the United Nations Convention on the Rights of People with Disabilities (article 27). However, as shown by the International Labour Office's paper on work for people with disabilities (ILO, 2015), this right follows from a wide range of international conventions, charters, agreements, and declarations. These are not rights in a strictly judicial sense (individual rights) but rather a duty for countries to implement an employment-for-all policy where people with disabilities have equal opportunities in the labour market. These international declarations have national policy parallels in a majority of countries (Parmenter, 2011), typically framed within an 'employment first' policy or policy aims regarding equal opportunities. The aim has also materialised in comparative statistics in Europe (Eurostat, 2015) and analyses of country performance on disability employment by the OECD (OECD, 2010).

The more concrete active labour market measures and supports for people with difficulties finding employment are partly related to the point about rights and policy aims. The supports comprise a number of different measures that vary between countries. However, as pointed out by Parmenter (2011), most countries apply an overriding structure of open (regular/competitive) employment, supported employment, sheltered employment, day activity centres, and no occupation. There are, though, national variations in the content or design of programs. For instance, in most countries, supported employment (SE) is based on long-term support in the employment situation, whereas in Norway this measure is short term. The use of ordinary workplaces for sheltered employment also varies. Thus, an outline of the supports and structures of the employment of people with intellectual disabilities needs to be rather concrete and culture-specific.

The last circle in our model refers to the issue that the majority of people with intellectual disabilities are generally seen as exempted from the duty to work. In most countries, there exists some kind of incapacity or disability benefit to which they are entitled. The generosity of the allowance varies across countries, but the point here is that even though people are exempted from the normative duty to work, this is not without social or moral costs. There is a duality: The allowance provides economic security, but one can nevertheless not simply be exempted. One is exempted because there is something 'seriously wrong with you', so serious that the 'employment first' imperative is disregarded. The benefit is thus likely to be associated with stigma and social devaluation and probably a set of stigma avoidance strategies from individuals. In sociological theory on social control, such as Parsons' (1951), one would argue that this stigma is an intrinsic part of the system, a discouragement 'intended' to maintain the motivation for work in the general population.

In brief, the context of the employment opportunities and choices for people with intellectual disabilities is complex, bringing in a wide set of social meanings. This chapter will explore two of the 'context circles': the two where there is a need for a more elaborate discussion. We need to go more in-depth into the social meaning and functions of work (section "The Social Meaning of Work"), and we need to be more concrete about the existing employment structure and supports (section "Employment Support and the Structure of Occupation for People with Intellectual Disabilities in Norway"). The impact of rights and the exemption from work will be discussed when we come to the analysis of the meaning of the occupation of people with intellectual disabilities (section "The Social Meaning of the Occupation of Intellectually Disabled People") and a set of illustrating case stories from the perspective of the individuals themselves (section "Individual Perceptions, Coping Strategies, and Self-Presentation"). These two sections will be the part of the chapter that addresses the inner circle in Fig. 1: peoples' experiences, coping strategies, and agency. This includes issues such as choice and self-determination, but also stigma management.

The Social Meaning of Work

Literature on the consequences of exclusion of people with disabilities from employment typically refers to the risk of poverty and dependence on social security benefits (Hyde, 1996). However, research on consequences of long-term *unemployment* in the general population tends to address the impact on health, self-esteem, psychosocial wellbeing, and the risk of losing the structure of the day and week (Waddell & Burton, 2006). This research also explores the role employment plays in adult life in modern societies.

The disadvantages for health are well documented, but there has been a question whether unemployment is cause or effect (unemployment causes health problems vs. people with health problems are more likely to be unemployed). Currently, most scholars agree that both processes apply (Dahl, van der Wel, & Harsløv, 2010; Waddell & Burton, 2006) and therefore that unemployment is a health hazard. In the context of this chapter, however, the possible reasons for negative health effects are the more interesting question. Could it be because of poverty? This is unlikely, since the negative effects are evident also in countries with generous unemployment benefits. Thus, the crucial point came to be: What is it about work that causes unemployment to have such a negative impact on peoples' lives?

The debate partly grew out of a classical study by Jahoda, Lazarsfeld, and Zeisel (1933) in the 1930s in Marienthal, an Austrian village struck by mass unemployment. This report and the later literature point to self-esteem, the structure of the day, access to social relations, social recognition, and importance for identity (Lysaght, Ouellette-Kuntz, & Lin, 2012; Timmons, Hall, Bose, Wolfe, & Winsor, 2011). This applies even though work can be boring, tiresome, and sometimes even dangerous. From the comprehensive body of research literature on work, Waddell and Burton (2006) summarise the following:

(a) Employment is the most important means of obtaining the economic resources which are crucial for full participation in society.
(b) Work meets important psychosocial needs in a society where paid employment is the norm.
(c) Work is central to identity, social roles, and social status.

One may add that it also provides a structure for the day and week and that not working may have moral costs since it infringes culturally mediated values ('not being a burden to others or society', 'everyone should contribute') and expectations mediated from the welfare system ('employment as first choice'). Borrowing concepts from Merton (1967), there is a distinction between manifest (intended and recognised) and latent (unintended and largely unrecognised) functions of work. Income is the typical example of a manifest function, whereas latent functions could be social relations, societal participation, or a feeling of being useful (Halvorsen, Bakken, & Fugelli, 1986). It could, however, sometimes be hard to judge whether a function is intended or not. Income is obvious, but what about the feeling of being useful? Our point is not that something is either manifest or latent but that the social functions of work go far beyond what is manifest.

As a background for the analysis of peoples' occupation, we need to ask not only which social functions it fulfils but also what work means: What are the defining criteria? The problem is elegantly illustrated in a saying attributed to Mark Twain: *Work and play are words used to describe the same thing under differing conditions.*[1] A chef works at a restaurant, but what is the activity when she makes dinner at home? Does the activity have to be paid in order to be seen as work? What about

---

[1] According to the *Online Etymology Dictionary.*

volunteer work or *housework*? Or did no one work until the introduction of capitalism and paid labour? We have no ambitions to clarify all the complexity of the concept of work in this chapter but make the point because the lack of clarity has consequences for the interpretation of the occupational role of people with intellectual disabilities. In this context, one of the points made by the philosopher Wittgenstein (1958) may be useful. He argues that for most words, it is not possible to give a precise definition. He uses *game* as an example: board games, card games, ball games, and Olympic Games. He claims that one cannot find a common set of criteria that defines games but that it is fairly easy to see 'family resemblances' and a complicated network of overlapping and crisscrossing similarities (pp. 31–32).

In the context of this chapter, this brings two ideas into the following analysis: The first is that whether something is regarded as work or not depends on the conditions, such as the place it is done or if it is paid. The second is that one will have to look for family resemblance and also to what extent the actors' narratives on their occupation refer to a family resemblance. This relates to a core point in normalisation theory: In order to counteract labelling or devaluating processes, special supports should be designed to resemble the ordinary as much as possible (Wolfensberger, 1972). Family resemblance with ordinary work is more likely to fulfil the typical functions of employment in everyday life.

We will return to interpretations of the work of people with intellectual disabilities shortly, but first we will outline the pattern of occupation of people with intellectual disabilities and the system of services intended to support them. Since this needs to be concrete and culture-specific, we use our home country, Norway, as an example.

Employment Support and the Structure of Occupation for People with Intellectual Disabilities in Norway

The Systems of Support

For many years, Norway has prioritised an 'employment first' policy. This has been explicit since the early 1990s (Stortingsmelding (White paper) 39, 1991–1992), but its history is in reality much longer. Among other things, such a policy means that the social security regulations and labour market measures should support the aims of (a) employment for all and (b) employment as the first choice for everyone. Keywords like 'workfare' are barely used, but the reality is the same, albeit balanced against the principle that people who cannot work are entitled to a decent income. The country is in general considered to have a wide range of active labour market measures intended to support among other people with disabilities in achieving paid employment (OECD, 2006). The national context is furthermore that unemployment is low and that the employment rate in the population at large is among the highest in the world (OECD, 2017). The disability employment rate is nevertheless mediocre (around the OECD average of 42–43%). This is why an OECD analysis concludes that *the key challenge for Norway is to understand why the existing frameworks, which look good, are not delivering* (2006, p. 14).

The system of supports is generic, in the sense that the same types of labour market supports are applied to all people with 'reduced work capacity'. The state Work and Welfare Administration (WWA) is responsible for both social security allowances and labour market measures, and the regulation of allowances and labour market supports is interdependent. The 'employment first' policy implies that no one is entitled to the disability pension before all available employment measures have been exhausted (Social Security Act § 12–5). The WWA is further-more obliged to support people with difficulties finding a job to get into employ-ment. According to the regulations of the WWA, people with 'reduced work capacity' have a right to a comprehensive work assessment and an action plan (Law on WWA, § 14a). It is the WWA's duty to try all available active labour market mea-sures and supports before considering the disability pension, which is considered a 'last resort'.

There is, however, an exception to the mandatory work assessment in 'obvious cases'. A diagnosis in itself is not a reason for classifying a case as obvious, but the regulations nevertheless mention people with intellectual disabilities as an example. There was a worrying change in the regulations in 2015. Before 2015, *severe* intel-lectual disability made a case obvious, but thereafter the qualifier *severe* was omit-ted (Circular on Social security Act, § 12–5). This has led to a practice whereby people with intellectual disabilities are put on a 'fast track' to disability pension (Wendelborg & Tøssebro, 2018): The majority are transferred to the disability pen-sion 'untried' at the age of 18–20 years. Some may not even have finished school yet. The allocation of the disability pension also turns the person into a 'low prior-ity' case among officials working with labour market supports (Spjelkavik, Børing, Frøyland, & Skarpaas, 2012). A study interviewing officials involved in work assessments in the WWA showed that they rarely serve or even meet people with intellectual disabilities (Proba, 2016).

The potential occupations of people with intellectual disabilities can, roughly speaking, be sorted into five types:

(a) Open labour market employment (with or without permanent support)
(b) Temporary labour market measures (including supported employment)
(c) Permanent sheltered work (segregated or not)
(d) Day activity centres
(e) None

  (a) Open labour market employment can be with or without supports from the WWA, such as permanent wage subsidies, combinations of allowances and pay, transport to work, mentors, and so on. The intention of the supports is to reduce employer costs for employees expected to have permanently reduced productivity.
  (b) Next, there is a wide range of temporary measures intended to improve peoples' work capacity/qualifications and/or to support/subsidise them

during a transition period to employment. The transition support could be temporary wage subsidies, funding of work-place accommodation, internships by regular employers, etc. In the international context, this toolbox is generally considered comprehensive. It also comprises supported employment (SE). This may seem somewhat unexpected since this support is long term in many countries (Parmenter, 2011). In Norway, it is short term (up to 3 years). However, it is necessary to distinguish between SE as a labour market measure and as a method of labour market inclusion. As a method, SE can in Norway be used within the framework of sheltered work. Both sheltered workshops and the WWA can use this method in order to facilitate the transition from segregated to ordinary (sheltered) settings. The WWA, however, rarely does this as it requires the follow-up and support of the user and employer over time, which conflicts with the WWA's standard procedures (Spjelkavik et al., 2012). Thus, non-segregated sheltered work is typically organised by sheltered workshops (vocational rehabilitation companies, VRC). Most people on temporary measures receive a temporary work assessment allowance.

(c) The permanent sheltered work is organised by VRCs. Such companies provide sheltered work but also other labour market supports. They work on contracts with the WWA. The companies were traditionally non-profit, but this has changed and a number of for-profit companies have recently entered this market. However, the for-profit companies are more involved in temporary measures, since it is less easy to make a business out of sheltered work. Sheltered work is typically in segregated settings but may be organised at ordinary workplaces with support from a VRC. Even though segregated sheltered work is generally considered 'old school', the rate of segregated to non-segregated sheltered employment is 9:1 among people with intellectual disabilities (Wendelborg & Tøssebro, 2018). People in sheltered work typically receive the disability pension but may receive 'encouragement pay' on top. This pay makes a slight difference for the monthly income, but more importantly it may also have a significant symbolic meaning due to family resemblance with regular jobs.

(d) Day activity centres are not considered a part of the labour market system but are regarded rather as social services – providing people with something to do during the day. These centres are organised by the local governments. The activities are typically segregated, but not necessarily so. There are cases, for instance, where people work with the local government internal postal service or help out in the canteen. People in day activity centres receive the disability pension. Some have encouragement pay on top, but this is less likely than in sheltered work.

Jobs for People with Intellectual Disabilities

There are no easily available statistics on the occupation of people with intellectual disabilities in Norway, but by drawing on several sources, it is possible to provide a fairly accurate picture. A study based on the 2014 public registers provides national data on people receiving any type of allowance or participating in any type of labour market measure (Wendelborg & Tøssebro, 2018). There is the reservation that some people with a mild intellectual disability may live without any of these types of support, but they are assumed to be few in number.[2] This may, though, lead to an underestimation of the number in open employment. However, according to the Wendelborg and Tøssebro study, the figures are 0.4% in open employment (with or without supports), 1.3% in temporary labour market measures, 22.7% in sheltered employment (2.4% in ordinary settings and 20.3% in segregated settings), 3.0% waiting, 3.1% in combination of employment (unclear what type) and disability pension, 5.3% not possible to classify, and the remaining 64.2% without employment. To what extent people without employment are occupied in day activity centres cannot be estimated from national registers, but other data sources suggest that about 15% are without employment and that about 50% are occupied at day activity centres (Reinertsen, 2012; Söderström & Tøssebro, 2011). The activities at such centres may resemble work (production of goods or services) or be more similar to leisure activities. About 50% of the people at activity centres are estimated to be occupied with work-type activities, but with a declining trend (Söderström & Tøssebro, 2011).

The overall picture is rather discouraging. Almost none are in open labour market employment, and the use of regular labour market measures is very limited. People with intellectual disabilities are in sheltered work (mostly segregated), in day activity centres, or without any occupation. In terms of employment rates, that is, all people in open employment, temporary labour market measures, and sheltered employment, the rate is about 25% – of whom about 80% are employed in a segregated setting. It is particularly discouraging to realise that supports that were introduced in the 1990s in order to facilitate inclusion by ordinary employers (Stortingsmelding (white paper) 39, 1991–1992), such as supported employment, currently only serve extremely few people with intellectual disabilities. The measures themselves have not been phased out but serve other groups with difficulties

---

[2] The registers of people of working age (18–66) were used. 0.54% of the population is registered with primary diagnoses related to ID (ICD 10: F70–79, F83, F84.0–84.4, Q90–95, 97–99). The figure is slightly lower than the only national epidemiological study (0.62%, Strømme & Valvatne, 1998) and a little further below typical findings in high-income countries (0.92%, Maulik, Mascarenhas, Mathers, Dua, & Saxena, 2011). People with ID may be unclassified in the register if they have (1) another primary diagnosis (such as CP, epilepsy, etc.) or (2) do not receive any of the WWA supports. This first point may lead to false negatives, whereas the second may lead to an underestimation of people with intellectual disabilities in open employment. This underestimation is likely to be minor and, in any case, comprised of people with a borderline intellectual disability.

in the labour market. There also appear to be economic incentives that discourage the VRCs from supporting people's move from sheltered to non-sheltered settings. The VRCs have productivity targets which are more difficult to achieve if the more productive workers leave – exactly the people with more possibilities in regular settings. With a term borrowed from Pierre Bourdieu's discussion of special education, one may call this a situation of being 'locked out and locked in' (Bourdieu, 1996).

The trajectory out of employment appears to start during secondary education. All people have the right to secondary education in Norway, and young people with intellectual disabilities typically take part in this. The education is intended to be a preparation for higher education or employment. However, a study of transition found that there was very limited contact between secondary schools and the WWA, making it unlikely that education was tailored to possible work opportunities for people with intellectual disabilities (Gjertsen & Olsen, 2013). Wendelborg, Gustavsson, and Tøssebro (forthcoming) have argued that the pattern resembles a vicious circle. Teachers in secondary education tend to look to employment opportunities for people with intellectual disabilities and conclude that only extraordinary cases will have any chance. Teachers thus see their task as finding something useful and nice to do for students with intellectual disabilities while they are enrolled in secondary education. The expectations and ambitions tend to be low, and the pupils are expected to be handed over to social services after graduation. One interviewee, a headmaster, used the term 'guests'. This implies that education for employment is not taken seriously and, consequently, the students do not reach their potential and are less equipped for options like open labour market jobs or mainstream labour market supports. From secondary school, they are on a track where most employment options, including non-sheltered labour market supports, are outside of the range of possible choices.

The generally discouraging picture does not imply that good examples are non-existent. A Danish recruitment project has provided more than 2500 regular, low-skilled jobs to people with intellectual disabilities with a small but real payment (on top of social security benefits).[3] A similar project has been initiated in Norway, and a large facility service company (cleaning, catering, security) and a hotel chain have signed up to the scheme.[4] Promising examples sometimes reach the media headlines and are as such important in the endeavour to change attitudes. The problem, so far, is not that good examples do not exist but that they don't seem to make much difference when it comes to the overall numbers. The innovations and good examples simply apply to too few people, and such patterns appear to repeat themselves. One saw similar encouraging examples after the deinstitutionalisation reforms in the 1990s. At that time, occupation tended to be sheltered workshops or activity units at the institutions. In the reform process, several efforts were introduced to remedy this, among others SE. The efforts were significant but were scarcely visible in overall figures on the employment of people with intellectual disabilities.

---

[3] www.klapjob.dk

[4] www.heltmed.no

Employment and Choice

The pattern in Norway appears to leave little space for choice. The trajectory appears to be set by the system rather than being responsive to peoples' choices. Existing data sources are also meagre on preferences and choice. However, a 2010 study of the living conditions of people with intellectual disabilities (Söderström & Tøssebro, 2011) provides indirect information. The primary caregiver among staff was asked what say the person himself/herself had regarding daytime occupation. Response options were as follows: took no part (43% of valid responses), was heard (14%), took part in the decision (20%), and decided himself/herself (23%). Twenty-two percent did not respond. The data was reanalysed for the purpose of this chapter, primarily to see if there was any relationship between type of employment and participation in decision-making.

There are two main findings: (1) People with no daytime occupation tended to use the extreme response options. Thirty-eight percent had no say and 46% decided themselves. (2) Among those in employment, the extent of choice increased with job 'normalization' (Pearson's $r = 0.40$, $p < 0.01$). This also applied after control for adaptive behaviour (beta = 0.15, $p = 0.01$). This second finding clearly suggests that if people have a choice, they prefer a less segregated type of work. Among people in non-segregated settings, 50% decided themselves and 27% took part, but this option was available only for a very small minority. Sheltered employment was also chosen by many (38% decided and 38% took part) and applies to more people. Day activity centres appear in general to be placements (71% had no say), and this is where the majority is occupied. This can hardly be interpreted any other way than that people prefer a less segregated and more normalised setting. Such a conclusion is in keeping with a finding of Beyer, Brown, Akandi, and Rapley (2010): People in supported employment report higher levels of quality of life than people in segregated settings.

The more unexpected outcome is the fact that close to 50% of those without any daytime activity chose this option. Does this mean that many people with intellectual disabilities do not want to work? We have no access to representative data that provides the opportunity to explore this issue, but qualitative data suggests that this choice is related to available options. When the possible choices are not seen as real work, but rather as some kind of 'pretend' activity, they prefer to be unoccupied. They want jobs, but these should be real jobs. It is thus a choice in a situation where all options are bad, that is, a dilemma. We will come back to this issue in the section on experiences and coping strategies (section "Individual Perceptions, Coping Strategies, and Self-Presentation").

Brief International Outlook

The Norwegian figures suggest that the employment rate among people with intellectual disabilities is about 25% if segregated sheltered employment is included in the figure. This is roughly in keeping with figures extracted from a literature review by Verdonshot et al. (2009). This is based on research from a number of countries, but a majority is from the USA and the UK. As for more details in international comparisons, Lysaght, Šiška, and Koenig (2015) argue that this only can be done with substantial reservations due to variations in operational definitions of both intellectual disabilities and employment. They found that between one-third and half of the population with intellectual disabilities are registered as participating in some form of work or production activities in Australia, Ireland, the UK, and the USA. However, these numbers include work for payment below minimum wages. If looking specifically for paid employment (more than symbolic pay), the impression of very low participation prevails in most national settings. In the USA, Bush and Tassé (2017) found that 13% were in paid community jobs, whereas in the UK, Hatton (2018) found that 5.7% of adults with intellectual disabilities had some form of paid employment. Working hours were typically less than 16 hours per week. Also from the UK, Melling, Beyer, and Kilsby (2011) report that rates for SE continues to be stable and low. In Ireland, McGlinchey, McCallion, Burke, Carroll, and McCarron (2013) found that less than 7% of people with intellectual disabilities were in paid employment and 12% in sheltered employment, whereas 73% were unemployed. From Australia, Tuckerman, Cain, Long, and Klarkowski (2012) suggest an increase in sheltered employment but very low rates of paid work.

Thus, even though systems of support and labour markets vary between countries, the extremely marginal position of people with intellectual disabilities appears to apply to all western countries. Details may vary, but the overall pattern is similar. Thus, the next sections on the social meaning, individual experiences, and coping strategies should be reasonably relevant also outside the specific details of the Norwegian setting.

The Social Meaning of the Occupation of Intellectually Disabled People

It is time to move towards the inner circle of Fig. 1: the individual experiences, choices, and coping strategies. The first step will, however, be with an outsider perspective. It is about making sense of the occupations described in the previous section in the context of the social meaning of work. The point of departure is that the majority (85%) of people with intellectual disabilities in Norway have a daytime occupation, but this is hardly what people in general would call work or employment. The majority are at day activity centres or in segregated, sheltered workshops.

When this is typically not perceived as work, it is not because of the activities. Activities are in a number of cases (but not always) work such as in catering, chopping and selling firewood, packaging, production of goods, postal services, cleaning, and so on. The perception of the activities as 'nonwork' is related to Twain's point about the impact of circumstances. The circumstances are low or no pay, and the activity is situated at a place not associated with employment. This transforms the occupation into some kind of undefined or liminal status – it is and is not work. This may undermine the social functions associated with employment. However, our point is not that lack of pay or a segregated setting necessarily undermines the activity as being work (cf. also McGlinchey et al., 2013), nor that it undermines all social functions of work, but there is definitely that risk. One thus has to look carefully at how such work is perceived, by the people themselves and their social environment.

Let us take a look at the social functions of work. Even though the work is segregated and with no pay, this does not have any consequences for the way the occupation structures the day, week, and year. The traditional argument for occupation in institutions was actually related to this: work as a means to avoid idleness. You leave the house and have something to do and it provides a structure to everyday life. Sheltered workshops and day activity centres also provide arenas for social relationships. The more segregated the setting is, the less likely is it that one can establish relationships with non-disabled people, and sometimes people at the day activity centre are also one's fellow residents. Thus, there may be limited opportunities for some types of new relationships, but the function in relation to social contacts is typically still there.

When it comes to functions such as support for self-esteem, identity, social status, having a valued social role, and a feeling of contributing, this is clearly more problematic if circumstances make work look like a social service. A segregated setting is less likely to contribute to a valued social role. However, the image of social service or 'pretend work' is from an outsider's perspective, but it may also affect people's own perspective. This is likely to happen because the perspective of others affects the opportunities for a positive self-presentation (Goffman, 1959), which is vital in social interactions. The opportunities for self-presentation are likely to be influenced by 'family resemblance' – to what extent the activities, pay, and place resemble typical conceptions of employment. Some people have sheltered employment by an ordinary employer and with a small encouragement payment on top of the disability pension. This is clearly more easily presented as work in comparison with occupation in an activity centre located at a welfare centre and with no pay at all. Thus, when moving on to the people's own experiences, agency, choice, and coping strategies, we need to take the aspect of family resemblance into account, including the possibilities for valued self-presentations, and also the functions of work that are not subverted by the social service 'invasion' of the occupation (for instance, structure of the day).

Individual Perceptions, Coping Strategies, and Self-Presentation

The following descriptions of individual perceptions, choices, coping strategies, and self-presentations are based on qualitative data from a set of studies the authors have carried out on intellectual disability and employment (Olsen, 2009). The majority of cases are from studies employing ethnographic fieldwork in a variety of work settings where people with intellectual disabilities work or have their daytime activities. The fieldwork consisted of observations of participants and semi-structured interviews with workers, staff (in sheltered workshops), co-workers (in integrated work settings), managers, staff at the local WWA, and coordinators of supported employment. Being part of the workplace over time provided the opportunity to meet representatives of the employers, parents/family members, and customers. A few of the examples are from another study with interviews carried out during less in-depth studies of the everyday life of people with intellectual disabilities.

The images presented by the people themselves show substantial variation. This is sometimes due to variation in the working situation but also peoples' perception or experience of it and how they use it in the presentation of themselves. We have chosen to present this variation in six types or categories. This is not an exhaustive list but describes some frequent or illuminating profiles. These are analytical and synthesised, but all quotations are from real individuals. The individuals are, however, not fixated in one profile. It may change over time, and individual narratives may have elements of more than one profile.

Work as a Stigma ('I Don't Look Upon This as Work')

The example of work as a stigma is from a sheltered workshop, where a group of men were producing wooden boxes for the transport of high-tech industrial products manufactured by a company nearby. When asked about payment, one of the men explains:

> Everyone here has a disability pension. There are restrictions on how much one can earn. Some people here are a bit angry about that, because they think it's difficult to tell their family, friends and people in the community. They think it is embarrassing. And they think it is difficult to explain if someone asks what they do at work. If you cannot answer properly, they think 'Wow, he doesn't know what he's making!' They get the impression that you don't do something useful.

The man sees his work as stigmatising. This applies even though he works full time, produces goods for the market, and in many respects has a great deal of responsibility. His 'embarrassment' is related to the sheltered/segregated setting and the minimal 'encouragement' payment (which for him and his colleagues is not encouraging at all). He has friends who work in ordinary settings, and he feels that his own employment is not 'real work'. He cannot use it to present himself as who he wants to be. He has instead developed a set of strategies to under-communicate that he works in a sheltered workshop. The name of the workplace, the payment, and references to his workmates are some of the things that 'reveal' the reality of his work – that it is not real work. In cases like this one, the employment can fulfil functions related to the structure of the day and social contacts, but not the set of psychosocial needs addressed in the literature on the social functions of work. It is rather a source of embarrassment – 'I don't look upon this as work'.

This illustration resembles Kittelsaa's (2011, 2014) description of the myriad strategies people with intellectual disabilities use in daily identity management to avoid a stigmatised status and Edgerton's (1967) discussion of the 'cloak of competence' – strategies in order not to disclose an embarrassing situation.

Work as Personal Development ('I Am Capable')

The perspective of a woman working in a catering service that is a part of a sheltered workshop is rather different:

> When I started working here, and got to see what they did, I understood that I had to behave and become a better person inside. That is important, in order to keep the job. I do not want anyone to take it from me, and I feel that I have become a better person.

The context of her occupation is not very different from the previous example. She works in a sheltered workshop for encouragement pay, and the activities resemble 'real' work. Her perception is, however, very different. Her narrative has a duality: It illustrates that it is important for her to have a job and also that this makes her a better person. She explicitly relates the positive aspects of the job to psychosocial functions of work, such as being a source of self-development. Work is a place to learn and develop. Even though it is less clear from the quote, she also relates the positive role of the employment to self-presentation and self-esteem. Through work she shows her abilities, that she is good and competent at something. Being good at work enhances her self-esteem.

We have found examples of this type of narrative among informants in different types of work settings, in integrated work settings, as well as in sheltered workshops and day activity centres. We cannot explain why some people find such circumstances positive, whereas others feel it embarrassing. It may be due to differences in expectations or self-image; that for her, the point was to show that she is able to do this, whereas for the man in the example above, his aspirations were to take on the typical adult role of a worker. Differences in aspirations may also be related to differences in earlier experiences of being treated with disrespect, being bullied, or facing hate speech. The point is nevertheless that for some people, and in different settings, work is seen as a positive source of self-development and a place to show other people that one is competent in regard to these tasks.

Work as Attractive Activity ('This Is Who I Am')

In some cases, the activity itself, or what the activity is associated with, appears to be the crucial point. A young man spent 12 hours a week at a regular office but found the work boring. He wanted to work with something more creative. The dream was to work for a radio channel. After many disappointments, he was provided the opportunity to work for a local radio as a volunteer. He now runs a live show every week with a partner. This gives him the opportunity to present himself as who he wants to be. It does not matter that the job is unpaid. He has his social security benefit and for him, pay does not define work or self-presentation. It is the activity that is attractive and provides the opportunity for self-development, social contacts, and self-presentation.

Another similar example is a young woman working in a store close to an equestrian centre. The job is in an integrated setting, but for no pay. Her work is as a shop assistant, and tasks are as in any shop. However, this shop is associated with who she wants to be – someone caring for and working with animals. The shop sells horse-riding equipment. Thus, the point is not the activity (shop assistant), but what it is associated with (animals). A third example could be the young man who did not care about having a job or what that meant, but he wanted to be seen as a real masculine man. Thus, even though it was unpaid and irregular, working on a fishing boat fitted well in with his self-image.

Work as a Social Arena ('Meeting Other People')

Work has social network functions. The workplace is a place to meet other people. Some young women were at a day activity centre, producing different types of textile work for sale. The centre had associates who were experienced designers, and the products were sold at high-quality design shops. One of the women explains:

> This is a workplace where I can do what I can. In my situation, I must have such a job because I cannot have a regular job. I could have worked in an office or something, but I like to have someone to talk to, so it is good for me to work here. [...] I am very happy to tell people about my work place.

Even though the women probably could have chosen a self-representation as 'fashion workers', this did not seem to be of much importance to them. In other similar cases, we have met people being proud of the fact that the textiles they produced were sold on the market. However, the one thing these women emphasised about the work was the opportunity to meet each other. They worked together every day and used this opportunity to discuss TV series, friends, and their activities outside of the workplace. Some of the women took part in organised leisure activities for people with disabilities, and they often discussed what to do in the evenings. The women organised their work and decided upon the speed and amount of what they produced each day. Even though highly competent in what they were doing, they would refer to it as a sort of voluntary activity. The social arena was important, whereas other functions of employment did not seem to matter much for these women. This may be related to their self-perception or ambitions (cf.: 'I cannot have a regular job'), but we do not know. It was the social aspects of work that were highlighted in their positive narrative, but their overall story about the work was also positive.

Work as Boring ('Rather This than Nothing at All')

Another widespread approach is to see work as something unwanted or boring, but nevertheless better than no activity. It is a way to socialise and be in some kind of activity. An example with a young man in a sheltered workshop may illustrate this:

- After having been out of work for some time, you started here again? Why was that?
- Yes, some… It goes a bit up and down.
- Did someone put a pressure on you to start again?
- Yeah, that as well. But I wanted to, also. I wanted to get out, not just sit at home.

The young man quoted here works in a workshop with quite repetitive work. He sees it as tiresome. In his case, he does not have many friends at the workplace, and he does not take much part in the social activities or discussions at coffee breaks or lunch. For him, the main point was 'not just to sit at home', whereas other examples also added the possibility to socialise. This man had stopped working for almost a year when we met him and had recently started again. For him, the work was a way of structuring the time, the day, the week, and the year, and it kept his mind busy. However, the question is whether the job could fulfil more social functions if it had been less repetitive and that the only alternative was 'to sit at home'. We cannot answer this since he has never tried other options, but the case illustrates that the problem is not always the context of the employment but also a rather repetitive content. Staff report that this problem is increasing because automation has led to fewer contracts with local businesses.

Exit from Work ('I Want to Work, But It Should Be Real Work')

The man we referred to in the section on stigma was concerned about the employment not being real work. Another middle-aged man had quit work for the same reason. He had a mild intellectual disability and lived semi-independently, and to us, it was quite puzzling when we realised that he had no daytime occupation. It should not be too hard to find an activity for him. When we asked him if he wanted a job, the response was:

> Yes, I want to work. But it should be paid. The kind of nonsense they offer me for next to nothing, that isn't work. It should be real work.

His point is clear. Work-like activities without core characteristics of work, such as pay, are not work. It is pretence. Most people would react like him. They would decline a job offer for no or minimal pay. The work does not have sufficient 'family resemblance' with the typical concept of work. For this man, pretend work was more embarrassing (cf. work as stigma) than being inactive. If work seems like pretence (or play in Twain's terms), the valued role of being employed is inverted.

We have met just a few people that have chosen this exit strategy: people that have chosen not to work and for whom the encouragement pay turns into the opposite. However, the statistics referred to above suggest that exiting employment is not that uncommon. It applies to about half of the 15% that have no daytime occupation. Interviews with staff actually suggest that with more self-determination, the figure could be higher: Some people are sent to daytime occupations against their preferences, due to lack of staff in their home setting.

The refusal to work could be seen as an ultimate self-determination situation. Despite the strong 'employment first' ideology mediated by the welfare system and the national culture, these people chose an exit strategy. This is, of course, possible only because their main income is from the disability pension, and remuneration is simply for encouragement. The interpretation should not be that many lack the motivation for employment but that they resist the options available for them. In the case referred to in this section, the options were resisted because it was not seen as real work. There may be other reasons, such as bad experiences at the work place, bullying, anxiety, poor individual tailoring, and so on. A young man with mental health difficulties that we met referred explicitly to such reasons for choosing the exit strategy. It nevertheless remains the case that the exit strategy appears to be a response to a situation where all options are bad options. As such, this coping strategy says more about the available occupation options than genuine access to choice about work.

What Works?

Ideally, the arguments and evidence presented should lead to or underpin conclusions regarding 'what works' with respect to providing people with intellectual disabilities jobs they value and that support a valued adult role. At one level, the recommendation is straightforward: provide jobs with more family resemblance with typical conceptions of employment. Although one should not underestimate that for many individuals, sheltered and/or segregated settings also provide the opportunity for presenting their occupation as work, the basic question is how to achieve more family resemblance with jobs in a competitive labour market with increasing productivity demands. There may be lessons to learn from good initiatives and examples, but as pointed out earlier, such examples tend to comprise few people and barely affect overall figures. Thus, the key appears to be within the realm of politics. The policies for employment, social security, and how the interdependency between the two is practised need to be addressed.

Most people with intellectual disabilities are likely to need social security allowances, such as a disability pension. But it is a political choice that this has the consequence that the support system skips the otherwise mandatory work assessment procedures and overlooks the general requirement that available employment measures should be exhausted. Furthermore, it is a less visible but nevertheless real administrative choice from employment service officials that people with a disability pension fall below the threshold for priority for employment supports. Thus, the link between disability pension and employment supports needs to be reformed. For officials working with employment support, the low priority of people with a disability pension is likely to be a response to their workload. According to Lipsky (1980/2010), officials with a heavy workload are likely to prioritise simpler cases and to disregard cases where possible (read: receives a disability pension). Thus, the employment supports for people with intellectual disabilities will probably need some kind of 'protection' within the generic employment support system, for instance, by establishing some kind of special task force whose explicit priority/task is employment supports for people with a disability pension.

There is probably also a need to develop the toolbox of possible employment supports. In the Norwegian setting, the introduction of long-term supported employment and combinations of pay and allowances in regular work settings are obvious candidates. Support from job coaches with labour market expertise and a network among employers will also possibly open opportunities in the regular labour market, subsidised or not. This has proven successful among other groups with reduced work capacity.

These proposals and concerns are not very innovative. A recent Public Committee Report (NOU (Norway's official reports), 2016) on services for people with intellectual disabilities called for (a) work assessment of everyone, (b) cutting the link between disability pension and low priority in the employment support system, (c) more jobs in sheltered employment (as alternative to activity centres), and (d) more use of supported and sheltered employment in regular work settings. To date, it is unknown whether this call for action will make any difference.

Conclusion: Self-Determination and Work

The structure of employment for people with intellectual disabilities suggests few available opportunities and thus little space for real choice. The few available options are generally at the margins of the labour market, and the current interdependency between social security and employment supports has negative unintended consequences regarding employment opportunities for people with intellectual disabilities.

Although the overall picture is discouraging, there are (a) good examples and (b) perceptions from people themselves that show considerable variation. At one extreme are people who see their occupation as stigmatising. Some of them continue working but use a strategy of under-communicating the type of employment. Others find the option of exiting from work less stigmatising. At the other extreme are people who have found an occupation that supports a self-presentation they identify with, whether it is as a volunteer at a radio station, on a fishing boat, or in a shop at an equestrian centre. In these cases, the circumstances do not necessarily resemble work, such as low or no pay, but the activity itself is associated with something they identify with. In between the extremes, one finds people who present a narrative of resignation ('rather this than nothing') and people enjoying certain functions of their occupation ('I am capable', 'meeting other people'). The examples used in this chapter are far from exhaustive when it comes to perceptions and coping strategies among people with intellectual disabilities, but illuminate the different ways in which people cope with the fact that they are excluded from a valued adult role. Furthermore, it should not be underestimated that the occupations in general fulfil some of the functions work has in adult everyday life, although it is more challenging when it comes to functions such as self-esteem, identity support, and the set of psychosocial needs outlined in the literature on the consequences of long-term unemployment.

In 1996, Hyde summed up the experiences after 50 years of UK policies to improve the employment situation of people with disabilities (the 1944 UK Disabled Person's (Employment) Act). The title of his paper was 'Fifty Years of Failure'. A similarly discouraging conclusion appears to apply to the policies to remedy the employment situation of people with intellectual disabilities in a number of countries, and in such a context the question of self-determination and choice is somewhat misplaced. The circumstances simply provide too few opportunities.

References

Beyer, S., Brown, T., Akandi, R., & Rapley, M. (2010). A comparison of quality of life outcomes for people with intellectual disabilities in supported employment, day services and employment enterprises. *Journal of Applied Research in Intellectual Disabilities, 23*, 290–295. https://doi.org/10.1111/j.1468-3148.2009.00534.x

Bourdieu, P. (1996). *Symbolsk makt. Artikler i utvalg* [Symbolic power. Selected articles]. Oslo, Norway: Pax.

Bush, K. L., & Tassé, M. J. (2017). Employment and choice-making for adults with intellectual disability, autism, and down syndrome. *Research in Developmental Disabilities, 65*, 23–34. https://doi.org/10.1016/j.ridd.2017.04.004

Butterworth, J., Hiersteiner, D., Engler, J., Bershadsky, J., & Bradley, V. (2015). National Core Indicators (c): Data on the current state of employment of adults with IDD and suggestions for policy development. *Journal of Vocational Rehabilitation, 42*(3), 209–220. https://doi.org/10.3233/jvr-150741

Dahl, E., van der Wel, K., & Harsløv, I. (2010). *Arbeid, helse og ulikhet* [Employment, health and inequality]. Oslo, Norway: The Norwegian Directorate of Health.

Edgerton, R. B. (1967). *The cloak of competence: Stigma in the lives of the mentally retarded.* Berkely, CA: University of California Press.

Eurostat. (2015). *Employment of disabled people. Statistical analysis of the 2011 Labour Force Survey ad hoc module.* Luxembourg, Europe: Publication Office of the European Union.

Gjertsen, H., & Olsen, T. (2013). *Broer inn i arbeidslivet* [Bridges to employment]. Bodø, Norway: Nordland Research Institute.

Goffman, E. (1959). *The presentation of self in everyday life.* New York, NY: Doubleday.

Greve, B. (2009). *The labour market situation of disabled people in European countries and implementation of employment policies: A summary of evidence from country reports and research studies.* Leeds, UK: University of Leeds and ANED. Retrieved from http://www.disability-europe.net/downloads/276-aned-task-6-final-report-final-version-17-04-09

Halvorsen, K., Bakken, O., & Fugelli, P. (1986). *Arbeidsløs i velferdsstaten* [Unemployment in the welfare state]. Oslo, Norway: Universitetsforlaget.

Hatton, C. (2018). Paid employment amongst adults with learning disabilities receiving social care in England: Trends over time and geographical variation. *Tizard Learning Disability Review, 23*(2), 117–122. https://doi.org/10.1108/tldr-01-2018-0003

Hedley, D., Uljarevic, M., Cameron, L., Halder, S., Richdale, A., & Dissanayake, C. (2017). Employment programmes and interventions targeting adults with autism spectrum disorder: A systematic review of the literature. *Autism, 21*(8), 929–941. https://doi.org/10.1177/1362361316661855

Hyde, M. (1996). Fifty years of failure: Employment services for disabled people in the UK. *Work, Employment & Society, 10*, 683–700. https://doi.org/10.1177/0950017096104004

ILO. (2015). *Decent work for persons with disabilities: Promoting rights on the global development agenda*. Geneva, Switzerland: International Labour Office.

Jahoda, M., Lazarsfeld, P., & Zeisel, H. (1933). *Die Arbeitdslosen von Marienthal* [The unemployed from Marienthal]. Leipzig, Germany: Hirzel.

Kittelsaa, A. M. (2011). *Vanlig eller utviklingshemmet? Selvforståelse og andres forståelser* [Ordinary or intellectually disabled? Self-identity and other peoples understandigs]. Bergen, Norway: Fagbokforlaget.

Kittelsaa, A. M. (2014). Self-presentations and intellectual disability. *Scandinavian Journal of Disability Research, 16*(1), 29–44. https://doi.org/10.1080/15017419.2012.761159

Kohli, M. (1985). Die Institutionalisierung des lebenslaufs. [The institutionalisation of the CV.]. *Kölner Zeitschrift für Soziologie und Sozialpsychologie, 37*, 1–29.

Kohli, M. (2007). The institutionalisation of life course: Looking back to look ahead. *Research in Human Development, 4*, 253–271. https://doi.org/10.1080/15427600701663122

Lipsky, M. (1980/2010). *Street-level bureacracy*. New York, NY: Russel Sage Foundation.

Lysaght, R., Ouellette-Kuntz, H., & Lin, C.-J. (2012). Untapped potential: Perspectives on the employment of people with intellectual disability. *Work, 41*, 409–422. https://doi.org/10.3233/WOR-2012-1318

Lysaght, R., Šiška, J., & Koenig, O. (2015). International employment statistics for people with intellectual disability. The case for common metrics. *Journal of Policy and Practice in Intellectual Disabilities, 12*(2), 112–119. https://doi.org/10.1111/jppi.12113

Maulik, P., Mascarenhas, M., Mathers, C., Dua, T., & Saxena, S. (2011). Prevalence of intellectual disability: A meta-analysis of population-based studies. *Research in Developmental Disabilities, 32*, 419–436. https://doi.org/10.1016/j.ridd.2010.12.018

McConkey, R., Kelly, F., Craig, S., & Keogh, F. (2017). A longitudinal study of post-school provision for Irish school-leavers with intellectual disability. *British Journal of Learning Disabilities, 45*(3), 166–171. https://doi.org/10.1111/bld.12190

McGlinchey, E., McCallion, P., Burke, E., Carroll, R., & McCarron, M. (2013). Exploring the issue of employment for adults with an intellectual disability in Ireland. *Journal of Applied Research in Intellectual Disabilities, 26*(4), 335–343. https://doi.org/10.1111/jar.12046

Melling, K., Beyer, S., & Kilsby, M. (2011). Supported employment for people with learning disabilities in the UK: The last 15 years. *Tizard Learning Disability Review, 16*(2), 23–32. https://doi.org/10.5042/tldr.2011.0165

Merton, R. (1967). Manifest and latent functions. In R. Merton (Ed.), *On theoretical sociology* (pp. 73–138). New York, NY: The Free Press.

NOU (Norway's Official Reports). (2016, no. 17). *På lik linje. Åtte løft for å realisere grunnleggende rettigheter for personer med utviklingshemming* [On equal terms. Eight measures to realize basic rights of people with intellectual disabilities]. Oslo, Norway: Departement of Children and Equality.

OECD. (2006). *Sickness, disability and work: Breaking the barriers*. Paris, France: Author.

OECD. (2010). *Sickness, Disability and Work. A synthesis of findings across OECD countries*. Paris, France: Author.

OECD. (2017). *OECD employment outlook*. Paris, France: Author. Retrieved from https://doi.org/10.1787/empl_outlook-2017-en

Olsen, T. (2009). *Versjoner av arbeid. Dagaktivitet og arbeid etter avviklingen av institusjonsomsorgen* [Versions of work. Daytime activities and work in the aftermath of the institutional reform for persons with intellectual disabilities] (PhD thesis). Uppsala, Sweden: Uppsala University.

Parmenter, T. (2011). *Promoting training av employment opportunities for people with intellectual disabilities: International experience.* (Employment working paper no. 103). Geneva, Switzerland: International Labour Office.

Parsons, T. (1951). *The social system.* London, UK: Routledge & Kegan Paul.

Proba. (2016). *Arbeidssituasjonen for personer med utviklingshemming* [The labour market situation of people with intellectual disablities]. Oslo, Norway: Proba.

Reinertsen, S. (2012). *Arbeids- og akttivitetssituasjonen blant mennesker med utviklingshemming* [Employment and occupation among people with intellectual disabilities]. Trondheim, Norway: NAKU.

Söderström, S., & Tøssebro, J. (2011). *Innfridde må eller brutte visjoner?* [Achieved aims or broken promises? The development of living conditions for intellectually disabled people]. Trondheim, Norway: NTNU Social Research.

Solvang, P. (1993). *Biografi, normalitet og samfunn* [Biography, normality and society]. Bergen, Norway: University of Bergen.

Spjelkavik, Ø., Børing, P., Frøyland, K., & Skarpaas, I. (2012). *Behovet for varig tilrettelagt arbeid* [The need for sheltered employment]. Oslo, Norway: Work Research Institute.

Stortingsmelding (White Paper), no. 39 (1991–1992). *Attføring og arbeid for yrkeshemmede* [Rehabilitation and employment for people with reduced work capacity]. Oslo, Norway: Department of Labour and Administration.

Strømme, P., & Valvatne, K. (1998). Mental retardation in Norway prevalence and sub-classification in a cohort of 30 037 children born between 1980 and 1985. *Acta Pædiatrica, 87,* 291–296. https://doi.org/10.1111/j.1651-2227.1998.tb01440.x

Timmons, J. C., Hall, A. C., Bose, J., Wolfe, A., & Winsor, J. (2011). Choosing employment: Factors that impact employment decisions for individuals with intellectual disability. *Intellectual and Developmental Disabilities, 49*(4), 285–299. https://doi.org/10.1352/1934-9556-49.4.285

Tøssebro, J. & Wik, S. (2015). *Funksjonshemmedes tilknytning til arbeidslivet* [Disabled people and employment]. Oslo, Norway: The Research Council of Norway.

Tuckerman, P., Cain, P., Long, B., & Klarkowski, J. (2012). An exploration of trends in open employment in Australia since 1986. *Journal of Vocational Rehabilitation, 37*(3), 173–183. https://doi.org/10.3233/JVR-2012-0612

Verdonshot, M. M. L., de Witte, L. P., Reichrath, E., Buntix, W. H. E., & Curs, L. M. G. (2009). Community participation of people with an intellectual disability: A review of empirical findings. *Journal of Intellectual Disability Research, 53*(4), 303–318. https://doi.org/10.1111/j.1365-2788.2008.01144.x

Waddell, G., & Burton, A. K. (2006). *Is work good for your health and well-being?* London, UK: TSO (The Stationery Office).

Wendelborg, C., Gustavsson, A., & Tøssebro, J. (forthcoming). Education and employment for intellectually disabled people – a vicious circle?

Wendelborg, C., & Tøssebro, J. (2018). *Personer med utviklingshemming og arbeid – arbeidslinje eller fast tack til kommunal omsorg?* [People with intellectual disabilities and employment – employment first or fast track til social services. *Fontene Forskning,* 11: 58–71.

Wittgenstein, L. (1958). *Philosophical investigations.* Oxford, UK: Basil Blackwell.

Wolfensberger, W. (1972). *Normalization.* Toronto, Canada: National Institute on Mental Retardation.

Choice, Relationships, and Sexuality: Sexual and Reproductive Health and Rights

Charlotta Löfgren-Mårtenson

The Swedish National Sexual and Reproductive Health and Rights (SRHR) Strategy lists persons with disability as a prioritized target group for knowledge development (National Board of Health and Welfare & Public Health Authority, 2014). The concept of SRHR is broad and includes equal opportunities, rights, and conditions of all people to have a safe and satisfying sexual life and to be able to decide about their own bodies without coercion, violence, or discrimination (The Swedish Government's Human Rights Website, 2017). Furthermore, access to health care and knowledge of sexuality are included in SRHR in order for all individuals to be able to take responsibility for their own sexual health and to be able to avoid situations or actions that could impair health (Public Health Agency of Sweden, 2018).

The WHO (2008) stresses the importance of key concepts such as *health inequities* and *inequality* in order to address differences and injustices between different groups of people and between different societies. Looking at people with intellectual disability (ID) as a group, comprehensive research studies suggest sexual vulnerability compared to other groups (e.g. Fitzgerald, 2011; Gougeon, 2009; Löfgren-Mårtenson, 2004; Kousmanen & Starke, 2015; McCarthy, 2014). One explanation is that people with ID have support needs related to abstraction, verbal, and communicative ability (Granlund & Göransson, 2011) and need specific supports to understand sexual norms, codes, and signals (Löfgren-Mårtenson, 2004). In addition, many people with ID have had insufficient sex education, leading to a lack of knowledge of sexuality, one's body, and relationships (Gougeon, 2009; Swango-Wilson, 2011). Persons with ID need lifelong support, and ensuring that supports address relationships and sexuality is critical (Löfgren-Mårtenson, 2004).

During the 1970s, living conditions changed through normalization and integration reforms in Scandinavia (Gustavsson, 1996/2000), as in most of the Western

C. Löfgren-Mårtenson (✉)
Faculty of Health and Society, Malmö University, Malmö, Sweden
e-mail: charlotta.lofgren-martenson@mau.se

© Springer Nature Switzerland AG 2020
R. J. Stancliffe et al. (eds.), *Choice, Preference, and Disability*, Positive Psychology and Disability Series, https://doi.org/10.1007/978-3-030-35683-5_13

society (e.g. McCarthy, 2014). Nevertheless, many people with ID still continue to live in a heteronormative and gender-stereotyped world where concerns are raised about risks for people with ID about unwanted pregnancies and sexual abuses (Desjardins, 2012; Löfgren-Mårtenson, 2004; McCarthy, 2014). Previous research has suggested that the normalization principle has a built-in stereotyped conception of gender (Angrosino & Zagnoli, 1992; Atkinson & Walmsley, 1995) which contributes to assumptions about people with ID needing to remain within certain understandings of "normal" in relation to gender and sexuality (Abbott & Howarth, 2007). In line with this, Swedish researchers have found that it can be difficult for youth with ID to come out as homo-, bi-, or transsexual (Löfgren-Mårtenson, 2009), which is confirmed in studies from the UK (e.g. Abbott & Howarth, 2007) and from Canada (Thompson, Bryson & Castell, 2001).

In general, people with ID tend to be seen as asexual and non-gendered (Grönvik, 2008). Barron (2002) analyzed in a Swedish context how women with ID reconstruct their identity based on notions of femininity. The informants often referred to biological aspects and traditional gender roles. Another Swedish study suggested that young women with ID challenge the traditional female passive role and take more initiatives to sexual activities than the young males with ID (Löfgren-Mårtenson, 2004). Young men with ID state that they are afraid of misconceptions about their sexuality and therefore act in a more passive way. Feelings of insecurity regarding not whether when but *if* sexual expressions are allowed were common among the young male informants (Löfgren-Mårtenson, 2004). A study from the UK showed more traditional gender roles, as well as widespread experiences of sexual assault and exploitation among female participants with ID. Women with ID rarely appear to expect positive experiences of sexual desire. Instead, they acceded to pleasure-less sexual acts with men in the apparent belief that this was their role as females (McCarthy, 1999). Fitzgerald (2011), in another study in the UK, found that the female participants with ID did not conceptualize themselves as sexual beings and that they tend to regard sex as "a dirty and inappropriate activity" (p. 7). Current Swedish research suggests experiences of sexual vulnerability and exploitation, such as a risk for prostitution in the participants with ID (Kousmanen & Starke, 2015). However, another Swedish study describes more positive outcomes with young females and males with ID describing pleasurable sexual experiences, even if these seldom include heterosexual intercourse (Löfgren-Mårtenson, 2004). Instead, experiences of masturbation, hugs, kisses, caresses, and petting seem to be more common. Overall, in a review of the research, McCarthy (2014) suggested that narratives from women with ID mostly contain negative experiences and perceptions of sexuality. She states: "…disempowerment is woven into every strand of the lives on many women with ID" (p. 130). And, knowledge on sexual and reproductive health and rights seem to be limited, which restricts opportunities for meaningful choice.

The aim of this chapter is to further review the SRHR concept in relation to people with ID and explore what is meant by the concept of SRHR in relation to persons with ID – and what implications this has for choice, relationships, and sexuality.

Review of the Existing Research on SRHR and Intellectual Disability

In this section, we provide a more systematic overview of key themes from the empirical data on SRHR that is emerging in multiple countries, including Australia, Canada, Ireland, the UK, and the USA. I selected recent articles and focused on identifying key themes across the articles, which we organized into two areas, aligned with the SHSR framework: (a) sexual health and rights, including sexual expressions and conduct and sexual identity and orientation, and (b) reproductive health and rights, including pregnancies and parenting and sexual knowledge and information.

Sexual Health and Rights

Sexual health is defined by the Swedish National SRHR Strategy as "a state of physically, emotionally, mental and social well-being related to sexuality, and not only the absence of disease, dysfunction or weakness" (National Board of Health and Welfare & Public Health Authority, 2014, p. 11). When it comes to sexual rights, the Swedish National SRHR Strategy stresses the right of all people to make decisions on their own body and sexuality.

Sexual Expressions and Conduct Despite ideological shifts, via normalization principles advancing the recognition of sexual autonomy for people with ID, the reviewed articles show continuing social and cultural barriers connected to sexual expressions and conduct (e.g., Ignagni, Fudge Schormans, Liddiard & Runswick-Cole, 2016; Healy, McGuire, Evans & Carley, 2009). Even though several studies address the importance of sexuality and of physical and emotional pleasure (e.g., Friedman, Arnold, Owen & Sandman, 2014; Turner & Crane, 2016), the review confirm that rules and restrictions still are present in the lives of people with ID, particularly in relation to sexual conduct (e.g. Ignagni et al., 2016; Kelly, Crowley, & Hamilton, 2009; Sullivan, Bowden, McKenzie & Qualy, 2013). Gomez (2012) address the history of sexual suppression of people with ID and states that it derives from "primal fear of difference" (p. 237). Fulfilling human rights therefore requires appropriate responses from service systems to support the sexual expression of people with ID. Concurrently, research show a great need among people with ID to have opportunities to express their choices and preferences and to be able to be heard (Friedman et al., 2014) and seen as "as normal as possible" and "to develop sexual identity as a 'normal' identity, in the context of the overshadowing ID identity" (Wilkinson, Theodore & Raczka 2015 p. 93). Nevertheless, young people with ID still face many obstacles, including stigma related to their ID. Karellou (2017) state in a Greek study that "limited progress has been made in supporting people with ID to create and sustain intimate personal relationships" (p. 217).

From the perspective of gender, Greenwood and Wilkinson (2013) point out the need for supporting the development of knowledge of sexual health among women with ID. They found higher prevalence of abuse and assaults in the target group compared to the rest of the population in their review. Furthermore, they address the need for optimizing choices and options for achieving sexual health among people with ID by encouraging professions to use a rights-based framework. Further, a limited number of studies focus on men with ID. Wilson, Parmenter, Stancliffe, and Shuttleworth (2011) use the notion *conditionally sexual* to describe the perceived limitations of men and teenage boys with moderate to profound ID. They continue by referring to an earlier review by Wilson, Parmenter, Stancliffe, Shuttleworth, and Parker (2010) that suggests that "sexual matters for men and boys with ID were often framed by a focus on socio-sexual pathologies such as criminal/anti-social behaviour and problematic sexual behaviour" (p. 277). There is an absence of studies within the discourse of the right of sexual pleasure for men with ID, while most studies focusing on, for example, "inappropriate" masturbation and "inappropriate" touching of female staff. However, one study in this review focuses a right-based approach to supporting the sexual fetish of a man with learning disability (Cambridge, 2013). This shows that sexual conduct that traditionally is categorized as "problematic" can be described in a more positive way and that more research and discussion of sexual health and the right of choice for both men and women with ID is needed.

Sexual Identity and Orientation Sexual expressions among lesbian, gay, bisexual and transgender (LGBT) people with ID still seems to be hidden and invisible, and this is a highly under-researched group. This seems to mainly be due to the largely heteronormative societal perspective and restrictive attitudes among staff members (Abbot, 2013; McClelland et al. 2012). Denial by others of their right to pleasure and the exercise of heightened external control over their sexuality are commonplace (McClelland et al., 2012). McClelland et al. (2012) state that "comparatively little is understood about their (LGBT people with ID) sexual experiences and sexual health needs" (p. 810) and that program initiatives and policy discussions concerning sexuality, safer sex, and sexual health often exclude LGBT people with ID. Furthermore, they point out multiple limitations for autonomy and choice in the lives of queer and trans young people labeled with ID, which results in having sex in places where they do not feel comfortable and limitations in the use of safe sex practices. McClelland et al. (2012) conclude: "Therefore, these youth are at heightened risk for compromised sexual health" (p. 809). From a gender perspective, it is also noticeable that the studies in this review on LGBT persons with ID concern men with ID, not women (e.g., Abbott, 2013).

Reproductive Health and Rights

Reproductive health is defined by the Swedish National SRHR Strategy as a state of physical, emotional, mental, and social well-being related to the reproductive system and all of its functions, not only the absence of diseases (National Board of

Health and Welfare & Public Health Authority, 2014, p. 11). *Reproductive right* is defined as the right of the individual to decide when and how many children the individual wants to have.

Pregnancies and Parenting The reviewed literature shows a long history of restrictive and negative attitudes toward sexuality among people with ID, especially when it comes to pregnancies and parenting (e.g., Gomez, 2012; Löfgren-Mårtenson, 2012; McConkey & Leavey, 2013; Rojas, Haya & Lazaro-Visa, 2014; Tilley, Walmsley, Earle & Atkinson, 2012). For example, women with ID were sterilized without consent during the early to mid-twentieth century and in some countries even longer (Tilley et al. 2012). As a consequence of worries about unwanted pregnancies and sexual vulnerability, many people with ID continued to be sheltered and overprotected with restricted choice options both in living arrangements and in community participation (Löfgren-Mårtenson, 2012; Pownall, Jahoda & Hastings, 2012). Additionally, choices and decisions about sexuality, intimate relationships, and contraception are controlled largely by caregivers instead of the persons with ID themselves (Greenwood & Wilkinson, 2013).

This review suggests that the majority of people with ID do not have children; however, many express longings for partners and family life (e.g. Löfgren-Mårtenson, 2012; Rojas et al. 2014). Greenwood and Wilkinson (2013) point out that pregnancy is possible for most women with ID and that it might be desired by some. It is difficult to say how many women with ID become pregnant or give birth, but it is estimated to be around 1.5% of adult women with ID (Greenwood & Wilkinson, 2013; Willems, Vries, Isarin & Reinders, 2007). Policies concerning pregnancy and parenting among the target group vary significantly around the world. For example, Dutch policy favors a right-based framework that suggests that any adult who desire to has the right to plan a pregnancy (Willems et al., 2007). However, no research shows evidence that this would lead to more or less or the same numbers of pregnancies in women with ID (Greenwood & Wilkinson, 2013). Being a parent with ID creates a need for societal support in order to meet the children's and family needs; however, support in this domain is typically lacking (Mayes, Llewellyyn & McConnell, 2011). Research has documented the "support gap" for parents with ID (Greenwood & Wilkinson, 2013). Of note is that the identified articles concerning parents with ID focuses only mothers and/or females with ID, not fathers and/or males with ID.

Sexual Knowledge and Information The Swedish National SRHR Strategy emphasizes the importance of sexual knowledge and comprehensive sex education for all people to be able to take responsibility for their own sexual health and to make informed choices and be able to avoid situations or actions that could impair health (National Board of Health and Welfare & Public Health Authority, 2014). Additionally, the strategy highlights the significance of addressing and including specific vulnerable groups, such as youth with disability. The reviewed literature suggests, however, that people with ID usually lack knowledge on sexuality, body, and relationships and that current sex education fails to address the specific support needs of children and adolescents with ID (Lafferty, McConkey & Simpson, 2012;

Löfgren-Mårtenson, 2012; Schaasfsma, Kok, Stoffelen & Curfs, 2017). The focus in sex education tends to be more on reproduction than on sexual health, which makes the information sometimes frightening and not perceived as relevant, particularly when people with ID lack a partner, lack experiences of sexual intercourse, and have not been exposed to options to consider the possibilities of parenthood in the future (Löfgren-Mårtenson, 2012). The reviewed studies also documented a lack of knowledge and several misconceptions concerning topics such as menstruation, sexual intercourse, pregnancy, and sexual orientation (Löfgren-Mårtenson, 2012; Schaasfsma et al., 2017). Furthermore, Swedish research suggests the dominance of a risk perspective in sex education focusing on negative aspects such as sexual abuse, sexually transmitted infections (STIs), and contraception (Löfgren-Mårtenson, 2012). The participants with ID instead wanted a focus on positive aspects of sexuality such as how to get a partner, what to do sexually with a partner, and how to achieve romantic and sexual relationships (Löfgren-Mårtenson, 2012). The same study also showed a heteronormative perspective in sex education, which leads to a focus on heterosexual conduct instead of a variety of sexual behavior and sexual identities (cf. Löfgren-Mårtenson 2012). An Irish study addressed the importance of including decision-making skills and safer sex skills in sex education as this increases the ability to recognize and report abuse by people with ID and to decrease sexual risks (Dukes & McGuire 2009). From a gender perspective, it is noteworthy that females with ID, not males with ID, are typically identified as potential victims (Dukes & Mcguire 2009).

What Works: The Importance of Sexual Agency

In conclusion, this chapter and the literature reviewed for this chapter suggest that the concept of SRHR in relation to persons with ID is important but also complex and diffuse. The concept is mostly described in general terms in the Swedish strategy and rarely connected directly to people with ID and the specific support needs that will be encountered to promote choice, responsibility, and sexuality. Therefore, its' relevance and significance is quite blurred. Furthermore, there are several barriers for people with ID to live a life that captures the meaning of the concept of SRHR. First, the environments' heteronormative attitudes and focus on protection are barriers. Wilkinson, Theodore, and Roman (2015) state that equality and protection need not be either/or priorities. However, there remains the need for considerable change in practice and policy if the principles of rights, choice, and inclusion are to be met in relation to sexual identity development in people with ID.

There are several areas in which additional research, policy, and practice development are needed. First, the findings that sexual orientation is rarely discussed in relation to the lives of people with ID are problematic. The literature suggests that homo- and bisexuality tend to be invisible (Löfgren-Mårtenson, 2009). Furthermore, research on same-sex relationships among women with ID is even more limited. In a UK study, Burns and Davies (2011) focus knowledge of homosexuality and attitudes toward homosexuality and gender role beliefs, not experiences of homosexuality and/or homo- and bisexual identity.

Second, the lack of comprehensive and relevant sex education is another barrier. This review showed not only limited sex education for children and adolescents with ID, but also a focus on risks, heterosexuality, intercourse, and pregnancy, which do not always meet their needs of (Löfgren-Mårtenson, 2012). A norm-critical perspective is suggested toward young people in the Swedish National SRHR Strategy in order to visualize, problematize, and change conceptions and norms that are part of discriminating societal structures (National Board of Health and Welfare & Public Health Authority, 2014). This review indicates that this should be an area of focus in sex education for people with ID. The Australian researchers Chivers and Mathieson (2000) highlighted the importance of providing educators who work with adolescents with ID with opportunities to reflect on the dominant professional discourse in which sexuality is seen as merely a biological function and where sex is focused on deleterious aspects and defines sex as equal to intercourse. They continued by suggesting that these social constructions of sexuality should be challenged and replaced by a discourse that includes desire, pleasure, and intimacy. Additionally, this could be one important strategy for switching the focus to the needs and actual preferences and choices of adolescents with ID.

Third, the invisibility of sexual agency among people with ID is a considerable hindrance. McKee et al. (2010) point out the importance of sexual agency, which they define as people "learn[ing] that they are in control of their own sexuality" (p. 16). In the psychological literature, cognate terms include sexual subjectivity, sexual citizenship, sexual self-efficacy, and sexual autonomy. There is obviously a large research gap on SRHR and people with ID, especially from the perspective of people with ID. Most research on sexuality and people with ID is from the perspectives of caregivers, staff members, teachers and personal assistants, and family. Methodological issues have been discussed regarding the inclusion of participants with ID (e.g., McCarthy, 1999); nonetheless, recently there is an increasing focus addressing the target group's own voices (e.g., McCarthy, 2014; Löfgren-Mårtenson, 2012; Turner & Crane, 2016). Sexual agency might be one of the most important areas to focus on to achieve relevance and significance of the SRHR for people with ID, creating opportunities for meaningful choice, relationships, and sexuality. However, as Gill (2015) states in his book *Already Doing It*, it is necessary to "recognize that people with intellectual disabilities are already active agents in their sexual expression, despite compromised privacy in living arrangements and systematic intrusions and oversights" (p. 6). In the same line, Fish (2016) states that most of the participants in her research study did want a sexual relationship, despite experiencing sexual abuse and violence in their pasts. Moreover, in the face of high levels of regulation in their restricted living arrangements (attributable to their perceived vulnerability), people with ID found ways to experience these intimate relationships. So there is already activism within the disability community on a large and small scale to confront sexual ableism. However, changes in policy and practice are needed to reduce the barriers to sexuality, change the focus on protection, and enhance the supports for sexual knowledge that impeded the achievement of SRHR in ways chosen by people with ID. This view of sexual agency might challenge the traditional definitions of sexual and reproductive health and rights but has the potential to fill the significance and relevance of the concept for people with ID. Sexual self-advocacy and the voice of people with ID in defining sexual self-advocacy need to be recognized as a central part of giving a meaning to the concept of SRHR for people with ID. In such work, an intersectional perspective, including factors such as ethnicity, gender, age, and social class that also influence SRHR, is important. Ultimately, addressing these critical issues has the potential to enhance choice, relationships, and sexuality for all people, including those with intellectual disability.

Disclosure Statement The author reports no potential conflict of interest.

Funding This work was supported by the Swedish Foundation for Humanities and Social Sciences and by Malmö University.

References

Articles Included in the Review

Abbott, D. (2013). "Nudge, nudge, wink, wink": Love, sex and gay men with intellectual disabilities – A helping hand or human right? *Special Issue: Human Rights, 57*, 1079–1087.∗
Abbott, D., & Howarth, J. (2007). Still off-limits? Staff views on supporting gay, lesbian and bisexual people with intellectual disabilities to develop sexual and intimate relationships. *Journal of Applied Research in Intellectual Disabilities, 20*, 116–126.
Angrosino, M. V., & Zagnoli, L. J. (1992). Gender constructs and social identity: Implications for community-based care of retarded adults. In T. Whitehead & B. Reid (Eds.), *Gender constructs and social issues* (pp. 40–69). Urbana, IL: University of Illinois Press.
Atkinson, D., & Walmsley, J. (1995). A women's place: Issues of gender. In T. Philpot & L. Ward (Eds.), *Values and visions: Changing ideas in in services for people with learning difficulties* (pp. 218–231). Oxford: Butterworth-Heinemann.
Barron, K. (2002). "Who am I?" Women with learning difficulties (re)constructing their self-identity. *Scandinavian Journal of Disability Research, 4*, 58–79.
Burns, J., & Davies, D. (2011). Same-sex relationships and women with intellectual disabilities. *Journal of Applied Research, 24*, 351–360.
Cambridge, P. (2013). A rights approach to supporting the sexual fetish of a man with learning disability: Method, process and applied learning. *British Journal of Learning Disabilities, 41*, 259–265.∗
Chivers, J., & Mathieson, S. (2000). Training in sexuality and relationships: An Australian model. *Sexuality and Disability, 18*, 73–80.
Desjardins, M. (2012). The sexualized body of the child: Parents and the politics of "Voluntary" sterilization of people labeled intellectually disabled. In: R. McRuer & A. Mollow (Eds.) *Sex and disability*. Durham and London: Duke University Press.
Dukes, E., & Mcguire, B. E. (2009). Enhancing capacity to make sexuality-related decisions in people with an intellectual disability. *Journal of Intellectual Disability Research, 53*, 727–734.∗
Fish, R. (2016). "They've said I'm vulnerable with men": Doing sexuality on locked wards. *Sexualities, 19*, 641–658.

Fitzgerald, C. (2011). "I don't know what a proper women means": What women with intellectual disabilities think about sex, sexuality and themselves. *British Journal of Learning Disability, 42*, 5–12.

Friedman, C., Arnold, C. K., Owen, A. L., & Sandman, L. (2014). "Remember our voices are our tools": Sexual self-advocacy as defined by people with intellectual and developmental disabilities. *Sexuality and Disability, 32*, 515–532.∗

Gill, M. (2015). *Already doing it: Intellectual disability and sexual agency*. Minneapolis, MN: University of Minnesota Press.

Gomez, M. T. (2012). The S words: Sexuality, sensuality, sexual expression and people with intellectual disability. *Sexuality and Disability, 30*, 237–245.∗

Gougeon, N. A. (2009). Sexuality education for students with intellectual disabilities, a critical pedagogical approach: Outing the ignored curriculum. *Sex Education, 9*, 277–291.

Granlund, M., & Göransson, K. (2011). Utvecklingsstörning [Developmental disability]. In L. Söderman & S. Antonsson (Eds.), *Nya Omsorgsboken [The new book of long-term care]* (pp. 12–19). Malmö, Sweden: Liber.

Greenwood, N. W., & Wilkinson, J. (2013). Sexual and reproductive health care for women with intellectual disabilities: A primary care perspective. *International Journal of Family Medicine, 2013*, 1–8.∗

Grönvik, L. (2008). Sexualitet och funktionshinder [Sexuality and Disability]. In: L. Grönvik & M. Söder (Eds.). *Bara funktionshindrad? Funktionshinder och intersektionalitet* [Disabled only? Disability and Intersectionality]. Malmö: Gleerups.

Gustavsson, A. (1996/2000). Integrering som motkultur – erfarenheter från den första integreringsgenerationen [Integration as a counterculture – experiences from the first integration generation]. I: T. Tabe & A. Hill (red.) *Boken om integrering. Idé, teori, praktik* [A reader on Integration. Ideas, Theory, Practice] Trelleborg: Studentlitteratur.

Healy, E., McGuire, B. E., Evans, D. S., & Carley, S. N. (2009). Sexuality and personal relationships for people with an intellectual disability. Part I: Service-user perspectives. *Journal of Intellectual Disability Research, 53*, 905–912.∗

Ignagni, E., Schormans, F., Liddiard, A., & Runswick-Cole, K. (2016). "Some people are not allowed to love": Intimate citizenship in the lives of people labeled with intellectual disabilities. *Disability & Society, 31*, 131–135.∗

Karellou, I. (2017). "It is only natural..." attitudes of young people with intellectual disabilities towards sexuality in Greece. *Journal of Mental Health Research in Intellectual Disabilities, 10*, 217–236.∗

Kelly, G., Crowley, H., & Hamilton, C. (2009). Rights, sexuality and relationships in Ireland: 'it'd be nice to be kind of trusted'. *British Journal of Learning Disabilities, 37*, 308–315.∗

Kousmanen, J., & Starke, M. (2015). Access to Sweden s legal system of crime victims with intellectual disability involved in prostitution activities. *Journal of Policy and Practice in Intellectual Disabilities, 4*(2), 255–265.

Lafferty, A., McConkey, R., & Simpson, A. (2012). Reducing the barriers to relationships and sexuality education for persons with intellectual disabilities. *Journal of Intellectual Disabilities, 16*, 29–43.∗

Löfgren-Mårtenson, L. (2004). "May I?" about sexuality and love in the new generation with intellectual disabilities. *Sexuality and Disability, 22*, 197–207.

Löfgren-Mårtenson, L. (2009). The invisibility of young homosexual women and men with intellectual disabilities. *Sexuality and Disability, 27*, 21–26.

Löfgren-Mårtenson, L. (2012). "I want to do it right!" A pilot study of Swedish sex education and young people with intellectual disability. *Sexuality and Disability, 30*, 209–225.∗

Mayes, R., Llewellyn, G., & McConnell, D. (2011). "That-s who I choose to be": The mother identity for women with intellectual disabilities. *Women's Studies International Forum, 34*, 112–120.∗

McCarthy, M. (1999). *Sexuality and women with learning disabilities*. London: Jessica Kingsley.

McCarthy, M. (2014). Women with intellectual disability: Their sexual lives in the 21st century. *Journal of Intellectual & Developmental Disability, 39*(2), 123–131.

McClelland, A., Flicker, S., Nepveux, D., Nixon, S., Vo, T., Wilson, C., … Travers, R. (2012). Seeking safer sexual spaces: Queer and trans young people labeled with intellectual disabilities and the paradoxical risks of restriction. *Journal of Homosexuality, 59*, 808–819.∗

McConkey, R., & Leavey, G. (2013). Irish attitudes to sexual relationships and people with intellectual disability. *British Journal of Learning Disabilities, 41*, 181–188.∗

McKee, A., Albury, K., Dunne, M., Grieshaber, S., Hartley, J., Lumby, C., & Mathews, B. (2010). Healthy sexual development: A multidisciplinary framework for research. *International Journal of Sexual Health, 22*, 14–19.

Pownall, J. D., Jahoda, A., Hastings, R. P., & Cambridge, P. (2012). Sexuality and sex education of adolescents with intellectual disability: Mothers attitudes, experiences, and support needs. *Intellectual & Developmental Disabilities, 50*, 140–154.∗

Public Health Agency of Sweden (2018). *Sexual and reproductive health and rights.* Retrieved from: https://www.folkhalsomyndigheten.se/the-public-health-agency-of-sweden/living-conditions-and-lifestyle/sexual-health/

Rojas, S., Haya, I., & Lazaro-Visa, S. (2014). "My great hope in life is to have a house, a family and a daughter": Relationships and sexuality in intellectually disabled people. *British Journal of Learning Disabilities, 44*, 56–62.∗

Schaafsma, D., Kok, G., Stoffelen, J., & Curfs, L. (2017). People with intellectual disabilities talk about sexuality: Implications for the development of sex education. *Sexuality and Disability, 35*, 21–38.∗

National Board of Health and Welfare & Public Health Authority (2014). *National strategy for sexual and reproductive health and rights.* Stockholm, Sweden: National Board of Health and Welfare.

Sullivan, F., Bowden, K., McKenzie, K. & Qualy, E. (2013). 'Touching people in relationships': a qualitative study of close relationships for people with an intellectual disability. *Journal of Clinical Nursing, 22*, 3456–3466.

Swango-Wilson, A. (2011). Meaningful sex education programs for individuals with intellectual/developmental disabilities. *Sexuality and Disability, 29*, 113–118.

The Swedish Government's Human Rights Website (2017). *Sexual and reproductive health and rights (SRHR).* Retrieved from: http://www.manskligarattigheter.se/en/human-rights/what-rights-are-there/sexual-and-reproductive-health-and-rights-srhr?searchstatisticsId=21936.

Thompson, A., Bryson, M., & Castell, S. (2001). Prospects for identity formation for lesbian, gay or bisexual persons with developmental disabilities. *International Journal of Disability, Developmental and Education, 48*, 53–65.

Tilley, E., Walmsley, J., Earle, S., & Atkinson, D. (2012). 'The silence is roaring': Sterilization, reproductive rights and women with intellectual disabilities. *Disability and Society, 37*, 413–426.∗

Turner, G. W., & Crane, B. (2016). Pleasure is paramount: Adults with intellectual disabilities discuss sensuality and intimacy. *Sexualities, 19*, 677–697.∗

WHO (2008). *Social determinants of health, Key concepts.* Retrieved from: https://www.who.int/social_determinants/thecommission/finalreport/key_concepts/en/

Wilkinson, V. J., Theodore, K., & Raczka, R. (2015). 'As Normal as Possible': Sexual identity development in people with intellectual disabilities transitioning to adulthood. *Sexuality and Disability, 33*(1), 93–105.∗

Willems, D. L., de Vries, J. N., Isari, J., & Reinders, J. S. (2007). Parenting by persons with intellectual disability: An explorative study in the Netherlands. *Journal of Intellectual Disability Research, 51*, 537–544.

Wilson, N.J., Parmenter, T.R., Stancliffe R.J., Shuttleworth, R.P. & Parker, D. (2010). A masculine perspective of gendered topics in the research literature on males and females with intellectual disability. *Journal of Intellectual and Developmental Disability, 35*(1), 1–8.

Wilson, N., Parmenter, T., Stancliffe, R., & Shuttleworth, R. (2011). Conditionally sexual: Men and teenage boys with moderate to profound intellectual disability. *Sexuality & Disability, 29*, 275–289.∗

The Choice of Becoming a Parent

Marjorie Aunos, Marja W. Hodes, Gwynnyth Llewellyn, Margaret Spencer,
Laura Pacheco, Gunnel Janeslätt, Beth Tarleton, Lydia Springer,
and Berit Höglund

> …When did you know you wanted to be a mother?
> Forever, I always wanted to be a mother; ever since I can remember.
>
> (Spencer, 2012)

Introduction

As disability and parenthood are both part of the human condition, it is reasonable to assume that there have always been parents with disabilities, in every society, at every time. Becoming a parent is an intense transition in a person's life and is often seen as a highly regarded social role. As such, many men and women with intellectual

M. Aunos (✉)
Brock University, Ontario, Canada

M. W. Hodes
Vrije Universiteit Amsterdam, Amsterdam, The Netherlands

G. Llewellyn
Faculty of Medicine and Health, The University of Sydney, Camperdown, NSW, Australia

M. Spencer
Faculty of Arts and Social Science, The University of Sydney, Camperdown, NSW, Australia

L. Pacheco
CUISSS-ODIM, Montreal, Quebec, Canada

G. Janeslätt
Department of Public Health and Caring Sciences, Uppsala University, Uppsala, Sweden

B. Tarleton
Norah Fry Centre for Disability Studies, School for Policy Studies, University of Bristol, Bristol, UK

L. Springer
SUF Kunskapscentrum, Uppsala, Sweden

B. Höglund
Department of Women's and Children's Health, Uppsala University, Uppsala, Sweden

© Springer Nature Switzerland AG 2020
R. J. Stancliffe et al. (eds.), *Choice, Preference, and Disability*, Positive
Psychology and Disability Series, https://doi.org/10.1007/978-3-030-35683-5_14

disability (ID), just like anyone else, have expressed a desire, hopes, and dreams about wanting to marry (or have a long-term relationship) and have a family of their own (Björnsdóttir, Stefansdóttir, & Stefansdóttir, 2017; Emerson, Honey, & Llewellyn, 2008; Healy, McGuire, Evans, & Carley, 2009; Lesseliers & Van Hove, 2002; Neuman & Reiter, 2017).

If parenting by persons with ID has been possible through history, choice and preference to become a mother are, on the other hand, a relatively recent concept for women in industrialized societies and particularly for women with disabilities. In many societies, the older generations arrange marriages for their young adult children, with partners thought suitable according to clan or class or family lines, as well as their likely capacity to produce healthy children (Beber & Biswas, 2009). Choice is ripped away from all women in all societies, particularly women with disabilities, who have been subjected to forced pregnancy as victims of ongoing sexual abuse or opportunistic rape in the community and institutional settings (Hughes et al., 2012). When adults with ID actively and purposefully choose to become parents, their choice to raise their children is often taken away, prematurely, without a clear understanding of what is happening or without having been given opportunities to showcase their capacity to parent (McConnell, Feldman, Aunos, & Prasad, 2011).

This chapter will examine the history and research concerning the choice to become a parent. We will highlight the articles of the United Nations' Convention on the Rights of Persons with disabilities that mention the choice for parenthood. The choices will be examined within a relational and cultural context, exploring the role that parents, caregivers, support workers, child protection services, and government play in the parenting choices that adults with ID make. We will describe approaches to providing education, services (including using specialized intervention and tools), and support for parenting choices.

Historical Perspective on the Choice to Parent

Historical understandings locate disability within individuals as an inherent (and permanent) characteristic of their being. When disability as a characteristic is understood as an "ailment" and ailments are devalued, disability becomes negative difference. Negative difference is the foundation of social stigma resulting in discrimination, disadvantage, and exclusion from society for those so stigmatized (Goffman, 1968). In the early phases of industrialization, exclusion took the form of institutionalization. The "feebleminded," blind, deaf, and lame were located "out of sight, out of mind" in state institutions or housed by state-supported charitable organizations. There was no choice about where to live and with whom. Presumably, there was also no choice about becoming a mother or father. The historical record is silent on how pregnancy was managed in institutions for "idiots" and the "insane," although pregnancy was likely to occur with no separation of men, women, and children (Swain, 2014).

With the Age of Enlightenment in the middle of the nineteenth century came the possibility of new psychological and educational interventions particularly for mental illness and ID. There were fewer "curative" successes than anticipated, institutions became overcrowded, and conditions declined. No longer was there a need to provide industrious occupation for adults with ID of childbearing age in institutional settings. This was prolific ground for the spread of eugenic ideas and the advent of "control and contain" legislation and practices (Cohen, 2016; Malacrida, 2015).

Parenting for people with ID first attracted the attention of researchers in the early decades of the twentieth century, hard on the heels of the eugenics movement prominent in industrialized countries at that time. Eugenics led to the involuntary sterilization of many women (and some men) with ID to protect society against what were considered the ravages of moral degeneration and unacceptable social costs of procreation (Cohen, 2016). Until sterilization laws were overturned, several generations of women (and some men) had no choice. Their capacity to bear children was involuntarily removed under the watchful eye of the (not so benevolent) state.

What about the mothers and fathers with ID who escaped the notice of the state? Perhaps their disability was overlooked because they were well-off and supported (or hidden) by their families; or ignored as destitute or homeless outcasts living on the fringes of society or isolated in rural settings; or at least for some, playing a useful role in their communities. Their histories with very few exceptions (e.g., Traustadóttir & Johnson, 2000; Traustadóttir & Sigurjónsdóttir, 2008) have not been written. In the latter part of the twentieth century, with the growing commitment to the idea that people with ID should live in a manner as nearly "normal" as possible, institutions, orphanages, and residential settings were emptied (Nirje, 1969). The former inmates of institutional "care" forged lives as workers and as parents getting by in the community as Edgerton famously said under a "cloak of competence" (Edgerton, 1967). Their choices to become parents were constrained only if they came to the notice of the authorities for being homeless, poor or frequenting unsafe violent neighborhoods. Finally, the (never institutionalized) parents with ID, or "forgotten generation" of children with borderline or mild ID, also blended into the community and only attracted official attention for the same reasons or for becoming pregnant (Tymchuk, Lakin, & Luckasson, 2001).

The Right to Choose

Each person with disabilities is equal before the law, can choose where they live and have the right to be protected from harm and discrimination and rendered assistance by their country (Art. 12, 19; The United Nations Convention on the Rights of Persons with Disabilities, 2008). Women and girls with disabilities, in particular, should be empowered (Art. 6), as they are often subject to multiple discrimination which directly impacts on their social and economic status, well-being, reproductive rights, and choices (Ross & Solinger, 2017).

Furthermore, the right to choose whether or not to have children, when and with whom, freely without being subject to discrimination, coercion or violence is protected (Art. 23). States should then ensure that persons with disability retain their fertility on an equal basis with others; freely enter into intimate partnerships and marriage of their choosing; and have access to *age appropriate* "family planning education" to enable them to decide if and when to have children, as well as to decide the number and spacing of their children. This requirement is further endorsed in Article 25 which calls upon state parties to provide persons with disability with affordable and accessible sexual and reproductive healthcare. By endorsing the rights of persons with disabilities to parent, this convention obligates states to provide "appropriate assistance to persons with disabilities in the performance of their child-rearing responsibilities" (Art. 23). It also asserts that the disability of a child and/or a parent should not be the grounds alone for the termination of parental rights.

With this convention in mind, people with ID, in 177 countries which ratified it, should be free to choose to become a parent and in making this choice should have access to the appropriate support for the upbringing and education of their child.

The Choice Is Made: Prevalence of Parents with Intellectual Disability

Even if a clear estimate of the prevalence of parents with ID is hard to obtain, there is good evidence to suggest a reasonable proportion of people with ID become parents. As an example, the fertility rate for women with ID in Ontario, Canada, was estimated to be 20.3 per 1000 women, which corresponds to half the fertility rate of women without ID (Brown, Lunsky, Wilton, Cobigo, & Vigod, 2016). In the United Kingdom, it is estimated that 0.9 per 1000 births are to a woman with ID (Goldacre, Gray, & Goldacre, 2014) and that out of the 1.2 million people with mild-moderate ID, 7% would be parents (Emerson & Hatton, 2014). In addition, a national representative household study in the United Kingdom ($N = 14,373$) found that 66% of the adults with ID had biological children (Emerson et al., 2015). An American study estimates that 1% of all deliveries in 2010 were from women with ID (Parish et al., 2015). In Australia, a large nationally representative household survey ($N = 61,900$, aged 15–64) found that 0.41% of the parent population were parents with ID (Man, Wade, & Llewellyn, 2017). In the Netherlands, a study suggests that 1.5% of people with ID will have children (Willems, De Vries, Isarin, & Reinders, 2007). A Swedish study reported 2% of children born every year have a mother with ID (Weiber, Berglund, Tengland, & Eklund, 2011).

Sexuality, Marriage, and Family Planning

Erroneous perceptions of asexuality or promiscuity have led to paternalistic and protectionist approaches that overshadow the normal development and expression of sexuality in adults with ID (Aunos & Feldman, 2002; Azzopardi-Lane & Callus, 2015; Sinclair, Unruh, Lindstrom, & Scanlon, 2015). Abiding by a paternalistic approach leads care givers, professionals, and substitute decision-makers to make decisions on behalf of people with ID without having consulted them (Heng & Sullivan, 2017). Although there is now more perceived openness towards the expression of their sexuality, attitudes about persons with ID being parents still remain negative and frequently prohibit parenthood (Cuskelly & Bryde, 2004; McGuire & Bayley, 2011). As a result, many adults feel justified in choosing secrecy as an attempt to avoid being told no, further limiting the availability of supports and information they could receive (Healy et al., 2009; Neuman & Reiter, 2017). This lack of knowledge affects their capacity to make informed decisions.

> I would like to tell about my desire to become a mother. But if I do, everyone is trying to convince me that I will never be able to take good care of my child. That I am not capable of raising my child. That is why I didn't tell anyone that I am pregnant. (woman with ID, 24 years old, 8 months pregnant; Hodes, 2015)

The Illusion of Choice: Favoring Ignorance and Control to Prevent Sexual Expression and Procreation

Most reported negative attitudes towards the sexuality of people with ID lie in the perception that pregnancy is a *risk* (Aunos & Feldman, 2002; Neuman & Reiter, 2017). Sexual education programs are available but generally lack information on different aspects leading to procreation and parenthood.

The concept of choice incorporates the notions of freedom and rights. Yet, women with ID feel that their sexuality is often controlled by others: either by the men who initiate it or by caregivers who discourage or prevent it from happening (Björnsdóttir et al., 2017; English, Tickle, & Das Nair, 2018). In addition, Many women with ID are likely to have reduced control over their bodies with little choice about becoming a mother due to partner violence and rape (McCarthy, Bates, Triantafyllopoulou, Hunt, & Milne Skillman, 2019; Pestka & Wendt, 2014).

Another form of control comes from the content of programs and information that is relayed to them. Masturbation training is often emphasized as a way to express sexuality, while intercourse is rarely mentioned (Gill, 2012). In some countries, even acknowledging female menstruation constitutes a taboo (Chou, Lu, Wang, Lan, & Lin, 2008). While most adults with ID would like programs to cover topics such as romantic versus non-romantic relationships, the main content is often aimed at contraception, biology, and the prevention of sexually transmitted diseases (English et al., 2018; Schaafsma, Kok, Stoffelen, & Curfs, 2015). As a result, people with ID generally lack knowledge, in comparison to the general population, on all aspects related to puberty, sexual hygiene, intimacy, intercourse, safe sex practices, pregnancy, childbirth, and family planning (Gilmore & Malcolm, 2014; Höglund & Larsson, 2019; Servais, 2006;). The lack of knowledge puts them at an increased risk for not recognizing abusive relationships and leads to misconceptions and missed opportunities to take appropriate actions to ensure proper healthcare (Frawley & O'Shea, 2018).

First-time mothers with ID are younger, have less social support, are more often unmarried and seldom declare a father present (Hindmarsh, Llewellyn, & Emerson, 2015; Mitra, Iezzoni, et al., 2015). Significantly more of them will report physical abuse and medical issues during their pregnancies. They are often significantly under the poverty line, with no employment opportunities. One study demonstrated that pregnancies in a group of teenagers with ID occurred due to a lack of knowledge about sexuality, contraceptives, and understanding of how they became pregnant (Dalmijn, 2017). Most of the girls were not actively trying to become pregnant, but the girls were happy that they were going to make the transition to parenthood. They imagined a perfect happy future as they longed for a normal family filled with love and tenderness.

> I was in shock when I discovered my pregnancy. But I was also very, very happy. From an early age I knew that I wanted to become a mum.
> Everyone was telling me that was not for me. And now I got it like a present! (young woman with ID, 17 years old; Hodes, 2015)

When people with ID are misinformed or not informed, when information is only given to them reactively, this puts them at higher risk for abuse, disease, and *unplanned* pregnancies.

Contraception, Sterilization, and Family Planning

Many countries have a history of systematic, non-consensual contraception and sterilization programs for people with ID (Glidden, 2016). Those pro-sterilization movements discarded rights and aimed at controlling the birth rate of women with ID (McCarthy, 2010). Even with regulations in place, unlawful sterilizations are still being reported (Mayes, Llewellyn, & McConnell, 2006), and many doctors still view sterilization as a good practice (Gilmore & Malcolm, 2014). Vasectomies are performed on men before they even demonstrate an interest in sexuality (Cuskelly & Bryde, 2004). Usually, these procedures are performed overtly, as consent is required, but studies have identified some covert and silent strategies routinely used to bypass informed consent, such as a third party (i.e., parents, caregivers, guardians) *convincing* adult children that sterilization is best for them (Desjardins, 2012; Glidden, 2016; Roets, Adams, & Van Hove, 2006). Other strategies include healthcare professionals withholding relevant information on the surgical procedure.

Disguised *Sterilization* Procedures

When tubal litigation and hysterectomies are not performed, long-term acting contraceptives (as opposed to short-term, compliance-based contraceptives) are prescribed, at the request of family members, caregivers or institutions but very seldom at the request of women themselves (Ledger, Earle, Tilley, & Walmsley, 2016; Patel, 2017; Van Schrojenstein Lantman-de Valk, Rook, & Maaskant, 2011; Wu, Zhang, Mitra, Parish, & Reddy, 2018; Zampas & Lamac̆ková, 2011). The use of a progestin shot, as a birth control method, is often the only option presented, introduced before puberty and without evidence of the young woman being sexually active (Dizon, Allen, & Ornstein, 2005). In addition, once contraceptives are prescribed, they tend to be re-prescribed automatically. Women with ID are thus often on contraceptives, sometimes without realizing it, up until their late 40s when fertility tends to decline (McCarthy, 2009a, 2009b, 2010).

As women often lack knowledge about their prescribed contraceptives, the choice of parenthood is taken away. These women are *chemically sterilized* without their *informed* consent. The impact of sterilization brings emotional distress: sadness, anger, and humiliation (Stefánsdóttir, 2014; Tilley, Walmsley, Earle, & Atkinson, 2012).

> Life should be like this. You are a child. And then you become a dad. And then my son becomes a dad. So I pass on life. And my family will exist for ever. And now you, you are destroying my whole family. You don't have the right to act like this. (young man, wishing to become a parent; Hodes, 2019)

Oppression and the Use of Alternative Birth *Control* Methods

Women and men with ID will often describe a context where their social network *subtly imposes* certain values or decisions on their body (Björnsdóttir et al., 2017). These women report feeling threatened by potential consequences that could occur if they disagreed with the plan presented before them. Moreover, when a woman with ID becomes pregnant, joy and celebration rarely occur (Höglund & Larsson, 2012; Homeyard, Montgomery, Chinn, & Patelarou, 2016; Malouf, McLeish, Ryan, Gray, & Redshaw, 2017; Walsh-Gallagher, Sinclair, & Mc Conkey, 2012). Instead, she is often *convinced* to give her child up for adoption or to have an abortion, even when she is in a relationship with the father (Mayes et al., 2006; Potvin, Barnett, Brown, & Cobigo, 2019). The subsequent grief following the loss of the child is seldom acknowledged, and more often than not, no support is offered to deal with her loss (Sheerin, Keenan, & Lawler, 2013). Subsequently, many have learnt to delay announcing their pregnancy to ensure they will not be asked or not be pressured to abort (Homeyard et al., 2016; Mayes et al., 2006). Delaying announcing the pregnancy means missed opportunities for antenatal care. Failure to receive early pregnancy support has been shown to have negative repercussions on the health and well-being of mothers with ID and is thought to contribute to poor birth outcomes for their babies (Mitra, Parish, Clements, Cui, & Diop, 2015).

Marriage and Family Planning

In families headed by persons with ID, marriages and relationships are usually described as supportive, and men/fathers are often considered as the main support to the mother and child (Booth & Booth, 2002; Mayes & Sigurjóndóttir, 2010). Many studies have found, however, that parenthood was rarely discussed between partners before pregnancy occurred, and only a few planned for it beforehand (Conder, Mirfin-Veitch, Sanders, & Munford, 2011; Mayes, Llewellyn, & McConnell, 2011; Mayes & Sigurjóndóttir, 2010; Mitra, Parish, et al., 2015; Theodore et al., 2018).

Most women require someone to facilitate contact with services (Burgen, 2010). Yet, formal family planning services are offered sporadically, and midwives and other healthcare practitioners report being overwhelmed and unprepared to support mothers with ID (Castell & Kroese, 2016; Höglund & Larsson, 2014; McGarry, Stenfert Kroese, & Cox, 2016). As such, women with ID are marginalized in accessing maternity services, and when *family planning* is offered, it serves as a discourse to discourage them from having a child (Walsh-Gallagher, Mc Conkey, Sinclair, & Clarke, 2011). Again, the lack of access highlights a missed opportunity to inform women adequately on sexual health, prenatal needs, genetic counseling, pregnancy, birthing, and other topics relevant to implementing a choice around parenthood (Höglund & Larsson, 2012).

In at least one study, women with ID reported being satisfied with the professional care they received during pregnancy and childbirth (Höglund & Larsson, 2014). However, most also report being dissatisfied due to the short-term nature of services, the lack of adaptation of material and the challenges in coordinating the numerous professionals (Malouf et al., 2017). Most report feeling that formal supports were at times excessive, intrusive, and too directive and perceived their maternal role to be often undermined (Walsh-Gallagher et al., 2012). The use of jargon and overuse of written material affected understanding and did not allow mothers to be in control of or even involved in decisions about their care (Bradbury-Jones et al., 2015; Redshaw, Malouf, Gao, & Gray, 2013). During labor, some even felt disempowered by the maternity service staff and fathers felt left out by professionals in regard to decisions involving pregnancy or birth (Mayes & Sigurjóndóttir, 2010). In addition, mothers with ID expressed difficulties trusting health professionals, as they felt disrespected when being told what to do instead of being invited to follow through with suggestions or recommendations (Homeyard et al., 2016). The anticipation of negative attitudes prevented some of them from accessing care in the first place or led them to withhold issues regarding their pregnancies to avoid feeling disempowered (Kopac & Fritz, 2004). In times of need, mothers also reported relying more on informal support (i.e., family members or their partner) even if they felt that support was unhelpful (Wilson, McKenzie, Quayle, & Murray, 2013).

Navigating a Pathway to Parenthood

A woman's choice to continue or terminate a pregnancy is influenced by multiple and complex factors including her values and beliefs, perceived threats, and support (McGaw & Cany, 2010; Nikkhesal, Nourizadeh, Dastgiri, & Mehrabi, 2018. It can further be complicated by negative attitudes and is often obstructed by cultural narratives and actions by family members, neighbors, and different systems (Mayes & Sigurjóndóttir, 2010; Sigurjónsdóttir & Traustadóttir, 2000). The discrimination experienced by parents with ID is based on their dual roles as a parent and person with ID (McConnell & Llewellyn, 2002; Rice & Sigurjónsdóttir, 2018). Llewellyn (2019) noted that a dominant theme in this literature is how parenting by people with disabilities is regarded with suspicion and negativity by people in the community, driven by the social stigma attached to stereotyped thinking about people with disabilities as lacking capacity and inherently defective, a point frequently reported by parents themselves. This issue remains one of the biggest impediments for persons with disabilities wishing to exercise their right to choose the valued social role of parenting.

The pervasive, negative cultural narratives that parents with ID face are undeniable; however, the choice to become a parent and their fight to keep their child/children has often been seen as the ultimate act of resistance (Malacrida, 2009; Pacheco & McConnell, 2017; Traustadóttir & Sigurjónsdóttir, 2010). As such, the decision to keep the baby or terminate the pregnancy is often described as a conscious choice, which often occurs following a discussion with at least one other person (Mayes et al., 2006; Walsh-Gallagher et al., 2012). Some parents with ID report that the decision to keep the baby was difficult and stressful as they had to face financial hardships or were worried for the health of baby due to the medication they were taking. But most reported being excited, joyful, and happy about becoming parents (Conder et al., 2011; Cuskelly & Bryde, 2004; Höglund & Larsson, 2012; Homeyard et al., 2016). Once the decision was made, these parents tried to prepare themselves for the baby's arrival, but most reported in hindsight not knowing at the time what that meant or feeling like their preparation would be in vain as child welfare would remove their child (Theodore et al., 2018).

Choice to Parent in the Context of Child Welfare

Compared to any other group of parents, parents with ID face some of the highest rates of child removal by child welfare authorities (Booth, Booth, & McConnell, 2005a, 2005b; McConnell et al., 2011; Willems et al., 2007). In addition, they are also much more likely to face a multiplicity of sociocultural and economic risk factors for inadequate parenting, including health problems, stress, depression, and histories of institutional or non-parental upbringing (Emerson & Brigham, 2013; Hatton & Emerson, 2003; Hindmarsh et al., 2015).

Many mothers felt the potential threat of child removal and experienced the pressure of unrealistic expectations (Mayes et al., 2011; Theodore et al., 2018). As child protection services become involved, these families are asked to participate in parenting capacity assessments despite the fact they often do not know what the reason for notification is (Azar, Maggi, & Proctor, 2013; Lightfoot, LaLiberte, & Cho, 2017). Informed consent is often not obtained before the assessment begins, and limits of confidentiality are not explained in a way that the parents can understand or retain (Budd, Felix, Sweet, Saul, & Carleton, 2006; Patel & Choate, 2014).

Furthermore, most assessments are not conducted according to best practices. Reasons for referral are not operationally defined, few (if any) adaptations are made during the process (Azar et al., 2013; Lightfoot et al., 2017), validated instruments are not used, and rarely do assessments include in vivo in context observations (McConnell & Llewellyn, 2002; Sigurjónsdóttir & Rice, 2017; Spencer, 2001). This approach results in overarching impressions being made with limited or unreliable data used for prediction of potential future risks to the child's well-being (Aunos & Pacheco, accepted; Cox, Kroese, & Evans, 2015; Kollinsky, Simonds, & Nixon, 2013) or in unrealistic recommendations (McConnell & Llewellyn, 2002; Sigurjónsdóttir & Rice, 2017; Spencer, 2001). Arbitrary time constraints imposed by courts are too limited to allow parents with ID to mobilize and access the support or services they need to provide contrary evidence (Booth et al., 2005a, 2005b; Zilberstein, 2016). Finally, more emphasis is placed on the parents' cognitive limitations in comparison to the family's socio-economic status or living circumstances (Alexius & Hollander, 2014). As the perspective of parents with ID is often not taken into consideration, they commonly feel shut out of decisions made for their children, yet again denying them the opportunity to choose and be involved (Tarleton, Ward, & Howard, 2006).

Support from Family and Friends

The presence of an informal support network seems critical in the evaluation of risk by child welfare authorities, and parents who have at least one significant involved person in their network have more chance of retaining custody of their children (Traustadóttir & Sigurjónsdóttir, 2008). Furthermore, receiving support not only influences the choice to keep (or not) the baby but also influences when they disclose their disability and their pregnancy and the types of services they receive. Often, it is the fear of losing custody that brings women with ID to make strategic choices in regard to whom they involve in their lives. The criteria for acceptance of assistance are conditional not only on it being deemed as helpful but also on the support persons respecting and affirming their maternal role and authority (Mayes, Llewellyn, & McConnell, 2008). As such, these significant persons have often been described as "the mother behind the mother" as they provide practical and emotional support, advocate, and protect the family while assisting parents in navigating services.

Cultural Differences and Values in the Concept of Choice

People with ID may not have the choice or may not be fully supported in their choices when it comes to parenthood. They are, more often than not, faced with judgment, stigma, and discrimination. Yet, in some cultures the notion of choice is experienced differently: marriage is often imposed or *guided* by family members, and pregnancy and parenthood are expected, irrespective of disability. In addition, arranged marriages of women with ID are common within some cultures, where the chosen marriage partner is unsuspecting of his wife's disability (Hepper, 1999). In these instances, it appears that the cultural status ascribed to marriage and children may take precedence over negative societal attitudes towards disability. For example, Pan and Ye (2012) reported that a shortage of "eligible" women in Rural China resulted in the "marrying off" of disabled women who, if non-disabled women were plentiful, may not have been considered worthy of marriage. Further, in Kahonde, McKenzie, and Wilson's South African study (2019), poorly resourced families expressed a desire for the young adults with ID to bear children who would become future caregivers. The opportunity to expand the family is exchanged for reducing the family's "burden of care" and upholding family traditions in the lives of women with ID (O'Hara & Martin, 2003; Groce, Gazzizova, & Hassiostis, 2014).

Having No Choice to Get Married and Have Children

Gender-specific roles and expectations are prescribed by cultural communities and family culture (Neculaesei, 2015; Shuttleworth & Kasnitz, 2006). There are also shared societal understandings of whom in the community is responsible for rearing children. In more highly industrialized societies, it is commonly believed that childrearing is the (almost) sole prerogative and responsibility of the biological mother and father. This restricts choices for parenting for people with ID, given implicit assumptions about disability as incompetence (McConnell, Llewellyn, & Ferronato, 2006). In lower- and middle-income societies, responsibility for childrearing is intimately connected with gender-based societal roles derived from how each society is organized according to inheritance, land ownership, clan status, occupation, and so on (Merton, 1946). In societies where both biological parents participate in full-time employment, grandparents may play a predominant role in parenting children at least in their early years prior to school entry (Purcal, Brennan, Cass, & Jenkins, 2014). Although the concept of shared care between family members and between generations is now commonplace in relation to separated or divorced families, within some cultural communities and where mothers and fathers are employed outside the home, extending the involvement of others in sharing parenting to parents with disabilities (including parents with ID), with rare exceptions, has yet to be considered (Llewellyn, 2019; Prilleltensky, 2004). There is a lot that can gleaned from the adage "it takes a village to raise a family" that many cultural communities abide by, for all families including families headed by parents with ID (O'Hara & Martin, 2003).

The way in which disability is perceived and treated and the opportunities that are afforded to persons with disabilities (i.e., getting married and having children) is also subject to cultural interpretation (Al-Aoufi, Al-Zyoud, & Shahminan, 2012; French Gilson & Depoy, 2000; Groce et al., 2014; Weaver, 2015). Women with ID's socialization towards motherhood can be impacted by several internal and external variables that can include culture, family beliefs and composition, birth order, religion, social class, and severity and visibility of the disability (Shuttleworth & Kasnitz, 2006). Within the field of parents and parenting with an ID, there have only been a few studies that have explored culture. When the parent has a mild ID, there is a tendency towards encouragement of marriage and having children. In Pacheco and McConnell's (2017) study of eight mothers with ID from different cultural communities in Canada, the women were encouraged and even expected to marry and have children according to their cultural traditions.

What Works: Supporting Decision-Making Skills and Parenting

There is limited research about how young people with ID can be supported so they can make well-informed decisions about sexuality, parenthood, and family life (Schaafsma, Stoffelen, Kok, & Curfs, 2013). However, it is well known that individuals with ID can understand and use adapted and specific information to assist with informed decision-making. As well, they can learn social skills and decision-making skills (Azar et al., 2013; Feldman, 1994), all of which can also be related to the area of sexuality and parenting. There is abundant evidence for the effectiveness of cognitive support to compensate for challenges in executive functioning in persons with ID (Gillespie, Best, & O'Neill, 2012). Examples of cognitive support that are effective to improve daily functioning are providing reminders, to-do lists for prioritizing, and step-by-step lists to know *how to* do things or using pictures and activity schedules to increase autonomy and participation (Feldman, 2010).

Some tools have been created to support the decision-making process in relation to parenthood. The intent and manner with which professionals use these tools will determine their usefulness and impact on adults with ID who have expressed their desire to become parents. It appears that professionals either believe persons with ID can parent adequately or they are convinced they cannot learn to do so. Depending on their mindset, the following tools can be used in a coercive or a supportive way. Obviously, the purpose of these tools is to support self-determination.

The program *Babyroute* (Tilburg, 2012) starts when a person or couple with ID first expresses their desire to become pregnant. This program allows for a close collaboration between the social and health services, child protection services, and midwives in order to guide potential future parents in their decision-making process and during pregnancy. The program was first initiated with the focus on risk factors (presuming it might be difficult to ask for support and the conviction that child protection services should be involved already for the unborn child). Later on, the program paid more careful attention to the protective factors like the availability of a supportive social network, asking for and accepting support, and the future parents were better involved in the program (Tilburg, 2012). When professionals are convinced that the person with ID in front of them should not be a parent (yet), the program *Do not become pregnant yet* (Rijlaarsdam, Van Rooij, & Fiedeldeij, 2017) could be used. This program offers tools to professionals to explain why becoming pregnant would not be a good decision (at this time). Results of this program were reported in the percentage of successful prevention of pregnancies because of the decision to start with contraceptives, supplied for free by the program. In a pilot with 30 women, 86% started with contraceptives (Rijlaarsdam et al., 2017).

To support the decision-making process to become a parent or not, there is a freely available toolkit (*Toolkit: Talking about children*; Hodes, 2010, 2012) (http://www.asvz.nl/specialismen/kinderwens-ouderschap/). This toolkit provides material that can be used to clarify the goals and desires of the person concerning their future (including sexuality and parenting goals) (e.g., *What I wish card game*). Another tool (*Who is there to support you?*) helps identify members of their support network who can (should) be involved during the decision-making process. Members of the informal support network can be included when appropriate. A third tool (e.g., *Do I know what that involves?*) helps people with ID become aware of what choosing to have a child entails.

Finally, to concretize the notion of parenthood, a new model providing knowledge using the *Do I know what that involves* game combined with providing experiences via the baby simulator was created for students in special schools aged 16–20 years, which showed promising results (Janeslätt, Larsson, Wickström, Springer, & Höglund, 2019). Real Care Baby is a computerized simulator that has been used for youth and young adults without disabilities in several countries in order to increase informed choice and in turn prevent teenage pregnancies. The baby simulator signals different needs that the caretaker must interpret and respond to (hunger, rocking, new diaper, etc.). The level of care of the simulator is registered, and after a completed session over many hours or a few days, a report is generated with data as to how well the caretaker has responded to the baby's needs. It is a learning aid designed to stimulate discussion about the pros and cons of having a baby and thus contributes to informed decisions about whether or not to have a child.

Research in this area is in its infancy and the tools presented above have not yet gotten through a rigorous validation process. More studies are needed to look at the effectiveness and usability of these tools regarding young adults with ID's decision-making process regarding pregnancy and parenthood, especially in a context where biaises and stereotypes still inform, too often, the behaviors of professionals involved with these (*potential*) future parents.

Parenting Intervention Programs

A positive alliance between parents and their workers is crucial in determining parenting goals but also moderates the effectiveness of interventions (Meppelder, Hodes, Kef, & Schuengel, 2014). Group interventions have also shown to reduce symptoms associated with psychological distress and isolation, while giving a sense of purpose to mothers with ID who participated (McConnell et al., 2016). A number of studies have targeted specific parenting skills (Wade, Llewellyn, & Matthews, 2008).

The *Step-by-Step* program (Feldman & Case, 1993; Feldman, Case, & Sparks, 1992) incorporates behavioral teaching strategies, such as modeling and positive reinforcement, in personalized, family-oriented, home-based format. Its content addresses the most vulnerable areas in childcare skills, safety, and parent-child interactions and is geared towards parents of children aged under 6 years. This program was built on research data that demonstrated positive effects on the learning and maintenance of basic child-care skills (Feldman, 1994). A study on a game-based intervention (module II of Step-by-Step) on parent-child interactions showed generalization within the game scenarios but was inconclusive in terms of transferability to in vivo situations (Tahir, Sword, & Feldman, 2015).

Parenting Young Children (PYC) (Starke, Wade, Feldman, & Mildon, 2013) is an intensive, family-tailored, home-based support program for parents with ID that focuses on parent-child interactions and childcare skills as per the *Step-by-Step* program. Its applicability and usefulness as per workers and parents' perceptions have been demonstrated.

A video-feedback intervention focusing on sensitive discipline and harmonious parent-child interaction in families with parents with ID *(Video-feedback to Promote Positive Parenting for parents with Learning Difficulties*; Hodes, Meppelder, De Moor, Kef, & Schuengel, 2017, 2018) demonstrated significantly reduced parenting stress for the entire intervention group. A Home Learning Program that targeted home safety skills demonstrated significant improvement in parents' ability to identify home dangers and apply appropriate actions (Llewellyn, McConnell, Honey, Mayes, & Russo, 2003).

A Cochrane review (Coren, Ramsbotham, & Gschwandtner, 2018) showed that three of these programs (Feldman et al., 1992; Hodes et al., 2017, 2018; Llewellyn et al., 2003) provide significant positive impact on learning new skills and improving parent-child interactions. Studies with more robust methodologies are also needed for parenting programs that are adapted to the specific needs of parents with ID. Having access to effective and evidence-based programs could influence the decision-making process towards becoming (or not) a parent.

Best Practices and Support Guidance for Professionals

England and Scotland have created good practice guidance (GPG) documents about working with parents with ID. Both of these documents recognize that parents with ID will require support, often over the longer-term, to make decisions and ensure positive outcomes for their children.

The English GPG (WTPN, 2016; wtpn.co.uk) is based on established principles of positive practice (Booth & Booth, 1998; McGaw & Newman, 2005; Tarleton et al., 2006). It recommends addressing both the needs relating to the parents' ID and the barriers parents face, such as unequal access to services and the negative attitudes they often experience towards their parenting, while focusing on the things that can be changed (such as inadequate housing) and support needs that can be met (such as equipment to help a parent measure baby feeds). Taking this positive approach forward, the Scottish GPG (SCLD, 2015) entitled "Supported Parenting" clearly recognizes "that parents have particular gifts as well as support needs, and that support should be tailored to build on parental capacity as well as addressing deficits" (p. 6).

The principles of Supported Parenting include that parents should have support available from pre-birth onwards and that they might need ongoing support at every stage of the child's development. Parents should be seen as a resource rather than a *problem*, and the support provided should be for the family (rather than individuals) and focus on building strengths. Supported parenting also recognizes that families are best supported in their existing social networks, including their own extended families, neighborhoods, and communities.

The GPGs recognize that parents should also have their own support needs assessed and met, promoting the need for joint commissioning of services based on strategies that have been agreed by adults and children's services and which include health, education, housing, as well as local voluntary and independent organizations.

Supporting parents means providing "accessible information and communication," using easy-read information leaflets, websites, and audiovisual information, as well as face-to-face discussions regarding available resources. Supporting parents also means coordinating referrals and assessment procedures that include a measure of their strengths and needs for the short and longer term. Parents should have access to independent advocacy when necessary (SCLD, 2015 p. 6, WTPN, 2016, p. 4).

In both countries, the GPGs are supported by regional and national laws and regulations. In England, the use of the GPG is supported by the Children Act (1989) which emphasizes the duty to keep children with their parents whenever possible and wider policy which endorses coordinated multiagency working. In April 2018, the GPG was endorsed by the president of the Family Division (family courts in England and Wales) resulting in all judges and legal professionals becoming aware the GPG and local authorities being asked in child protection proceedings whether they have followed the GPG.

Enabling Self-Determination: Collaboration Between Organizations

Without inter-sector collaboration and effective communication among professionals who work with parents with ID, the quality of services offered is affected (Weiber, Eklund, & Tengland, 2016). Working in a long-term, proactive, multiagency way to meet parents' support needs has demonstrated benefits and improved outcomes for their children (Tarleton & Porter, 2012). Having professionals who have strong commitments towards family unity and mutual control over decision-making processes leads to more positive outcomes for families (Aunos & Pacheco, 2013). The need for collaboration between organizations has become increasingly evident. National and international initiatives are underway to develop service pathways and tools that can be used to support families and enable the decision-making processes around family planning.

Conclusion

Throughout history, there have been many instances of discriminatory practices as people with ID were ostracized, placed in institutions, segregated and sterilized without consent. Paternalistic views continue to belittle them and affect their agency, by limiting their capacity to make choices, even sometimes on everyday life matters.

Around the choice of parenthood, there exists a dichotomy, where control and resistance interplay. Many people with ID experience significant barriers to exercising their reproductive choices, starting from even before puberty. Information is withheld, they are either prevented from choosing to have a relationship or told who to marry, told the kind of sexual acts they should or should not do, and convinced that pregnancy and parenthood are not the best option for them (or expected to have many children). Additionally, when pregnant, services are often not adapted, further limiting their opportunity to choose. Resistance to this oppressive context is expressed through people with ID choosing to have children. To every control mechanism, they find ways to resist. To break free of the controls, they will hide their pregnancy to ensure they bring their baby to term, even if by doing so, they are affecting their health, social conditions, and the outcomes and lives of their (*possible, future*) children.

Parenting with disability is possibly the last bastion for delivering equal opportunities, self-determination, and for including people with disabilities in valued social roles (Kirshbaum & Olkin, 2002).

References

Al-Aoufi, H., Al-Zyoud, N., & Shahminan, N. (2012). Islam and the cultural conceptualisation of disability. *International Journal of Adolescence and Youth, 17*, 205–219. https://doi.org/10.10 80/02673843.2011.649565

Alexius, K., & Hollander, A. (2014). Care assessments concerning involuntary removal of children from intellectually disabled parents. *Journal of Social Welfare and Family Law, 36*, 295–310.

Aunos, M., & Feldman, M. A. (2002). Attitudes toward sexuality, sterilisation, and parenting rights of persons with intellectual disabilities. *Journal of Applied Research in Intellectual Disability, 15*, 285–296.

Aunos, M., & Pacheco, L. (2013). Changing perspective: Workers' perceptions of inter-agency collaboration with parents with an intellectual disability. *Journal of Public Child Welfare, 7*, 658–674. https://doi.org/10.1080/15548732.2013.852153

Aunos, M., & Pacheco, L. (accepted). Able or unable: How do professionals determine the parenting capacity of mothers with intellectual disabilities. *Journal of Public Child Welfare.*

Azar, S. T., Maggi, M. C., & Proctor, S. N. (2013). Practices changes in the child protection system to address the needs of parents with cognitive disabilities. *Journal of Public Child Welfare, 7*, 610–632.

Azzopardi-Lane, C., & Callus, A. M. (2015). Constructing sexual identities: People with intellectual disability talking about sexuality. *British Journal of Learning Disabilities, 43*, 32–37.

Beber, E., & Biswas, A. B. (2009). Marriage and family life in people with developmental disability. *International Journal of Culture and Mental Health, 2*, 102–108. https://doi.org/10.1080/17447140903205317

Björnsdóttir, K., Stefansdóttir, A., & Stefansdóttir, G. V. (2017). People with intellectual disabilities negotiate autonomy, gender and sexuality. *Sexuality & Disability, 35*, 295–311. https://doi.org/10.1007/s11195-017-9492-x.

Booth, T., & Booth, W. (2002). Men in the lives of mothers with intellectual disabilities. *Journal of Applied Research in Intellectual Disabilities, 15*, 187–199.

Booth, T., Booth, W., & McConnell, D. (2005a). The prevalence and outcomes of care proceedings involving parents with learning difficulties in family courts. *Journal of Intellectual Disability Research, 18*, 7–17.

Booth, T., Booth, W., & McConnell, D. (2005b). Care proceedings and parents with learning difficulties: Comparative prevalence and outcomes in an English and Australian court sample. *Child and Family Social Work, 10*, 353–360.

Booth, W., & Booth, T. (1998). *Advocacy for parents with learning difficulties.* Brighton, UK: Pavilion Publishing.

Bradbury-Jones, C., Breckenridge, J. P., Devaney, J., Kroll, T., Lazenbatt, A., & Taylor, J. (2015). Disabled women's experiences of accessing and utilising maternity services when they are affected by domestic abuse: A critical incident technique study. *BMC Pregnancy & Childbirth, 15*, 181. https://doi.org/10.1186/s12884-015-0616-y

Brown, H. K., Lunsky, Y., Wilton, A. S., Cobigo, V., & Vigod, S. N. (2016). Pregnancy in women with intellectual and developmental disabilities. *Journal of Obstetrics and Gynaecology Canada, 38*, 9–16. https://doi.org/10.1016/j.jogc.2015.10.004

Budd, K. S., Felix, E. D., Sweet, S. C., Saul, A., & Carleton, R. A. (2006). Evaluating parents in child protection decisions: An innovative court-based clinic model. *Professional Psychology: Research and Practice, 37*, 666–675.

Burgen, B. (2010). Women with cognitive impairment and unplanned or unwanted pregnancy: A 2-year audit of women contacting the pregnancy advisory service. *Australian Social Work, 53*, 18–34. https://doi.org/10.1080/03124070903471033

Castell, E., & Kroese, B. S. (2016). Midwives' experiences of caring for women with learning disabilities – a qualitative study. *Midwifery, 36*, 35–42.

Children Act 1989. https://www.legislation.gov.uk/ukpga/1989/41/contents

Chou, Y. C., Lu, Z.-Y. J., Wang, F. T. Y., Lan, C.-F., & Lin, L.-C. (2008). Meanings and experiences of menstruation: Perceptions of institutionalized women with an intellectual disability. *Journal of Applied Research in Intellectual Disabilities, 21*, 575–584.

Cohen, A. (2016). *Imbeciles: The supreme court, American eugenics, and the sterilization of Carrie Buck*. New York, NY: Penguin Press.

Conder, J., Mirfin-Veitch, B., Sanders, J., & Munford, R. (2011). Planned pregnancy, planned parenting: Enabling choice for adults with a learning disability. *British Journal of Learning Disabilities, 39*, 105–112. https://doi.org/10.1111/j.1468-3156.2010.00625.x

Coren, E., Ramsbotham, K., & Gschwandtner, M. (2018). Parent training interventions for parents with intellectual disability. *Cochrane Database of Systematic Reviews, 7*, CD007987. https://doi.org/10.1002/14651858.CD007987.pub3

Cox, R., Kroese, B. S., & Evans, R. (2015). Solicitors' experiences of representing parents with intellectual disabilities in care proceedings: Attitudes, influence and legal processes. *Disability & Society, 30*, 284–298. https://doi.org/10.1080/09687599.2015.1005730

Cuskelly, M., & Bryde, R. (2004). Attitudes towards the sexuality of adults with an intellectual disability: Parents, support staff, and a community sample. *Journal of Intellectual & Developmental Disability, 29*, 255–264.

Dalmijn, E. W. (2017). Tienerzwangerschap en tienerouderschap in Nederland. [Teenage pregnancies and teenage parenthood in the Netherlands]. *Jeugdbeleid, 11*, 9–15. https://doi.org/10.1007/s12451-017-0132-3

Desjardins, M. (2012). The sexualized body of the child: Parents and the politics of voluntary sterilization of people labeled intellectual disabled. In R. McRuer & A. Mollow (Eds.), *Sex and disability* (pp. 69–85). Durham, NC: Duke University Press.

Dizon, C., Allen, L., & Ornstein, M. (2005). Menstrual and contraceptive issues among young women with developmental delay. *Journal of Paediatric and Adolescent Gynaecology, 18*, 157–162.

Edgerton, R. B. (1967). *The cloak of competence. Stigma in the lives of the mentally retarded*. Berkeley, CA: University of California Press.

Emerson, E., & Brigham, P. (2013). Health behaviours and mental health status of parents with intellectual disabilities: Cross sectional study. *Public Health, 127*, 1111–1116.

Emerson, E., & Hatton, C. (2014). *Health inequalities and people with intellectual disabilities*. Cambridge: Cambridge University Press.

Emerson, E., Honey, A., & Llewellyn, G. (2008). *The well-being and aspirations of Australian adolescents and young adults with a long-term health condition, disability or impairment*. Canberra, Australia: Australian Research Alliance for Children and Youth. https://www.aracy.org.au/publications-resources/area?command=record&id=118

Emerson, E., Llewellyn, G., Hatton, C., Hindmarsh, G., Robertson, J., Man, W. Y. N., & Baines, S. (2015). The health of parents with and without intellectual impairment in the UK. *Journal of Intellectual Disability Research, 59*, 1142–1154.

English, B., Tickle, A., & Das Nair, R. (2018). Views and experiences of people with intellectual disabilities regarding intimate relationships: A qualitative metasynthesis. *Sexuality & Disability, 36*, 149–173. https://doi.org/10.1007/s11195-017-9502-z

Feldman, M. A. (1994). Parenting education for parents with intellectual disabilities: A review of outcome studies. *Research in Developmental Disabilities, 15*, 299–332. https://doi.org/10.1016/0891-4222(94)90009-4

Feldman, M. (2010). Parenting education programs. In G. Llewellyn, R. Traustadóttir, D. McConnell & H. B. Sigurjónsdóttir (Eds.), *Parents with ID: past, present and futures* (pp. 121–136). West Sussex, UK: Wiley-Blackwell.

Feldman, M. A., & Case, L. (1993). *Step-by-step child-care: A pictorial manual for parents, child-care workers, and babysitters*. Toronto, ON: Authors.

Feldman, M. A., Case, L., & Sparks, B. (1992). Effectiveness of a child-care training program for parents at-risk for child neglect. *Canadian Journal of Behavioural Science/Revue canadienne des sciences du comportement, 24*, 14–28.

Frawley, P., & O'Shea, A. (2018). Sexual lives and respectful relationships: A rights based approach. *Intellectual Disability Australasia, 39*, 22–24.

French Gilson, S., & Depoy, E. (2000). Multiculturalism and disability: A critical perspective. *Disability & Society, 15*, 207–218. https://doi.org/10.1080/09687590025630.

Gill, M. (2012). Sex can wait, masturbate: The politics of masturbation training. *Sexualities, 15*, 472–493.

Gillespie, A., Best, C., & O'Neill, B. (2012). Cognitive function and assistive technology for cognition: a systematic review. *Journal of the International Neuropsychological Society, 18*, 1–19. https://doi.org/10.1017/S1355617711001548

Gilmore, L., & Malcolm, L. (2014). "Best for everyone concerned" or "Only as a last resort"? Views of Australian doctors about sterilisation of men and women with intellectual disability. *Journal of Intellectual & Developmental Disability, 39*, 177–187. https://doi.org/10.3109/136 68250.2013.877125

Glidden, L. M. (2016). Removing reproductive, sexual, and child-rearing rights of women with ID: Congratulated, condoned and condemned. In J. R. Lutzker, K. Guastaferro, & M. L. Benka-Coker (Eds.), *Maltreatment of people with intellectual and developmental disabilities* (pp. 163–188). Washington, DC, USA: AAIDD.

Goffman, E. (1968). *Stigma. Notes on the management of spoiled identity.* Harmondsworth, England: Penguin.

Goldacre, A. D., Gray, R., & Goldacre, M. J. (2014). Childbirth in women with intellectual disability: Characteristics of their pregnancies and outcomes in an archived epidemiological dataset. *Journal of Intellectual Disability Research, 59*, 1–11. https://doi.org/10.1111/jir.12169

Groce, N. E., Gazzizova, D., & Hassiostis, A. (2014). *Forced marriage among persons with intellectual disability: Discussion paper. Leonard Chesire disability and inclusive development center.* London, UK: University College.

Hatton, C., & Emerson, E. (2003). The relationship between life events and psychopathology amongst children with intellectual disabilities. *Journal of Applied Research in Intellectual Disabilities, 17*, 109–117.

Healy, E., McGuire, B. E., Evans, D. S., & Carley, S. N. (2009). Sexuality and personal relationships for people with an intellectual disability. Part I: Service-user perspectives. *Journal of Intellectual Disability Research, 503*, 905–012. https://doi.org/10.1111/j.1365-2788.2009.01203.x.

Heng, J., & Sullivan, W. F. (2017). Ethics of decision making and consent in people with intellectual and developmental disabilities. In M. L. Wehmeyer, I. Brown, M. Percy, K. A. Shogren, & W. L. A. Fung (Eds.), *A comprehensive guide to intellectual and developmental disabilities: Second edition* (pp. 655–664). Baltimore, MA: Paul H. Brookes Publishing.

Hepper, F. (1999). A woman's heaven is at her husband's feet'? The dilemmas for a community learning disability team posed by the arranged marriage of a Bangladeshi client with intellectual disability. *Journal of Intellectual Disability Research, 43*, 558–561.

Hindmarsh, G., Llewellyn, G., & Emerson, E. (2015). Mothers with intellectual impairment and their 9-month-old infants. *Journal of Intellectual Disability Research, 59*, 541–550. https://doi.org/10.1111/jir.12159

Hodes, M. W. (2010, 2012). *Toolkit: Talking about children.* Sliedrecht, The Netherlands: ASVZ.

Hodes, M. W. (2015). *Talking with future moms* (Unpublished proceedings of an ASVZ parenting support group). The Netherlands: Hoogvliet.

Hodes, M. W. (2019). *Discussion with a general practitioner* (Unpublished citation from ASVZ clinical work). Rotterdam, The Netherlands.

Hodes, M. W., Meppelder, M., De Moor, M., Kef, S., & Schuengel, C. (2017). Alleviating parenting stress in parents with intellectual disabilities: A randomized controlled trial of a video-feedback intervention to promote positive parenting. *Journal of Applied Research in Intellectual Disabilities, 30*, 423–432. https://doi.org/10.1111/jar.12302

Hodes, M. W., Meppelder, M., De Moor, M., Kef, S., & Schuengel, C. (2018). Effects of video-feedback intervention on harmonious parent-child interaction and sensitive discipline of parents with intellectual disabilities: A randomized controlled trial. *Child: Care, Health and Development, 44*, 304–311. https://doi.org/10.1111/cch.12506

Höglund, B., & Larsson, M. (2012). Struggling for motherhood with an intellectual disability – a qualitative study of women's experiences in Sweden. *Midwifery, 29*, 1–7. https://doi.org/10.1016/j.midw.2012.06.014

Höglund, B., & Larsson, M. (2014). Professional and social support enhances maternal well-being in women with intellectual disability – a Swedish interview study. *Midwifery, 11*, 1118–1123. https://doi.org/10.1016/j.midw.2014.03.018.

Höglund, B., & Larsson, M. (2019). Midwives' work and attitudes towards contraceptive counselling and contraception among women with intellectual disability: Focus group interviews in Sweden. *Europe Journal of Contraception Reproduction Health Care, 24*, 39–44. https://doi.org/10.1080/13625187.2018.1555640

Homeyard, C., Montgomery, E., Chinn, D., & Patelarou, E. (2016). Current evidence on antenatal care provision for women with intellectual disabilities: A systematic review. *Midwifery, 32*, 45–57.

Hughes, K., Bellis, M. A., Jones, L., Wood, S., Bates, G., Eckley, L., … Officer, A. (2012). Prevalence and risk of violence against adults with disabilities: A systematic review and meta-analysis of observational studies. *The Lancet, 379*, 1621–1629.

Janeslätt, G., Larsson, M., Wickström, M., Springer, L., & Höglund, B. (2019). An intervention using the parenting toolkit "children – what does it involve?" And the real-care-baby simulator among students with intellectual disability – a feasibility study. *Journal of Applied Research Intellectual Disabilities, 32*, 380–389. https://doi.org/10.1111/jar.12535

Kahonde, C. K., McKenzie, J., & Wilson, N. J. (2019). Discourse of needs versus discourse of rights: Family caregivers responding to the sexuality of young south African adults with intellectual disability. *Culture, Health & Sexuality, 21*, 278–290.

Kirshbaum, M., & Olkin, R. (2002). Parents with physical, systemic or visual disabilities. *Sexuality and Disability, 20*, 65–80.

Kollinsky, L., Simonds, L. M., & Nixon, J. (2013). A qualitative exploration of the views and experiences of family court magistrates making decisions in care proceedings involving parents with learning disabilities. *British Journal of Learning Disabilities, 41*, 86–93. https://doi.org/10.1111/j.1468-3156.2012.00726.x

Kopac, C. A., & Fritz, J. (2004). The availability and accessibility of gynaecological and reproductive services for women with developmental disabilities: A nursing perspective. *Clin Excell Nurse Practitioners, 8*, 35–42.

Ledger, S., Earle, S., Tilley, E., & Walmsley, J. (2016). Contraceptive decision-making and women with learning disabilities. *Sexualities, 19*, 698–724.

Lesseliers, J., & Van Hove, G. (2002). Barriers to the development of intimate relationships and the expression of sexuality among people with developmental disabilities: Their perceptions. *Research & Practice for Persons with Severe Disabilities, 27*, 69–81.

Lightfoot, E., LaLiberte, T., & Cho, M. (2017). A case record review of termination of parental rights cases involving parents with a disability. *Children and Youth Services Review, 79*, 399–407. https://doi.org/10.1016/j.childyouth.2017.06.037

Llewellyn, G. (2019). Parents with disabilities. In M. H. Bornstein (Ed.), *Handbook of parenting* (Vol. 4. Social and cultural conditions of parenting, 3rd ed.). New York, NY: Routledge Publishers.

Llewellyn, G., McConnell, D., Honey, A., Mayes, R., & Russo, D. (2003). Promoting health and home safety for children of parents with intellectual disability: A randomized controlled trial. *Research in Developmental Disabilities, 24*, 405–431.

Malacrida, C. (2009). Performing motherhood in a disablist world: Dilemmas of motherhood, femininity and disability. *International Journal of Qualitative Studies in Education, 23*, 99–117.

Malacrida, C. (2015). *A special hell: Institutional life in Alberta's eugenic years*. Toronto, ON: University of Toronto Press.

Malouf, R., McLeish, J., Ryan, S., Gray, R., & Redshaw, M. (2017). 'We both just wanted to be normal parents': A qualitative study of the experience of maternity care for women with learning disability. *BMJ Open, 7*, e015526. https://doi.org/10.1136/bmjopen-2016-015526

Man, N. W., Wade, C., & Llewellyn, G. (2017). Prevalence of parents with intellectual disability in Australia. *Journal of Intellectual & Developmental Disability, 42*, 173–179. https://doi.org/10.3109/13668250.2016.1218448

Mayes, R., Llewellyn, G., & McConnell, D. (2006). Misconception: The experience of pregnancy for women with intellectual disabilities. *Scandinavian Journal of Disability Research, 8*, 120–131. https://doi.org/10.1080/15017410600774178

Mayes, R., Llewellyn, G., & McConnell, D. (2008). Active negotiation: Mothers with intellectual disabilities creating their social support networks. *Journal of Applied Research in Intellectual Disabilities, 21*, 341–350. https://doi.org/10.1111/j.1468-3148.2008.00448.x

Mayes, R., Llewellyn, G., & McConnell, D. (2011). "That's who I choose to be": The mother identity for women with intellectual disabilities. *Womens Studies International Forum, 34*, 112–120. https://doi.org/10.1016/j.wsif.2010.11.001

Mayes, R., & Sigurjóndóttir, H. (2010). Becoming a mother – becoming a father. In G. Llewellyn, R. Traustadóttir, D. McConnell, & H. Sigurjonsdóttir (Eds.), *Parents with intellectual disabilities: Past, present & futures* (pp. 17–33). Oxford, UK: Wiley-Blackwell.

McCarthy, M. (2009a). Contraception and women with intellectual disabilities. *Journal of Applied Research in Intellectual Disabilities, 22*, 363–369.

McCarthy, M. (2009b). 'I have the jab so I can't be blamed for getting pregnant': Contraception and women with learning disabilities. *Women's Studies International Forum, 32*, 198–208. https://doi.org/10.1016/j.wsif.2009.05.003

McCarthy, M. (2010). The sexual lives of women with learning disabilities. In G. Grant, P. Ramcharan, M. Flynn, & M. Richardson (Eds.), *Learning disability: A life cycle approach* (2nd ed., pp. 259–268). Maidenhead, England: Open University Press.

McCarthy, M., Bates, C., Triantafyllopoulou, P., Hunt, S., & Milne Skillman, K. J. J. (2019). "Put bluntly, they are targeted by the worst creeps society has to offer": Police and professionals' views and actions relating to domestic violence and women with intellectual disabilities. *Journal of Applied Research in Intellectual Disabilities, 32*, 71–81.

McConnell, D., Feldman, M., Aunos, M., Pacheco, L., Savage, A., Hahn, L., … Park, E. (2016). Ameliorating psychosocial risk among mothers with intellectual impairment. *Community Mental Health Journal, 52*, 944–953. https://doi.org/10.1007/s10597-015-9979-9

McConnell, D., Feldman, M., Aunos, M., & Prasad, N. (2011). Parental cognitive impairment and child maltreatment in Canada. *Child Abuse and Neglect, 35*, 621–632. https://doi.org/10.1016/j.chiabu.2011.04.005

McConnell, D., & Llewellyn, G. (2002). Stereotypes, parents with intellectual disability and child protection. *Journal of Social Welfare and Family Law, 24*, 297–317.

McConnell, D., Llewellyn, G., & Ferronato, L. (2006). Context contingent decision-making in child protection practice. *International Journal of Social Welfare, 15*, 230–239.

McGarry, A., Stenfert Kroese, B., & Cox, R. (2016). How do women with an intellectual disability experience the support of a doula during their pregnancy, childbirth and after the birth of their child? *Journal of Applied Research in Intellectual Disabilities, 29*, 21–33.

McGaw, S., & Cany, S. (2010). Supported decision making for women with intellectual disabilities. In G. Llewellyn, R. Traustadóttir, D. McConnell, & H. B. Sigujónsdóttir (Eds.), *Parents with intellectual disabilities. Past, present and futures*. West Sussex, UK: Wiley-Blackwell.

McGaw, S., & Newman, T. (2005). *What works for parents with learning disabilities?* Ilford, England: Barnardo's.

McGuire, B. E., & Bayley, A. A. (2011). Relationships, sexuality and decision-making capacity in people with an intellectual disability. *Current Opinion in Psychiatry, 24*, 398–402. https://doi.org/10.1097/YCO.0b013e328349bbcb

Meppelder, M., Hodes, M. W., Kef, S., & Schuengel, C. (2014). Parents with intellectual disabilities seeking professional parenting support: The role of working alliance, stress and informal support. *Child Abuse & Neglect, 38*, 1478–1486. https://doi.org/10.1016/j.chiabu.2014.04.006; PUBMED: 24856130.

Merton, R. K. (1946). *Social theory and social structures*. New York, NY: Free Press.

Mitra, M., Iezzoni, L. I., Zhang, J., Long-Bellil, L. M., Smeltzer, S. C., & Barton, B. A. (2015). Prevalence and risk factors for postpartum depression symptoms among women with disabilities. *Journal of Maternal and Child Health, 19*, 362–372.

Mitra, M., Parish, S. L., Clements, K. M., Cui, X., & Diop, H. (2015). Pregnancy outcomes among women with intellectual and developmental disabilities. *American Journal of Preventive Medicine, 48*, 300–308.

Neculaesei, A. N. (2015). Culture and gender role differences. *Cross-Cultural Management Journal, 1*, 31–35.

Neuman, R., & Reiter, S. (2017). Couple relationships as perceived by people with intellectual disability – implications for quality of life and self-concept. *International Journal of Developmental Disabilities, 63*, 138–147.

Nikkhesal, N., Nourizadeh, R., Dastgiri, S., & Mehrabi, E. (2018). The factors affecting women's decision about unplanned pregnancy: A hierarchical modeling strategy. *International Journal of Women's Health and Reproduction Sciences, 6*, 483–490.

Nirje, B. (1969). The normalization principle and its human management implications. In R. B. Kugel & W. Wolfensberger (Eds.), *Changing residential patterns for the mentally retarded*. Washington, DC: President's Committee on Mental Retardation.

O'Hara, J., & Martin, H. (2003). Parents with learning disabilities: A study of gender and cultural perspectives in East London. *British Journal of Learning Disabilities, 31*, 18–24.

Pacheco, L., & McConnell, D. (2017). Love and resistance of mothers with intellectual disability from ethnocultural communities in Canada. *Journal of Applied Research in Intellectual Disability, 30*, 501–510.

Pan, L., & Ye, J. (2012). Sexuality and marriage of women with intellectual disability in male-squeezed rural China. *Sexuality and Disability, 30*, 149–160.

Parish, S. L., Mitra, M., Son, E., Bonardi, A., Swoboda, P. T., & Igdalsky, L. (2015). Pregnancy outcomes among US women with intellectual and developmental disabilities. *American Journal on Intellectual and Developmental Disabilities, 120*, 433–443. https://doi.org/10.1352/1944-7558-120.5.433

Patel, P. (2017). Forced sterilization of women as discrimination. *Public Health Reviews, 38*, 15. https://doi.org/10.1186/s40985-017-0060-9

Patel, S., & Choate, L. (2014). Conducting child custody evaluations: Best practices for mental health counselors who are court-appointed as child custody evaluators. *Journal of Mental Health Counseling, 36*, 18–30.

Pestka, K., & Wendt, S. (2014). Belonging: Women living with intellectual disabilities and experiences of domestic violence. *Disability & Society, 29*, 1031–1045.

Potvin, L. A., Barnett, B. M., Brown, H. K., & Cobigo, V. (2019). "I didn't need people's negative thoughts": Women with intellectual and developmental disabilities reporting attitudes toward their pregnancy. *Canadian Journal of Nursing Research*. https://doi.org/10.1177/0844562118819924

Prilleltensky, O. (2004). My child is not my carer: Mothers with physical disabilities and the well-being of children. *Disability and Society, 19*, 209–223.

Purcal, C., Brennan, D., Cass, B., & Jenkins, B. (2014). Grandparents raising grandchildren: Impacts of life course stage on the experiences and costs of care. *Australian Journal of Social Issues, 49*, 467–488.

Redshaw, M., Malouf, R., Gao, H., & Gray, R. (2013). Women with disability: The experience of maternity care during pregnancy, labour, birth and the postnatal period. *BMC Pregnancy & Childbirth, 13*, 174. http://www.biomedcentral.com/1471-2393/13/174

Rice, J., & Sigurjónsdóttir, H. B. (2018). Notifying neglect: Child protection as an application of bureaucratic power against marginalized parents. *Human Organization, 77,* 112–121.

Rijlaarsdam, C., Van Rooij, I., & Fiedeldeij. (2017). Kwetsbare vrouwen best over te halen tot anti-conceptie. [Vulnerable women can be persuaded towards contraceptives]. *Medisch Contact, 3,* 18–20.

Roets, G., Adams, M., & Van Hove, G. (2006). Challenging the monologue about silent steriliza-tion: Implications for self-advocacy. *British Journal of Learning Disabilities, 34,* 167–174. https://doi.org/10.1111/j.1468-3156.2006.00415.x

Ross, L., & Solinger, R. (2017). *Reproductive justice: An introduction* (Vol. 1). Oakland, CA: University of California Press.

Schaafsma, D., Kok, G., Stoffelen, J. M., & Curfs, L. M. (2015). Identifying effective methods for teaching sex education to individuals with intellectual disabilities: A systematic review. *Journal of Sex Research, 52,* 412–432.

Schaafsma, D., Stoffelen, J. M. T., Kok, G., & Curfs, L. M. G. (2013). Exploring the development of existing sex education programmes for people with intellectual disabilities: An intervention mapping approach. *Journal of Applied Research in Intellectual Disabilities, 26,* 157–166.

SCLD. (2015). *Supported parenting. Refreshed Scottish good practice guidelines for supporting parents with a learning disability.* Glasgow, UK: SCLD. http://www.bristol.ac.uk/media-library/sites/sps/documents/wtpn/2016%20WTPN%20UPDATE%20OF%20THE%20GPG%20-%20finalised%20with%20cover.pdf

Servais, L. (2006). Sexual health care in persons with intellectual disabilities. *Mental Retardation and Developmental Disabilities Research Reviews, 12,* 48–56.

Sheerin, F. K., Keenan, P. M., & Lawler, D. (2013). Mothers with intellectual disabili-ties: Interactions with children and family services in Ireland. *British Journal of Learning Disabilities, 41,* 189–196. https://doi.org/10.1111/bld.12034

Shuttleworth, R., & Kasnitz, D. (2006). Cultural context of disability. In G. Albrecht (Ed.), *Encyclopedia of disability* (pp. 330–337). Thousand Oaks, CA: Sage.

Sigurjónsdóttir, H. B., & Rice, J. G. (2017). 'Framed': Terminating the parenting rights of parents with intellectual disability in Iceland. *Journal of Applied Research in Intellectual Disabilities, 30,* 543–552.

Sigurjónsdóttir, H. B., & Traustadóttir, R. (2000). Motherhood, family and community life. In R. Traustadóttir & K. Johnson (Eds.), *Women with intellectual disabilities: Finding a place in the world* (pp. 253–270). London: Jessica Kingsley Publishers.

Sinclair, J., Unruh, D., Lindstrom, L., & Scanlon, D. (2015). Barriers to sexuality for individuals with intellectual and developmental disabilities: A literature review. *Education and Training in Autism and Developmental Disabilities, 50,* 3–16.

Spencer, M. (2001). Proceed with caution: The limitations of current parenting capacity assess-ments. *Developing Practice, 1,* 16–24.

Spencer, M. (2012). *We are a family. Intellectual disability rights service.* Retrieved 17 April 2019 from https://m.youtube.com/watch?v=yhGEdYvkaas

Starke, M., Wade, C., Feldman, M. A., & Mildon, R. (2013). Parenting with disabilities: Experiences from implementing a parenting support programme in Sweden. *Journal of Intellectual Disabilities, 17,* 145–156.

Stefánsdóttir, G. V. (2014). Sterilisation and women with intellectual disability in Iceland. *Journal of Intellectual & Developmental Disability, 39,* 188–197. https://doi.org/10.3109/13668250.2014.899327

Swain, S. (2014). *History of inquiries reviewing institutions providing care for children.* Royal Commission into Institutional Responses to Child Sexual Abuse, Commonwealth of Australia, viewed 3rd March, 2019. http://www.childabuseroyalcommission.gov.au/documents/pub-lished- research/historical-perspectives-report-3-history-of-inquir.pdf

Tahir, M., Sword, C., & Feldman, M. A. (2015). Evaluation of a game-based parent education intervention to increase positive parent-child interactions in parents with learning difficulties. *Behaviour Analysis: Research and Practice, 15,* 187–200.

Tarleton, B., & Porter, S. (2012). Crossing no man's land: A specialist support service for parents with learning disabilities. *Child & Family Social Work, 17*, 233–243.

Tarleton, B., Ward, L., & Howard, J. (2006). *Finding the right support: A review of issues and positive practice in supporting parents with learning difficulties and their children*. Bristol, UK: University of Bristol. www.baringfoundation.org.uk/FRSupportSummary.pdf

The United Nations Convention on the Rights of Persons with Disabilities (2008). *Convention on the rights of persons with disabilities*. https://www.un.org/development/desa/disabilities/convention-on-the-rights-of-persons-with-disabilities.html

Theodore, K., Foulds, D., Wilshaw, P., Colborne, A., Lee, J. N. Y., Mallaghan, L., & Skelton, J. (2018). 'We want to be parents like everybody else': Stories of parents with learning disabilities. *International Journal of Developmental Disabilities, 64*, 184–194. https://doi.org/10.108 0/20473869.2018.1448233

Tilburg, M. (2012). Babyroute, een goede start. *Notitie Samenwerking met zwangere vrouwen en partners met een (lichte) verstandelijke beperking en hun toekomstig kind*. [Baby route, a healthy start. Report on collaboration with pregnant couples with ID concerning their future child]. Retrieved 7 May 2019 from https://www.kennispleingehandicaptensector.nl/images/KGS/images/Nieuws/Kinderwens%20Zwangerschap%20en%20Anitconceptie%20Rieanne%20v%20Laarhoven.pdf

Tilley, E., Walmsley, J., Earle, S., & Atkinson, D. (2012). 'The silence is roaring': Sterilization, reproductive rights and women with intellectual disabilities. *Disability & Society, 27*, 413–426. https://doi.org/10.1080/09687599.2012.654991

Traustadóttir, R., & Johnson, K. (2000). *Women with intellectual disabilities: Finding a place in the world*. London, UK: Jessica Kingsley Publishers.

Traustadóttir, R., & Sigurjónsdóttir, H. B. (2008). The 'mother' behind the mother: Three generations of mothers with intellectual disabilities and their family support networks. *Journal of Applied Research in Intellectual Disabilities, 21*, 331–340. https://doi.org/10.1111/j.1468-3148.2008.00450.x

Traustadóttir, R., & Sigurjónsdóttir, H. B. (2010). Parenting and resistance: Strategies in dealing with services and professionals. In G. Llewellyn, R. Traustadóttir, D. McConnell, & H. Sigurjónsdóttir (Eds.), *Parents with intellectual disability: Past, present and futures* (pp. 1–14). West Sussex, UK: Wiley-Blackwell.

Tymchuk, A. J., Lakin, K. C., & Luckasson, R. (2001). *The forgotten generation: The status and challenges of adults with mild cognitive limitations*. Baltimore, MA: Paul H. Brookes. (387 pages).

Van Schrojenstein Lantman-de Valk, H. M. J., Rook, F., & Maaskant, M. A. (2011). The use of contraception by women with intellectual disabilities. *Journal of Intellectual Disability Research, 55*, 434–440. https://doi.org/10.1111/j.1365-2788.2011.01395.x

Wade, C., Llewellyn, G., & Matthews, J. (2008). Review of parent training interventions for parents with intellectual disability. *Journal of Applied Research in Intellectual Disabilities, 21*, 351–366.

Walsh-Gallagher, D., Mc Conkey, R., Sinclair, M., & Clarke, R. (2011). Normalising birth for women with a disability: The challenges facing practitioners. *Midwifery, 29*, 294–299. https://doi.org/10.1016/j.midw.2011.10.007

Walsh-Gallagher, D., Sinclair, M., & Mc Conkey, R. (2012). The ambiguity of disabled women's experiences of pregnancy, childbirth and motherhood: A phenomenological understanding. *Midwifery, 28*, 156–162.

Weaver, H. N. (2015). Disability through a native American lens: Examining influences of culture and colonization. *Journal of Social Work in Disability & Rehabilitation, 14*, 148–162. https://doi.org/10.1080/1536710X.2015.1068256

Weiber, I., Berglund, J., Tengland, P. A., & Eklund, M. (2011). Children born to women with intellectual disabilities–5-year incidence in a Swedish county. *Journal of Intellectual Disability Research, 55*, 1078–1085.

Weiber, I., Eklund, M., & Tengland, P. (2016). The characteristics of local support systems, and the roles of professionals, in supporting families where a mother has an intellectual disability. *Journal of Applied Research in Intellectual Disabilities, 29*, 197–210. https://doi.org/10.1111/jar.12169

Willems, D. L., De Vries, J. N., Isarin, J., & Reinders, J. S. (2007). Parenting by persons with intellectual disability: An explorative study in the Netherlands. *Journal of Intellectual Disability Research, 51*, 537–544.

Wilson, S., McKenzie, K., Quayle, E., & Murray, G. C. (2013). The postnatal support needs of mothers with an intellectual disability. *Midwifery, 29*, 592–598. https://doi.org/10.1016/j.midw.2012.05.002

WTPN. (2016). *Working together with parents network (WTPN) update of the DH/DfES good practice guidance on working with parents with a learning disability (2007)*. Bristol, UK: University of Bristol. http://www.bristol.ac.uk/media-library/sites/sps/documents/wtpn/2016%20WTPN%20UPDATE%20OF%20THE%20GPG%20-%20finalised%20with%20cover.pdf

Wu, J., Zhang, J., Mitra, M., Parish, S. L., & Reddy, G. K. M. (2018). Provision of moderately and highly effective reversible contraception to insured women with intellectual and developmental disabilities. *Obstetrics & Gynecology, 132*, 565–574.

Zampas, C., & Lamacˇková, A. (2011). Forced and coerced sterilization of women in Europe. *International Journal of Gynecology & Obstetrics, 114*, 163–166. https://doi.org/10.1016/j.ijgo.2011.05.002

Zilberstein, K. (2016). Parenting in families of low socioeconomic status: A review with implications for child welfare practice. *Family Court Review, 54*, 221–231.

Adults with Intellectual Disability: Choice and Control in the Context of Family

Bernadette Curryer, Angela Dew, Roger J. Stancliffe, and Michele Y. Wiese

Introduction

An awareness and insight about the interaction between adults with intellectual disability and their family are essential to understanding the experience and enactment of self-determination. Family, particularly parents and siblings, are a primary source of support for many adults with intellectual disability throughout their life. The United Nation's Convention on the Rights of Persons with Disabilities (UNCRPD) recognizes as a general principle "Respect for inherent dignity, individual autonomy including the freedom to make one's own choices, and independence of persons" (United Nations, 2006, p. 5). However, reliance on family support to enact such freedom results in a strong family influence, and at times limitations, on choice and decision-making. A number of western countries have an increased focus on individualized funding for people with disability, requiring lifestyle choices around the setting and realization of goals and plans. The natural authority of the family (Kendrick, 1996), recognized as a counterbalance to governmental or service provider influence (Curryer, Stancliffe, & Dew, 2015), may in effect support or restrict the self-determination of adults with intellectual disability.

B. Curryer (✉)
Centre for Disability Research and Policy, Faculty of Health Sciences, University of Sydney, Sydney, NSW, Australia
e-mail: bcur3628@uni.sydney.edu.au

A. Dew
Disability and Inclusion, School of Health and Social Development, Faculty of Health, Deakin University, Melbourne, VIC, Australia

R. J. Stancliffe
Centre for Disability Research and Policy, The University of Sydney, Sydney, NSW, Australia

M. Y. Wiese
School of Social Sciences and Psychology, Western Sydney University, Sydney, NSW, Australia

© Springer Nature Switzerland AG 2020
R. J. Stancliffe et al. (eds.), *Choice, Preference, and Disability*, Positive Psychology and Disability Series, https://doi.org/10.1007/978-3-030-35683-5_15

This chapter will explore the following:

- Self-determination theory and how it may be viewed in the context of family relationships
- The concept of adulthood and how it pertains to adults with intellectual disability
- The experience of exercising choice and control by adults with intellectual disability within the context of family
- The role, influence, and strategies of parents and the factors that have an impact on their level of support for the exercise of choice and control by their adult children with intellectual disability
- The role of siblings
- What works in terms of increasing choice and control within the family

Brief scenarios are used to demonstrate the issues discussed and to encourage the reader to think about the practical expression of these issues. While not based on specific people, the scenarios are constructed from the general experiences of people with intellectual disability, as observed by the authors.

Self-determination Theory

In this chapter, we draw on the tripartite ecological theory of self-determination (Abery & Stancliffe, 2003) to help understand the experience of choice and control in the context of family. This theory recognizes that self-determination is relevant to all people, but the tripartite theory has been developed and evaluated mostly in relation to people with disability, particularly intellectual and developmental disability. As discussed later in the chapter, our own research and that of others point to a degree of shared choice and control between adults with intellectual disability and their close family members, in particular, parents and siblings.

Two features of the tripartite theory make it particularly relevant to the experience of self-determination by adults with intellectual disability within the family. Firstly, as an *ecological* theory, the tripartite theory places consistent emphasis on the importance of the interaction between the person and the environment, including the family environment. For example, everyday environments that provide frequent opportunities to express preferences and to make choices support the development of greater self-determination, which in turn may help create even more such opportunities.

Secondly, one component of the tripartite theory involves "the amount of control desired" (Abery & Stancliffe, 2003, p. 44). That is, there is a recognition that often people do not wish to exercise total control over every aspect of their life and may voluntarily cede some degree of control to others who they consider more experienced or knowledgeable. Deciding which aspects of life one wishes to control, the amount of control to exercise, and who to ask for help are, in themselves, all manifestations of self-determination. For example, many people choose to follow recommendations from health professionals, rather than deciding independently how to deal with a health condition. In addition, while sufficient choice is important for quality of life, excessive choice can be stressful and is associated with reduced well-being (Schwartz & Ward, 2004). For this reason as well, individuals may seek to manage such stress by asking for assistance from others about certain choices. However, notions of voluntariness and reversibility are important in such circumstances, as noted by Abery and Stancliffe (2003, p. 49) who stated that:

> Individuals who exercise low levels of personal control are self-determined only in cases where they voluntarily cede control over decision-making (and can take back personal control whenever they wish).

Beyond notions of others having greater knowledge, parental authority over younger children, and the role of disability service staff in supporting service users, the tripartite theory has not focussed in depth on who should provide support for preference, choice, and control. By contrast, mainstream self-determination theory identifies *relatedness* as one of three basic needs, with an emphasis on the importance of close, trusting relationships with others (Ryan & Deci, 2017). To date, self-determination theories as they relate to people with intellectual disability, including the tripartite ecological theory of self-determination, have placed little explicit emphasis on the role of trusting relationships in the exercise of choice and self-determination (Curryer et al., 2015). Our research on choice and control by adults with intellectual disability in the context of family indicates that such relationships are important (Curryer, Stancliffe, Dew, & Wiese, 2018) and, depending on how they are enacted, may enhance or constrain choice.

Adulthood

> The path to adulthood in contemporary western society is defined as a more individualized, complex, and unpredictable process than before due to changes in social and institutional structures. (Midjo & Aune, 2018, p. 34).

Exploration of the concept of adulthood is important when considering the exercise of choice, preference, and control. Achieving adult status is typically commensurate with full attainment of the right to control of one's life. However, the transition to adulthood for young people evolves over a number of years, and there are significant differences in the way individuals—with and without disability—experience this transition. The attitudes and perceptions of family members regarding the transition to adulthood of their son or daughter with intellectual disability are important. Family members potentially play a crucial role in supporting the person to develop attributes of self-determination which facilitate their attainment of adult roles and responsibilities. In what some parents have described as the "black hole of transition" (Biswas, Tickle, Golijani-Moghaddam, & Almack, 2017, p. 103), the current policy, service provision and community focus on autonomy and self-determination for young adults with intellectual disability, can be worrying and frustrating for parents as they assess their son's or daughter's preparedness and capacity to take their place in the adult world (Biswas et al., 2017).

What Will Trang Do After He Finishes School?

Trang is 18 years old with a passion for football. He has Down syndrome and has been attending a local special school following access to early intervention since the age of 2. School has been a big part of Trang's and his mother's lives. Trang's mother has been an active member of the parent's association and a regular attendee at their family support group.

Trang will shortly complete his final year of school. Individualized funding means a greater range of choices are available, but these require goal-setting, planning, and ongoing coordination. The amount of paid support Trang can receive after he finishes school will vary depending on what option is chosen. Trang and his family are still considering what he will do next. His options include a transition to work program, disability-specific sheltered work, trying to find mainstream employment, or attendance at a disability day program.

- How do you think Trang and his family feel about these important decisions?
- What may be some of their concerns?
- How will Trang's preferences and choices influence what he does next?
- How will Trang know what he wants?

Defining at what point a person is deemed to be an "adult" is contested and may have implications for parental support towards self-determination. For example, in a small qualitative study exploring 12 white British parents' views of the transition to adulthood of their 11 sons and daughters with severe intellectual disability, Biswas et al. (2017) identified 3 main markers of transition to adulthood: (a) physical/bodily changes denoting sexual maturity, (b) age of legal majority (typically 18 or 21 years), and (c) social markers, including milestones and attributes such as getting a job and moving out of home. Within western cultures, these markers may be considered universal regardless of disability; however, as Biswas et al. (2017) stated, parents in their study used comparisons with non-disabled peers to reveal that "if a parent struggles to notice signs of adult development in their child, they may be less inclined to make any changes to encourage their child's transition to adulthood" (p. 102).

In addition to the biological changes that occur with puberty, and legal age criteria, there are two broad schools of thought in western society, not mutually exclusive, which identify when a person may be considered to have achieved the social markers of "adult" status and deemed able to exercise control over their life choices. First, adult status is attributed to the attainment of transition milestones, such as leaving school and getting a full-time job, going on to further education, leaving the parental home to establish an independent residence, entering a romantic relationship, and becoming a parent (Hendry & Kloep, 2010; Janus, 2009; van Naarden Braun, Yeargin-Allsopp, & Lollar, 2006; Wells, Sandefur, & Hogan, 2003). Hendry and Kloep (2010) identified from a sample of 38 non-disabled young adults aged 17–20 living in South Wales, UK, that employment was viewed as the primary marker of transition to adulthood, regardless of living situation (still in the parental home or living independently). The authors also identified the importance of considering socio-economic status, culture, and life experiences in relation to adult-milestone achievement. Given that attaining employment is often difficult for people with intellectual disability, reliance upon this marker is problematic for assessing a person's level of self-determination. Indeed, UK disability scholar Mark Priestly (2003) warned that relying on achievement of milestones, including but not restricted to employment, to determine adulthood discriminates against those who may never achieve some or any of these milestones.

Does Being an Adult Mean Living an Adult Lifestyle?
Bev is just about to turn 21 and is looking forward to a birthday dinner with her family.
  Bev:

- Lives with her parents, with no plans or options to move out
- Attends a disability day program from 9 am to 3 pm each weekday (same as school hours)
- Is dropped off and picked up by her mother each day
- Does not have access to her bank account, but Mum does give her "pocket money".
- Has a boyfriend, although she is only allowed to see him once a week, when her Mum and his group home staff arrange it

- How "adult" is Bev's lifestyle?
- How are Bev's lifestyle preferences and choices supported?
- How does Bev know what kind of lifestyle she would prefer?
- How likely is it that Bev's parents will support her to achieve a lifestyle of her preference if it is not one with which they agree?

Priestly's (2003) warning is seemingly borne out in a study conducted by Wells et al. (2003) using longitudinal data from two large US national surveys, the National Longitudinal Transition Study of Special Education Students, 1987–1991 ($N = 5297$), and the National Educational Study of 1998 ($N = 12,490$) to examine educational attainment, competitive employment, residential independence, and family formation (marriage and parenthood) for people with a disability aged between 18 and 26. The authors reported that having a disability negatively affected the socio-economic and personal outcomes experienced, as 40% of those who attended special education continued to live at home with parents and were not involved in education or employment after leaving school. In contrast, according to the Australian Bureau of Statistics *Australian Social Trends* report (2009), 23% of young people in the general community continued to live at home with their parents, and the majority of these were either employed and/or studying. In relation to their study, Wells et al. (2003) stated:

> Disability and type of disability profoundly impact youths' early steps toward adulthood, and among young persons with disabilities, the effects of disability and the type of disability greatly overshadow those of race and ethnicity, family structure, and number of siblings. (p. 826).

Shogren and Shaw (2017) analysed the National Longitudinal Transition Study-2 data to investigate the relationship between race/ethnicity, gender, and family income on self-determination and early adulthood outcomes for 1250 students with diverse disabilities. With respect to income, the authors reported low levels of financial independence among the cohort, linked to lack of employment opportunities. Family income was the major variable in students' post school outcomes, with higher family income facilitating access to programs.

The second school of thought in relation to achievement of adulthood is the development of personal qualities. Those recognized as indicative of adult status include accepting responsibility for one's actions and decisions, making independent decisions, becoming self-sufficient, and gaining financial independence (Arnett, 1998, 2000). In describing development of these personal qualities in early adulthood among the general US population of young adult college students aged 21–28, Arnett used the term *emerging adulthood*. Arnett concluded that the acquisition of the individual qualities of self-sufficiency, responsibility, and independent control over decisions and finances was more important in conceiving oneself as an adult than the achievement of specific events such as marriage, having children, or establishing a career.

This view of adulthood may be more inclusive of people with disability as it is possible, although sometimes difficult, to exercise agency while relying on others to carry out activities necessary to achieve life goals (Galambos, Darrah, & Magill-Evans, 2007). For example, a Norwegian study by Midjo and Aune (2018) identified the key role that mothers play in coordinating tasks and taking responsibility for their young adult son or daughter with disability's transition to live independently outside the family home. The concerns mothers expressed about this transition included their young adult child's ability to take care of themselves, eat a healthy diet, have friendships, be safe, and manage their finances. Despite these concerns, many mothers in this study recognized their young adult son's or daughter's competence in learning new skills and ensured he or she actively engaged in future planning, while at the same time recognizing his or her need for some ongoing assistance in certain areas of life. Development of personal qualities, as described by Arnett (1998, 2000), speaks directly to the focus of this book on preference, choice, and self-determination, as these qualities are indicative of choice and control.

Experience of Choice and Control Within the Context of Family

Importance of Family

From the research of lived experience, it is clear that family relationships have a major impact on the lives of adults with intellectual disability. Family are seen as central players in the lives of adults with intellectual disability and are recognized as having a crucial impact on their family member's happiness, through the provision of care and support (Haigh et al., 2013; Widmer, Kempf-Constantin, Robert-Tissot, Lanzi, & Carminati, 2008). Adults with intellectual disability recognize a natural tie between themselves and the family members involved in their lives, seeing these as valuable relationships offering reciprocal benefits (Curryer et al., 2018).

Taking Control, Having Choice

Increased choice and control is promoted as a goal and expected outcome of contemporary disability supports, including those involving individualized disability funding. Across the western world, individualized funding examples include Australia's National Disability Insurance Scheme, direct payments through Canada's Community Living British Columbia, personal budgets in Ireland, and self-directed US Medicaid Home and Community-Based Services funding (Friedman, 2018). Funding, assessed on an individual basis, may require the setting of goals, development of a plan, and identification of support requirements. For people with intellectual disability, taking control in such complex systems may be difficult. The presence of a strong advocate, often the family, may be important if funding commensurate with the person's lifestyle choices is to be provided.

In a study about the lived experience of choice and decision-making by adults with intellectual disability, Curryer et al. (2018) reported that making choices and decisions gave the participants a sense of achievement. These adults recognized that at times they made mistakes and believed these should be accepted as part of the learning process. Participants thought they learned about choice preference not only through the act of making their own choices but also by watching the choice-making of others. Family members were acknowledged as important role models, both about what should and should not be done. A sense of increased choice and control was reported by these adults as they grew older. Parents were viewed as less controlling, with siblings often seen as encouraging parents to let go and allow the individual to try new things. The experience of increased adult responsibility resulted in a self-reported sense of pride which they wanted family to recognize and share. Participants were keen to prove to family that they could successfully control their lives (Curryer et al., 2018).

Self-awareness, knowing what they liked and having the confidence to speak up, was identified by adults with intellectual disability as a way of taking control. By having people around—frequently family members—who listened to them, and to whom they could speak honestly and openly, they were able to demonstrate their ability to take some control over life and actively participate in mutual decision-making (Curryer et al., 2018). An interdependent decision-making process, characterized by seeking advice and discussing options until a decision is reached (Bach, 2009), is evident in many of the experiences described. Family support was recognized as integral to the individual's ability to practise and develop skills necessary for self-determined behaviour. The skills required for self-determination include choice and decision-making, goal setting, and problem-solving (Wehmeyer, 2003).

Accepting Limitations to Control

Despite many positive family support experiences reported, the autonomy and independence referred to by the UN Convention (United Nations, 2006) are not always reflected in actual experience. Common barriers to control, identified by adults with intellectual disability, include overprotection by parents, a need to constantly prove their ability, and support which does not meet needs (Haigh et al., 2013; Jahoda & Markova, 2004; Shogren & Broussard, 2011).

When Choices Don't Work

David has just moved into a small, separate unit in the back yard of his parents' house. He decides to invite his mother and father, both of whom are keen home cooks, to dinner. He chooses to try a new chicken recipe as he really wants to cook more for himself.

When his parents arrive, he serves the dinner, but the chicken is not cooked through so cannot be eaten. His mum suggests that perhaps he should just reheat frozen meals rather than try to cook full meals. His Dad offers to go and get a pizza.

- What message might David take from this reaction?
- How could this impact David's experience of self-determination?
- What could be done instead to support David's preference and choice to learn to cook?

In our recent study examining the experience of choice and control by adults with intellectual disability (Curryer et al., 2018), participants generally reported satisfaction with the level of control they had in their lives, despite acknowledging limitations placed on their choice and decision-making. Some participants described both recognizing and accepting their family as either the final decision-maker or gatekeeper of what choices they could make independently. Participants lived in a variety of situations; some remained within the family home, while others lived on their own or in disability service-run group homes. Family involvement, the degree of which varied according to the living situation and closeness of the relationship, was reported in some day-to-day decisions, such as what to eat, but more often in major life decisions such as employment, living situation, and relationships. The final decision-making role was not given to just anyone in the family, only to someone trusted. This trusted relationship appeared to create a sense that, even when family did step in and restrict or override an individual's choice-making, this was seen as a sign of love and ultimately accepted by the adult with intellectual disability (Curryer et al., 2018).

Supporting Choice and Control: Roles and Strategies of Parents

Family support for the self-determination of an adult with intellectual disability is, for many families, an ongoing struggle as they try to balance the rights of the individual to control their own life with concerns over the potential consequences of choices. This is particularly true when choices are viewed as unwise or different from those preferred by the family. Families are aware that any consequences may affect not only the individual but often the parent providing support and even the family as a whole. Examples range from relatively minor inconveniences such as providing transport if a bus is missed or financial support if money is spent imprudently to possible major family involvement in supporting the upbringing of a child. Concern about consequences may result in varying family support, ranging from proactive empowerment with exploration of options and consideration of the consequences to fear-based protection and restriction of options (Curryer et al., 2018).

For people with high support needs around decision-making, choice-making supporters are required to acknowledge, interpret, and then act on the will and preference expressed. Preference may not be verbalized, instead communicated through informal methods such as body language. A close relationship, together with a positive assumption about the capacity of the person to make their own decisions, is required for effective support (Watson, 2016). However, it is unclear to what degree concerns for consequences influence the way family may enact the will of the person. Unlike support workers who generally attempt to take a neutral position about options, family support for options is impacted by the vision they hold about the individual's life (Bigby, Whiteside, & Douglas, 2017).

Setting Limits to Choice and Control

In-depth knowledge and an understanding of a person's preferences, together with a sense of responsibility to protect, are reasons given as to why parents feel justified in making choices on behalf of their adult children with intellectual disability (Dyke, Bourke, Llewellyn, & Leonard, 2013; Foley, 2013). Limiting choice and control is often based on their perception of their adult child with intellectual disability, citing the individual's vulnerability, previous poor decision-making, and inability to fully understand consequences (Murphy, Clegg, & Almack, 2011; Power, 2008; Saaltink, MacKinnon, Owen, & Tardif-Williams, 2012). As the degree of complexity and risk involved in a decision increases, so does the family's belief that they need to intervene (Mitchell, 2012). There may also be a tension between the parental vision for their adult child's life and the actual preferences of the individual (Reindl, Waltz, & Schippers, 2016) with any choices or decisions not in line with family values and norms particularly prone to limitation or overrule (Saaltink et al., 2012).

Balancing Choice and Risk

Claire, 19, loves music, and her favourite band has just announced a tour. She wants to go to one of their concerts with her boyfriend from the disability-specific sheltered workshop where she works. They want to purchase standing room tickets at the front of the stadium, nearest to the band.

When she asks her mother to help her to order the tickets online, a process she finds confusing, her mother agrees. However, Claire's mother insists that she goes too, saying she will drive them, rather than have them go on public transport at night, and that the seated tickets towards the back are better as they will be more comfortable. Claire's mother goes ahead and orders the seated tickets that she prefers.

- How do you think Claire might feel about her mother's help?
- Why do you think her mother overrode Claire's preference?
- Were the mother's actions reasonable?
- How can perceived dangers be balanced with choice and preference?
- Whose preference should take precedence?

Factors which may impact on the degree of support for the individual's choices include:

- The family's values and beliefs around the concept of self-determination and the level of support for an individual's right to a life of their choosing (Knox & Bigby, 2007; Mitchell, 2012)
- The perceived capacity of the individual to make these choices, including their decision-making and problem-solving skills and level of understanding of consequences (Mitchell, 2012; Murphy et al., 2011; Saaltink et al., 2012)
- The type of decision and level of complexity and risk (Mitchell, 2012)

- Any potential consequences and on whom these consequences will fall
- How close these choices are to the wishes and beliefs of the family, including cultural considerations (Reindl et al., 2016; Saaltink et al., 2012)
- The level of practical or emotional support the choice requires
- The legal status of the individual, including whether they are under guardianship (Stancliffe, Abery, Springborg, & Elkin, 2000).

Influencing Choice

Parents may have significant influence over the choices of an adult with intellectual disability due to their valued position and ongoing support role. Many people with intellectual disability do not live with a partner or have children and remain in the family home for longer (Heller et al., 2011). Adults with intellectual disability have identified a smaller number of supportive family members and may feel less connected to the extended family than the general population (van Asselt-Goverts, Embregts, & Hendriks, 2013; Widmer et al., 2008). In western countries, such as Australia, most of the family support falls to parents, with the mother usually identified as the primary caregiver (Australian Bureau of Statistics, 2014).

Who Has Control?
Leanne requires support in some aspects of daily living such as housework, cooking, and shopping. Leanne's mother has always arranged and attended medical appointments with her.

Leanne has recently started a relationship with Brett and has begun to talk about getting married and having a baby. She wants to have her birth control implant removed, but her mother is refusing to organize an appointment or accompany her to the doctor.

- What might Leanne's mother's concerns be about Leanne's choice to have a baby?
- In what way is Leanne's mother exercising control over Leanne and Brett's future lives?
- How might Leanne's choice and the mother's concerns be negotiated?
- What about Brett's view and choices, how could these be considered?

The influence of parents may be felt in a number of ways, some quite subtle, yet still impacting on the options available and choices made. These include the following:

- The filtering of options—this may occur through identification and discussion of options preferred by parents, excluding those options not supported by the parents.

Reduced access to information, enhanced by issues such as low literacy, lack of internet access, or not knowing where or how to access information may limit the awareness of alternative options by adults with intellectual disability.

- Failure to provide the support required to successfully carry out options that they, the parents, do not agree with, including removal of assistance around transport, communication, or access to financial resources, knowing that without such support, the person would not be able to undertake preferred action.
- An expectation and acceptance that parents will make, or at least give approval, to any decisions, as this is the way things have always been done and no one challenges or questions this.

The desire of an adult with intellectual disability to please family may also increase the likelihood that they will choose the option preferred and put forward by family. Acceptance of the family's choice may be enhanced by their wish and need for ongoing support and care.

Role of Siblings

Siblings experience the longest and most durable family relationship (Cicirelli, 1995). Given their often close ages, siblings frequently share experiences and confidences that mean they advocate for each other with parents. The broader sibling literature where disability is not present suggests that in childhood, sibling relationships are both egalitarian, with siblings forming a child's first peer group (Sanders, 2004), and hierarchical as older siblings act as role models for younger ones (Howe & Recchia, 2005; McHale & Crouter, 2005; Stoneman & Brody, 1993). In adulthood, sibling relationships become increasingly voluntary and, where they are maintained, provide continuity across the life course not evident in any other relationship (Connidis, 2001). Siblings therefore have the potential to be hugely influential in each other's lives. Nonetheless, the majority of siblings will not be required to make decisions on behalf of their brothers and sisters as; if circumstances indicate a need for this, a spouse or adult child will more likely do so.

In contrast to the relational approach taken in the broader sibling research, historical scholarship investigating the relationship between siblings where one has an intellectual or developmental disability has focused on the (often negatively perceived) psychosocial impact of disability on non-disabled siblings (see reviews by Damiani, 1999; Dew, Balandin, & Llewellyn, 2008; Meyers & Vipond, 2005). More recent sibling disability research (e.g. Atkin & Tozer, 2013; Dew, Llewellyn, & Balandin, 2013; Meltzer, 2017; Meltzer & Kramer, 2016) has sought a nuanced relational understanding of siblingship beyond the traditional discourses around burden, developmental gaps, or caring duties.

Indeed, the long-standing nature of the relationship very often means that siblings know their brother or sisters' life history, health information, service usage, and preferences (Dew et al., 2013). Siblings often assume a role as a critical advocate for the choice, control, inclusion, and effective communication of their brother or sister with intellectual disability (Bigby, Webber, & Bowers, 2014; Dew, Balandin, & Llewellyn, 2011).

Alongside a long-term shared understanding, Tozer and Atkin (2015) suggested that the role of non-disabled siblings in the life of their brother or sister with intellectual disability may involve a degree of obligation or duty, especially as parents age and may no longer be able to provide support in the ways they previously did. This increased sense of obligation is heightened due to many people with life-long cognitive disability not marrying or having children, thus placing greater reliance on siblings (Bigby, 2000). Increased obligation later in life has the potential to fundamentally change the nature of the relationship between siblings with and without disability.

A substantial body of work around future planning by ageing parent carers of an adult son or daughter with intellectual disability by US researchers Tamar Heller and colleagues (Heller & Arnold, 2010; Heller & Kramer, 2009), Marsha Seltzer and colleagues (Orsmond & Seltzer, 2000, 2007; Seltzer, Greenberg, Krauss, Gordon, & Judge, 1997; Seltzer, Greenberg, Orsmond, & Lounds, 2005; Seltzer & Krauss, 1993), and Australian Christine Bigby and colleagues (Bigby, 1997; Bigby, 2000; Bigby et al., 2014) identifies the lack of formal planning by parents and an, often unstated, reliance on siblings to take over caregiving roles. As parental health deteriorates, siblings gradually take on greater responsibility for supporting their brother or sister with intellectual disability. However, this often occurs in a de facto fashion with little negotiation between parents and siblings or indeed between siblings with and without disability. The evidence suggests that siblings provide more emotional than practical support and typically sisters provide more support than brothers (Orsmond & Seltzer, 2000). However, once parents are no longer able to do so, non-disabled siblings find themselves making decisions and/or engaging in caregiving tasks that were previously their parent's domain, and this may cause discomfort for siblings both with and without disability. Indeed, as indicated by Dew et al. (2008), the "quantum and type of support may extend well beyond what is typically expected of a sibling relationship" (p. 487).

Future Considerations

Salma, 42, has an intellectual disability and lives with her now elderly mother. Her sister, Laila, 45, lives an hour's drive away and usually drops in every Sunday and takes Salma out for a few hours, often having afternoon tea at a local café. They have done this for many years and both look forward to the outing.

Recently their mother's health has deteriorated, and the need for her to enter an aged care facility is suggested by her doctor. Their mother is refusing to leave Salma alone and won't discuss moving until Salma's future living situation is settled. Salma wants to stay in the family home; however Laila realizes that Salma will need much more support from her beyond a weekly outing. Laila does not know how this can fit in with her life which includes two teenage sons, a husband, and full-time work.

- How might Laila approach both Salma and their mother to explore options that reflect Salma's preferences and are sustainable into the future?
- If Salma's choice is not supported by either her mother or Laila, how might a solution be negotiated?
- As Laila's role changes, what is the potential impact on the sisters' relationship?

Acting as arbiters and advocates, the egalitarian nature of sibling relationships built over a lifetime means non-disabled siblings are in an ideal position to negotiate with parents and foster opportunities for their brother or sister with intellectual disability to identify their preferences, exercise choice, and control and have a greater degree of self-determination.

Increasing Choice and Control Within the Family Context: What Works

Little is known about what works to support adults with intellectual disability to have greater choice and control within their family relationships. The maintenance of strong, positive family relationships is important to the quality of life of people with intellectual disability and has been recognized by both people with intellectual disability (Curryer et al., 2018; Haigh et al., 2013; Miller, Cooper, Cook, & Petch, 2008; van Asselt-Goverts et al., 2013) and their families (Dyke et al., 2013; Saaltink et al., 2012). Therefore, efforts to support growing self-determination should not jeopardize these important relationships.

Environmental factors, including the family, have been identified as having more impact on the expression of self-determination than individual characteristics (Caouette, Lachapelle, Moreau, & Lussier-Desrochers, 2018; Wehmeyer & Garner, 2003). The cultural belief system of the family, particularly about roles and autonomy of family members, has an impact on both the understanding and exercise of self-determination (Abery & Stancliffe, 2003). In comparison to western cultures, many non-western cultures have a concept of self that is closely linked to the family and one's role within the family, with less recognition of individualism or autonomy (McCarthy, 2012); therefore, support for individually focused self-determination may not be considered. Cultural views about gender roles and vulnerability may also have an impact on the level of support for self-determination of the individual. As identified in the tripartite ecological theory of self-determination, self-determination is the result of interaction between an individual and their environment (Abery & Stancliffe, 2003). The family often plays a major role in the establishment and maintenance of links with, and between, the multiple settings in which the person with intellectual disability lives his or her life. It is often the family who take on the responsibility for the identification of choice options and ensuring ongoing contact and access to those chosen. Examples may include applying for funding, meeting and assessing suitability of disability service providers, and identifying a range of other study, work, or recreational opportunities. The family has, therefore, an opportunity to not only exert influence directly on the individual but also have an indirect influence on their choice and control within these settings.

While families may be in a prime position to influence the development and exercise of self-determination in their family members with intellectual disability, little is known about how they do this, what support they may need, and any cultural implications (Wehmeyer, 2014). Research focused on self-determination and intellectual disability has generally taken place in non-family settings such as schools or disability services (Carter et al., 2013). The little research that has been done within the family context indicates that families generally have a more negative view about self-determination by people with intellectual disability than disability support workers (Martínez-Tur et al., 2018). Open communication about self-determination between disability workers and families increased positive attitudes in family members about self-determination and resulted in a corresponding increase in frequency of exercising choice and preference by the person with intellectual disability within the family home (Martínez-Tur, Moliner, Peñarroja, Gracia, & Peiró, 2015). Similarly, a classroom-based competency building program with a group of young adults, together with family education focussed on understanding self-determination, its importance, and strategies for development and exercise, showed a significant increase in personal control within the context of family life (Abery, Rudrud, Arndt, Schauben, & Eggebeen, 1995).

A study of parent-initiated supported living schemes in the Netherlands identified that families are eager to organize living environments that work towards increased autonomy for their sons or daughters with intellectual disability but found the practicalities of supporting autonomy challenging (Reindl et al., 2016). Residences, set up by parent groups to provide an alternative to state-run homes for adults with intellectual disability, were generally small in size and usually provided both private and communal areas. However, overprotection, paternalistic attitudes, and system limitations continued to restrict the development and expression of residents' choice and control. Parents found it difficult to allow their son or daughter greater autonomy when they believed ongoing guidance was required. Staff were able to assist by educating parents about self-determination, providing self-advocacy training for residents and mediation of issues as they arose. A model of interdependence, where self-determination is not characterized by lack of assistance but rather by support that is personalized and self-directed, was suggested by Reindl et al. (2016). This vision of interdependence recognizes the complexity of parent/adult child relationships, particularly where intellectual disability is an additional element.

These findings suggest that assisting families to develop a more positive view about self-determination is an effective method of increasing choice and control of adults with intellectual disability. This may be achieved through formalized education programs or more informally by disability services encouraging and facilitating open discussion about self-determination with families. Reportedly, the program described by Abery et al. (1995) was particularly helpful in assisting family members "to establish a balance between togetherness and self-determination" (p. 177).

Conclusion

This chapter has highlighted a number of issues about the navigation of choice and control by people with intellectual disability within the family context. Two things are evident: choice and decision-making opportunities are highly valued by people with intellectual disability, but so too is family (Miller et al., 2008). This chapter has shown that maintaining strong familial relationships, while exercising choice and control, can be challenging for all. Given that both are valued, much remains to be learnt about how people with intellectual disability navigate the development of self-determination within the family and its cultural context.

Reliance on markers of typical adult status or the individual's personal qualities, to identify the rite of passage to self-determination, can be problematic when applied to people with intellectual disability. This can translate to limited opportunity to practise a range of typical life choice-making opportunities. The family, including parents and siblings, have a critical role in facilitating choice-making experiences across all life domains. This chapter has demonstrated though that such facilitation is not straightforward, with the potential consequences of unwise choices having far-reaching effects for not only the individual with intellectual disability but also their family. Families can act as both enhancer and constrainer of self-determination by their member with intellectual disability. Future research needs to prioritize the evidence base about strategies and resources families can use to proactively support the development of self-determination by their family member with intellectual disability.

References

Abery, B., Rudrud, L., Arndt, K., Schauben, L., & Eggebeen, A. (1995). Evaluating a multicomponent program for enhancing the self-determination of youth with disabilities. *Intervention in School and Clinic, 30*(3), 170–179. https://doi.org/10.1177/105345129503000307

Abery, B. H., & Stancliffe, R. J. (2003). A tripartite-ecological theory of self-determination. In M. L. Wehmeyer, B. H. Abery, D. E. Mithaug, & R. J. Stancliffe (Eds.), *Theory in self-determination: Foundations for educational practice* (pp. 43–78). Springfield, IL: Charles C. Thomas.

Arnett, J. J. (1998). Learning to stand alone: The contemporary American transition to adulthood in cultural and historical context. *Human Development, 41*, 295–315.

Arnett, J. J. (2000). Emerging adulthood: A theory of development form the late teens through the twenties. *American Psychologist, 55*, 469.

Atkin, K., & Tozer, R. (2013). Personalisation, family relationships and autism: Conceptualising the role of adult siblings. *Journal of Social Work, 14*(3), 225–242. https://doi.org/10.1177/1468017313476453

Australian Bureau of Statistics. (2009). *Australian Social Trends, Home and Away: The living arrangements of young people.* (Cat.No 4102.0) Retrieved from http://www.abs.gov.au/ausstats/abs@.nsf/Lookup/4102.0Main+Features50June+2009

Australian Bureau of Statistics. (2014). *Intellectual disability Australia 2012* (Cat No.4433.0.55.003). Retrieved from http://www.abs.gov.au/ausstats/abs@.nsf/Lookup/4433.0.55.003main+features252012

Bach, M. (2009). *The right to legal capacity under the UN Convention on the rights of persons with disabilities: Key concepts and directions from law reform.* Retrieved from Institute for Research and Development on Inclusion and Society (IRIS) website: http://irisinstitute.ca/the-work-we-do/publications/

Bigby, C. (1997). Parental substitutes? The role of siblings in the lives of older people with intellectual disability. *Journal of Gerontological Social Work, 29*(1), 3–21.

Bigby, C. (2000). *Moving on without parents: Planning, transitions and sources of support for middle-aged and older adults with intellectual disability.* Baltimore, MD: Paul H. Brookes.

Bigby, C., Webber, R., & Bowers, B. (2014). Sibling roles in the lives of older group home residents with intellectual disability: Working with staff to safeguard wellbeing. *Australian Social Work, 68*(4), 453–468. https://doi.org/10.1080/0312407X.2014.950678

Bigby, C., Whiteside, M., & Douglas, J. (2017). Providing support for decision making to adults with intellectual disability: Perspectives of family members and workers in disability support services. *Journal of Intellectual & Developmental Disability, 44*, 1–14. https://doi.org/10.310 9/13668250.2017.1378873

Biswas, S., Tickle, A., Golijani-Moghaddam, N., & Almack, K. (2017). The transition into adulthood for children with a severe intellectual disability: Parents' views. *International Journal of Developmental Disabilities, 63*(2), 99–109. https://doi.org/10.1080/20473869.2016.1138598

Caouette, M., Lachapelle, Y., Moreau, J., & Lussier-Desrochers, D. (2018). Descriptive study of caseworkers' practices to support the development of self-determination of adults with intellectual disabilities. *Journal of Policy and Practice in Intellectual Disabilities, 15*(1), 4–11. https://doi.org/10.1111/jppi.12217

Carter, E. W., Lane, K. L., Cooney, M., Weir, K., Moss, C. K., & Machalicek, W. (2013). Parent assessments of self-determination importance and performance for students with autism or intellectual disability. *American Journal on Intellectual and Developmental Disabilities, 118*(1), 16–31. https://doi.org/10.1352/1944-7558-118.1.16

Cicirelli, V. (1995). *Sibling relationships across the life span.* New York, NY: Plenum Press.

Connidis, I. (2001). *Family ties & aging.* Thousand Oaks, CA: Sage.

Curryer, B., Stancliffe, R. J., & Dew, A. (2015). Self-determination: Adults with intellectual disability and their family. *Journal of Intellectual & Developmental Disability, 40*(4), 394–399. https://doi.org/10.3109/13668250.2015.1029883

Curryer, B., Stancliffe, R. J., Dew, A., & Wiese, M. Y. (2018). Choice and control within family relationships: The lived experience of adults with intellectual disability. *Intellectual and Developmental Disabilities, 56*(3), 188–201. https://doi.org/10.1352/1934-9556-56.3.188

Damiani, V. (1999). Responsibility and adjustment in siblings of children with disabilities: Update and review. *Families in Society, 80*(1), 34–40.

Dew, A., Balandin, S., & Llewellyn, G. (2008). The psychosocial impact on siblings of people with lifelong physical disability: A review of the literature. *Journal of Developmental and Physical Disabilities, 20*, 485–507.

Dew, A., Balandin, S., & Llewellyn, G. (2011). Using a life course approach to explore how the use of AAC impacts on adult sibling relationships. *Augmentative and Alternative Communication, 27*, 245–255.

Dew, A., Llewellyn, G., & Balandin, S. (2013). Exploring the later life relationship between adults with cerebral palsy and their non-disabled siblings. *Disability & Rehabilitation, 36*, 756–764.

Dyke, P., Bourke, J., Llewellyn, G., & Leonard, H. (2013). The experiences of mothers of young adults with an intellectual disability transitioning from secondary school to adult life. *Journal of Intellectual & Developmental Disability, 38*(2), 149–162. https://doi.org/10.3109/1366825 0.2013.789099

Foley, S. (2013). Reluctant 'jailors' speak out: Parents of adults with Down syndrome living in the parental home on how they negotiate the tension between empowering and protecting their intellectually disabled sons and daughters. *British Journal of Learning Disabilities, 41*(4), 304–311. https://doi.org/10.1111/j.1468-3156.2012.00758.x

Friedman, C. (2018). Participant direction for people with intellectual and developmental disabilities in Medicaid Home and Community Based Services waivers. *Intellectual and Developmental Disabilities, 56*(1), 30–39. https://doi.org/10.1352/1934-9556-56.1.30

Galambos, N., Darrah, J., & Magill-Evans, J. (2007). Subjective age in the transition to adulthood for persons with and without motor disabilities. *Journal of Youth Adolescence, 36*, 825–834.

Haigh, A., Lee, D., Shaw, C., Hawthorne, M., Chamberlain, S., Newman, D. W., … Beail, N. (2013). What things make people with a learning disability happy and satisfied with their lives: An inclusive research project. *Journal of Applied Research in Intellectual Disabilities, 26*(1), 26–33. https://doi.org/10.1111/jar.12012

Heller, T., & Arnold, C. (2010). Siblings of adults with developmental disabilities: Psychosocial outcomes, relationships, and future planning. *Journal of Policy and Practice in Intellectual Disabilities, 7*(1), 16–25.

Heller, T., & Kramer, J. (2009). Involvement of adult siblings of persons with developmental disabilities in future planning. *Intellectual and Developmental Disabilities, 47*, 208–219.

Heller, T., Schindler, A., Palmer, S. B., Wehmeyer, M. L., Parent, W., Jenson, R., ... O'Hara, D. M. (2011). Self-determination across the life span: Issues and gaps. *Exceptionality, 19*, 31–45. doi:https://doi.org/10.1080/09362835.2011.537228

Hendry, L., & Kloep, M. (2010). How universal is emerging adulthood? An empirical example. *Journal of Youth Studies, 13*, 169–179.

Howe, N., & Recchia, H. (2005). Playmates and teachers: Reciprocal and complementary interactions between siblings. *Journal of Family Psychology, 19*, 497–502.

Jahoda, A., & Markova, I. (2004). Coping with social stigma: People with intellectual disabilities moving from institutions and family home. *Journal of Intellectual Disability Research, 48*(8), 719–729.

Janus, A. (2009). Disability and the transition to adulthood. *Social Forces, 88*(1), 99–120.

Kendrick, M. (1996). The natural authority of families. *Crucial Times*, (6), 6. Retrieved from http://cru.org.au/resources-and-publications/crucial-times/

Knox, M., & Bigby, C. (2007). Moving towards midlife care as negotiated family business: Accounts of people with intellectual disabilities and their families "just getting along with their lives together". *International Journal of Disability, Development and Education, 54*(3), 287–304. https://doi.org/10.1080/10349120701488749

Martínez-Tur, V., Estreder, Y., Moliner, C., Gracia, E., Pătraş, L., & Zornoza, A. (2018). Dialogue between workers and family members is related to their attitudes towards self-determination of individuals with intellectual disability. *Journal of Intellectual & Developmental Disability, 43*(3), 370–379. https://doi.org/10.3109/13668250.2017.1416256

Martínez-Tur, V., Moliner, C., Peñarroja, V., Gracia, E., & Peiró, J. M. (2015). From service quality in organisations to self-determination at home. *Journal of Intellectual Disability Research, 59*, 882–890. https://doi.org/10.1111/jir.12190

McCarthy, J. R. (2012). The powerful relational language of 'family': Togetherness, belonging and personhood. *The Sociological Review, 60*(1), 68–90. https://doi.org/10.1111/j.1467-954X.2011.02045.x

McHale, S. M., & Crouter, A. (2005). Sibling relationships in childhood: Implications for life-course study. In V. Bengston, A. Acock, K. Allen, P. Dilworth-Anderson, & D. Klein (Eds.), *Sourcebook of family theory and research* (pp. 184–190). Thousand Oaks, CA: Sage Publications.

Meltzer, A. (2017). 'I couldn't just entirely be her sister': The relational and social policy implications of care between young adult siblings with and without disabilities. *Journal of Youth Studies, 20*(8), 1013–1027. https://doi.org/10.1080/13676261.2017.1287889

Meltzer, A., & Kramer, J. (2016). Siblinghood through disability studies perspectives: Diversifying discourse and knowledge about siblings with and without disabilities. *Disability & Society, 31*(1), 17–32.

Meyers, C., & Vipond, J. (2005). Play and social interactions between children with developmental disabilities and their siblings: A systematic literature review. *Physical and Occupational Therapy in Pediatrics, 25*(1/2), 81–103.

Midjo, T., & Aune, K. E. (2018). Identify constructions and transition to adulthood for young people with mild intellectual disability. *Journal of Intellectual Disabilities, 22*(1), 33–48. https://doi.org/10.1177/1744629516674066

Miller, E., Cooper, S.-A., Cook, A., & Petch, A. (2008). Outcomes important to people with intellectual disabilities. *Journal of Policy and Practice in Intellectual Disabilities, 5*(3), 150–158.

Mitchell, W. (2012). Parents' accounts: Factors considered when deciding how far to involve their son/daughter with learning disabilities in choice-making. *Children and Youth Services Review, 34*(8), 1560–1569. https://doi.org/10.1016/j.childyouth.2012.04.009

Murphy, E., Clegg, J., & Almack, K. (2011). Constructing adulthood in discussions about the futures of young people with moderate-profound intellectual disabilities. *Journal of Applied Research in Intellectual Disabilities, 24*(1), 61–73. https://doi.org/10.1111/j.1468-3148.2010.00565.x

Orsmond, G., & Seltzer, M. (2000). Brothers and sisters of adults with mental retardation: Gendered nature of the sibling relationship. *American Journal on Mental Retardation, 105*, 486–508.

Orsmond, G., & Seltzer, M. (2007). Siblings of individuals with autism spectrum disorders across the life course. *Mental Retardation and Developmental Disabilities Research Reviews, 13*, 313–320.

Power, A. (2008). Caring for independent lives: Geographies of caring for young adults with intellectual disabilities. *Social Science & Medicine, 67*(5), 834–843.

Priestly, M. (2003). *Disability: A life course approach*. Cambridge, UK: Polity Press.

Reindl, M. S., Waltz, M., & Schippers, A. (2016). Personalization, self-advocacy and inclusion: An evaluation of parent-initiated supported living schemes for people with intellectual and developmental disabilities in the Netherlands. *Journal of Intellectual Disabilities, 20*(2), 121–136. https://doi.org/10.1177/1744629516631449

Ryan, R. M., & Deci, E. L. (2017). *Self-determination theory: Basic psychological needs in motivation, development, and wellness*. New York, NY: The Guildford Press.

Saaltink, R., MacKinnon, G., Owen, F., & Tardif-Williams, C. (2012). Protection, participation and protection through participation: Young people with intellectual disabilities and decision making in the family context. *Journal of Intellectual Disability Research, 56*(11), 1076–1086. https://doi.org/10.1111/j.1365-2788.2012.01649.x

Sanders, R. (2004). *Sibling relationships: Theory and issues for practice*. New York, NY: Palgrave Macmillan.

Schwartz, B., & Ward, A. (2004). Doing better but feeling worse: The paradox of choice. In P. A. Linley & S. Joseph (Eds.), *Positive psychology in practice* (pp. 86–104). Hoboken, NJ: Wiley.

Seltzer, M., Greenberg, J., Krauss, M., Gordon, R., & Judge, K. (1997). Siblings of adults with mental retardation or mental illness: Effects on lifestyle and psychological well-being. *Family Relations, 46*, 395–405.

Seltzer, M., Greenberg, J., Orsmond, G., & Lounds, J. (2005). Life course studies of siblings of individuals with developmental disabilities. *Mental Retardation, 43*, 354–359.

Seltzer, M., & Krauss, M. (1993). Adult sibling relationships of persons with mental retardation. In Z. Stoneman & P. Berman (Eds.), *The effects of mental retardation, disability, and illness on sibling relationships: Research issues and challenges* (pp. 99–115). Baltimore, MD: Paul H. Brookes.

Shogren, K., & Shaw, L. (2017). The impact of personal factors on self-determination and early adulthood outcome constructs in youth with disabilities. *Journal of Disability Policy Studies, 27*(4), 223–233. https://doi.org/10.1177/1044207316667732

Shogren, K. A., & Broussard, R. (2011). Exploring the perceptions of self-determination of individuals with intellectual disability. *Intellectual and Developmental Disabilities, 49*(2), 86–102. https://doi.org/10.1352/1934-9556-49.2.86

Stancliffe, R. J., Abery, B. H., Springborg, H., & Elkin, S. (2000). Substitute decision-making and personal control: Implications for self-determination. *Mental Retardation, 38*(5), 407–421.

Stoneman, Z., & Brody, G. (1993). Sibling relations in the family context. In Z. Stoneman & P. Berman (Eds.), *The effects of mental retardation, disability, and illness on sibling relationships: Research issues and challenges* (pp. 3–30). Baltimore, MD: Paul H. Brookes.

Tozer, R., & Atkin, K. (2015). 'Recognized, valued and supported'? The experiences of adult siblings of people with autism plus learning disability. *Journal of Applied Research in Intellectual Disabilities, 28*(4), 341–351. https://doi.org/10.1111/jar.12145

United Nations. (2006). *Convention on the rights of persons with disabilities and optional protocol*. Retrieved from http://www.un.org/disabilities/documents/convention/convoptprot-e.pdf

van Asselt-Goverts, A. E., Embregts, P., & Hendriks, A. H. C. (2013). Structural and functional characteristics of the social networks of people with mild intellectual disabilities. *Research in Developmental Disabilities, 34*(4), 1280–1288. https://doi.org/10.1016/j.ridd.2013.01.012

van Naarden Braun, K., Yeargin-Allsopp, M., & Lollar, D. (2006). A multi-dimensional approach to the transition of children with developmental disabilities into young adulthood: The acquisition of adult social roles. *Disability and Rehabilitation, 28,* 915–928.

Watson, J. (2016). Assumptions of decision-making capacity: The role supporter attitudes play in the realisation of Article 12 for people with severe or profound intellectual disability. *Laws, 5*(1), 6.

Wehmeyer, M. (2003). A functional theory of self-determination: Definition and categorization. In M. Wehmeyer, B. H. Abery, D. E. Mithaug, & R. J. Stancliffe (Eds.), *Theory in self-determination: Foundations for educational practice* (pp. 174–181). New York, NY: Charles C. Thomas.

Wehmeyer, M. (2014). Self-determination: A family affair. *Family Relations, 63*(1), 178–184. https://doi.org/10.1111/fare.12052

Wehmeyer, M. L., & Garner, N. W. (2003). The impact of personal characteristics of people with intellectual and developmental disability on self-determination and autonomous functioning. *Journal of Applied Research in Intellectual Disabilities, 16*(4), 255–265. https://doi.org/10.1046/j.1468-3148.2003.00161.x

Wells, T., Sandefur, G., & Hogan, D. (2003). What happens after the high school years among young persons with disabilities? *Social Forces, 82,* 803–832.

Widmer, E. D., Kempf-Constantin, N., Robert-Tissot, C., Lanzi, F., & Carminati, G. G. (2008). How central and connected am I in my family? Family-based social capital of individuals with intellectual disability. *Research in Developmental Disabilities, 29*(2), 176–187.

Choice as People Age with Intellectual Disability: An Irish Perspective

Mary-Ann O'Donovan, Philip McCallion, Darren McCausland, and Mary McCarron

Introduction

The ageing of people with intellectual disability is a relatively new phenomenon and a great success story of modern time (McCallion & McCarron, 2004). Historically, life expectancy for people with Down syndrome was 9 years of age (Glasson, Hussain, Dye, & Bittles, 2017), with most recent estimates of life expectancy for this population extending to 60 and 70 years of age and overall life expectancy for people with intellectual disability comparable to the general population of people without intellectual disability (Haveman et al., 2011). With this success, great challenges exist for the health and social care sector in understanding and responding to the changing needs of people with intellectual disability as they age. With the historical segregation of people with intellectual disability, through institutionalised living, education and healthcare, generations of people with intellectual disability have been completely disenfranchised from their lives, with little, if any autonomy, control or choice in where and how they live their lives (Smyth & Bell, 2006; Stancliffe et al., 2011).

More recently, there has been a theoretical, political and sociological shift in how disability is perceived, underscored by challenges to the medicalisation of disability and the repositioning of disability as socially constructed (Oliver, 1990). However, the social construction of disability itself continues to be debated (Owens, 2015; Shakespeare & Watson, 2002). With extended life expectancy, disability across the life course is beginning to receive attention in the academic literature, yet recognition in policy is not comparable. This chapter explores the experience of choice in

M.-A. O'Donovan (✉) · D. McCausland · M. McCarron
Trinity College, Dublin, Ireland
e-mail: odonovm3@tcd.ie

P. McCallion
Temple University, Philadelphia, PA, USA

the lives of people with intellectual disability ageing in Ireland. Data from the Intellectual Disability Supplement to the Irish Longitudinal Study on Ageing (IDS-TILDA) is examined through the lens of current theoretical debates on ageing and choice and within the context of the Irish policy environment.

Policy for Ageing and Disability in Ireland

Internationally, underpinned by the UNCRPD, person-centredness, autonomy and the right to live a life of one's choosing are associated with a good quality of life. Ratification of the UNCRPD was much delayed in Ireland, occurring in 2018, with the optional protocol yet to be ratified. However, a plethora of national disability policy and strategies preceded this ratification, guiding practice and service delivery in the Irish health and social care landscape. Two landmark publications advanced the shift in disability policy and advocacy. The 1996 'A Strategy for Equality' report by the Commission on the Status of People with Disabilities highlighted the challenges and barriers encountered by people with disabilities (Commission on the Status of People with Disabilities, 1996). Later, the National Disability Strategy (NDS) 2004 which was a turning point for the disability sector, services and the lives of people with disabilities in Ireland (Department of Justice, Equality and Law Reform, 2004). The aim was to advance inclusion of people with disabilities in society, and, in addition to a commitment for multi-annual funding, sectoral reviews and reports, it brought with it the first Disability Act (2005) in Ireland (Government of Ireland, 2015).

The position of older people with disabilities, people with intellectual disability and subsequently older people with intellectual disability were not drawn out extensively in these policy and legislative documents. Yet, evidence attests to the unique experience of older people with intellectual disability. Within the health policy sphere, the National Positive Ageing Strategy (2013) in Ireland presents a vision for growing older in Ireland (Department of Health, 2013). There is a strong focus on the promotion of well-being and quality of life for older people. However, people with intellectual disability and their needs as they age are not featured explicitly in this policy. In fact, policies to inform practice to support the ageing and health of people intellectual disability do not exist in Ireland.

However, what is central within many recent policy and strategic documents is the importance of a person-centred approach to care and support (Department of Health, 2012; Government of Ireland, 2015; Health Information and Quality Authority, 2013; Health Service Executive, 2011, 2012). At the heart of a person-centred approach is discovering how a person wants to live their life in addition to ascertaining the supports required to make that possible (McCarron et al., 2018; National Ageing Research Institute, 2006; National Disability Authority, 2005). Thus, from a policy perspective, person-centeredness raises the importance of self-determination in all areas of the life of the older person with intellectual disability.

Theories for Ageing and Disability

Ageing itself is a dynamic process (Kahlin, Kjellberg, & Hagberg, 2016). Different theories on ageing and how it impacts on the person offer both negative and positive perspectives. Disengagement theory (Cumming & Henry, 1961) proposes that ageing signifies a natural gradual withdrawal from society, bringing with it reduced activity and interaction with others and a decreased quality of life. These potential risks were somewhat highlighted in a recent longitudinal study of ageing in Ireland (McCrory, Leahy, & McGarrigle, 2014) but were also seen as constructed in a more positive approach to ageing (Cornwell, Laumann, & Schumm, 2008).

More positive outlooks on ageing are proposed by activity theory (Havighurst, 1963), in which continued well-being is associated with continued activity through older age, and in continuity theory (Atchley, 1989), which proposes continued involvement in established roles in life as a mediator to the process of ageing, protecting against reduced self-esteem (Coleman, Ivani-Chalian, & Robinson, 1993). In addition, the Selective Optimization with Compensation Framework (Baltes & Baltes, 1990) considers positive ageing as healthy adaptation through the selective maintenance of more valued activities and relinquishing of less valued activities.

The lesson from these outlooks is that ageing can be a positive experience in which quality of life is maintained. Though there are no specific theories of ageing as applied to people with intellectual disability, there is support (Schalock et al., 2002) for the view that a critical aspect of quality of life, and maintaining quality of life as one ages, is self-determination and choice (The WHOQOL Group, 1998; United Nations, 2006). Also, the frameworks above offer additional mechanisms to begin the process of understanding ageing for this population. One lens that has begun to be applied to the ageing of people with intellectual disability is that of the life course.

The Life Course for People with Intellectual Disability

Elder (1998) highlighted the importance of human agency (inclusive of autonomy, choice and control) within the theory of the life course. The life course as described by Elder is '…a sequence of socially defined events and roles that the individual enacts over time' (Giele & Elder, 1998). Events and role transitions are typically demarcated by age, though age is not necessarily the best marker (Cain, 2009; van Staa, van der Stege, Jedeloo, Moll, & Hilberink, 2011).

Having a lifelong disability can impact on the life course (Harrison, 2003; Raymond, Grenier, & Hanley, 2014), with the disability itself likely to carry different import at different life stages (Priestley, 2002). In addition, people with disabilities may not be provided the opportunity to participate in 'expected' life course events and transitions, for example, having a partner (Slota & Martin, 2003) or family, owning own home and attending higher education. This can lead to people with disabilities being exempted from expected life course events typically available to the general population (Slota & Martin, 2003). This exclusion from the normative life course and its transitions is underpinned by exclusion from choice and the opportunity for developing choice-making skills.

The positioning of choice in the life course for people with disabilities specifically was further highlighted by the work of Heller and Harris (2012), whose framework for understanding the life course of people with disabilities identifies six stages of the life course with four interdependent themes present at each stage. Self-determination and participation are one of the core themes. Choice and control are seen as central to the experience of true participation (Kahlin et al., 2016), while self-determination, a psychological construct positioned within the concept of human agency (Walker et al., 2011), incorporates both control and choice of people to determine the lives that they lead. It is the issue of choice within the broader construct of self-determination which is the primary focus of this chapter.

Choice and People Ageing with Intellectual Disability

Choice has been defined as 'an opportunity to make a selection free from coercion' (Brown & Brown, 2009). In the general population, the type and level of choices a person is faced with and the ability and opportunity to make these decisions usually develop over the life course, with more responsibility for and involvement in decisions as the individual moves from child to adulthood (Burton-Smith, Morgan, & Davidson, 2005). Exercising choice is more complex for people with intellectual disability (Stancliffe et al., 2011), who usually have fewer opportunities for choice (Burton-Smith et al., 2005).

For many people with intellectual disability, the opportunity to exercise and develop choice-making skills and become self-determined individuals has been denied (Burton-Smith et al., 2005; Heller et al., 2011). Absence or restriction to exposure to decision-making in early life may act as an impediment for decision-making at later life (Smyth & Bell, 2006). In addition, this lack of early life experience may also serve to inhibit transition to adulthood (Jenkinson, 1993). So, two issues arise: how people age is informed by their personal life course and how ageing is experienced impacts on how choice and control are experienced in later life (Kahlin et al., 2016). For these reasons, understanding the availability of and opportunity for choice for people with intellectual disability as they age, and in the context of increasing life expectancy, is of critical importance.

Through the lens of the life course, it has been demonstrated that choice-making and, more broadly, self-determinism are something that can be developed over the life of an individual (Heller et al., 2011). Evidence supports this learning and acquiring of self-determination skills for people with intellectual disability (Wehmeyer & Bolding, 2001), including for older people with intellectual disability (Heller et al., 2011). Choice is one element of self-determination, with a positive relationship shown to exist between choice-making skills for people with intellectual disability and being more self-determined (Wehmeyer & Garner, 2003), also an important dimension of quality of life (Sexton, O'Donovan, Mulryan, McCallion, & McCarron, 2016).

Access to choice and control over one's life are fundamental human rights and are explicitly outlined in Article 12 of the UNCRPD. In addition to being a rights issue, choice is also a key contributor to positive quality of life. The issue of access to and opportunity for choice is less prominent in the general gerontology literature. There is an absence of specific choice measurement scales in many of the longitudinal studies in ageing and in measurements of quality of life. Sexton et al. (2016) highlighted the absence of choice measures in the general population study examined.

Similarly, any choice questions tend to focus specifically on healthcare decision-making or lifestyle health behaviour choices. This is in contrast to the measurement of involvement in everyday and key life choices in studies of people with intellectual disability. This assumes and implies that the vast majority of the general population have access to and make these choices. There are exceptions, and daily decision-making in life is beginning to receive some attention in the literature (Feinberg & Whitlatch, 2001; Menne & Whitlatch, 2007; Sexton et al., 2016). The field of capacity assessment for older people, particularly in the area of health- and finance-related decision-making, is one growing area of research (Moye & Marson, 2007). Of note is the work by Reed, Mikels, and Simon (2008), which indicates that in the general population, older people prefer fewer options from which to choose when compared to a younger cohort. There is also an emerging commonality in the identification of associations between access to choice opportunities and where people age and live (Harris, 2003; Kahlin et al., 2016; McCausland, McCallion, Brennan, & McCarron, 2018; O'Donovan, Byrne, McCallion, & McCarron, 2017). However, the range of choice measures that have developed in the context of people with intellectual disability attests to both the greater importance and complexity of the issue for this population (O'Donovan et al., 2017).

Choice and People Ageing with Intellectual Disability in Ireland

In Ireland, the health and ageing of people with intellectual disability are being tracked through the Intellectual Disability Supplement to the Irish Longitudinal Study on Ageing (IDS-TILDA). This study has been running since 2007 with three waves of data collection gathered, with first data collection in 2010/2011. A national sample of people with the full range of intellectual disability aged 40 years and over and living in a variety of settings (institution, community group home, family and independent) was included (McCarron et al., 2011). Full details of the methodology and conceptual framework guiding study design as well as overall key findings are outlined in the wave reports (Burke, McCallion, & McCarron, 2014;

Table 1 Profile of sample respondents for each wave

	Wave 1	Wave 2	Wave 3	Present
Total	753	708	609	594
Age				
<50	38.2 (288)	28.1 (197)	11.8 (72)	0
50–64	45.6 (343)	50.8 (356)	62.6 (381)	65.3 (388)
65+	16.2 (122)	21.1 (148)	25.6 (156)	34.7 (206)
Missing		8		
Gender				
Male	44.5 (335)	44.1 (312)	44.2 (269)	44.4 (264)
Female	55(418)	55.9 (396)	55.8 (340)	55.6 (330)
ID				
Mild	24 (167)	24.2 (158)	24.8 (139)	25.4 (139)
Moderate	46.5 (323)	46.5 (304)	46.2 (259)	45.7 (250)
Severe/profound	29.5 (205)	29.4 (192)	29.1 (163)	28.9 (158)
Missing	58	54	13	47
Type of residence				
Independent	17.1 (129)	16.3 (115)	15.6 (95)	15.5 (92)
CGH	35.6 (268)	43.5 (307)	40.4 (246)	40.9 (243)
Residential	47.3 (356)	40.2 (284)	44 (268)	43.6 (259)

McCarron et al., 2011; McCarron, Haigh, & McCallion, 2017). Baseline data for the original sample of 753 people with intellectual disability is presented in Table 1.

Choice experience and opportunity for older people with intellectual disability have been examined across the waves of data for IDS-TILDA. The daily choice inventory scale, developed by Heller, Miller, and Hsieh (2000) and adapted for use in an Irish context within the IDS-TILDA study, reflects this variety in the application of choice by people with intellectual disability. Within this scale, choice for people with intellectual disability takes the form of self or independent choice, supported choice with an advocate, parent, keyworker, or other guardian supporting the person with intellectual disability to make a choice or proxy choice where the person with intellectual disability is not involved in the choice-making but the decision is made completely by a third party. Some key findings based on analysis of this scale are presented in this section.

The basic requirement for choice by people with intellectual disability appears to be the individual's right and entitlement to make a choice. The IDS-TILDA data shows that self-choice is higher for people living at home or independently compared with people living in community group homes or residential settings (McCausland et al., 2018; O'Donovan et al., 2017). In addition, people with mild intellectual disability were more likely to make choices for themselves (McCausland et al., 2018; O'Donovan et al., 2017).

The IDS-TILDA data concurs with previous work by Ticha, Hewitt, Nord, and Larson (2013) on adults aged 18 years and over. Figure 1 illustrates the two types of choice that seem to exist for older people with intellectual disability: everyday choices and key life choices (O'Donovan et al., 2017).

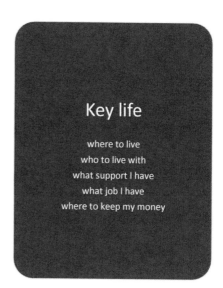

Fig. 1 Two levels of choice

The data showed a high level of interconnectedness between the two domains of choice and links with literature on self-determination, such as Abery and Stancliffe (2003), which suggests a high correlation between everyday decisions and people with intellectual disability being more self-determined (O'Donovan et al., 2017). Further investigation into how choice in one life domain can impact on choice opportunity in another domain is required (O'Donovan et al., 2017). Nevertheless, the data do attest to variation in how choice is exercised in the lives of people with intellectual disability, and this is explored further next.

Change in Self-Choice Experience over a 10-Year Time Frame

The choice experience reported by the IDS-TILDA participants over three time points shows that self-choice was persistently available to a greater percentage of older people with intellectual disability living independently/with family than people in residential or community group homes. With the exception of the choice of what clothes to wear, which was comparable between those living in independent/family settings and community group home but much lower for those in institutional settings.

There was a greater percentage of self-choice reported for key life decisions of where you live, who you live with and where you keep your money after 10 years regardless of where the person was living. People had less involvement into the type of support they received, and this was indicated by lower self-choice on the variable 'who chooses the support you receive'. More variability in change was identified in everyday decisions with no consistent trend in the change pattern. For example,

Table 2 Percentage self-choice by type of residence at wave 1 and wave 3

	Independent/ family		Community group home		Residential institute	
	W1	W3	W1	W3	W1	W3
Everyday choice						
What food do you eat?	53.5	55.3	36.0	46.5	21.5	29.3
What food is cooked in your home?	35.7	30.9	18.0	16.9	2.7	7.0
What clothes do you wear?	68.8	65.3	65.3	66.8	29.8	38.2
Who do you spend your free time with?	63.8	65.6	45.2	53.3	27.7	43.3
Where do you go in your free time?	66.4	54.8	31.7	33.9	22.1	25.5
How do you spend your money?	26.6	44.7	43.4	30.7	27.4	11.4
What time do you go to bed?	85.9	88.4	81.6	88.5	62.0	70.8
What TV shows do you watch?	91.0	n/a	78.2	n/a	50.0	n/a
How do you decorate your room?	59.2	62.4	48.5	48.4	15.4	54.9
Key life decisions						
What job do you have?	50.0	49.4	36.4	35.7	18.5	26.0
Where do you live?	44.4	48.9	11.0	19.3	3.7	7.3
Who do you live with?	38.3	43.7	1.9	7.6	1.1	3.1
What support do you receive?	30.3	23.1	7.2	4.1	2.8	1.5
Where do you keep your money?	41.4	46.3	16.4	18.9	2.6	5.3

there was an increase in the percentage of respondents reporting who they spend free time with across the type of residence and where to go in free time (for those in community group home and residential) as well as increased percentage reporting self-choice in bedtime and decorating bedrooms (Table 2).

Predictors of Choice

Analysis of IDS-TILDA data shows that choice is a multifactorial concept, with a range of factors influencing choice-making for older people with intellectual disability, including demographic, individual and social variables (McCausland et al., 2018). When examined according to *key life choice* and *everyday choice*, crucial differences were found in the factors associated with each of type of choice.

The type of residence was the strongest predictor in the model exploring key life decisions, whereby individuals living in independent/family settings were significantly more likely to exercise this type of choice than people in institutional residences. However, a multifactorial analysis also identified other significant predictors, including the level of intellectual impairment, Instrumental Activities of Daily Living (IADL) functioning, residential proximity to family, contact with family, having friends other than the co-residents and literacy. For everyday choice, Activities of Daily Living (ADL) functioning was the strongest predictor, whereas here the type of residence was not a significant factor. Additional predictors of everyday choice included the level of intellectual disability, family contact, IADL functioning, age and having non-resident friends.

So while there were some crucial differences, there were also a number of common factors that predicted better choice across the two domains of choice (McCausland et al., 2018). The data demonstrate that people with intellectual disability are more likely to have the opportunity to exercise choice in more independent community settings. This suggests that access to the appropriate required supports related to personal ability and policies promoting independent community living, in addition to supports outside the home, provide the best environment for self-determination (McCausland et al., 2018). The impact of active support in increasing choice for people with intellectual disability was borne out in the work by Beadle-Brown, Hutchinson, and Whelton (2012).

What Works

The evidence presented in this chapter highlights key messages for policymakers and practitioners.

First, choice for older people with intellectual disability has been shown to be multifactorial in nature with a breadth of predictors that influence choice-making for older people with intellectual disability. This has implications for the nature of supports required and the importance of continuing to resource these supports to facilitate older people to make choices of import in their lives.

Second, the supports needed are advocacy (through family or independently), access to personalised budgets, supportive living environments and opportunity for enhanced engagement with Instrumental Activities of Daily Living. These resources are practical ways in which older people with intellectual disability can be supported in choice-making across key life and everyday choices.

Conclusion

As noted by Brown and Brown (2009), choice for people with intellectual disability is intertwined with the concepts of rights and entitlement. The right to live a life of one's choosing is underpinned by the UNCRPD. Yet historically people with intellectual disability have been excluded from choice-making within and about their lives. The IDS-TILDA data reported here which spans a 10-year time frame attests to the exclusion from choice-making and that it continues for some older people with intellectual disability. Yet others are participating and making choices in key life and everyday decisions for themselves or with support.

Change in the experience of self-choice has been examined. In particular, there has been increases in self-choice in key life areas of where to live, who to live with and where to keep money, regardless of the type of living arrangement. However, a reduction over time was found in reporting self-choice in other areas, and the experience of no choice particularly in key life areas persists.

The IDS-TILDA data also demonstrate that the opportunity for and experience of choice for older people with intellectual disability are multidimensional and multifactorial. Although the type of residence was the main predictor for key life decisions, need for assistance with ADLs was the main predictor for everyday decisions, although neither was the sole predictors of choice. Both of these main predictors may be influenced, where people live by policy responses and the need for ADL assistance with additional supports. The current focus on person-centredness, a key feature of many national policies, offers an additional mechanism to highlight choice desires, more specifically to guide the application of needed supports and to highlight where policy responses should be targeted. In this way, people with intellectual disability will have greater opportunities to participate in and choose life that they desire and deserve.

References

Abery, B. H., & Stancliffe, R. J. (2003). A tripartite theory of self-determination. In M. L. Wehmeyer, B. H. Abery, D. E. Mithaug, & R. J. Stancliffe (Eds.), *Theory in self-determination: Foundations for educational practice* (pp. 43–78). Springfield, IL: Charles C Thomas Publisher.

Atchley, R. C. (1989). A continuity theory of normal aging. *The Gerontologist, 29*, 183–190.

Baltes, P. B., & Baltes, M. M. (1990). Psychological perspectives on successful aging: The model of selective optimization with compensation. *Successful Aging: Perspectives from the Behavioral Sciences, 1*, 1–34.

Beadle-Brown, J., Hutchinson, A., & Whelton, B. (2012). Person-centred active support – Increasing choice, promoting independence and reducing challenging behaviour. *Journal of Applied Research in Intellectual Disabilities, 25*(4), 291–307.

Brown, I., & Brown, R. I. (2009). Choice as an aspect of quality of life for people with intellectual disabilities. *Journal of Policy and Practice in Intellectual Disabilities, 6*(1), 11–18.

Burke, E., McCallion, P., & McCarron, M. (2014). *Advancing years, different challenges: Wave 2 IDS-TILDA: Findings on the ageing of people with an intellectual disability.* Dublin, Ireland: School of Nursing and Midwifery, Trinity College Dublin.

Burton-Smith, R., Morgan, M., & Davidson, J. (2005). Does the daily choice making of adults with intellectual disability meet the normalisation principle? *Journal of Intellectual and Developmental Disability, 30*(4), 226–235.

Cain, L. D., Jr. (2009). Life course and social structure. In W. R. Heinz, J. Hiunink, & A. Weymann (Eds.), *The life course reader: Individuals and societies across time* (pp. 53–65). Frankfurt, Germany/New York, NY: Campus Verlag.

Coleman, P. G., Ivani-Chalian, C., & Robinson, M. (1993). Self-esteem and its sources: Stability and change in later life. *Ageing and Society, 13*, 171–192.

Commission on the Status of People with Disabilities. (1996). *A strategy for equality: Summary of the report of the commission on the status of people with disabilities.* Dublin, Ireland: Stationery Office.

Cornwell, B., Laumann, E. O., & Schumm, L. P. (2008). The social connectedness of older adults: A national profile. *American Sociological Review, 73*, 185–203.

Cumming, E., & Henry, W. E. (1961). *Growing old: The process of disengagement.* New York, NY: Basic Books.

Department of Health. (2012). *Value for money and policy review of disability services in Ireland*. Dublin, Ireland: The Stationery Office.

Department of Health. (2013). *The national positive ageing strategy*. Dublin, Ireland: Department of Health.

Department of Justice, Equality and Law Reform. (2004). *National disability strategy*. Dublin, Ireland: Author.

Elder, G.H., Jr. (1998). The Life course as developmental theory. *Child Development, 69*(1), 1–12.

Feinberg, L. F., & Whitlatch, C. J. (2001). Are persons with cognitive impairment able to state consistent choices? *The Gerontologist, 41*, 374–382. https://doi.org/10.1093/geront/41.3.374

Giele, J. Z., & Elder, G. H., Jr. (Eds.). (1998). *Methods of life course research: Qualitative and quantitative approaches*. London, UK: Sage.

Glasson, E., Hussain, R., Dye, D., & Bittles, A. (2017). Trends in ageing for people with down syndrome: A 56-year cohort study in Western Australia. *Innovation in Aging, 1*(1), 1334.

Government of Ireland. (2005). *Disability act*. Dublin, Ireland: Stationary Office.

Government of Ireland. (2015). *Assisted decision-making (capacity act 2015)*. Dublin, Ireland: Stationary Office.

Harris, T. (2003). Time to make up your mind: why choosing is difficult. *British Journal of Learning Disabilities, 31*, 3–8.

Harrison, T. (2003). Women aging with childhood onset disability: A holistic approach using the life course paradigm. *Journal of Holistic Nursing, 21*(3), 242–359.

Haveman, M., Perry, J., Salvador-Carulla, L., Noonan-Walsh, P., Kerr, M., Van Schrojenstein Lantman-de Valk, H., ... Weber, G. (2011). Ageing and health status in adults with intellectual disabilities: Results of the European POMONA II study. *Journal of Intellectual and Developmental Disability, 36*(1), 49–60.

Havighurst, R. J. (1963). Successful aging. *Processes of Aging: Social and Psychological Perspectives, 1*, 299–320.

Health Information and Quality Authority. (2013). *National standards for residential services for children and adults with disabilities*. Dublin, Ireland: Health Information and Quality Authority.

Health Service Executive. (2011). *Time to move on from congregated settings: A strategy for community inclusion*. Dublin, Ireland: Author.

Health Service Executive. (2012). *New directions – Review of HSE day services and implementation plan 2012–2016*. Dublin, Ireland: Author.

Heller, T., & Harris, T. (2012). *Disability through the lifecourse*. Los Angeles: Sage Publications.

Heller, T., Miller, A. B., & Hsieh, K. (2000). Later-life planning: Promoting knowledge of options and choice-making. *Mental Retardation, 38*(5), 395–406.

Heller, T., Schindler, A., Palmer, S. B., Wehmeyer, M. L., Parent, W., Jenson, R., ... O'Hara, D. M. (2011). Self-determination across the life span: Issues and gaps. *Exceptionality, 19*(1), 31–45.

Jenkinson, J. C. (1993). Who shall decide? The relevance of theory and research to decision making by people with an intellectual disability. *Disability, Handicap & Society, 8*(4), 361–375.

Kahlin, I., Kjellberg, A., & Hagberg, J.-E. (2016). Choice and control for people ageing with intellectual disabilities in group homes. *Scandinavian Journal of Occupational Therapy, 23*(2), 127–137.

McCallion, P., & McCarron, M. (2004). Ageing and intellectual disabilities: A review of recent literature. *Current Opinion in Psychiatry, 17*(5), 349–352.

McCarron, M., Haigh, M., & McCallion, P. (Eds.). (2017). *Health, wellbeing and social inclusion: Ageing with an intellectual disability in Ireland. Evidence from the first ten years of the intellectual disability supplement to the Irish longitudinal study on ageing (IDS-TILDA)*. Dublin, Ireland: School of Nursing and Midwifery, Trinity College Dublin.

McCarron, M., Sheerin, F., Roche, L., Ryan, A. M., Griffiths, C., Keenan, P., ... McCallion, P. (2018). *Shaping the future of intellectual disability nursing in Ireland*. Health Services Executive: Dublin, Ireland.

McCarron, M., Swinburne, J., Burke, E., McGlinchey, E., Mulryan, N., Andrews, V., ... McCallion, P. (2011). *Growing older with an intellectual disability in Ireland in 2011: First results from the Intellectual Disability Supplement to The Irish Longitudinal Study on Ageing (IDS-TILDA)*. Dublin, Ireland: School of Nursing and Midwifery, Trinity College Dublin.

McCausland, D., McCallion, P., Brennan, D., & McCarron, M. (2018). The exercise of human rights and citizenship by older adults with an intellectual disability in Ireland. *Journal of Intellectual Disability Research, 62*(10), 875–887.

McCrory, C., Leahy, S., & McGarrigle, C. (2014). What factors are associated with change in older people's quality of life? In A. Nolan, C. O'Regan, C. Dooley, D. Wallace, A. Hever, H. Cronin, et al. (Eds.), *The over 50s in a changing Ireland: Economic circumstances, health and wellbeing* (pp. 153–187). Dublin, Ireland: The Irish Longitudinal Study on Ageing.

Menne, H. L., & Whitlatch, C. J. (2007). Decision-making involvement of individuals with dementia. *The Gerontologist, 47*, 810–819. https://doi.org/10.1093/geront/47.6.810

Moye, J., & Marson, D. C. (2007). Assessment of decision-making capacity in older adults: An emerging area of practice and research. *The Journals of Gerontology: Series B, 62*(1), 3–1. https://doi.org/10.1093/geronb/62.1.P3

National Ageing Research Institute. (2006). *What is person-centred health care? A literature review*. Melbourne, Australia: Victorian Government Department of Human Services.

National Disability Authority. (2005). *Guidelines on person centred planning in the provision of services for people with disabilities in Ireland*. Dublin, Ireland: Author.

O'Donovan, M.-A., Byrne, E., McCallion, P., & McCarron, M. (2017). Measuring choice for adults with an intellectual disability – A factor analysis of the adapted daily choice inventory scale. *Journal of Intellectual Disability Research, 61*, 471–487.

Oliver, M. (1990). The social construction of the disability problem. *The Politics of Disablement*, 78–94. https://doi.org/10.1007/978-1-349-20895-1_6

Owens, J. (2015). Exploring the critiques of the social model of disability: The transformative possibility of Arendt's notion of power. *Sociology of Health and Illness, 37*, 385–403.

Priestley, M. (2002). *From womb to tomb: Disability, social policy and the life course*. Leeds, UK: Centre for Disability Studies University of Leeds.

Raymond, E., Grenier, A., & Hanley, J. (2014). Community participation of older adults with disabilities. *Journal of Community and Applied Social Psychology, 24*, 50–62.

Reed, A., Mikels, J., & Simon, K. (2008). Older adults prefer less choice than younger adults. *Psychology and Ageing, 23*(3), 671–675.

Schalock, R. L., Brown, I., Brown, R., Cummins, R. A., Felce, D., Matikka, L., … Parmenter, T. (2002). Conceptualization, measurement, and application of quality of life for persons with intellectual disabilities: Report of an international panel of experts. *Mental Retardation, 40*, 457–470.

Sexton, E., O'Donovan, M.-A., Mulryan, N., McCallion, P., & McCarron, M. (2016). Whose quality of life? Measures of emotional wellbeing and self-determination in research with older adults with and without intellectual disabilities. *Journal of Intellectual and Developmental Disability, 41*(4), 324–337.

Shakespeare, T., & Watson, N. (2002). The social model of disability: an outdated ideology? *Research in Social Science & Disability, 2*, 9–28.

Slota, N., & Martin, D. (2003). Methodological considerations in life course theory research. *Disability Studies Quarterly, 23*(2), 19–29.

Smyth, C. M., & Bell, D. (2006). From biscuits to boyfriends: The ramifications of choice for people with learning disabilities. *British Journal of Learning Disabilities, 34*, 227–236.

Stancliffe, R. J., Lakin, K. C., Larson, S., Engler, J., Taub, S., & Fortune, J. (2011). Choice of living arrangements. *Journal of Intellectual Disability Research, 55*(8), 746–762.

The WHOQOL Group. (1998). The World Health Organization quality of life assessment (WHOQOL): Development and general psychometric properties. *Social Science & Medicine, 46*, 1569–1585.

Ticha, R., Hewitt, A., Nord, D., & Larson, S. (2013). System and individual outcomes and their predictors in services and support for people with IDD. *Intellectual and Developmental Disabilities, 51*(5), 298–315.

United Nations. (2006). *Convention on the rights of persons with disabilities*. New York, NY: United Nations.

van Staa, A., van der Stege, H. A., Jedeloo, S., Moll, H. A., & Hilberink, S. R. (2011). Readiness to transfer to adult care of adolescents with chronic conditions: Exploration of associated factors. *The Journal of Adolescent Health, 48*(3), 295–302.

Walker, H. M., Calkins, C., Wehmeyer, M. L., Walker, L., Bacon, A., Palmer, S. B., … Johnson, D. R. (2011). A social-ecological approach to promote self-determination. *Exceptionality, 19*(1), 6–18.

Wehmeyer, M. L., & Bolding, N. (2001). Enhanced self-determination of adults with intellectual disability as an outcome of moving to community-based work or living environments. *Journal of Intellectual Disability Research, 45*(5), 371–383.

Wehmeyer, M. L., & Garner, N. W. (2003). The impact of personal characteristics of people with intellectual and developmental disability on self-determination and autonomous functioning. *Journal of Applied Research in Intellectual Disabilities, 16*, 255–265.

End-of-Life Choices

Michele Y. Wiese and Irene Tuffrey-Wijne

Introduction

Not everyone wishes to engage with the topic of death. This in itself is a choice. It is, however, only a choice if it is informed. While acknowledging that capacity to make decisions is variable for each individual and presenting situation, we uphold the United Nations Convention on the Rights of the Person with Disability position that every person has the right to make his or her own decisions, and, unless otherwise established, the capacity to do so must be presumed (Turner, 2007; United Nations, 2006). With sufficient information, many people with intellectual disability can make an informed choice about the extent to which they choose to engage with the end-of-life topic and make decisions about it.

End-of-life decisions, sometimes emotionally laden and often deeply personal, may not be agreeable to all. This does not mean that the person does not have the capacity to make these decisions. Further, decision making about the end of life isn't always just the province of the person themselves. There are many instances where others need to make choices too. For example, if the person wishes to be cared for at home when dying, those who may be expected to provide this care may need to decide about their capacity to do so.

For the purposes of this chapter, we define end-of-life decisions as any decision pertaining to the dying and death period. These could be decisions made when the person has a life-limiting illness, or is well but contemplating their future dying and death.

M. Y. Wiese (✉)
Western Sydney University, Sydney, NSW, Australia
e-mail: m.wiese@westernsydney.edu.au

I. Tuffrey-Wijne
Kingston University and St. George's, University of London, London, UK

© Springer Nature Switzerland AG 2020
R. J. Stancliffe et al. (eds.), *Choice, Preference, and Disability*, Positive
Psychology and Disability Series, https://doi.org/10.1007/978-3-030-35683-5_17

Understanding and Opportunity

The available research shows that people with intellectual disability have variable understanding of death and end-of-life planning (Stancliffe, Wiese, Read, Jeltes, & Clayton, 2016). People with intellectual disability are not routinely afforded the opportunity to make end-of-life decisions (Voss et al., 2017; Wicki, 2018; Wiese, Stancliffe, Read, Jeltes, & Clayton, 2015). This is due to a number of factors. First, caregivers express concern that talking about end of life may do harm or that the person with intellectual disability may not be able to cope (Wiese, Dew, Stancliffe, Howarth, & Balandin, 2013). Second, there is evidence to suggest that caregivers may feel uncomfortable or ill-equipped to engage with people with intellectual disability about dying and death (Tuffrey-Wijne & Rose, 2017; Wiese et al., 2013). Recent research, however, has shown that talking about the end of life is not harmful and does not cause any lasting adverse distress for people with intellectual disability or disability care staff (Stancliffe, Wiese, Read, Jeltes, & Clayton, 2017). As for many, when talking about the end of life, some individuals may become upset, and therefore sensitivity is required.

The following real-life case and the questions that follow illustrate the range of issues and end-of-life decisions that could potentially arise for a person with intellectual disability and their caregivers (Box 1).

Box 1 Pete Carpenter Case Study[1]
Pete Carpenter was 66 years old when he was diagnosed with advanced lung cancer. Pete had severe intellectual disability. His vocabulary was limited to short, simple sentences. Pete lived in a staffed residential home with two other people. He had grown up in the family home, where he had seen his father die a painful cancer death. His sister visited Pete occasionally but found his final illness extremely difficult to cope with, leading to fewer visits. Pete had many friends and enthusiasms. He seemed happy in his home and loved going to his day centre, a retirement project which he called 'work'.

The cancer diagnosis was given to his staff, who were told that his prognosis was just a few months. It was difficult to know how much Pete would be able to understand about his illness and about the options available to him. The staff at his home felt panicked about their ability to keep Pete pain-free and give him the right medication at the right time. Difficult childhood experiences had taught Pete not to complain of pain. Pete's bedroom was upstairs, and there was no lift, which became a problem as he lost strength to climb the stairs. His housemates were distressed seeing Pete ill. They were frightened of what might happen to him but did not want to talk about this.

---

[1] This is an anonymised real-life case study, described in detail in (Tuffrey-Wijne, 2010).

There were many decisions and choices to be made by Pete as well as the people supporting him, such as:

- *Should Pete be told that he has cancer?* Should he be told that he is dying? If so, who should tell him and how?
- *Who should be involved in making decisions about Pete's treatment and care?* How much can Pete be involved? If he can't make his own decisions, who would he like to make decisions for him?
- *What are his treatment options?* Should Pete undergo radiotherapy? Does he have pain? How would staff know? How can his symptoms be treated?
- *Can Pete stay at home?* Would he want to? Would it be possible? What are his options? Does he need to be in hospital? Does he need to go into a hospice? Does he need to move to another home, more suited to his increased nursing care needs? What outside professional support is available at home? How about palliative care?
- *Who does Pete want to have around him?* Does he want friends to visit? Does he want to stay at home or keep going to his day centre?
- *Does Pete want to be involved in planning his own funeral?* Would he have opinions about the music, the flowers, the coffin?
- *Would Pete want to bequeath treasured possessions?* Does he have a legal will or should he seek legal advice? Is there someone special he would like to leave his treasured record collection to? Where do these things get written down?
- *To what extent could Pete consider decisions about organ donation?* Can he donate his organs and/or tissues? Would he understand what that means, and would he want to?
- *Does Pete want to complete an advance care plan?* Who could support him to do that?

Breaking Bad News

Even if a person with intellectual disability has variable understanding of death and lacks understanding and insight and the capacity to gain such understanding, that person can still be involved by taking a central place in best-interest decisions.

There is consistent evidence in the literature that many people with intellectual disability are not told about their own dying (Tuffrey-Wijne, 2013b; Tuffrey-Wijne & Rose, 2017; Wiese et al., 2013). While it is now less common than in the past that people with intellectual disability are not informed about the death of a loved one and not involved in funerals, talking about expected death (i.e. understanding and talking about the possibility of dying) is much more problematic. Healthcare professionals tend to leave such conversations to family and disability care staff, as was the case for Pete Carpenter; and as previously described, family and disability care staff also tend to avoid talking about dying with people with intellectual disability (Ryan, Guerin, Dodd, & McEvoy, 2011; Tuffrey-Wijne & Rose, 2017).

One of this chapter's authors, Irene Tuffrey-Wijne, has carried out a program of research about breaking bad news, resulting in a model and guidelines for people with intellectual disability (Breaking Bad News, n.d.; Tuffrey-Wijne, 2013a, 2013b). This research found that reasons for non-disclosure include:

- Preventing distress ('what's the point of upsetting him?').
- Too difficult to be the bearer of bad news (especially for family members and disability care staff working in intellectual disability services, who are not used to breaking bad news and who may be emotionally close to the person).
- The potential bearer of bad news lacks knowledge (doctors may leave disclosure about expected death to those who know the person well but do not provide sufficient support and information to staff and relatives).
- The person is unable to understand.
- The person lacks a sense of time.
- There are conflicting views (family members or care staff may be opposed to disclosure).

The main reasons for disclosure were:

- The person has a right to know, especially if they have capacity.
- Understanding the events and changes in their life can help people cope.
- The importance of being involved in planning and decision making, including planning how to use the time that is left and having opportunities to say goodbye.

A Model for Breaking Bad News

Bad news situations are usually complex, constituting a wide range of different chunks of knowledge and information. In Pete Carpenter's case, the bad news could be summarised as 'You have incurable cancer', but this is clearly not sufficient. Does Pete know what cancer is? Does he understand that some, but not all, people die of cancer? Does he know the implications of such a diagnosis? Can he oversee the future to such an extent that he can plan ahead? And if the answer to any of these questions is 'no', how can he be helped to understand and cope with the inevitable changes in his life over the coming months?

Breaking bad news to people with intellectual disability, in this context their own life-limiting illness, is not a singular event or a linear process but a gradual building of knowledge in ways that can be unpredictable and must involve all caregivers. Understanding grows over time if it is consistently supported by everyone involved. There are four key components to this (Tuffrey-Wijne, 2013a):

1. Building a Foundation of Knowledge Gradually and over time, people with intellectual disability build their understanding of the way their situation is changing because of the bad news. There is no sudden understanding of the whole situation; rather, people are helped to understand and cope with a changing and changed reality. Complex information should be broken down into small, singular chunks. These can be given to the person one by one and built on as the person's foundation of knowledge grows. It is important to consider what 'background knowledge' the person already possesses and to ensure that the new information fits this existing framework of background knowledge. It is also important to start building knowledge early, ideally when the person is young and well (Wiese et al., 2015).

2. Understanding How much someone is able to understand at a particular point in time will influence decisions about when and which aspects of the bad news are to be imparted. Assessment of capacity to understand and consideration of jurisdictional laws on mental capacity are important (Purser, Magner, & Madison, 2015). People's capacity to understand will be enhanced by having information in a familiar format, for example, using simple words, pictures, photos, objects of reference, demonstration, etc.

3.People Collaboration is key. An interdisciplinary approach is needed to meet the complex needs of people who are reaching the end of life. This should include health and social care professionals, families and disability care staff. Everyone involved should be aware of what is happening, why and with whom. It should also be clear to everyone what their role and authority are and where to get support. This is particularly important for junior staff who may be most likely to be asked questions and most likely to lack the confidence to answer them.

4.Support The person with intellectual disability will clearly need psychological and emotional support, but so does everyone else involved. Families, friends and disability care staff may be particularly affected by the illness and the person's impending death (Box 2).

Box 2 Pete Carpenter Case Study Part 2

Pete's background knowledge included the experience of his father's cancer. He knew the word 'cancer' and presumably knew that people could die of it. He had also experienced the deaths of several friends and housemates and had been to their funerals. He had always seemed frightened of death. His residential home was close to the cemetery, and he could become distressed if a funeral hearse went past. His disability care staff and family decided that Pete should be told by a doctor that he had cancer. He did not appear to take this in, but over the subsequent weeks the staff were able to relate his symptoms of tiredness and breathlessness to 'cancer'. They also reassured him as much as possible that he could have pain medication, so he did not have to be in pain like his father had been. Knowing about his childhood experience of pain was important in helping him cope with pain now. Contrary to expectation, Pete remained calm and appeared accepting of his situation throughout his final months. The disability care staff team was supported to care for Pete at home by the local palliative care nurses.

Could Breaking Bad News Be Harmful?

As a matter of course, people with intellectual disability have the same rights to information about their illness as the general population. the research shows that having conversations about the end of life with people with intellectual disability is not harmful (Stancliffe et al., 2017). The difficulty, however, is determining how much a person with intellectual disability can, and wants to, be involved in discussions and decisions. Even if someone cannot, or does not want to, think about their situation, it is still important that they understand what is happening on a day-to-day basis. Conflicting messages or even un-truths ('don't worry, you are fine!') can be distressing, especially if the person feels anything but fine.

It is important to consider the possible reasons for non-disclosure very carefully. If someone is unable to indicate how much they want to know, it is useful to think about the test for capacity: can this person *understand, retain* and *balance* the information (Mental Capacity Act (England & Wales), 2005; Purser et al., 2015)?

Understanding the information: If someone is truly unable to understand what is being said, he/she likely won't be harmed by people trying to explain. It is almost inevitable that some of the explanations will not be understood. It is important to try and simplify the information and to find out how he/she has interpreted it.

Retaining the information: People with intellectual disability are likely to need a lot of repetition. For resources about how to do this, see the *Handy teaching skills* module on the website *Talking End of life with people with intellectual disability* (TEL) (https://www.caresearch.com.au/TEL/; Wiese et al., 2018). Giving information that someone won't remember is not necessarily harmful, but if repeated information is distressing every time, it may be worth considering how important it is that the person understands it.

Balancing the information: This is the ability to understand the implications of the information. It includes the ability to put information into the perspective of 'time' and the ability to see 'the bigger picture'. People with severe and profound intellectual disability may not be able to understand abstract concepts that happen in the future. If this is the case, it is best to limit information to the immediate future, for example, what will happen today and tomorrow. People with autistic spectrum disorder may find it particularly difficult to cope with information that is not concrete and certain (and very often, information about terminal illness and prognosis is uncertain).

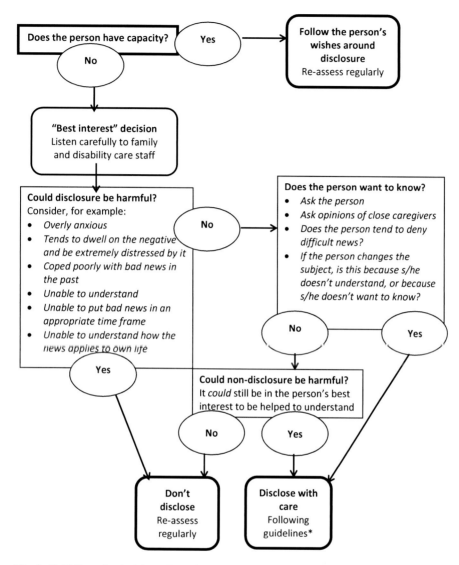

Fig. 1 Guidelines for decisions about (non-)disclosure of bad news around life-limiting illness and death to people with intellectual disability (Tuffrey-Wijne, 2013)

The flow chart in Fig. 1 summarises Tuffrey-Wijne's guidelines for decisions about disclosure of bad news around life-limiting illness and death to people with intellectual disability (Tuffrey-Wijne, 2013) (Fig. 1).

Palliative Care and End-of-Life Care

The life expectancy of people with intellectual disability has improved in recent decades, although it is still around 20 years below that of the general population (Bittles et al., 2002; Patja, Iivanainen, Vesala, Oksanen, & Ruoppila, 2000). People with mild and moderate levels of intellectual disability are more likely to live into old age than people with severe and profound levels of intellectual disability. The leading causes of death in people with intellectual disability are respiratory disease, heart and circulatory disorders and cancer (Heslop et al., 2013; O'Leary, Cooper, & Huges-McCormack, 2018). Dementia is common among people with intellectual disability, in particular among people with Down syndrome (Strydom et al., 2010). People with intellectual disability are therefore increasingly likely to die of conditions usually associated with older age, which are often preceded by a period of ill-health. This period increasingly means the need for palliative care as the end of life approaches.

Palliative care has been defined as follows:

> The active, total care of patients whose disease is not responsive to curative treatment. Palliative care takes a holistic approach, addressing physical, psychosocial and spiritual care, including the treatment of pain and other symptoms. Palliative care is interdisciplinary in its approach and encompasses the care of the patient and their family and should be available in any location including hospital, hospice and community. Palliative care affirms life and regards dying as a normal process; it neither hastens nor postpones death and sets out to preserve the best possible quality of life until death. (European Association for Palliative Care, n.d.)

There are significant challenges in providing palliative care to people with intellectual disability. The European Association of Palliative Care published a White Paper with consensus norms of what good palliative care for this population looks like. Thirteen norms were developed, summarised in Box 3. Support for the person's involvement in end-of-life decision making is a key part of these international norms (Tuffrey-Wijne & McLaughlin, 2015) (Box 3).

Box 3
People with intellectual disability should have:
1. Equity of access to palliative care services
2. Understanding of and support for their communication needs
3. Recognition by health and social care providers of when the need for palliative care arises, prompting a person-centred plan for palliative care support
4. Assessment of physical, emotional, social and spiritual needs
5. Recognition, assessment and management of pain and other symptoms; this should include collaboration between those who know the person well and those who are experts in symptom management
6. All necessary support, including advocacy, to enable involvement in end-of-life decision making and a recognition of the value of their life and their right to life
7. Involvement of those who matter: families, friends and disability care staff
8. Services that collaborate with all others involved and share expertise

9. Support for families, friends and disability care staff
10. Opportunities to prepare for death
11. Bereavement support, including a recognition of a higher risk of compli-
    cated grief

Service providers should:

12. Provide staff education and training and death education for people with
    intellectual disabilities
13. Prioritise equitable palliative care for people with intellectual disabilities,
    including forward planning and providing adequate resources

Tuffrey-Wijne & McLaughlin, (2015)

The Place of Care When Dying

For the general population, the place of care is found to be influenced by a number
of factors including the length of illness and presence of symptoms, the dying person's preferences, together with environmental factors such as social support and
home-care availability (Gomes & Higginson, 2006).

Of these, the environmental factors are the most influential. This is even more
likely to be true for people with intellectual disability, who may live in supported
accommodation settings that are not designed or suited to increased care needs.
Having a choice about the place of care at the end of life requires the availability of
at least two high-quality options. To have a real choice, the person would need to
understand those options. For example, people with intellectual disability may
know what a hospital is but may be less likely to understand what a hospice is or
what it would be like to receive their care in a residential care home such as a nursing home. Our own research has found that many people with intellectual disability
who reach the end of life have few, if any, options open to them (Tuffrey-Wijne, 2009).

There should be no assumptions about what is the best place of care for people
with intellectual disability at the end of life – including the assumption that 'home
is best'. There are some challenging questions to be asked when we say that people
with intellectual disability should be enabled to receive their dying care at home.
For example, where is 'home' for a person who may have spent part of their lives in
institutional or residential care? While supported accommodation staff may feel that
they are offering people a 'home for life', we cannot always assume that this is
indeed possible nor that people themselves would choose this option. Alternatively,
if the person who is dying has lived with their family all their life, a challenging
question might be: is being cared for at home possible if the family caregivers are
themselves ageing?

Tuffrey-Wijne's research has found that a good place of care, and ultimately a
good death, requires the following components (Tuffrey-Wijne, 2009):

- *Familiar or safe surroundings with familiar people.* Some people do not feel safe at home and would rather be somewhere else. This could be, for example, if caregivers convey a feeling of being frightened themselves or if the setting is unsuitable for increased care needs. What seems important is that people are in a place where their physical needs can be met and close bonds with family, friends and disability care staff can continue until the moment of death and beyond. While continuing close bonds are easiest at home, these can also be achieved elsewhere if other care needs need to be prioritised. The real-life case in Box 4 offers an illustration (Box 4).
- *Freedom from pain and anxiety.* This is likely to require input from specialists, such as the palliative care team. Deaths at home need intensive support and good collaboration. Even if this is in place, and the death is anticipated, it is not unusual for caregivers to be taken by surprise, with the final days extremely difficult with which to cope.
- *Extensive support for caregivers.* Caregivers need to know what is happening and what to expect. They need to see that the person is treated with respect. They also need recognition and support for their own emotions and grief. If that is not available, the place of care may be good for the dying person, but it may be unacceptable for caregivers (Box 5).

Box 4 Lilly Lamb Case Study[3]
Lilly had moderate intellectual disability. She was confused about being at home when she was clearly ill. 'I have pain', she said, 'I should be in hospital'. She was transferred to a hospice and loved it there. There was space for her wheelchair and hoist. 'It's handy', she said.

Box 5 Pete Carpenter Case Study Part 3
Pete Carpenter died at his supported accommodation home. It seemed to be a 'good death' for him: pain-free, in a familiar environment with people he trusted. But the toll on care staff and fellow residents was heavy. Staffing levels were not adjusted quickly enough to cope with his changing needs. When he became unable to walk the stairs, his bed was moved into the downstairs living room, which upset the other residents. One of the housemates told her day care staff, 'It's all right for you, you go home to your own house at the end of the day. I have to sit there and watch it'. It was considered lucky that Pete died at a weekend when both his housemates were away. There was no plan B, but the situation at home was quickly becoming unsustainable.

Guidance on Decision Making Around the Best Place of Care

A research team in the Netherlands has developed evidence-based guidance for disability care staff and healthcare professionals (Bekkema, Tuffrey-Wijne, Wagemans, Hertogh, Francke, & de Veer, 2015). The guide identifies four important considerations, which echo the findings of Tuffrey-Wijne's research.

1. *Familiarity*. It is particularly important for people with intellectual disability to be around people who understand them and are able to quickly pick up signs, for instance pain or discomfort.
2. *The team's expertise*. The first step for a professional team is to determine the care requirements, the expertise they already have, the additional know-how they will need to bring in and whether 24-h care can be provided.
3. *The home environment setup*. Is the home properly equipped for providing palliative care? For example, is there room to put a raised (or lowered) bed and to receive visitors? Are there patient hoists available, and is it possible to install medical equipment?
4. *Fellow residents or family members (for people living together)*. Palliative care for a person with intellectual disability living with other people can be valuable to both the dying person and others living in the shared home. Yet, caregivers of the dying person need to continually ask themselves if they can balance the required care activities with their other responsibilities. In the case of disability care staff, whether they can also maintain standards of care to other residents. For family caregivers, whether they can maintain their usual household tasks and family routines.

It is important to take into account *everyone's* perspectives and choices. This includes, first of all, the perspective of the person with intellectual disability who is dying. As we have seen, this may not be what others expect, so careful listening to verbal and non-verbal communication is important. Families, disability care staff and healthcare professionals may all have different views on what is best for the dying person. Ideally, all these perspectives will be listened to and taken into consideration, leading to a joint decision-making process about care – whatever the setting. For complex decisions such as these, it is helpful to have a coordinator, for example, a team leader, case manager, palliative care expert or care staff member, to coordinate the decision-making process and to ensure that all the appropriate people are involved.

Funeral Wishes

The research shows that at least some people with intellectual disability can consider choices about funerals and that the personal experience of having attended funerals can be a catalyst to consider one's own (Bekkema, Veer, & Hertog, 2016).

Making choices about funeral wishes is not just about whether a cremation or burial is preferred. A person with intellectual disability may wish to also consider where the funeral ceremony might be held, the preferred location of the grave or ashes, special guests, the music, flowers, any readings and the things that the person might like to take with them, including treasured possessions or preferred clothing to wear. All these are valid choice opportunities. Given time and adequate information to think about these things, a person with intellectual disability may have strong preferences. Facilitating these choice-making opportunities is a demonstration of the value placed upon the person's preferences and offers a remembrance to those left behind after the funeral. The real-life case in Box 6 demonstrates the range of funeral choices in action. A pseudonym has been used to protect the person's identity (Box 6).

Box 6 Dale Case Study

Dale has pancreatic cancer and knows he has a few months left to live. He has a photograph in his wallet of the place where his dead mother's ashes are spread. He told his disability care staff he would like to have his ashes spread there also. He has a favourite shirt that he has chosen to wear when he dies, and he does not want any sad music. All these choices are now formally documented in Dale's personal file at his supported accommodation home. His disability care staff reported relief knowing Dale's choices and anticipated that this will mean the funeral will truly represent Dale and his preferences.

For people without pre-existing knowledge or experience with funerals, and thereby the available choices, a helpful place to start is to understand the difference between cremation and burial. Resources that caregivers might use to help a person with intellectual disability understand these concepts include *The Books Beyond Words* series: *When Mum Died* (https://booksbeyondwords.co.uk/bookshop/paperbacks/when-mum-died?rq=when%20mum%20died; Hollins & Sireling, 2004b), which illustrates a cremation, and *When Dad Died* (https://booksbeyondwords.co.uk/bookshop/paperbacks/when-dad-died?rq=when%20dad%20died; Hollins & Sireling, 2004a), which illustrates a burial, as well as the *Funeral Wishes* module on the website *Talking End of life with people with intellectual disability* (TEL) (https://www.caresearch.com.au/TEL/; Wiese et al., 2018). The research suggests that helpful ways of discussing the topic could include introducing it as a hypothetical and drawing on previous experiences where funerals were attended to provide real examples (McKenzie, Mirfin-Veitch, Conder, & Brandford, 2017).

Bequeathing

For the purposes of this chapter, we define bequeathing as to pass or hand down (Macquarie Dictionary, 2018). In contemporary society the term is often associated with a legal will. Any person can make a will, but its legal standing may be challenged if the will-maker's mental capacity is challenged (see also discussion about capacity at the beginning of this chapter). Mental capacity is usually presumed, but if challenged, then the person's ability to understand the general nature of will-making and communicating their intentions is determined by a suitably qualified clinician, usually in consort with legal expertise. Further detail about mental capacity is not offered in this chapter, with the exception of offering helpful resources (Intellectual Disability Rights Service, 2018; New South Wales Government Attorney General's Department, 2009).

Operating from the premise that mental capacity is presumed under common law, a person with intellectual disability is thereby presumed to be able to make decisions about bequeathing. Like other decisions, bequeathing is an important human right (Purser et al., 2015). It offers reassurance to the person that the things he or she loves best are going to those most cared about. For those left behind, it can be an honour to receive these things and to have a lasting memory about the person who died. There are two important issues for caregivers to consider when supporting a person with intellectual disability to make decisions about bequeathing: (1) documenting the decisions and (2) ensuring the decisions made by the person are not subject to influence by others, that is, they are autonomous.

1.Documenting the Decisions Bequeathing decisions are usually documented via a legal will or through the individual's person-centred planning. The key difference between the two is that the legal will is binding and is often written by a legal professional and, if challenged, the person's decision-making ability may be subject to mental capacity assessment (Intellectual Disability Rights Service, 2018; Purser et al., 2015). Even if the person is deemed to not have the mental capacity to make a legal will, this does not preclude them from making bequeathing decisions that could be planned for and documented through person-centred planning.

Irrespective of whether the bequeathing is organised through legal will-making or person-centred planning, the important thing is that the bequeathing decisions are documented. Legal wills can be obtained with the advice of a lawyer. Inclusion Ireland also has helpful information in accessible format for people with disability about will-making (Inclusion Ireland, n.d.). Using person-centred planning approaches, there is no single way of documenting bequeathing wishes. There are, however, available templates which can be used by the person with intellectual disability to document bequeathing decisions (My end of life choices, n.d.; When I Die, n.d.). These templates are best completed with support. The *Bequeathing* module on the website *Talking End of life with people with intellectual disability* (TEL) offers an example of how to support a person with intellectual disability understand and make decisions about bequeathing (https://www.caresearch.com.au/TEL/; Wiese et al., 2018).

2.Ensuring Autonomous Decisions Anecdotal evidence suggests that disability support staff are concerned that assisting people to make decisions may be viewed as coercion, perhaps for personal gain. We propose that while disability support professionals are ideally placed to teach the concept of bequeathing, they should not be solely involved in assisting that person to document their decisions. Irrespective of whether documentation is done via a legal will or person-centred planning approaches, a team approach should be taken, with the person with intellectual disability at the centre of all decision making (Wiese et al., 2018).

Organ and Tissue Donation

Organ donation is the process whereby organs including the kidneys, lungs, heart, liver and pancreas are transplanted from a dead person (the donor) to a recipient who is very ill or dying from organ failure. Tissue donation is a similar process but includes heart valves, bone tissue, skin, eye and pancreas tissue (Australian Government Organ and Tissue Authority, 2018).

The extent to which people with intellectual disability understand the concept of organ and tissue donation and the decision to donate is not yet well understand in the research literature. While any one can make a decision to donate, particular sensitivities and vigilance around mental capacity are suggested (Malhotra, Balhara, & Varghese, 2004).

There are limited resources about organ and tissue donation. The following are suggested from the United Kingdom and Australia (NHS Blood and Transplant, n.d.; Wiese et al., 2018).

Advance Care Planning

Advance care planning is a process whereby the person makes choices about future care in anticipation of reduced decision-making capacity. Choices might include who would be the decision-maker on the person's behalf and preferred medical care based on the person's individual values and goals (Sudore et al., 2017). In the general community, the research shows that documenting and upholding the dying person's future care preferences results in enhanced care quality and self-control for the dying person. For those left behind, improved satisfaction and reduced stress, anxiety and depression have been reported (Bischoff, Sudore, Miao, Boscardin, & Smith, 2013; Detering, Hancock, Reade, & Silvester, 2010).

To date, there is no available research about the outcomes of advance care planning for people with intellectual disability or the extent to which people with intellectual disability can understand the process. However, positive outcomes have been reported by caregivers (Pueyo et al., 2015; Voss et al., 2017). A recent study by McKenzie, Mirfin-Veitch, Conder and Brandford (2017) showed that pacing the introduction of information, caregiver facilitation skills, supporting decision making and covering all necessary content were important to people with intellectual disability who participate in advance care planning. To work well for all, clarity about family and professional roles in advance care planning is needed (Voss et al., 2017).

One potentially sensitive content area of advance care planning is decision making about do not resuscitate (DNR). There is limited research about DNR decision making by, or for, people with intellectual disability (Tuffrey-Wijne et al., 2014; Wagemans et al., 2017). The available research suggests that DNR decision making is a contested and complex area with reported conflicts between physicians and family, lack of certainty about the decision-maker role and inconsistent policy guidance (Tuffrey-Wijne et al., 2014; Wagemans et al., 2017).

What Works

There is much still to be learnt about how people with intellectual disability can be assisted to understand and make choices about the end of life. Notwithstanding, we offer some guidance about what works based on the available evidence presented in this chapter:

- People with intellectual disability must understand what dying and death are before they can make decisions about the end of life.
- There are many topics associated with decision making about the end of life. These include palliative care, place of care, funeral wishes, bequeathing, organ and tissue donation and advance care planning.
- Caregivers play a critical role to support people with intellectual disability understand and make choices about the many topics associated with end of life.
- Caregivers need to provide the framework whereby people with intellectual disability can document their decisions.
- Caregivers need to provide a structure whereby if the person changes their mind, decisions can be reviewed and changed.
- There are a range of available resources for caregivers to support people with intellectual disability to engage with the end-of-life topic. These are variously referred to throughout these chapter and are summarised here:

  - *Breaking bad news to people with intellectual disability* (Breaking bad news, n.d., http://www.breakingbadnews.org)
  - *Making a will* (Inclusion Ireland, n.d., http://www.inclusionireland.ie/makingawill)

- A template to document end-of-life choices (My end of life choices, n.d., https://www.caresearch.com.au/tel/tabid/4658/Default.aspx)
- A template to document end-of-life choices (When I Die, n.d., https://www. pcpld.org/wp-content/uploads/when_i_die_2_0.pdf)
- *Organ and tissue donation: A leaflet for people with learning disabilities* (NHS Blood and Transplant, n.d., file://ad.uws.edu.au/dfshare/ HomesHWK$/30044211/My%20Documents/Literature/NHS%20Organ%20 and%20tissue%20donation%20leaflet.pdf)
- *Talking end of life with people with intellectual disability (TEL)* (Wiese et al., 2018, https://www.caresearch.com.au/TEL/)
- Selected works from the *Books beyond Words* series (Hollins & Sireling, 2004a, https://booksbeyondwords.co.uk/bookshop/paperbacks/when-dad-died?rq=when%20dad%20died; Hollins & Sireling, 2004b, https://booksbe-yondwords.co.uk/bookshop/paperbacks/when-mum-died?rq=when%20 mum%20died; Hollins & Tuffrey-Wijne, 2009, https://booksbeyondwords. co.uk/bookshop/paperbacks/am-i-going-die
- Software resource to assist children and adults with learning disability to understand their life-limiting illness (PicTTalk, n.d., https://www.keele.ac.uk/ nursingandmidwifery/research/picttalk/)
- Resources for people with learning disabilities (Palliative Care for People with Learning Disabilities Network, 2018, https://www.pcpld.org)

Conclusion

Every person has the right to make his or her own decisions, and this includes those about the end of life. Choice making about dying and death is an emerging area of intellectual disability research and practice. The issues are many, including the person's capacity to understand this sensitive and challenging topic, the important support role of caregivers and the limitations of the available research. For people with intellectual disability to enact self-determination, making decisions about the end of life represents perhaps the final but no less important opportunity to state preference and for caregivers to validate the person's individuality and value.

References

Australian Government Organ and Tissue Authority. (2018). *About donation*. Retrieved from https://donatelife.gov.au/about-donation/get-facts/facts-and-statistics

Bekkema, N., de Veer, A. J. E., & Hertog, C. M. P. M. (2016). *Perspectives of people with mild intellectual disabilities on care relationships at the end of life: A group interview study*. Palliative Medicine, Advance online publication. doi:https://doi.org/10.1177/0269216316640421

Bekkema, N., Tuffrey-Wijne, I., Wagemans, A., Hertogh, C. M. P. M., Francke, A. L., & de Veer, A. J. E. (2015). *Decision-making about the best place of palliative care for people with intellectual disability: A guide for care staff and healthcare professionals providing palliative care for people with intellectual disability*. Retrieved from https://www.nivel.nl/sites/default/files/bestanden/Handreiking-decisionmaking-palliative-care-disabilities.pdf

Bischoff, K. E., Sudore, R. L., Miao, Y., Boscardin, W. J., & Smith, A. K. (2013). Advance care planning and quality of end-of-life care in older adults. *Journal of the American Geriatrics Society, 61*, 209–214. https://doi.org/10.1111/jgs.12105

Bittles, A. H., Petterson, B. A., Sullivan, S. G., Hussain, R., Glasson, E. J., & Montgomery, P. D. (2002). The influence of intellectual disability on life expectancy. *Journal of Gerentology: Medical. Sciences, 57A*(7), M470–M472.

Books Beyond Words. (n.d.). Retrieved from https://booksbeyondwords.co.uk/

Breaking Bad News. (n.d.). Retrieved from http://www.breakingbadnews.org

Detering, K. M., Hancock, A. D., Reade, M. C., & Silvester, W. (2010). The impact of advance care planning on end of life care in elderly patients: Randomised controlled trial. *British Medical Journal, 340*(c1345), 1–9. https://doi.org/10.1136/bmj.c1345

European Association for Palliative Care. (n.d.). *Definition of palliative care (English)*. Retrieved from https://www.eapcnet.eu/about-us/what-we-do

Gomes, B., & Higginson, I. J. (2006). Factors influencing death at home in terminally ill patients with cancer: Systematic review. *BMJ, 55*(February), 1–7. https://doi.org/10.1136/bmj.38740.614954.55.

Heslop, P., Blair, P., Fleming, P., Hoghton, M., Marriott, A., & Russ, L. (2013). *Confidential inquiry into premature deaths of people with learning disabilities (CIPOLD)*. Retrieved from Bristol, UK.

Hollins, S., & Sireling, L. (2004a). *When Dad died (Books beyond Words series)*. London, UK: The Royal College of Psychiatrists. Retrieved from https://booksbeyondwords.co.uk/bookshop/paperbacks/when-dad-died?rq=when%20dad%20died

Hollins, S., & Sireling, L. (2004b). *When Mum died (Books beyond Words series)*. London, UK: The Royal College of Psychiatrists. Retrieved from https://booksbeyondwords.co.uk/bookshop/paperbacks/when-mum-died?rq=when%20mum%20died

Hollins, S., & Tuffrey-Wijne, I. (2009). *Am I going to die? (Books beyond Words series)*. London, UK: RCPsych Publications and St George's University. Retrieved from https://booksbeyondwords.co.uk/bookshop/paperbacks/am-i-going-die

Inclusion Ireland. (n.d.). *Making a will*. Retrieved from http://www.inclusionireland.ie/makingawill

Intellectual Disability Rights Service. (2018). *Wills for people with intellectual disability*. Retrieved from http://www.idrs.org.au/publications/read-factsheet.php?factsheet=wills-for-people-with-intellectual-disability

Macquarie Dictionary. (2018). Retrieved from https://www.macquariedictionary.com.au/

Malhotra, S., Balhara, Y., & Varghese, S. (2004). Organ donation in mental retardation: A clinical dilemma. *Indian Journal of Medical Sciences, 58*(10), 444.

McKenzie, N., Mirfin-Veitch, B., Conder, J., & Brandford, S. (2017). "I'm still here": Exploring what matters to people with intellectual disability during advance care planning. *Journal of Applied Research in Intellectual Disabilities, 30*(6), 1089–1098. https://doi.org/10.1111/jar.12355

Mental Capacity Act (England & Wales). 2005. Retrieved from https://www.legislation.gov.uk/ukpga/2005/9/pdfs/ukpga_20050009_en.pdf

My end of life choices. (n.d.). Retrieved from https://www.legislation.gov.uk/ukpga/2005/9/pdfs/ukpga_20050009_en.pdf https://www.caresearch.com.au/tel/tabid/4658/Default.aspx

New South Wales Government Attorney General's Department. (2009). *Capacity toolkit*. Sydney, NSW: New South Wales Government. Retrieved from https://www.justice.nsw.gov.au/diversityservices/Documents/capacity_toolkit0609.pdf

NHS Blood and Transplant. (n.d.). *Organ and tissue donation: A leaflet for people with learning disabilities*. Retrieved from file://ad.uws.edu.au/dfshare/HomesHWK$/30044211/My%20Documents/Literature/NHS%20Organ%20and%20tissue%20donation%20leaflet.pdf

O'Leary, L., Cooper, S. A., & Huges-McCormack, L. (2018). Early death and causes of death of people with intellectual disability: A systematic review. *Journal of Applied Research in Intellectual Disabilities, 31*(3), 325–342. https://doi.org/10.1111/jar.12446

Palliative Care for People with Learning Disabilities Network. (2018). Retrieved from https://www.pcpld.org

Patja, K., Iivanainen, M., Vesala, H., Oksanen, H., & Ruoppila, I. (2000). Life expectancy of peo-
    ple with intellectual disability: A 35-year follow-up study. *Journal of Intellectual Disability
    Research, 44*(5), 591–599.
picTTalk. (n.d.). *About PicTTalk*. Retrieved from https://www.keele.ac.uk/nursingandmidwifery/
    research/picttalk/
Pueyo, C. B., Tuneu, N. C., Gomez, A. B., Vila, M. C., Carrascosa, L. M., & Martinez, C. M.
    (2015). P-49 advance care planning for persons with severe intellectual disabilities: A case
    report of Vic. Catalonia, Spain. *BMJ Supportive & Palliative Care Supplement, 2*(5), A58.
    https://doi.org/10.1136/bmjspcare-2015-000978.179
Purser, K., Magner, E. S., & Madison, J. (2015). A therapeutic approach to assess legal capacity in
    Australia. *International Journal of Law and Psychiatry, 38*, 18–28. https://doi.org/10.1016/j.
    ijlp.2015.01.003
Ryan, K., Guerin, S., Dodd, P., & McEvoy, J. (2011). End-of-life care for people with intellectual
    disabilities: Paid career perspectives. *Journal of Applied Research in Intellectual Disabilities,
    24*(3), 199–207.
Stancliffe, R. J., Wiese, M. Y., Read, S., Jeltes, G., & Clayton, J. (2017). Assessing knowledge and
    attitudes about end of life: Evaluation of three instruments designed for adults with intellectual
    disability. *Journal of Applied Research in Intellectual Disabilities, 30*(6), 1076–1088. https://
    doi.org/10.1111/jar.12358
Stancliffe, R. J., Wiese, M. Y., Read, S., Jeltes, G., & Clayton, J. M. (2016). Knowing, planning for
    and fearing death: Do adults with intellectual disability and disability staff differ? *Research in
    Developmental Disabilities, 49-50*, 47–59. https://doi.org/10.1016/j.ridd.2015.11.016
Strydom, A., Shooshtari, S., Lee, L., Raykar, V., Torr, J., Tsiouris, J., … Maaskant, M. (2010).
    Dementia in older adults with intellectual disabilities – Epidemiology, presentation, and diag-
    nosis. *Journal of Policy and Practice in Intellectual Disabilities, 7*(2), 96–110.
Sudore, R. L., Lum, H. D., You, J. J., Hanson, L. C., Meier, D. E., Pantilat, S. Z., … Helyalnd,
    D. K. (2017). Defining advance care planning for adults: A consensus definition from a multi-
    disciplinary Delphi panel. *Journal of Pain and Symptom Management, 53*(5), 821–832.e821.
Tuffrey-Wijne, I. (2009). The preferred place of care for people who are dying. *Learning Disability
    Practice, 12*(6), 16–21.
Tuffrey-Wijne, I. (2010). *Living with learning disabilities, dying with cancer: Thirteen personal
    stories*. London, UK: Jessica Kingsley.
Tuffrey-Wijne, I. (2013a). *How to break bad news to people with intellectual disabilities: A guide
    for careers and professionals*. London, UK: Jessica Kingsley.
Tuffrey-Wijne, I. (2013b). A new model for breaking bad news to people with intellectual disabili-
    ties. *Palliative Medicine, 27*(1), 5–12.
Tuffrey-Wijne, I., Goulding, L., Gordon, V., Abraham, E., Giatras, N., Edwards, C., … Hollins, S.
    (2014). The challenges in monitoring and preventing patient safety incidents for people with
    intellectual disabilities in NHS acute hospitals: Evidence from a mixed-methods study. *BMC
    Health Services Research., 14*, 432. https://doi.org/10.1186/1472-6963-14-432
Tuffrey-Wijne, I., & McLaughlin, D. (2015). *Consensus norms for palliative care of people with
    intellectual disabilities in Europe: EAPC white paper*. Retrieved from https://eapcnet.files.
    wordpress.com/2016/02/white-paper-id-shot-2015-11-25-at-14-01-48.png
Tuffrey-Wijne, I., & Rose, T. A. (2017). Investigating the factors that affect the communication
    of death-related bad news to people with intellectual disability by staff in residential and sup-
    ported living services: An interview study. *Journal of Intellectual Disability Research, 61*(8),
    727–736. https://doi.org/10.1111/jir.12375
Turner, F. J. (2007). Implications of the Mental Capacity Act 2005 on advance care planning at the
    end of life. *Nursing Standard, 22*(2), 35–39.
United Nations. (2006). *Convention on the rights of persons with disabilities*. Retrieved from
    http://www.un.org/disabilities/convention/conventionfull.shtml
Voss, H., Vogel, A., Wagemans, A. M. A., Francke, A. L., Job, P., Metsemakers, F. M., … de Veer,
    A. J. E. (2017). Advance care planning in palliative care for people with intellectual disabili-

ties: A systematic review. *Journal of Pain and Symptom Management, 54*(6), 938–960. https://doi.org/10.1016/j.jpainsymman.2017.04.016

Wagemans, A. M. A., van Schrojenstein Lantman-de Valk, H. M. J., Proot, I. M., Bressers, A. M., Metsemakers, J., Tuffrey-Wijne, I., … Curfs, L. M. G. (2017). Do-Not-Attempt resuscitation orders for people with intellectual disabilities: Dilemmas and uncertainties for ID physicians and trainees. The importance of the deliberation process. *Journal of Intellectual Disability Research, 61*(3), 245–254. https://doi.org/10.1111/jir.12333

When I Die. (n.d.). Retrieved from https://www.pcpld.org/wp-content/uploads/when_i_die_2_0.pdf

Wicki, M. T. (2018). Advance care planning for persons with intellectual disabilities. *The Journal of Gerontopsychology and Geriatric Psychiatry, 31*, 87–95. https://doi.org/10.1024/1662-9647/a000187

Wiese, M., Dew, A., Stancliffe, R. J., Howarth, G., & Balandin, S. (2013). "If and when?": Experiences of community living staff engaging older people with intellectual disability to know about dying. *Journal of Intellectual Disability Research, 57*(10), 980–992.

Wiese, M., Stancliffe, R. J., Read, S., Jeltes, G., & Clayton, J. M. (2015). Learning about dying, death and end-of-life planning: Current issues informing future actions. *Journal of Intellectual & Developmental Disability, 40*(2), 230–235. https://doi.org/10.3109/13668250.2014.998183

Wiese, M. Y., Stancliffe, R. J., Wagstaff, S., Tieman, J., Jeltes, G., & Clayton, J. (2018). *Talking End of Life…with people with intellectual disability (TEL)*. Retrieved from https://www.care-search.com.au/TEL/

Part IV
Implications for Policy and Practice

Policies and Practices to Support Preference, Choice, and Self-Determination: An Ecological Understanding

Roger J. Stancliffe, Karrie A. Shogren, Michael L. Wehmeyer, and Brian H. Abery

Policies and Practices to Support Preference, Choice, and Self-Determination: An Ecological Understanding

This chapter begins with an examination of the centrality of preference, choice, and self-determination in long-standing notions of citizenship and rights, ideas codified recently in the Convention on the Rights of Persons with Disabilities (CRPD; United Nations [UN], 2006). For much of the current chapter, we draw together key ideas presented throughout the book by identifying broad themes related to factors that facilitate or impede the realization of these rights across the lifespan. Throughout this final chapter, we frequently refer to individual chapters that illustrate the broader themes.

This effort is necessarily complex because of the multiplicity of factors involved at many different levels of the environment, ranging from individual supports for identifying and communicating preference (chapter "Preference Assessments, Choice, and Quality of Life for People with Significant Disabilities"), the family's role in influencing self-determination (chapter "Adults with Intellectual Disability: Choice and Control in the Context of Family"), to issues of national policy concerning guardianship (chapter "Choice Within the Israeli Welfare State: Lessons Learned

R. J. Stancliffe (✉)
Centre for Disability Research and Policy, The University of Sydney,
Sydney, NSW, Australia
e-mail: roger.stancliffe@sydney.edu.au

K. A. Shogren
Kansas University Center on Developmental Disabilities, University of Kansas,
Lawrence, KS, USA

M. L. Wehmeyer
Beach Center on Disability, University of Kansas, Lawrence, KS, USA

B. H. Abery
Institute on Community Integration, University of Minnesota, Minneapolis, MN, USA

© Springer Nature Switzerland AG 2020
R. J. Stancliffe et al. (eds.), *Choice, Preference, and Disability*, Positive
Psychology and Disability Series, https://doi.org/10.1007/978-3-030-35683-5_18

from Legal Capacity and Housing Services"), education (chapter "Choices and Transition from School to Adult Life: Experiences in China"), employment (chapter "Employment Opportunities for People with Intellectual Disabilities"), and disability services funding and delivery (chapter "Choice, Preference, and Disability: Promoting Self-Determination Across the Lifespan"). Like several of the book's chapters (e.g., chapters "Choices, Preferences, and Disability: A View from Central and Eastern Europe" and "Adults with Intellectual Disability: Choice and Control in the Context of Family"), we have used the multilevel ecological model developed by Bronfenbrenner (e.g., Bronfenbrenner, 1994, 2005) as an organizing framework within which to place the many factors influencing choice and self-determination. For those seeking more information about this approach, we refer readers to Abery and Stancliffe's (2003) ecological theory of self-determination and to the discussion in the chapters "Choices, Preferences, and Disability: A View from Central and Eastern Europe" and "Adults with Intellectual Disability: Choice and Control in the Context of Family" of the applicability of this theory to various aspects of choice and self-determination by people with intellectual disability.

Finally, we place preference, choice, and self-determination in a broader context by recognizing that the developments and issues described throughout this book form part of an international movement away from a deficits-based understanding of disability and toward a strengths-based approach. As befits a text that forms parts of a book series on *Positive Psychology and Disability*, we end by briefly considering how these issues align with the emerging discipline of positive psychology.

Citizenship, Rights, and Ableism

Since the time of ancient Greece, the concept of *citizenship* has implied the capability of individuals to express their preferences, make their own choices, and exercise control over their lives. First articulated in the writings of Locke and Hobbes, the notion that all people, irrespective of their particular social context, have the same inherent rights (Petman, 2009) underlies much of what we know about self-determination. The CRPD (United Nations, 2006) was adopted by the United Nations General Assembly in 2006 and has been ratified by almost 160 countries. Article 12 of the *Convention* guarantees both equal recognition before the law and the legal capacity to exercise self-determination (United Nations, 2006). Countries that have ratified the Convention are required to recognize that persons with disabilities enjoy a legal right to exercise control on an equal basis with others in all aspects of life, as well as to take steps to support this right. The social-ecological model of disability underlying the CRPD leads to the explicit recognition that some people with disabilities will require support if they are to exercise choice but that nonetheless they have *both* the capacity and right to do so.

Despite the ratification of international treaties like the CRPD, there has rarely been a system to ensure that governments take steps to guarantee those rights. Lang, Kett, Groce, and Trani (2011) argued that, in spite of the good intentions underlying the CRPD, there remains a significant gap in implementation. Lang and colleagues attribute this to a number of factors including (a) insufficient national disability policies that support effective implementation of the Convention; (b) a lack of congruence between policy and practice; and (c) the absence of will for implementation on the part of governments and civil society. Societal challenges to the exercise of choice and control and their impact of the lives of people with disabilities are explored by a number of chapter authors in this book. Holler, Werner, Tolub, and Pomerantz (chapter "Choice Within the Israeli Welfare State: Lessons Learned from Legal Capacity and Housing Services") describe the current legislative and policy factors that have led to persons with intellectual disability in Israel having few choices for truly inclusive housing. Tichá and coauthors (chapter "Choices, Preferences, and Disability: A View from Central and Eastern Europe") explore the societal underpinnings of the limited progress people with disabilities have made in expressing preference and choice in the context of growing up and living in Central and Eastern Europe. Additionally, Tøssebro and Olsen (chapter "Employment Opportunities for People with Intellectual Disabilities") and Löfgren-Mårtenson (chapter "Choice, Relationships, and Sexuality: Sexual and Reproductive Health and Rights"), respectively, discuss the cultural, ideological, and policy underpinnings of the limited choices and rights persons in the Scandinavian countries have with respect to employment and sexual and reproductive rights. In each of these cases, policies theoretically supportive of the enhanced exercise of control and self-determination exist, but implementation has occurred with low levels of fidelity, and/or there has been a lack of effective monitoring and enforcement.

Minkowitz (2017) and Werner (2012) argued that we must better understand both the barriers that exist to effective implementation of the CRPD and the need for improved monitoring of implementation efforts. Many of these barriers exist at the macrosystem level (Garbarino, 2017). The *macrosystem* – one of the levels of Bronfenbrenner's ecological model (1994) – refers to the values and ideology of a culture and the patterns of organization that characterize it. In most countries, societal attitudes with respect to persons with disabilities remain "ableist" with high levels of discrimination in favor of nondisabled people. And the impact of ableism extends beyond acts of discrimination to the way a culture views people with disabilities. Both practices and dominant attitudes continue to devalue, marginalize, and limit the potential of people with disabilities. Many of these forms of discrimination are normalized and integrated into a culture's understanding (or, more accurately, disregard) of the experiences of people with disabilities. Campbell (2008, 2009) and others (e.g., Dunn & Andrews, 2015; Hehir, 2005) suggested that when cultures view people with disabilities as in need of being "fixed" and as unable to function as full members of society, they are marginalized to the extent that their human rights are at risk.

Macrosystem factors also have an impact on the ability of people with disabilities to defend their civil liberties and to pressure government and society at large to acknowledge and support their rights to choice and control. Grugel and Piper (2009) maintain that the disability movement, specifically self-advocacy groups nationally and internationally, has failed to connect disability rights to both national and international development goals. Although a unique aspect of the development of the CRPD was the active involvement of disability organizations, it has been relatively rare for people with a variety of disabilities to come together nationally or internationally to successfully apply political pressure on governments. In order to effectively advocate in a collaborative manner, however, resources are required, specifically funding. In most cases, disability organizations have yet to receive this support either from governments or society at large. At least part of the reason for these difficulties stems from limited government interest in disability issues.

As Grugel and Piper (2009) argue, the effectiveness of lobbying efforts centered on human rights is contingent upon whether an issue "catches the public imagination" and is believed to have high moral claims. As a result of the "othering" (i.e., devaluing) of people with disabilities within society, the actual implementation of disability-focused treaties (or lack thereof) has received far less attention from the government and general public than the civil rights of persons from different racial and cultural groups or women. Societal attitudes and the approach taken by most governmental agencies have resulted in a situation for the self-advocacy movement similar to the one Piven and Cloward (1971, 2012) described many years ago regarding how governments regulate people who are socioeconomically disadvantaged in such a manner that makes it extremely difficult for them to change their lives for the better.

One must also consider that in many societies, it is not just people with disabilities who struggle to advocate for their rights but the population as a whole. Over the past two centuries, governments in many countries, either through force or psychological means, have effectively suppressed the will of the people to advocate for themselves (see Tichá et al.'s chapter "Choices, Preferences, and Disability: A View from Central and Eastern Europe"). As a result, parent and professional groups as well as others with the moral authority have failed to challenge ableist attitudes, the lack of fidelity with which the CRPD has been implemented, and the ineffectiveness of legislation designed to support choice and control for persons with disabilities.

In spite of the challenges, there do appear to be changes at the macrosystem (i.e., societal level) in many countries in the capacity and willingness of the general population to challenge those in power and to advocate for the rights of people with disabilities. Recent peaceful revolutions in Armenia in the Spring of 2018 and Ukraine a few years earlier have shown that populations can rise when their rights fail to be respected by the governments that are supposed to protect them. In these countries, significantly more effort is now being devoted to enforcing disability rights and providing opportunities for choice-making and personal control than in years past.

These are not the only countries that have witnessed an evolution in disability rights. In their chapter "Choice, Preference, and Disability: Promoting Self-Determination Across the Lifespan", Laragy and Fisher described how, in spite of a number of challenges, the *Australian National Disability Insurance Scheme* provides more choice for people with disabilities who now have individualized disability funding. Xu and colleagues in their chapter "Choices and Transition from School to Adult Life: Experiences in China" discuss recent regulations in the People's Republic of China including the *Regulation on the Education for People with Disabilities* legislation (2017 revision) that have created more opportunities for people with disabilities to access school-based vocational training resulting in greater opportunities for choice of post-school employment. Abery and Tichá (personal communication, 2019) reported that in the Russian Federation, Republics of Georgia, and Armenia, as well as Ukraine and the Czech Republic, parents and people with disabilities are now organizing at the local and national level and applying political pressure to their representatives to pass new legislation to provide greater opportunities for choice and self-determination to people with disabilities, enforce violations of the rights of people with disabilities, and provide government incentives to public and private organizations whose policies and regulations both directly and indirectly increase opportunities for choice and control.

Although, in some countries, it may take a generation before the right to choice and control is fully extended to people with disabilities, significant changes in many nations are in process. The systemic theft of the right to self-determination of people with disabilities is becoming less frequent with recent events demonstrating that with the appropriate supports, most people with disabilities, even people with intensive support needs, can make informed choices over most areas of life (Abery, Olson, Poetz, & Smith, 2019; Shogren, Wehmeyer, Martinis, & Blanck, 2018). If policy related to choice and control is to be effective, it needs to be proposed with and based on the perspective of people with disabilities, accepted by the society at a macrosystem level, implemented with high fidelity, and then monitored and evaluated closely and with adequate rigor.

Barriers to Choice Across Contexts and Across the Lifespan

As described in the previous section, the freedom to make choices is a fundamental human right of all persons, including people with disabilities. In fact, the first guiding principle of the CRPD is "respect for inherent dignity, individual autonomy *including the freedom to make one's own choices*, and independence of persons [italics added]" (UN, 2006). However, as noted throughout this text, there are significant and pervasive barriers within and across communities and societies that can restrict the opportunities that people with disabilities have to (a) make choices and (b) access effective supports for actualizing their choices. The previous section highlighted the role of policy and policy change in removing barriers to choice but also emphasized that changes in policy alone are not enough; just as important is the "nuts and bolts" of policy implementation and the spirit with which changes are integrated into supports provided. From an ecological systems perspective (Bronfenbrenner, 2005), however, change cannot only occur at the macrosystem level. Instead, changes are also needed at the microsystem (e.g., individual, family) and mesosystem (e.g., community, support organizations) levels to make sustainable changes that will enhance choice opportunities. Barriers to choice must be broken down across ecological systems to actualize the values of policy, including the CRPD, and to support the advocacy of people with disabilities for choice opportunities (as described in the chapter "Reflections on Choice: The Stories of Self-Advocates" by Smith, Cocchiarella & Schaper).

One goal of this text and its chapters was to explicate barriers, across contexts, to the expression of preferences and choice in people with disabilities and highlight solutions that are emerging and establish what is working and what can work to actualize the right to choice and self-determination. A unique aspect of this text is the focus of barriers across cultural contexts; the text includes chapters from authors exploring issues related to choice from Australia, Israel, Central and Eastern Europe, China, Norway, Sweden, Canada, Ireland, the Netherlands, the UK, and the USA. Several of these authors explore specific barriers to choice that are influenced by country and cultural factors. For example, issues in Israel related to housing options and the use of plenary guardianship are highlighted in the chapter "Choice Within the Israeli Welfare State: Lessons Learned from Legal Capacity and Housing Services" by Holler et al., exploring both how changes can be made and how such change can be slow to be adopted within communities because of expectations, lack of education, and the absence of alternative models of delivering supports.

Other chapters focus on specific life domains, again highlighting barriers as well as strategies for change. For example, the chapter "Preference, Choice, and Self-Determination in the Healthcare Context" by Abery and Anderson focuses on issues related to choice and preference in the healthcare context, emphasizing health provider education. In their chapter "Employment Opportunities for People with Intellectual Disabilities", Tøssebro and Olsen discuss issues related to employment, including the role of expectations and supports. The unique barriers to choice in relation to sexuality and reproductive health are described in the chapter "Choice, Relationships, and Sexuality: Sexual and Reproductive Health and Rights" by Löfgren-Mårtenson, and specific barriers that people with intellectual disability face with respect to parenthood are described in the chapter "The Choice of Becoming a Parent" by Aunos and colleagues. For example, the use of sterilization or contraception imposed on women (and some men) with intellectual disability and the removal of the choice of being a parent, often without consent, emphasize the need to focus on the right of people with disabilities in health and healthcare to make decisions about their lives. Recognizing that both opportunities and barriers to choice change across the lifespan, chapters also focus on childhood and adolescence (chapter "The Development of Choice-Making and Implications for Promoting Choice and Autonomy for Children and Youth with Intellectual and Developmental Disabilities" by Wehmeyer and Shogren) as well as through adulthood and into aging (chapter "Choice as People Age with Intellectual Disability: An Irish Perspective" by O'Donovan, McCallion, McCausland & McCarron). Specific issues to consider in terms of end-of-life decision-making, an area often under considered in planning supports for people with intellectual disability, are highlighted by Wiese and Tuffrey-Wijne (chapter "End-of-Life Choices").

Overall, there remains significant and ongoing work to be done to remove barriers to choice opportunities and expression for people with disabilities across contexts. The ongoing presence of low expectations, absent or limited supports, poverty, restricted education and community living options and opportunities, and increased exposure to social and economic risk factors in disability communities interact with the opportunities and supports that enable people with disabilities to actualize their right to be self-determined individuals, engaged in choices and decisions about their lives, consistent with the values of the CRPD and each of its articles. Ultimately, to actualize change in choice opportunities across contexts and across the lifespan for people with disabilities, there is a need for an ongoing paradigm shift in how people with disabilities are understood and more importantly supported to be active members of their community and society and to break down "attitudinal and environmental barriers that hinders full and effective participation in society on an equal basis with others" (United Nations, 2006).

What We Know About What Works

In this section, we consider the issue of what works to support greater choice and control by people with disability. Our approach is to identify several key issues and illustrate them with examples drawn mostly from the book's chapters, not to repeat all of the specific strategies presented in the various chapters.

Research and Rights

As researchers ourselves, we place high value on high-quality research evidence for guiding policy and practice. We also recognize that there are many areas, especially concerning disability research, where such evidence is limited, of indifferent technical quality, or simply unavailable. In supporting people with disability, we cannot be frozen into inaction by the absence of the highest-quality research but, instead, need to act in a person-centered manner based on the best available evidence. Nor can we afford to be passive about the need for good-quality research. We should advocate for socially important research to help guide better disability practice and policy.

Many reforms arise from a rights-based outlook rather than an evidence-based approach. For example, as described in the chapters "Supported Decision Making" and "Choice Within the Israeli Welfare State: Lessons Learned from Legal Capacity and Housing Services", the motivation to reform paternalistic guardianship laws and move toward supported decision-making fundamentally derives from a recognition of the right of people with cognitive impairment to exercise choice and control in their lives. Nevertheless, both chapters also ably illustrate the importance of research and evaluation of the outcomes of such reforms to guide practice and to determine how well the intended aims are achieved in reality. In short, we see rights-based and evidence-based approaches as being complementary, not in opposition. For example, good research can help describe and quantify the extent of the violation of rights and so provide clear evidence of the need for reform.

An Ecological Approach

The various chapters in this book show clearly the importance of support to acquire relevant personal skills, knowledge, and attitudes to achieve choice and control, as well as having a supportive context in which to enact these capacities. More than 25 years ago Foxx, Faw, Taylor, Davis, and Fulia (1993) provided a classic demonstration of this dilemma relating to choosing where to live. Choice of where and with whom to live is such a critical issue that the CRPD (UN, 2006) explicitly states in Article 19a that "Persons with disabilities have the opportunity to choose their place of residence and where and with whom they live on an equal basis with others and are not obliged to live in a particular living arrangement."

Foxx et al. (1993) taught adults with intellectual disability living in a residential facility the skills to participate fully in the decision about where they would live when they moved to a community living setting. In a multicomponent intervention, Foxx et al. (1993) supported each individual to (a) identify their personal community living preferences, (b) ascertain their ten strongest preferences, and (c) learn how to ask questions of community living staff about the availability of their preferences in various community living settings. The participants acquired these skills well, but regrettably, the disability service environment did not enable them to participate meaningfully in making the actual decision. As Foxx et al. (1993, p. 247) noted, their participants "All had histories in which the decisions as to where they lived were based more on facility openings than their expressed choices or preferences. This placement model was and still is being followed at the facility." That is, the preference and information-gathering skills were necessary but not sufficient to empower participants. While some details may differ 25 years later, the importance of a supportive context remains as relevant as ever.

Yogi Berra once famously said, "In theory there is no difference between theory and practice. In practice there is." When it comes to choice-making by people with disabilities, that difference is context. As just illustrated, choices occur in a social, environmental, economic, and policy context. Given the support needs of many people with intellectual disability to access choice, communicate preference, experience alternatives, understand consequences, and implement choices, the role of those providing support is particularly significant. These supporters can enable or inhibit choice, but supporters too operate within a broader legal, service, and policy context. In thinking about what works to enhance choice, all of these factors are at play, often simultaneously. Indeed, it is frequently the case that a single factor (e.g., better staff training) will make a positive difference only if other key contextual factors (e.g., policies, funding) are also aligned. This very complexity and interdependence requires an ecological understanding of how these factors fit together. As noted at the beginning of this chapter, we draw on the multilevel ecological model of the environment described by Bronfenbrenner (1994, 2005) and Garbarino (2017) to help organize these ideas. We recognize the inherent complexity and interactivity of such an ecological approach. Nevertheless, for the sake of clarity of presentation, we will examine the various supports and interventions in contextual groups. These groupings are organized on the basis of who or what is the target and the nature of the support/intervention.

Microsystem interventions

The microsystem represents people, places, and events that the individual with disability experiences directly.

Supports and interventions targeted at the person with disability These methods include teaching people with disability about choice-making or communicating choices. In their chapter "Preference Assessments, Choice, and Quality of Life for People with Significant Disabilities", Cannella-Malone and Sabielny advocate starting small with people with significant disabilities and offering simple here-and-now choices within the context of everyday activities, such as choice of available snacks and continuing to build as learning occurs. Another aspect is helping the person to communicate their choice. This may include teaching the person to use technology to communicate their preferences and choices.

Another approach is providing people with accessible information to assist with informed choices. This can vary from simple awareness of possible outcomes to more directly experiencing the consequences of certain choices. For example, in their chapter "The Choice of Becoming a Parent", Aunos and colleagues describe several effective approaches to support people with intellectual disability for them fully understand the choice about becoming a parent. These include, as part of a freely available toolkit (Toolkit: Talking about children; Hodes, 2010, 2012), an activity game (e.g., Do I know what that involves?) to assist people with intellectual disability to understand clearly what having a child involves. Experiential opportunities using a Real Care Baby simulator can facilitate informed choice about having a baby (Janeslätt, Larsson, Wickström, Springer, & Höglund, 2019).

Interventions targeted at caregivers Many interventions have been described and evaluated that aim to increase choice by training caregivers to identify and make available preferred items and activities, offer more choices, and support choice more effectively. For example, in their chapter "Preference Assessments, Choice, and Quality of Life for People with Significant Disabilities", Cannella-Malone and Sabielny focus on fundamental issues of preference and choice involving people with very significant disabilities. They describe well-researched methods for identifying preferences and presenting choices that caregivers can be trained to use. Caregivers may also need training in how to recognize individual nonverbal behaviors that indicate preference and choice (e.g., pointing, grasping, vocalizing, eye gaze). Cannella-Malone and Sabielny recommend that caregivers routinely offer choices throughout the day (e.g., about personal care) and offer control over the sequencing of activities through the use of techniques such as pictorial schedules that can be rearranged.

Having identified preferences, it is important to ensure that people with intellectual disability have consistent opportunities and appropriate support to participate in preferred activities and to choose among activities. As noted by Stancliffe in his chapter "Choice Availability and People with Intellectual Disability", staff training interventions such as Active Support (Beadle-Brown, Hutchinson, & Whelton, 2012) and teaching staff to routinely offer a choice of leisure activities (Wilson, Reid, & Green, 2006) have each been shown to increase both activity participation and choice.

Choice and relationships Choice and relationships in the context of family relationships are examined in detail by Curryer, Dew, Stancliffe, and Wiese (chapter "Adults with Intellectual Disability: Choice and Control in the Context of Family") and in other contexts (friends, roommates, disability staff by Stancliffe in his chapter "Choice Availability and People with Intellectual Disability"). Both chapters show that relationships can fundamentally affect choice. The absence of sustained, meaningful relationships can also affect choice. Bigby and Douglas in their chapter "Supported Decision Making" make the excellent point that effective support for decision-making requires that the supporter knows the person well. Sadly, there are people with cognitive disabilities who currently have few social connections. This limits opportunities to access supported decision-making, as having someone with in-depth knowledge of the person's preferences and experiences is critical. This dilemma reminds us of several key issues: (a) the importance of sustained relationships as a context for choice and (b) the fact that approaches that usually enhance choice may not work for every individual, especially if there are fundamental problems, such as having no real friends, that require attention.

Environmental interventions In his chapter "Choice Availability and People with Intellectual Disability", Stancliffe noted the consistent evidence of greater availability of choice to adults with intellectual disability living in smaller and more individualized living arrangements, such as one's own home (e.g., Houseworth, Tichá, Smith, & Ajaj, 2018; Stancliffe et al., 2011). An implication is that if people in other more restrictive living arrangements move to their own home, they would likely have access to more choice. However, there are numerous factors that can prevent such a change from taking place.

Holler and colleagues in their chapter "Choice Within the Israeli Welfare State: Lessons Learned from Legal Capacity and Housing Services" point out that in Israel, housing provision for people with intellectual disability is strongly influenced by the availability of housing, resources, and services and is dominated by administrative processes and committees that actually make the final housing decision. Moreover, there remains a heavy reliance on housing people in institutions, which bring about a pervasive loss of personal control over almost all life choices. Holler and colleagues remind us that, even in community-based settings, when a disability service agency controls the setting, there is a consequent loss of control over fundamental issues such as choice of housemates and sharing one's bedroom or not. Holler et al. also point to the Israeli regulatory environment for disability services that focuses on protection, with little attention to or enforcement of resident choice and control. These authors also note the unaffordability of private rental housing for people with intellectual disability unless they have financial support from their family. In short, this multiplicity of environmental barriers means that most people have no feasible option to live in their own home and so are denied the benefits of increased choice and control that characterize this living arrangement.

Policy and funding   A number of the good practices identified throughout the book require supportive policy, funding, training, and monitoring. In their chapter "Choice, Preference, and Disability: Promoting Self-Determination Across the Lifespan", Laragy and Fisher report evidence that Australia's National Disability Insurance Scheme with its individualized funding appears to have resulted in improved choice for many people. However, these authors also warn that governmental budget restrictions could undermine such progress.

Major policy change and law reform are sometimes essential. For example, restrictive practices such as widespread use of plenary guardianship (e.g., see the chapter "Choice Within the Israeli Welfare State: Lessons Learned from Legal Capacity and Housing Services") may require changed policy and law reform. In Israel, where guardianship law reform was enacted recently, Holler et al. propose that it is too early to tell whether these reforms will result in beneficial changes. The new laws do give recognition to supporters, but it is unclear how supported decision-making will be implemented. The law requires that supporters undergo some training, but the effect of this training is currently unknown. Well-intentioned reform requires careful monitoring and well-resourced implementation. It is naïve to assume that law reform alone will change entrenched practices and beliefs.

In their chapter "The Choice of Becoming a Parent" on parenting, Aunos et al. note that in the UK, good practice guidance documents have been developed to guide professionals on best practice for working with parents with intellectual disability. Importantly, they also note that these documents are supported by laws and regulations and have been endorsed at the highest level of the family courts.

Overall, it seems clear from the issues examined throughout the book's chapters that preference, choice, and self-determination require us to think in an ecological manner by taking into account factors at all levels of the person's environment, from individual characteristics and personal supports at the microsystem level, to funding, policy, and system-level issues at the macrosystem level.

The Future of Choice, Preference, and Disability

We want to leave the readers of this text with thoughts about what the future holds with regard to choice and people with disability. We have emphasized in this chapter that international treaties on human rights, policy, legal reforms, and legislative statutes are, in essence, necessary but not sufficient for change with regard to choice and preference. Still, it is clear that a future in which the choices and preferences of people with disability are recognized and valued necessitates a meaningful role for policy and legislative action.

In an ongoing case in which one of the editors of this text has been involved, a number of people with intellectual disability filed a class action lawsuit against a US state alleging that the state unnecessarily segregates individuals with intellectual and developmental disabilities in nursing facilities, in violation of the Olmstead ruling from the Americans with Disabilities Act. The US Department of Justice (DOJ) joined the action against the state, which is currently awaiting a ruling from a federal court. One of the primary focus areas for the case on the part of the plaintiffs and the DOJ was that of informed choice; that the state had fundamentally denied the plaintiffs the opportunity to learn about options pertaining to where they might live and, in other cases, had ignored the preferences of people with regard to living somewhere other than the nursing facility (see https://www.ada.gov/olmstead/olmstead_cases_list2.htm for more information and other similar cases). Research on choice and preferences cited throughout this text was entered into testimony, illustrating the symbiotic relationship between research and policy in bringing about change.

The rate of change as effected by research and policy on choice and preference has, however, proven to be painfully slow, as is evident from discussions in most of the chapters in this text. We have referred to the Australian National Disability Insurance Scheme (NDIS) several times in this chapter, and it is overviewed by Laragy and Fisher in their chapter "Choice, Preference, and Disability: Promoting Self-Determination Across the Lifespan". Despite difficulties in implementing such a large-scale reform effort, it seems evident that people with disability have increased choice opportunities as a result of these policy changes. There have been related policy initiatives throughout the world that have at their core put in place practices that enable people with disabilities and their families to "operationalize" choices and preferences by providing them more control over funding for services and supports. The US Department of Health and Human Services, Administration for Community Living (ACL) has, in fact, put consumer choice and control at the forefront of program initiatives for aging and developmental disability services in the USA (https://acl.gov/programs/consumer-control). The levers that the ACL is using (through its discretionary and regulatory funding mechanisms) include emphases on person-centered planning, supported decision-making, and individualized budgeting (e.g., consumer-controlled funding). So, although change is slow, it seems that one takeaway message from the chapters in this text is that change is indisputably possible and the demand for change inescapable. Choice and control have become ensconced in human rights (CRPD), policy, and legislation that, ultimately, will create meaningful opportunities for self-determination.

One of the areas emphasized by ACL and discussed in the chapters "Supported Decision Making" and "Choice Within the Israeli Welfare State: Lessons Learned from Legal Capacity and Housing Services" in this text is that of addressing the overly broad use of guardianship practices around the world. Supported decision-making as an alternative to guardianship is beginning to take root throughout much of the world and seems likely to continue to grow as a means of supporting choice and self-determination for people with disabilities, and particularly people with intellectual and developmental disabilities, through the provision of supports that enable them to participate meaningfully in decisions that impact the quality of their lives (Shogren et al., 2018).

The US National Council on Disability (NCD 2018) issued a report in 2018 titled "Beyond Guardianship: Toward Alternatives that Promote Greater Self-Determination for People with Disabilities" that lays out multiple alternatives, legal and practice, that reduce the use of guardianship. Another report was issued by NCD in 2019 titled "Turning Rights into Reality: How Guardianship and Alternatives Impact the Autonomy of People with Intellectual and Developmental Disabilities." This report calls for stakeholders in the USA to collect data on the use of guardianship, to address misperceptions about autonomy and people with disabilities, and calls on the nation to address the "school-to-guardianship" pipeline (National Council on Disability, 2019, p. 14).

Moving from legal, policy, and human rights issues, there are several "big picture" issues that may accelerate the pace of change. First and foremost, as mentioned previously in this chapter and by Shogren in her chapter "Self-Determination, Preference, and Choice" there is a need for an ongoing paradigm shift in how people with disabilities are understood and to break down barriers to full participation and citizenship. There are now widely adopted models of disability which emphasize that disability is a function of the relationship between the person's capacities and the demands of the environment or context, rather than as a fault or defect within the person (Buntinx, 2013). The most prominent of such models is the World Health Organization's International Classification of Functioning, Disability, and Health (ICF; World Health Organization, 2001), which suggests that impairments to health can result in limitations in activities and restricted participation, where activity refers to the execution of a task or action by a person and participation is defined as involvement in a life situation.

Essentially, the ICF suggests that disability exists only in the gap between the person's abilities and capacities and the demands of the environment. To the degree that the environment can be designed to enable successful functioning and supports provided to enhance personal capacity and reduce or eliminate the gap between what a person can do and what is needed to function successfully in typical environments and contexts, then disability becomes, essentially, irrelevant (Buntinx, 2013). Strengths-based approaches to disability are replacing deficits-based approaches worldwide. These strengths-based approaches emphasize personal capacity, self-determination, and, of course, choice and control (Wehmeyer, 2019).

One effect of the shift to a strengths-based approach to disability is that, increasingly, research and practice have begun to align supports and services in disability to the still emerging discipline of positive psychology (Shogren, Wehmeyer, & Singh, 2017; Wehmeyer, 2013). Positive psychology is "the pursuit of understanding optimal human functioning and well-being" (Wehmeyer, Little, & Sergeant, 2009, p. 357). During his term as president of the American Psychological Association, Seligman (1999) called for a "reoriented science that emphasizes the understanding and building of the most positive qualities of an individual" (p. 559) or, simply, a psychology which he called positive psychology. Topics in positive psychology well-being and positive emotions include resilience, creativity, character strengths, optimism, hope, and self-determination (Snyder & Lopez, 2009). Research in disability has, over time and at an increasing rate, begun to focus on issues in positive psychology based upon strengths-based approaches to disability (Shogren, Wehmeyer, Pressgrove, & Lopez, 2007; Shogren et al., 2017; Wehmeyer, 2013). Issues of choice and control are at the heart of many positive psychological constructs, and as research and practice in disability expand a focus on strengths and positive characteristics of people with disabilities, the momentum toward choice and control will be accelerated.

Finally, one cannot speak about the future of any disability-related endeavor without examining the role of technology in that future. There are a myriad of ways in which technology advances enhance choice and control for people with disability. From apps that improve a person's capacity to more independently make decisions, to GPS enhanced technology that supports people to navigate in their community more independently, to technology supports that enable people to be more successful in employment settings, technology will enable people with disabilities to exert greater control in their lives, express preferences, and live more self-determined lives (Wehmeyer, Tanis, Davies, & Stock, in press).

Conclusions

We hope that the chapters in this text serve to highlight the critical importance of a focus on choice and preference for people with disabilities, the barriers to such a focus, and, ultimately, provide a path to achieving the vision of the CRPD to promote the full dignity, participation, and self-determination of people with disabilities.

References

Abery, B. H., Olson, M. R., Poetz, C. L., & Smith, J. G. (2019). Self-determination and self-advocacy: It's my life. In A. S. Hewitt & K. M. Nye-Langerman (Eds.), *Community living and participation for people with intellectual and developmental disabilities* (pp. 117–140). Washington, D.C.: American Association on Intellectual and Developmental Disabilities.

Abery, B. H., & Stancliffe, R. J. (2003). A tripartite-ecological theory of self-determination. In M. L. Wehmeyer, B. H. Abery, D. E. Mithaug, & R. J. Stancliffe (Eds.), *Theory in self-determination: Foundations for educational practice* (pp. 43–78). Springfield, IL: Charles C. Thomas.

Beadle-Brown, J., Hutchinson, A., & Whelton, B. (2012). Person-centred active support – Increasing choice, promoting independence and reducing challenging behaviour. *Journal of Applied Research in Intellectual Disabilities, 25*(4), 291–307.

Bronfenbrenner, U. (1994). Ecological models of human development. In T. Husen & T. N. Postlethwaite (Eds.), *International encyclopedia of education* (Vol. 3, 2nd ed., pp. 1643–1647). Oxford, UK: Pergamon Press/Elsevier Science.

Bronfenbrenner, U. (Ed.). (2005). *Making human beings human: Bioecological perspectives on human development.* Thousand Oaks, CA: Sage.

Buntinx, W. H. E. (2013). Understanding disability: A strengths-based approach. In M. L. Wehmeyer (Ed.), *The Oxford handbook on positive psychology and disability* (pp. 7–18). Oxford, UK: Oxford University Press.

Campbell, F. (2009). *Contours of ableism: The production of disability and abledness.* New York, NY: Palgrave Macmillan.

Campbell, F. A. K. (2008). Exploring internalized ableism using critical race theory. *Disability and Society, 23,* 151–162.

Dunn, D. S., & Andrews, E. E. (2015). Person-first and identity-first language: Developing psychologists' cultural competence using disability language. *American Psychologist, 70*(3), 255.

Foxx, R. M., Faw, G. D., Taylor, S., Davis, P. K., & Fulia, R. (1993). "Would I be able to..."? Teaching clients to assess the availability of their community living life style preferences. *American Journal on Mental Retardation, 98,* 235–248.

Garbarino, J. (2017). *Children and families in the social environment: Modern applications of social work.* New York, NY: Routledge Publishing.

Grugel, J., & Piper, N. (2009). Do rights promote development? *Global Social Policy, 9*(1), 79–98.

Hehir, T. (2005). *New directions in special education: Eliminating ableism in policy and practice.* Cambridge, MA: Harvard Education Press.

Hodes, M. W. (2010, 2012). *Toolkit: Talking about children.* Sliedrecht, The Netherlands: ASVZ.

Houseworth, J., Tichá, R., Smith, J., & Ajaj, R. (2018). Developments in living arrangements and choice for persons with intellectual and developmental disabilities, *Policy Research Brief 27*(1)., University of Minnesota, Institute on Community Integration. Downloaded from https://ici.umn.edu/products/view/972

Janeslätt, G., Larsson, M., Wickström, M., Springer, L., & Höglund, B. (2019). An intervention using the Parenting Toolkit "Children - What does it involve?" and the Real-Care-Baby simulator among students with intellectual disability - A feasibility study. *Journal of Applied Research Intellectual Disabilities, 32,* 380–389.

Lang, R., Kett, M., Groce, N., & Trani, J. F. (2011). Implementing the United Nations Convention on the rights of persons with disabilities: Principles, implications, practice and limitations. *Alter, 5*(3), 206–220.

Minkowitz, T. (2017). CRPD and transformative equality. *International Journal of Law in Context, 13*(1), 77–86.

National Council on Disability. (2018). *Beyond guardianship: Toward alternatives that promote greater self-determination for people with disabilities.* Washington, D.C.: Author.

National Council on Disability. (2019). *Turning rights into reality: How guardianship and alternatives impact the autonomy of people with intellectual and developmental disabilities.* Washington, D.C.: Author.

Petman, J. (2009). The special reaching for the universal: Why a special convention for persons with disabilities? In J. Kumpuvuori & M. Scheinin (Eds.), *United Nations Convention on the Rights of Persons with Disabilities–Multidisciplinary Perspectives* (pp. 20–33). Helsinki, Finland: The Center for Human Rights of Persons with Disabilities in Finland (VIKE).

Piven, F. F., & Cloward, R. (2012). *Regulating the poor: The functions of public welfare.* New York, NY: Vintage.

Piven, F. F., & Cloward, R. A. (1971). *Regulating the poor: The functions of public welfare.* New York, NY: Vintage, Random House.

Seligman, M. E. P. (1999). The President's address. *American Psychologist, 54,* 559–562.

Shogren, K. A., Wehmeyer, M. L., Martinis, J., & Blanck, P. (2018). *Supported decision-making: Theory, research, and practice to enhance self-determination and quality of life.* Cambridge, UK: Cambridge University Press.

Shogren, K. A., Wehmeyer, M. L., Pressgrove, C. L., & Lopez, S. J. (2007). The application of positive psychology and self-determination to research in intellectual disability: A content analysis of 30 years of literature. *Research and Practice for Persons with Severe Disabilities, 31*, 338–345.

Shogren, K. A., Wehmeyer, M. L., & Singh, N. (2017). *Handbook of positive psychology in intellectual and developmental disabilities: Translating research into practice.* New York, NY: Springer.

Snyder, C. R., & Lopez, S. J. (2009). *Oxford handbook of positive psychology* (2nd ed.). Oxford, UK: Oxford University Press.

Stancliffe, R. J., Lakin, K. C., Larson, S. A., Engler, J., Taub, S., & Fortune, J. (2011). Choice of living arrangements. *Journal of Intellectual Disability Research, 55*(8), 746–762.

United Nations [UN]. (2006). *Convention for the Rights of Persons with Disabilities.* Available online: http://www.un.org/disabilities/convention/conventionfull.shtml (accessed on 28 May 2019).

Wehmeyer, M. L. (2013). *Oxford handbook of positive psychology and disability.* Oxford, UK: Oxford University Press.

Wehmeyer, M. L. (2019). *Strengths-based approaches to educating all learners with disabilities: Beyond special education.* New York, NY: Teachers College Press.

Wehmeyer, M. L., Little, T., & Sergeant, J. (2009). Self-determination. In S. Lopez & R. Snyder (Eds.), *Handbook of positive psychology* (2nd ed., pp. 357–366). Oxford, UK: Oxford University Press.

Wehmeyer, M. L., Tanis, S., Davies, S. K., & Stock, S. E. (in press). The role of applied cognitive technology and assistive technology in supporting the adaptive behavior of people with intellectual disability. In P. Sturmey & R. Lang (Eds.), *Handbook of adaptive behavior.* New York, NY: Springer.

Werner, S. (2012). Individuals with intellectual disabilities: A review of the literature on decision-making since the Convention on the Rights of People with Disabilities (CRPD). *Public Health Reviews, 34*(2), 14.

Wilson, P. G., Reid, D. H., & Green, C. W. (2006). Evaluating and increasing in-home leisure activity among adults with severe disabilities in supported independent living. *Research and Training in Developmental Disabilities, 27*(1), 93–107.

World Health Organization. (2001). *International classification of functioning, disability, and health.* Geneva, Switzerland: Author.

Index

© Springer Nature Switzerland AG 2020
R. J. Stancliffe et al. (eds.), *Choice, Preference, and Disability*, Positive
Psychology and Disability, https://doi.org/10.1007/978-3-030-35683-5